CONSERVATISM IN CANADA

With the electoral success of the Harper Conservatives federally and of a number of conservative parties provincially, the topic of conservatism is more important to our understanding of Canadian party politics than ever before. This timely volume presents the first comprehensive examination of Canadian conservatism in a generation – a period during which its nature has changed substantially.

Conservatism in Canada explores the ideological character of contemporary Canadian conservatism, its support in the electorate, its impact on public policies such as immigration and foreign policy, and its articulation at both federal and provincial levels. The essays include comparisons with other countries, including the United States, the United Kingdom, and Australia, as well as specific examinations of conservatism in Ontario, Alberta, and Quebec.

Featuring contributions by both established and new scholars in the fields of political science and public policy, this volume makes a significant contribution to our understanding of the changing nature of Canadian conservatism and its broader implications for the future of this country.

JAMES FARNEY is an assistant professor in the Department of Political Science at the University of Regina. He is the author of *Social Conservatives and Party Politics in Canada and the United States*.

DAVID RAYSIDE is a professor in the Department of Political Science and an associate of the Mark S. Bonham Centre for Sexual Diversity Studies at the University of Toronto. He is the author of *Queer Inclusions, Continental Divisions: Public Recognition of Sexual Diversity in Canada and the United States*.

Conservatism in Canada

EDITED BY JAMES FARNEY
AND DAVID RAYSIDE

UNIVERSITY OF TORONTO PRESS
Toronto Buffalo London

© University of Toronto Press 2013
Toronto Buffalo London
www.utppublishing.com
Printed in Canada

ISBN 978-1-4426-4668-1 (cloth)
ISBN 978-1-4426-1456-7 (paper)

Library and Archives Canada Cataloguing in Publication

Conservatism in Canada / edited by James Farney and
David Rayside.

Includes bibliographical references and index.
ISBN 978-1-4426-4668-1 (bound). – ISBN 978-1-4426-1456-7 (pbk.)

1. Conservatism – Canada – History.   2. Conservative Party of Canada.
I. Rayside, David M. (David Morton), 1947–, editor of compilation.   II. Farney,
James Harold, editor of compilation

JC573.2.C3C65 2013   320.520971   C2013-903850-7

This book has been published with the help of a grant from the Canadian Federation
for the Humanities and Social Sciences, through the Awards to Scholarly Publications
Program, using funds provided by the Social Sciences and Humanities Research
Council of Canada.

University of Toronto Press acknowledges the financial assistance to its publishing
program of the Canada Council for the Arts and the Ontario Arts Council.

University of Toronto Press acknowledges the financial support of the Government of
Canada through the Canada Book Fund for its publishing activities.

Contents

List of Figures

List of Tables

Preface

This volume is rooted in two beliefs. The first is that Canadian conservatism is a complex, shifting phenomenon, which enjoys recurrent electoral success and a strong, if sometimes counter-intuitive, influence on public policy. The second is that it is the collective responsibility of political scientists to enhance our understanding of the set of ideas and political parties grouped under the label "conservative" with analytical rigour. Whatever our own proclivities, we need to explore the roots and transformations of these ideas, the character and appeal of the parties and groups claiming to embody them, and the extent to which public policy is shaped by them.

As editors, we have tried to meet this challenge by gathering a group of contributors diverse in their own political leanings and methodological preferences and then asked them to examine different aspects of Canadian conservatism in the light of different analytical frameworks and, for some, various international comparisons. These distinct contributions were then brought together through sustained conversation, in part through joint participation in annual meetings of the Canadian Political Science Association, and in part through what we might describe as an assertive editorial process.

James has come to this project with roots in rural Alberta. His earliest political memories are of community meetings motivated by the agricultural depression of the mid-1980s – meetings that embodied the populist and regional disenfranchisement that created the Reform Party. The nature and legacy of this populism occasioned episodic political involvement and continues to be one source of his interest in he Canadian right. The other is the tension between his religious commitments, the outreach of conservative parties to religious communities (which many close to him found profoundly appealing), and the neoliberal reality of conservative governance. Sorting through these tensions occupied much of his doctoral research and culminated in *Social Conservatism and Party Politics in Canada and the United States* (University of Toronto Press, 2012).

David's roots lie in post–Second-World-War Montreal and in the highly politicized environment of the 1960s and 1970s, a period when many social and political traditions were under what he considered justifiable attack. After completing graduate school and joining the Political Science Department at the University of Toronto, he became politically active on lesbian and gay rights issues and by the mid-1980s was writing in the area. His scholarly (and activist) engagement with questions of sexual diversity since then has required understanding the sources of opposition to those rights. His exploration of conservatism has also been nurtured by a longstanding interest in the play of ideas and activism in Canadian party politics, and by more recent work on the role of faith in parties on the right.

We met while one of us (David) was graduate director in the University of Toronto's Political Science Department and the other (James) was starting his PhD there. Later, David was one of the external readers on James's dissertation. After that dissertation defence, talk fell to an orphan project that had come about through happenstance at the 2008 CPSA meetings in Vancouver. James and Andrej Zaslov (then at Laurier, now at Nijmegen) had independently organized panels examining Canadian conservatism. David Laycock, over a late morning beer, suggested that those panels could form the core of an edited volume. Andrej's move to Europe led to him withdrawing from the project, but he had organized a very good group of papers and the project seemed worth pursuing. Over lunch with Don Forbes, Linda White, Laycock, and Rayside after his defence, talk turned to how best James might continue the project. David, because of (or perhaps in spite of) his previous experience shepherding edited volumes, saw an opportunity to explore his interest in the Canadian right and so agreed to join in. A follow-up set of panels was organized for the 2010 CPSA meetings in Montreal – panels that form the core of the present volume. Following that, additional contributors were recruited to fill in what we saw as obvious gaps.

We have much to be thankful for in the completion of this volume. We first acknowledge the thoughtfulness and work of our many contributors. Andrej Zaslov, Don Forbes, Linda White, Rob Vipond, and

David Laycock all deserve a hearty thanks for their early encouragement, as do the chairs, discussants, and participants at the 2008 and
2010 conference panels at which early versions of these chapters were
presented. The preparation of this book has benefited from the assis-   ·
tance of Ben Peel and Jerry Sabin. The folks at University of Toronto
Press have been wonderful to work with, especially our extraordinary
editor Daniel Quinlan. We also benefited enormously from anonymous
reviewers who took great care in their evaluation of all parts of the
large manuscript.

And finally, we thank those who have to live most closely to and
continuously with the kind of work patterns that get projects like this
completed. To Christina, Bridget, and Gerry we say, once again, the
warmest possible thank you.

James Farney, Regina
David Rayside, Toronto

CONSERVATISM IN CANADA

1 Introduction: The Meanings of Conservatism

JAMES FARNEY AND DAVID RAYSIDE

A volume of essays about conservatism is risky anywhere, and no less so in Canada. In the contemporary period, the term is applied to very different ideological and policy positions, some of them philosophically contradictory. In this volume we have embraced this variety by seeking out authors with a range of perspectives and substantive interests. Some are interested in conservatism as a set of ideas, others in political parties on the right. Some conceive of conservatism as concerned primarily with limiting the scope of state authority, emphasizing free choice and individualism. Other analyses focus on moral traditionalism or on immigration controversies and emphasize those currents of conservatism that focus on order, authority, and tradition. Still others see conservatism as a pragmatic mixture of policy positions designed to appeal to a range of electoral constituencies sizeable enough to provide legislative majorities.

As shepherds of the flock of writers we present in this volume, in this introduction we seek to lay out the complexity of the terrain we call *Canadian conservatism*. We start with what we believe are first principles, by characterizing the layers of meaning embodied in *conservative*. We then lay out what we see as the major currents of contemporary political conservatism. And finally, we raise questions about whether there is a distinctiveness to Canadian conservatism. Part of the last will be a brief consideration of Canadian party systems, the extent to which clear-cut conservative alternatives are discernable within them, and whether this has any influence on public policy. We will return to these themes in the conclusion to this volume, drawing lessons more explicitly from our fellow contributors.

Our writers, and conservatives themselves, use a variety of terms to describe what they observe in others or believe themselves – *toryism, neoliberalism, neoconservatism* – that variety illustrating the multidimensionality of both the ideas and the parties under examination here. In our own contributions to this volume, we use the term *neoliberalism* to identify free market values and a preference for low taxes and circumscribed state authority – ideas that we see as preeminent among contemporary Canadian conservatives. Other writers, here and elsewhere, use the term *neoconservative* to denote the same ideas, and still others use that term to characterize the combination of free market liberalism and moral traditionalism. We have deliberately avoided disciplining the writers in this volume to a common language, in part to display the uncertainties and variations associated with the central term under examination here. In other words, by combining these various articles in one place, we have illustrated the varieties of conservatism at play in contemporary Canadian politics and served up a range of views on how much the election of conservative governments produces a coherent set of public policies.

Conservatism as an Ideological Type

Even settling on a single definition of conservatism as a theoretical framework is more difficult than it seems. Everyday references to this term or to others defining overall conceptions of society and politics, like *socialism* or *liberalism*, frequently employ very different ideas, particularly as we move from one time or place to another. In trying to understand the breadth of this phenomenon, we might begin with Michael Freeden in treating conservatism as an ideological family, where considerable internal diversity is bounded by (1) "resistance to change, however unavoidable, unless it is perceived as organic and natural," and (2) "an attempt to subordinate change to the belief that the laws and forces guiding human behavior have extra-human origins."[1] In Freeden's analysis such laws can come from religion, custom, or the free market, creating some common ground that conservatives drawing from a number of different traditions can all claim as their own.

The first philosophical variant to consider might be referred to as *classical* conservatism, or what is commonly referred to in Canada and Britain as *toryism*. This is an analytical framework that conceives of society as a hierarchically ordered and organically interdependent whole, governed or shaped by norms that are imputed with truthfulness from scripture, natural law, or the test of time. As Canadian writer Charles Taylor has put it, "Everything starts with continuity ... the tory sees society as an organic unity in which everyone has his duties as well as his rights ... [They] have a sense of reverence ... Defending human dignity, they also recognize human fallibility: man is *not* the measure of all they survey ... They know that we are part of some larger order, which we can only dimly comprehend, and which must command our highest allegiance."[2]

Tory conservatism has no inherent antipathy to the deployment of state power, but Taylor also points out that conservatives see humankind as naturally allegiant to or supported by "smaller communities" defined by region, occupation, culture, or other characteristics. Gad Horowitz has a similar view, characterizing tory, or "feudal," values as centred on the organic, corporate, and hierarchical community.[3]

In the eighteenth and nineteenth centuries, one important challenge to conservatism came from reformism and revolution embodied in major currents of liberal individualism, and collectivist ideas based on class conflict. Some liberal frameworks called for democratic reform, but a good deal of nineteenth century liberalism in effect supported new forms of inequality based on free market values and therefore belonged on what we would now call the political right.[4] With the emergence of industrialization, the disruption of traditional seats of privilege, and the increasing power of liberal political ideas, "conservative" politicians and writers like Edmond Burke developed new frameworks that pragmatically combined ideas of continuity and hierarchy on the one hand, and property rights on the other.[5] The willingness to change gradually so as to accommodate new ideas and social forces, to bend rather than break, became something of a hallmark of British conservatism and was deeply influential on its English-Canadian offshoot.

Other reactions were, of course, possible. Leaving aside simple authoritarian reactions against change, which were politically important in fascism and other forms in Europe, the most important embodiment of classical conservatism was the Roman Catholic Church, which railed against liberalism as well as socialism. The great 1891 papal encyclical *Rerum Novarum* was not intended primarily to attack liberalism – that was the job of the 1864 encyclicals *Quanta Cura* and *The Syllabus of Errors*. But it does contain this condemnation of what we might call the free market in the name of a more collectivist and organic vision of society:

In any case we clearly see, and on this there is general agreement, that some opportune remedy must be found quickly for the misery and wretchedness pressing so unjustly on the majority of the working class ... [By] degrees it has come to pass that working men have been surrendered, isolated and helpless, to the hardheartedness of employers and the greed of unchecked competition. The mischief has been increased by rapacious usury, which, although more than once condemned by the Church, is nevertheless, under a different guise, but with like injustice, still practiced by covetous and grasping men. To this must be added that the hiring of labor and the conduct of trade are concentrated in the hands of comparatively few; so that a small number of very rich men have been able to lay upon the teeming masses of the laboring poor a yoke little better than that of slavery itself.[6]

In the late nineteenth century, and even more widely as the twentieth century passed, most writers who identified themselves as conservative (and most Catholics) reached some form of accommodation to free market liberalism, while retaining tory elements.

In Canada, the idea of a tory "touch" has provided one of the key heuristics for understanding our political culture and the evolution of the party system.[7] Two classic accounts of Canadian party politics and political culture – those of Gad Horowitz and Seymour Martin Lipset – stress the continuing influence of this tory touch, even as genuine tories have become very rare birds indeed. Horowitz, who asserts the importance of a tory touch in the formative years of Canadian political history, recognizes that we are dealing with currents that are not unalloyed. What this produced was a belief in or acquiescence to social stratification and hierarchy, a prioritization of order and stability, and an emphasis on continuity, and at the same time an openness to expanding the power of the state, in part born of more traditional tory notions of authority, in part a function of the necessities of a frontier on the edge of the growing American colossus. Lipset sees Canada as born of "counter-revolution" rather than revolution.[8] Canadians are, he argues, more deferential to authority and less intensely individualistic. From that would naturally emerge a form of conservatism that retained elements of toryism alongside some elements of free-market liberalism.

One descendant of this tory influence in the second half of the twentieth century was a political current given the curious and distinctly Canadian label of *red tory*. This represents (or represented) a set of beliefs that support the provision of collective goods by the state, including those welfare state policies that ensure basic human dignity. The "red" label implies a dedication to significantly redistributive politics that may well not be applicable to most of those to whom the label has been attached, but it accurately identifies a willingness to place some limits on the free market, which, left to its own, results in unacceptable levels of deprivation. Red toryism has been a declining force on the Canadian right, particularly since the 1970s. From that time on, the Canadian right was more clearly defined by an intermixing of or coalition between neoliberals who emphasize freeing the market from government interference, alongside populists and moral conservatives.

To different degrees, and for reasons ranging from political style to ideological commitment, neoliberals, populists, and moral conservatives are hard to fit coherently into the box formerly labelled *tory*, however successful their political partnership under that label has been. So, to understand its contemporary usage, we must recognize that the very label *conservative* is used in very different and occasionally contradictory ways. We recognize that if overall resistance to change once served as a unifying idea for conservatives, it does not so serve now. For some it still harkens to an earlier time (real or imagined), but for others change that is induced by the marketplace is eagerly embraced. Such diverse currents can be found in conservatism in almost all democratic political systems and represented by one or more parties on the right, the centre, and at times even those otherwise identifying themselves on the left of the political spectrum. There may well be a distinctively Canadian combination of these values in Canada as a whole, though we also recognize that there are some differences across regions in this country, and major changes over recent decades in the prominence of one or another current. Understanding the nature of these differences and changes is the central goal of this volume.

Moral and Social Traditionalism

Conservatism still marks out an adherence to traditional norms in some areas, most notably associated with family life. In part driven by support for continuity, social stability, and notions of constraint, family structures are seen as naturally centred on the complementary but distinct roles of men and woman. The family unit's core mission is procreative, and it includes the transmission of time-honoured values to children.

For some conservatives, these and associated values are derived from faith and religious authority. For others, they are thought to be rooted in naturalness, timelessness, and functionality. For both, state authority may be invoked to defend traditional values or ensure their legitimacy, though some conservatives may believe that moral "regulation" is better left to religious or community mechanisms.

At the core of social or moral traditionalism is a resistance to ideas of gender equality and arguments that place an emphasis on rights rather than responsibilities. In some respects moral traditionalists are wary of "modernity," or at least those aspects of modernization that have produced what is seen as dislocation, uprootedness, and selfish individualism.

Neoliberalism

In the late twentieth century and early twenty-first, conservative economic stances are informed predominantly by a belief in providing maximum leeway for individual choice and the free market. This calls for cutting government regulation and taxation, reducing state social spending, and privatizing state-owned enterprises.

At the core of this revival of radically individualistic, nineteenth-century liberalism is the argument that individuals should be as free from constraint as possible, including the constraint implied by high levels of taxation. Accompanying this is the view that market forces constitute the most efficient mechanism for producing and distributing goods and services, and for ensuring economic prosperity. State provision of goods and services, beyond the most essential tasks associated with guaranteeing security, is inherently inefficient. Redistributive social policy constitutes a form of social engineering that creates economic inefficiencies, devalues work, and flies in the face of real-life differences in motivation and talent.

Populism

The idea that citizens should have a direct say in policymaking, or that established political institutions and political parties are inherently suspect, does not in itself belong to left or right. After all, in the late nineteenth and early twentieth centuries, populism was often associated with attacks on the wealthy and on large corporations in defence of the disadvantaged. In the 1960s and 1970s, too, there were calls for direct democracy inside political parties in both Canada and the United States that came from progressives as well as conservatives.

However, most populist surges in the last quarter-century in North America and Europe have come from the right. And, for some rightist movements and parties, the populism of their appeals is a key motivator for grassroots activists. This derives in part from a suspicion of the state, and for all those institutions entangled in it, and a scepticism directed at "experts" and the media. It marshals the language of "common sense" as justifying a bypass of the usual policymaking channels. Populism still exists on the left, evident, for example, in some currents of the 2011 Occupy movement. But the wider spread of populism on the right derives in part from the longer-term expansion of state authority over the twentieth century and the development (however unevenly) of the post–Second-World-War welfare state. The kind of populist communitarianism that once could be sustained in an agrarian society was harder to muster as a plausible political platform in a more thoroughly urbanized society.

Nationalist Views of Immigrants and Minorities

Nationalism, too, has no inherent association with any part of the political spectrum, but in most political settings over the last century its more assertive forms are likely to come from parties associated with the right. It has become a vehicle for legitimizing a focus on military expenditures and celebrating military glories. It has also served as a framework for emphasizing the importance of assimilating immigrants and minorities.

So while nationalism is not necessarily founded on notions of an authentic culture, language, religion, or ethnicity, it often enough is in its conservative variants, and becomes exclusionary of any group seen as "other." In immigrant societies like those in North America, conservative nationalism is more likely to be built on a clear sense of what *America*, or *Canada* means, accompanied by expectations of assimilation of those ideas among newcomers. Whether officially approved levels of immigration are high or low, such nationalism will often focus on the particular threat posed by illegal immigration and favour punitive measures to confront it.

The Link between Conservative Ideas and Party Politics

Political parties are almost all coalitions of interests, beliefs, and constituencies. They rarely represent purely principled positions on any one issue dimension. Parties sometimes have their origins in social movements that have a firm allegiance to a coherent set of principles. This can be said of various socialist or social democratic parties born in the late nineteenth century or through the twentieth. Other parties may well include grassroots members and leaders whose roots lie in ideologically driven social movement activism and who remain "believers" operating in what they recognize are environments where not everyone agrees. Almost all parties combine a mixture of policy ideas and do so with a pragmatic eye to what will gain or secure votes. Some of these operate with only the loosest of ideological commitments. This is an approach embodied historically in the Progressive Conservatives and still in the federal Liberals, who in the past functioned as competing teams of "ins" and "outs," each seeking to outbid the other for electoral support in a competition often described as brokerage politics.

What core beliefs, if any, do we find when we look at conservative parties in the early twenty-first century? Across North America and Europe, we most certainly find neoliberal policies. The Republican Party in the United States and the Conservative Party of Canada place free market ideas at the centre of their policy repertoires, and their records in government demonstrate the primacy of those policies over others.[9] The same is true, though often not in as radical a form, in Europe. Even Catholic parties, which historically have supported the welfare state and echoed a certain guardedness about unfettered markets, have embraced a broad form of neoliberalism, especially when facing social democratic or socialist parties.[10]

In North America, moral traditionalism is also part of the policy mix of rightist parties. This is obviously true in the Republican case, where opposition to abortion and to rights protections for sexual minorities remains strong and visible. There is little doubt that the Conservative Party of Canada has significant representation of such beliefs in its leadership and grassroots, but it is much relegated to the sidelines in the party's electoral presentation of itself, and largely too in its government policies. In western Europe, and especially northwestern Europe, issues of moral regulation have receded even more from public policy debates than in Canada. British Conservatives are not alone in having moved substantially to the centre on most of the hot button moral issues on which they once staked out more firmly traditionalist stances. Catholic parties still call for policies reflecting traditionalist notions of family, and resist public recognition of sexual diversity. But their resistance to change on the latter is sometimes tempered in the face of very strong majority support for change.

Far right parties are typically more preoccupied with immigration and ethnocultural minorities than with moral regulation. The conservative parties in Europe that are most strongly identified with anti-immigrant politics have a range of outlooks on the free market, moral regulation, and populism.[11] Centre-right parties have been drawn into more exclusionary or restrictive policies on immigration and ethnic minorities. The same is true of some parties on the left, but the shift is more evident and widespread on the right.

So we find a range of policy mixes in conservative parties, with significant variations across countries and among parties within single systems. We do see a general convergence towards one or another version of neoliberalism, but we find it difficult to generalize cross-nationally about how that policy direction is combined with others. This is no less true of the Canadian case than others. Even within Canada, our unusually federalized party system results in provincial parties often being quite distinct from their federal cousins, and provincial party alignments often bearing little resemblance to those at the federal level.

Canadian parties at the federal level and in several provinces have also experienced reconfigurations as radical as any other country in the liberal democratic world. The most dramatic illustration of electoral volatility is the 1993 federal election, which saw the Progressive Conservatives go from governing party to two seats in Parliament. More than once, governing parties in western Canadian provinces have quickly slipped into near oblivion, replaced by new parties or parties previously on the sidelines of provincial life.

The frequency of major realignment in federal politics since the nineteenth century has meant that analysts now talk of us witnessing the "fourth" party system.[12] For most of the twentieth century, national politics had been dominated by two parties, the Progressive Conservatives on the centre-right and the Liberals on the centre-left, each brokering a variety of interests and ideas with coalitions that shifted significantly from time to time, but with the broad patterns roughly stable. The social democratic New Democratic Party and its predecessors represented the most consistent third-party presence in Ottawa.

From the mid-1970s on, both major parties started shifting towards an embrace of neoliberal premises, though without a sharp break from past policy commitments. The Liberals had long included within their ranks a "business" liberal current emphasizing the free market alongside a reformist current supporting the welfare state.[13] Conservatives had long represented a mixture of centrist tory ideas and more right-wing free market liberal individualism.[14] The early 1990s saw neoliberals more clearly gaining ascendancy in both parties. On top of that, strains were appearing within the Progressive Conservative coalition under Prime Minister Brian Mulroney. That coalition essentially disintegrated in the 1993 election, with the western-based Reform Party on the right and the Bloc Québécois on the left increasing their legislative representation substantially.

Reform brought together an even firmer commitment to neoliberalism than manifest in the Progressive Conservatives, and in particular to the reduction in scope of federal government activity. It also represented a clearly conservative voice on moral issues, displayed most assertively in opposition to lesbian and gay rights. There were currents within Reform sceptical of high immigration levels, and even more so of official policies that protected ethnocultural minority rights and bilingualism, though the party's leadership kept such opinions subdued.

The Liberals benefitted most from the division on the right between PCs and Reform. The party retained its own coalition of left and right liberalism, though after winning office in 1993, the latter were most firmly in control. As Patten argues, in 1995 Finance Minister Paul Martin presented what was "arguably the most economically conservative budget of the postwar period."[15]

The transition to a new party system was effected by decade's end with the creation of the Conservative Party of Canada. This was an amalgamation of the PCs and the Canadian Alliance, successor to Reform, with policy dominance effected by those who came from the Reform/ Alliance side. The selection of Stephen Harper as leader signalled a neoliberal free market emphasis as radical as in any major party in recent Canadian history. Harper-led minority governments were elected in 2006 and 2008, and then in 2011 the Conservatives won a majority in Parliament. The economic crisis and recession limited the government's capacity to act on its fiscally conservative instincts, and opinions continue to vary on how ideologically driven the party's leadership is, but we see fiscal conservatism as still core to the party's ideological mix. Moral conservatism remained an important current within the party and was evident in policy gestures meant to secure the loyalty of that base, but was very much secondary to policies that prioritized tax cuts and federal government expenditure cuts. Anti-immigrant sentiments have been almost entirely absent from the party's platforms or policies.

Recent Conservative governments have adopted aggressive policies towards illegal immigrants and have emphasized the integration of immigrant beliefs into what are portrayed as traditional and patriotic Canadian values, though government spokespeople would claim that this is simply a new form of incorporating diversity. The most important action on the immigration file by the current government has been its dramatic increase in the proportion of immigrants accepted on work, rather than family reunification or refugee, visas – a move with broad acceptance in the business community and very much in keeping with the party's neoliberal priorities.

Carty, Cross, and Young point out that there are more populist elements in party organizational changes in this most recent system, more so for the Conservatives now than in the PC past.[16] For the CPC, this is a remnant of the populism that was an important rhetorical current in the Reform Party. On the other hand, the remaining formal commitments to populist measures coexist with unprecedented levels of top-down leadership control over the party and government policymaking.

The realignment and repositioning that occurred through the course of the 1990s produced a clearer "sorting" of the electorate than in the past. The Liberals, for now much diminished by their poor showing in the 2011 election, continue to draw support from a broad ideological range, but the Conservatives are now more obviously drawing voters who place themselves on the right. When the 2004 Canadian election study asked those who identify with each national party to place themselves as "left," "right," or "centre," 56 per cent of Conservatives said "right," and only 9 per cent said "left.[17] Among Liberals, 31 per cent said "left," 29 per cent "right," and 32 per cent "centre." Among NDP identifiers, 11 per cent placed themselves on the right; among Blocistes, 19 per cent. We also now find that a strong majority (two-thirds) of evangelical Christians support the Conservative Party.[18]

We can hear some echoes of the changes embodied in the fourth Canadian party system at the provincial level. In most provinces, parties on the right have more firmly taken up neoliberal positions than before. This was dramatically true of Ontario's Progressive Conservatives from 1990s on, under the leadership of Mike Harris. It was also true of Ralph Klein's PCs in Alberta from the same period onward, and a firm commitment to free market values is at the core of the Wild Rose Alliance. We see a similar shift in the British Columbia Liberal Party as it gained strength by representing all those forces opposed to the provincial NDP. While he was in the Quebec premier's office, Jean Charest would have liked to pull the provincial Liberals' economic policy more radically to the right than he realized he could manage and still retain power provincially.

Like their federal counterpart, provincial parties on the right have mostly sidelined moral traditionalism or highly contained it. It remains electorally most visible in Alberta and Saskatchewan, but even there the most powerful of the parties on the right realize that most of their supporters do not prioritize these issues. Moral traditionalism remains an important minority current at the popular level and finds representation in provincial or territorial legislatures (least so in Quebec). But it rarely constitutes an important influence on party election platforms or in policymaking by conservative parties. There are occasionally rhetorical and policy nods to traditionalist values, and as with the CPC, a few issues (like "law and order") are marshalled to appeal to a broad spectrum of voters, including many who would hold to traditional values on gender and sexuality.

What Our Authors Contribute

The authors whom we have corralled into contributing original articles for this volume come from a variety of approaches to the study of politics. Some are theorists or writers interested primarily in the play of ideas within Canadian conservatism. Nelson Wiseman explores the roots of such ideas across the country. Clark Banack examines the particular and important case of Alberta. James Farney tracks the recent development of populist ideas within Canadian parties of the right.

Others are more interested in mass behaviour, with the values and attitudes held by citizens. Chris Cochrane uses World Values Surveys to explore the meanings attached to "left" and "right" in Canadian politics and points to a conclusion that is an important theme throughout this volume – that at the voter level, conservatism on economic issues does not necessarily coincide with other attitude sets that are politically combined by North American parties on the right. Andrea Lawlor and Éric Bélanger focus on Quebec's conservatives, looking especially at those who vote for the Conservative Party of Canada federally and the now-defunct ADQ provincially.

Several writers focus their attention on the Conservative Party of Canada. Tom Flanagan's analysis provides an overview of the party under Steven Harper's leadership. Steve Patten looks at the strength of neoliberalism within the party, and Jonathan Malloy at the role of moral conservatism. Inder Marwah, Phil Triadofiloulous, and Stephen White explore immigration and citizenship policy; Alan Bloomfield and Kim Nossal cover foreign policy (comparing the Conservatives with their Australian counterparts). Karen Bird and Andrea Rowe focus on gender-related policies that have emerged from the Conservative Party and governments controlled by it. John Frendreis and Ray Tatalovich do not focus on just the Conservatives but engage in a comparative analysis of the role of party in fiscal politics in Canada and the United States over the last century and a half.

Several other writers focus on provincial politics. We have already identified the contributions of Nelson Wiseman (on provincial politics in general), Clark Banack (on Alberta), and Lawlor and Bélanger (on Quebec). In addition, David Stewart and Anthony Sayers, like Banack, engage the Albertan case, using survey evidence to challenge many of the stereotypes associated with that province. David Rayside tracks the persistence of moral traditionalism in Ontario's party system, and particularly in the PCs, despite the primacy given to neoliberalism. Complementing Lawlor and Bélanger, Brian Tanguay examines the place of conservatism in Quebec's party politics.

In our conclusion, we return to some of the big themes that we and our colleagues have introduced, with a particular view to understanding how a multifaceted conceptualization of Canadian conservatism will help us understand the situation of the current majority government and its provincial counterparts. Recognizing the primacy of neoliberalism as an ideological commitment amongst all Canadian conservatives, we try to establish if there are distinctively Canadian dimensions to this widespread phenomenon, and to what extent this ideological direction is evident in the campaigning and governing of parties on the right in this country.

NOTES

1 Michael Freeden, *Ideologies and Political Theory: A Conceptual Approach* (Oxford: Clarendon, 1996), 344.

2 Charles Taylor, *Radical Tories: The Conservative Tradition in Canada* (Toronto: Anansi, 1982), 213.

3 This appears in his justifiably famous article, "Conservatism, Liberalism, and Socialism in Canada: An Interpretation," *Canadian Journal of Economics and Political Science* 32, no. 2 (1966): 143–71.

4 A classic treatment of the philosophical development of such ideas is C.B. Macpherson, *The Political Theory of Possessive Individualism: Hobbes to Locke* (Oxford: Oxford University Press, 1964).

5 On Burke's ideas, see F.P. Lock, *Edmond Burke* (Oxford: Clarendon, 2006), 2; and for an American perspective, see Russell Kirk, ed., *Edmund Burke: A Genius Reconsidered*, rev. ed. (Wilmington: Intercollegiate Studies Institute, 1997).

6 "Encyclical of Pope Leo XIII on Capital and Labor," paragraph 3, http://www.vatican.va/holy_father/leo_xiii/encyclicals/documents/hf_l-xiii_enc_15051891_rerum-novarum_en.html.

7 For the classic statement of this view, see Horowitz, "Conservatism, Liberalism and Socialism in Canada." Historian Donald Creighton also implied this view in his monumental biography, *John A. Macdonald* (Toronto: Macmillan of Canada, 1952), 2.

8 Seymour Martin Lipset, *Revolution and Counter-Revolution* (New Brunswick: Transaction, 1988); and Lipset, *Continental Divide: The Values and Institutions of the United States and Canada* (New York: Routledge, 1990).

9 Some Canadian observers will see the Conservative Party as having abandoned any serious commitment to neoliberalism (e.g., Andrew Coyne and others). On the other hand, we believe that the party leadership retains a strong commitment to lower taxes and a constrained federal government, though it is willing to work incrementally towards that goal in ways that do not jeopardize its electoral strength. In this we agree with David Laycock, *The New Right and Democracy in Canada: Understanding Reform and the Canadian Alliance* (Don Mills: Oxford University Press, 2002); and Steve Patten (chapter 4 in this volume).

10 Martin Conway, "The Age of Christian Democracy," in *European Christian Democracy*, ed. Thomas Kselman and Joseph A. Buttigieg, 44–67 (Notre Dame: University of Notre Dame Press, 2003); and Kees van Kersbergen, "The Distinctiveness of Christian Democracy," in *Christian Democracy in Europe*, ed. David Hanley, 31–47 (London: Pinter, 1994).

11 Hans George Betz and Stefan Immerfall, eds., *The New Politics of the Right: Neo-Populist Parties and Movements in Established Democracies* (New York: St Martin's, 1998).

12 Steve Patten, "The Evolution of the Canadian Party System," in *Canadian Parties in Transition*, 3rd ed., ed. Alain-G. Gagnon and A. Brian Tanguay, 55–81 (Peterborough: Broadview, 2007); R.K. Carty, William Cross, and Lisa Young, "Building a Fourth Canadian Party System," in *Party Politics in Canada*, 8th ed., ed. Hugh G. Thorburn and Alan Whitehorn, 33–48 (Toronto: Prentice-Hall, 2001).

13 See Reginald Whitaker, *The Government Party: Organizing and Financing the Liberal Party of Canada, 1930-1958* (Toronto: University of Toronto Press, 1977); and Joseph Wearing, *The L-Shaped Party: The Liberal Party of Canada, 1958–1980* (Toronto: McGraw-Hill Ryerson, 1981).

14 See Colin Campbell and William Christian, *Parties, Leaders, and Ideologies in Canada* (Toronto: McGraw-Hill Ryerson, 1995), 26. See also Stephen Clarkson, "The Liberal Party of Canada," 231–47; and Peter Woolstencroft, "Staying Alive: The Progressive Conservative Party Fights for Survival," in Thorburn and Whitehorn, *Party Politics in Canada*, 248–63.

15 Patten, "Evolution of the Canadian Party System," 75.

16 Cross and Young, "Building a Fourth Canadian Party System."

17 Lawrence Leduc, "Realignment and Dealignment in Canadian Federal Politics," in Gagnon and Tanguay, *Canadian Parties in Transition*, 171.

18 Ipsos-Reid, 2004 survey.

PART ONE

Philosophical, Attitudinal, and Religious Foundations

2 The Structure and Dynamics of Public Opinion

CHRISTOPHER COCHRANE

There are a number of sweeping cross-national and cross-time studies of public opinion. These studies interpret the contours of opinion change somewhat differently, but their findings converge on a central point: public opinion in advanced industrial countries is moving leftward. Unprecedented economic and physical security, rising levels of formal education, and declining religiosity have transformed opinion landscapes right across the advanced industrial world.[1] People are less preoccupied with economics and law and order, turning instead to such post-material considerations as leisure time, free speech, political influence, and urban aesthetics.[2] People are less tolerant of authority, more tolerant of diversity, and substantially more likely to support gay rights, abortion, euthanasia, and environmentalism.[3]

General leftward shifts in public opinion, however, have not been reflected in voting choices. Comparative studies of party platforms and governing coalitions indicate that right-wing parties are receiving as many votes, winning as many seats, and participating in government as often as they used to.[4] Left-wing parties have not cashed in on the tide of public opinion that has swung in their favour, and right-wing parties have not fallen apart. What explains the apparent discrepancy between the dominant accounts of opinion change and the robust electoral showing of right-wing parties?

This chapter argues that the electoral struggles of the political left, and the longevity of the political right, stem in part from a fundamental asymmetry at the elite level between the left and the right in the ways that individuals organize their opinions about multiple issues. Each individual holds opinions about more than one issue. In other words, public opinion is multidimensional. There is not one dimension of opinions that matters, but many dimensions. From this standpoint, there is nothing about the trajectory of opinion change at the aggregate level that tells us anything about the connections between opinions at the individual level. Outside of the political elite, most citizens hold "mixed opinions" – they hold right-wing opinions about some issues and left-wing opinions about others. However, political elites, particularly on the left, are more likely to combine their moral and economic positions into a coherent set of political viewpoints. Whatever advantage the left gains from the popularity of its positions on individual issues, it loses to the laws of probability when combining them.

Evidence of Opinion Change

Public opinion in Canada and other Western countries has changed considerably on a number of issues over the past quarter century. Notably, opinions about euthanasia, abortion, and especially homosexuality changed drastically throughout the 1980s and 1990s, with citizens not just in Canada, but in the United States and Western Europe as well, expressing increasing levels of support for women's rights to abortion and for the rights of gays of lesbians. Respondents in each wave of the World Values Survey were asked to indicate their opinions about abortion, homosexuality, and euthanasia on scales that range from 1 (never justifiable) to 10 (always justifiable). Thus, higher positions on this scale indicate increasingly favourable views about these three subjects. Figure 2.1 plots in cross-time perspective the average positions of Canadians, Western Europeans, and Americans on each of these survey items. In all three cases and on all three issues, the results indicate that publics became increasingly more supportive across time. The results are particularly pronounced on the issue of homosexuality. In 1981, 51 per cent of Canadian respondents expressed the view that homosexuality was "never justifiable." By 2005, just 20 per cent of Canadians shared that opinion. The results are no less pronounced in Europe (47% to 16%) or the United States (65% to 33%). Certainly, there may be short-term fluctuations in opinions about these issues, and there is no guarantee that any of these cross-time trends will continue. Even so, public opinion on so-called moral issues, and particularly homosexuality, has moved sharply leftward over the past quarter-century.

Less impressive, but notable nonetheless, is the shift in economic outlooks. Compared to 1990, Canadians in 2006 were less supportive of private industry, more supportive of income equality, and

Figure 2.1. Changing Opinions about Abortion, Homosexuality, and Euthanasia, 1981–2005

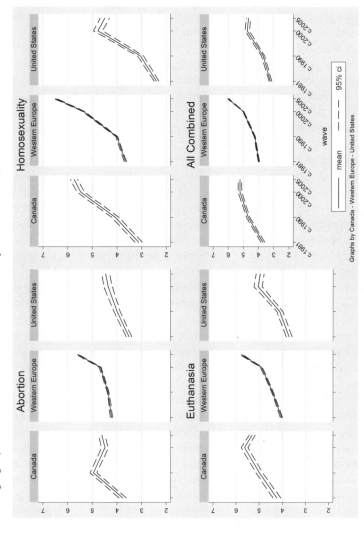

Source: World Values Survey (1981–2006)

substantially less likely to agree that people should look after themselves, rather than have the government do it.[5] These opinions are also plotted on ten-point scales in the World Values Survey. The mean positions of Canadians, Western Europeans, and Americans in 1990, 2000, and 2005 are summarized in figure 2.2. Lower scores indicate increasingly left-leaning positions, and higher scores indicate the opposite. Thus, the trajectories in figure 2.2 are invariably leftward. To be sure, the effect is modest compared to moral values, and Canada is still a fiscally conservative country, all things considered. Even so, the magnitude of cross-time change is not insignificant. In 1990, 21 per cent of Canadians felt strongly that incentives for individual effort should be increased at the expense of income equality. By 2005, only 5 per cent of Canadians expressed this same view. In 1990, 30 per cent of Canadians felt strongly that private ownership of business and industry should be increased. That figure fell to less than 12 per cent by 2005. And in 1990, 30 per cent of Canadians thought that people, rather than government, should take more responsibility for themselves. Fifteen years later, that figure had dropped to less than 7 per cent. Simply, Canada is a less conservative country today than it used to be. In this respect, Canadians are not unlike their counterparts in the United States and Western Europe.

Many scholars attribute these shifts to underlying structural shifts in the economy, including generational changes in public opinion, which stem from long-term socioeconomic transformations from an agrarian, to a manufacturing, to a service economy.[6] These modernization theories assign a great deal of importance to the role of the economy in shaping the broader environment of mass opinion. The shift from a manufacturing to a service economy, for example, generated an increasing demand for skills associated with university education. A university education, in turn, is associated with increasingly left-wing opinions about a range of issues, especially so-called moral issues like homosexuality and abortion. Even so, underlying structural changes explain only a part of the value change story. Indeed, opinions about these issues have changed among citizens in all educational categories, and cross-time change in levels of education account for only some of the cross-time change in opinions about homosexuality (about 12%) and abortion (about 67%). The role of social movements, certainly, cannot be discounted in these numbers. Whatever the precise mechanisms driving these trends, there is no question that opinions about controversial moral and economic issues have undergone a profound shift

Figure 2.2. Changing Opinions about Income Inequality, the Private Sector, and Government Welfare, 1981–2005

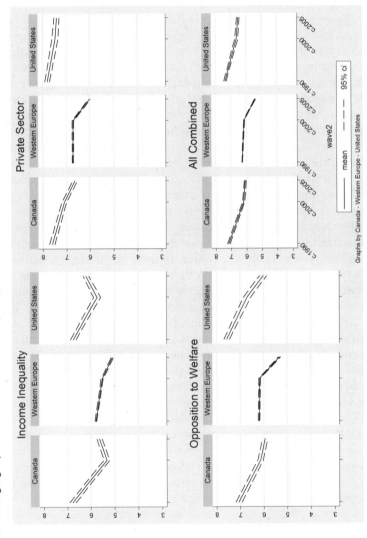

Source: World Values Survey (1981–2006)

over the past three decades. Surely, this has translated into heightened electoral success for left-wing parties. Or has it?

Left-Wing and Right-Wing Electoral Performance

Figure 2.3 plots the election results for left-wing and right-wing political parties in national parliamentary elections in nineteen Western democratic countries between 1945 and 2005. The left-right scores of these parties are assigned by the Comparative Manifesto Research Project (CMRP), a systematic content analysis of party election platforms in democratic countries since 1945. In the CMRP, party platforms are quantified in left/right terms according to coding criteria that classify, line by line, the percentage of a party election platform that is devoted to supporting left-wing and right-wing positions on a range of issues. As Budge and Klingemann explain, "The [left/right] scale generally opposes emphases on peaceful internationalism, welfare and government intervention on the left, to emphases on strong defense, free enterprise and traditional morality on the right."[7] In this scale, the proportion of left-wing phrases is subtracted from the proportion of right-wing phrases. Thus, higher values suggest increasingly right-wing platforms, and lower values suggest increasingly left-wing platforms.

Parties with generally left-wing scores are plotted in figure 2.3A and parties with generally right-wing scores are plotted in figure 2.3B. In both cases, the year of the election is reflected along the horizontal axis, and the proportion of the popular vote that each party received is plotted along the vertical axis. The points in the graphs therefore correspond to the percentage of the popular vote that each individual political party received in a national election during that year. The two trend lines in the graph represent separate measures of electoral success.[8] The top trend line is the estimated probability that any given left-wing or right-wing political party occupied a position in their national executive at some point after the election of that year and before the next election (i.e., whether the election got the party into office), and the bottom trend line depicts the estimated average share of the popular vote that political parties received during elections in that year. Together, these estimates provide a two-pronged measure of party success. On this point, notice that results in the figures indicate that right-wing parties are performing at least as well as their counterparts on the left. Indeed, the top trend line declines for parties on the left and not for parties on the right. If anything, left-wing political parties have become

Figure 2.3. Vote Share and Executive Power for Left-Wing and Right-Wing Parties, 1945–2005

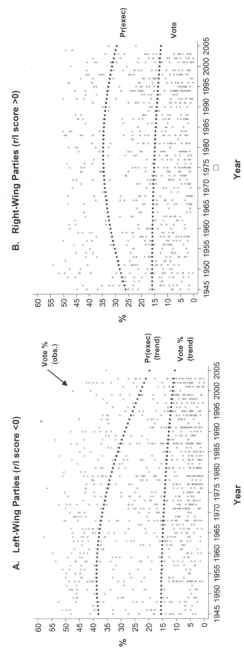

A. Left-Wing Parties (r/l score <0)

B. Right-Wing Parties (r/l score >0)

Sources: Data from Budge and Klingemann (2001); Klingemann et al. (2006); Müller and Strom (2000); EJPR Political Data Yearbooks

Notes:

1 Cross-national coverage includes Australia, Austria, Belgium, Canada, Denmark, Finland, France, Germany, Great Britain, Iceland, Italy, Luxembourg, Netherlands, New Zealand, Norway, Sweden, Switzerland, and the United States. Iceland and New Zealand are missing on Pr(exec).

2 Right-Left (r/l score) outlined by Budge and Klingemann (2001, 22).

3 A party is coded 1 on executive if it held a formal position in the Cabinet (White House in United States) at any point between one election (t_0) and the next election at (t_1).

4 The data are grouped on party (panel) and election date (time).

less likely to govern and right-wing parties *more* likely to govern. Even so, the magnitude of this difference does not achieve conventional levels of statistical significance.

This general pattern certainly reinforces the anecdotal evidence. In Canada, the New Democratic Party (NDP) performed abysmally in three successive elections between 1993 and 2000, setting a new record in the process for the party's worst election result since its founding in 1932 (as the CCF). Denmark, Sweden, and Switzerland are now governed by right-wing parties, and, if not for a peculiarity of the electoral system, Norway would be as well. Between 1998 and 2001, the leading left-wing parties in Sweden, Norway, and Denmark all experienced among their poorest electoral showing in nearly eighty years.[9] The far-right Swiss People's Party (SVP) is now the dominant electoral force in Switzerland, far outstripping its main left-wing opponent, the Social Democrats (SPS).

Where stories of right-wing success are not as obvious, they rarely seem far from the surface. In Belgium, the green parties AGALEV and ECOLO were crushed in the 2003 election; by contrast, the extreme right Vlaams Bloc has increased its share of the popular vote in all but one election since 1978. Republicans presidents have occupied the White House for twenty of the past thirty years. Even so, George W. Bush was the first Republican in nearly a half-century to preside while his party controlled majorities in both house of Congress. In Austria, the left-wing Austrian Social Democratic Party (SPO) was excluded from Cabinet after the 1999 election (and again after the 2002 election) for the first time since 1966 and only the second time since 1945. The SPO was replaced in Cabinet by the far-right Freedom Party (FPO). In general, established right-wing political parties are holding their own against their longstanding left-wing rivals. And new-right authoritarian parties are outperforming their new-left ecological counterparts in all but a handful of countries.

Left/Right Asymmetry

A number of reasons could account for the paradox between the standard account of a leftward shift in mass opinion and the observed reality of no such shift in voter preferences. Certainly, one possibility is that issue opinions simply do not matter that much in affecting vote choice. Indeed, an extensive literature suggests that the role of issue positions is vote choice is minimal.[10] "Many citizens," Converse argues, "... do not have meaningful beliefs, even on issues that have formed the basis for intense political controversy among elites, for substantial periods of time."[11]

But even among citizens who do possess meaningful opinions about the issues, few of them actually organize their opinions in such a way that they would be able to project these preferences onto the political landscape. The overwhelming majority of people hold left-wing opinions about some issues and right-wing positions about other issues. As a result, they have to choose in the ballot box between their preferences about different issues. When voters with left-wing economic positions and right-wing moral positions cast a vote for a left-wing party, they bring with them into that party's support base a set of moral issues that are wholly at odds with the party's positions.[12] The constrained choice environment of party competition limits the extent to which voters are able to express their policy preferences in a ballot box. As we shall see, this may be particularly the case for citizens with left-wing preferences, as there seems to be a mass-elite dichotomy on the political left when it comes to the way that leftists bundle together their preferences about multiple issues.

Theory and Hypotheses

Opinions about multiple issues are bound into bundles by underlying influences that affect simultaneously the preferences of individuals about more than one issue. A prominent approach to studying opinion clusters in political science has involved specifying in advance how citizens *should* organize their opinions and then searching for explanations to account for the failure of many citizens to organize their opinions in these particular ways. Converse, for example, argues that levels of government taxation and spending were "logically" connected. Thus, he reasons, the opinions of citizens who supported lower taxes and higher spending were correspondingly illogical. For Converse, these kinds of opinions were effectively meaningless, beyond a reflection of unsophistication and political disinterest.[13]

The argument proposed here, however, is different. Rather than assuming a natural connection between opinions about multiple issues, the argument here is that there is no natural, logical, or normative connection between opinions about any two issues. In this scenario, there would be no way to predict people's opinion about one issue on the basis of knowledge about their opinion on any other issue. Or, to put it another way, there would be no "constraint" between issues.[14] This analytical question is quite different from the one that Converse set out to address some half century ago. In Converse's case, there were reasons to expect that people should organize their preferences about issues into coherent bundles, and the interesting analytical question was why so many people failed to do so. In the current analysis, however, this logic is turned upside down. The underlying assumption is that there is no a priori reason to expect that people should organize their preferences about issues into coherent bundles, and the analytical question is why so many people *do make these connections across issue domains*. This is more than a difference of style. It changes altogether the empirical endeavour.

The core argument proposed here is that opinion clusters form when underlying predispositions interact with social sources of information to affect simultaneously the opinions of individuals about more than one issue. Economic insecurity, for example, is an underlying influence that generates for many citizens left-wing opinions about social welfare and, at least in certain information environments, right-wing opinions about immigration.[15] An abstract commitment to equality, similarly, generates left-wing opinions about wealth redistribution, and it also moves leftward opinions about gays and lesbians, women, and immigrants. These kinds of connections between general predispositions and specific policy issues are not made naturally or inevitably by citizens.[16] Rather, they arise when people are exposed to arguments that couch an issue position in terms of a big idea that they are predisposed to accept. From this standpoint, it is not just information that matters, and it is not just predisposition; rather, it is the interaction of the two.

A broad commitment to equality is a well-known influence on the political left.[17] But what about the political right? Indeed, just because a commitment to equality underlies left-wing positions about a range of issues, it is a fundamental mistake to suppose that it is simply the opposite of equality, or inequality, that underlies right-wing positions on these issues. Conservatives do not wake up in the morning and ask, "How can I promote human inequality today?" By contrast, right-wing opinions stem from altogether different commitments to religion, economic growth, and majority social, racial, or ethnic groups. Taken together, the underlying sources that constrain right-wing opinions are qualitatively different from those that constrain left-wing opinions. Left-wingers and right-wingers think about policy in terms of different big ideas, and these big ideas, in turn, apply to more than one issue.

People who think about issues from the standpoint of altogether different big ideas are not only likely to disagree in their opinions about those issues, they are also likely to disagree regarding how those issues fit together logically with other issues in the political environment.

Figure 2.4 outlines some of the prominent sources of left-wing and right-wing opinions on seven broad policy domains: income equality, welfare programs, taxes vs government spending, abortion rights, same-sex marriage, and multiculturalism. These issues figure prominently in conventional understanding of left/right disagreement. In virtually all studies of the political left, an underlying commitment to equality turns out to underlie – for politically engaged segments of the electorate – left-wing positions about each of these issues. A commitment to equality affects opinions about wealth redistribution, welfare programs, women's rights, gay and lesbian rights, immigration, and cultural diversity. On the political right, a commitment to free-market materialism generates right-wing opinions about income equality and taxes vs spending. A commitment to religion typically generates right-wing opinions about abortion and gay rights. And out-group intolerance is associated with negative opinions about people who are different, including, typically, gays, lesbians, racial minorities, and immigrants.

However, when it comes to each of these sources of right-wing opinion, notice the range of opinions that each of these influences does not affect. Free-market materialism is not associated with increasingly right-wing opinions about abortion rights, same-sex marriage, immigration, or multiculturalism. Religion is not associated with right-wing opinions about income equality, welfare programs, immigration, or multiculturalism. And out-group intolerance is not associated with right-wing opinions about economics and abortion, even though it does affect opinions about same-sex marriage, because those who dislike people who are different from themselves tend to dislike gays and lesbians, as well as immigrants and racial minorities.[18] It is worth emphasizing that the argument proposed here is not that right-wingers are materialistic, religious, and intolerant. Indeed, the main point is that materialistic conservatives are no more likely than others to be religious or intolerant; religious conservatives are no more likely to be materialistic or intolerant; and intolerant conservatives are no more likely to be materialistic or religious. Taken together, we have theoretical reasons to expect that the single key source of left-wing opinions – namely, equality – affects a range of issues different from each of the

Figure 2.4. Left/Right Predispositions and Policy Preferences about the Economy, Morality, and Diversity

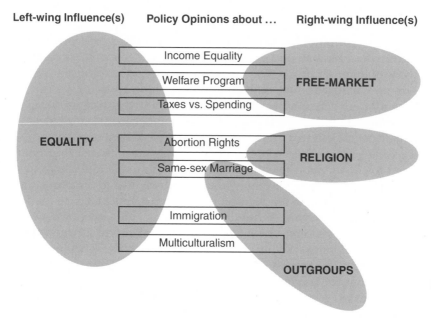

key sources of right-wing opinions: free-market materialism, religion, and out-group intolerance.

Observable Implications

The observable implications of this core argument have previously been tested against the patterns of activist preferences within Canadian political parties, as well as in the patterns of party policy in cross-national perspective.[19] In both cases, the evidence is consistent with the expectation that preferences about economic and social policy are bound more tightly by those on the political left than by those on the political right. The following analysis extends the implications of this argument to the patterns of public opinion in twenty democratic countries, as well as Northern Ireland: Austria, Belgium, Britain, Canada, Denmark, Finland, France, Germany, Iceland, Ireland, Italy, Luxembourg, Malta, Netherlands, Norway, Portugal, Spain, Sweden, Switzerland, and the

United States. In the population as a whole, across all of these countries, there is a clear connection between the left/right self-placement of survey respondents on the one hand, and their opinions about the economy and social morality. Yet, knowing that opinions about these issues are all connected to the left/right continuum is not the same as knowing whether these opinions are connected to each other. Indeed, there is little evidence of a connection in the population as a whole between opinions on the economic and moral dimensions.

The lack of a connection in the population as a whole between opinions about economics and morality is not surprising. First, many citizens lack meaningful opinions about issues. When interviewers ask these respondents about policy issues in the course of a public opinion survey, many respondents are simply "answering a question" rather than "revealing a preference."[20] In other words, many respondents have no fixed preference on the issue that the question is asking about, but they answer the question anyway for the sake of satisfying the interviewer's request for an answer. Second, there are numerous sources of influence that bear down on the opinions of each individual. For example, some citizens support redistributive economic policies because they are poor and would stand to gain financially from welfare policies. Many of these citizens also support heightened restrictions on immigration, in part because they perceive immigrants as competitors for wages and housing at the bottom of the socioeconomic hierarchy.[21] Other citizens, however, express support for wealth redistribution out of an abstract commitment to equality. Their commitment to wealth redistribution stems not from economic self-interest or financial insecurity, but from an ideological commitment to the secular-egalitarian principles that lie at the core of left-wing ideology. This commitment to equality, far from underlying right-wing opinions about immigration, has precisely the opposite effect – it generates left-wing opinions about immigration. Thus, two common sources of left-wing economic opinions, financial insecurity and egalitarianism, generate altogether opposing positions when it comes to immigration. It is hardly surprising, then, that left-wing opinions about the economy are not associated, in the population at large, one way or the other, with left-wing opinions about immigration or morality.

Despite the lack of a connection between economic and social positions at the mass level, there are nonetheless reasons to expect connections between these issues among the political elite, at least among those who are simultaneously politically engaged and on the left.

Politically engaged left-wingers, in particular, are anomalous in an important respect: they are affluent and well educated, yet they still support income equality and wealth redistribution. Income does not at all predict market outlooks among the most highly engaged left-wingers. More generally, politically engaged citizens tend to be more ideologically oriented than are the ideologically "naive" citizens who are typical of the electorate as a whole. Ideology motivates political interest, and political interest, in turn, can reinforce and shape ideology. As the argument outlined above suggests, the dominant ideological commitment on the left – equality – applies with equal facility to economic, social, and immigration issues. By contrast, the big ideas on the right – free-market materialism, religion, and out-group intolerance – do not apply individually to the full range of these issues. Thus, the expectation is that politically engaged left-wingers will bundle together their economic, social, and immigration positions, but politically engaged right-wingers will not.

Evidence

Figure 2.5 summarizes the results of formalizing these hypotheses by specifying latent variable structural equation models and then fitting these models to politically engaged Canadians on the left and the right. The summary statistics for the model of the whole are underneath the figures.[22] The most interesting results stem, first, from the connection between the observed variables (the variables represented by rectangles) and the underlying latent variables (the variables represented by circles), and second, from the relationships between the latent variables themselves. In the first case, notice that the two latent variables – "economic opinions" and "moral opinions" – have three and four indicators, respectively. Opinions about euthanasia, homosexuality, and abortion load strongly on "moral opinions," and opinions about the private sector, income equality, welfare, and competition load (somewhat less strongly) on "economic opinions." The numbers atop the arrows connecting the latent and observed variables are the standardized factor loadings (i.e., correlation coefficients). Standardized factor loadings closer to 1 indicate a stronger connection between the latent variable and the observed opinion. Standardized factor loadings closer to 0 indicate little connection.

For those on the left, economic opinions correlate with moral opinions ($r = .40, p < .001$). Thus, the results for those on the left are consistent

Figure 2.5. The Structure of Moral and Economic Opinions for Politically Interested Leftists and Rightists in Canada

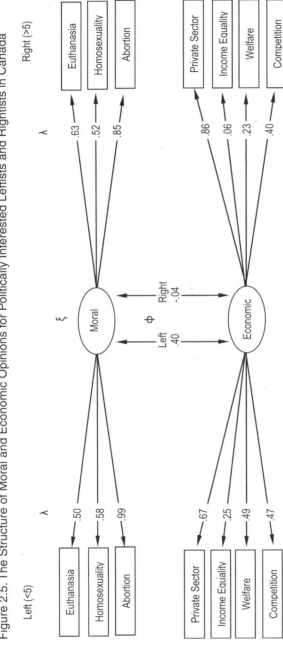

Source: World Values Survey (Canada) (2000 and 2005)
Notes:
1 Results are standardized solutions from confirmatory factor analysis, using maximum likelihood estimation.
2 Number of observations = 413 for Left; 1055 for Right.
3 Analysis confined to politically interested respondents, defined as those with at least some interest in politics (> 2 on a 1–4 scale of political interest).

with the central expectations. There is a connection among politically engaged leftists between their opinions about economics and morality. The results are different, however, for those on the right. Like their counterparts on the left, their opinions about income equality, the private sector, the welfare state, and competition are connected to one another via general economic orientations. And "moral opinions" link answers to questions about abortion, homosexuality, and euthanasia. Yet there is no connection between these different kinds of right-wing opinions. Indeed, the correlation between economic and moral opinions is actually negative ($r = -.04$, $p = .310$). There is, in other words, no unifying latent structure that connects moral and economic opinions for those on the right. There is an economic right and a moral right.

The evidence in the comparative case is not at all different from the Canadian evidence. Like Canadians, respondents in the United States and Western Europe tend to organize their opinions about these issues in clear bundles of moral and economic opinions, but they do not, on the whole, bind together into a single coherent bundle their opinions about moral and economic issues. For most people, moral and economic issues are separate domains of consideration. The exception, again, is among politically engaged left-wingers. Indeed, by repeating the above analysis on the comparative data, the correlation between the social and economic opinions of engaged left-wingers is significant and positive ($r = .20$, $p < .001$). By contrast, the correlation is negative for the population as a whole ($r = -.06$, $p < .001$), and it is non-existent for those who are politically engaged and on the right ($r = .00$). This comparative evidence is consistent with the patterns of public opinion in Canada. Simply, activists on the political left often think about economic and moral issues as if they belong to a single domain of consideration; activists on the right, and citizens in general, do not.

Implications

Left-wing coherence at the elite level has consequences for left-wing parties. Left-wing parties are constrained by the preferences of their activists from adopting non-left-of-centre positions on economic, social, or even immigration issues. Cuts to social welfare, restrictions on abortion, and anti-immigrant positions are all outright unacceptable to sizeable proportions of left-wing activists. Nonetheless, many citizens in the electorate hold left-wing positions on economic issues and right-wing positions on social issues; likewise, many hold left-wing positions on social morality and right-wing positions about the economy. As a result, many of the citizens who agree with left-wing parties on economic issues disagree with left-wing parties on social issues, and many who agree with left-wing parties on social issues disagree with left-wing parties on economic issues. What left-wing parties gain in the popularity of their positions on individual policy dimensions they lose to the probability calculus of combining together in their policy platforms issue dimensions, which are independent of each other in the electorate as a whole. There are many people who agree with left-wing parties on one dimension; there are few who agree with left-wing parties on multiple dimensions.

The situation is somewhat different for parties on the right. In this case, there are no connections among the right-wing elite when it comes to opinions about economic and moral issues. Many economic conservatives accord little importance to social issues; many social conservatives accord little weight to economic issues. As a result, right-wing parties in many contexts enjoy a greater degree of freedom than their counterparts on the left when it comes to manoeuvring strategically on economic and social issues. Even in circumstances where fiscal and social conservatives have to work together – such as Single Member Plurality (SMP) electoral systems, which reward parties for the number of constituencies that they win, rather than for their overall share of the popular vote, and where vote splitting therefore has particularly catastrophic effects for the electoral prospects of parties – the tension between economic and moral conservatives may generate centralizing pressures in the party as a whole. Presumably, fiscal conservatives do not want to lose electoral support by adopting non-mainstream positions on social issues of which they care little, and social conservatives are unlikely to risk losing voters by taking extreme positions on economic issues of which they care little. It is possible, over time, that the pull of partisanship in multidimensional right-wing parties may bring into alignment the social opinions of fiscal conservatives and the economic opinions of social conservatives. All things being equal, however, the pull of ideologues in multidimensional right-wing parties is unlikely to match the pull of ideologues in a multidimensional left-wing party.

Conclusion

Citizens in Canada, the United States, and Western Europe are more likely today than perhaps at any point in recent history to agree with left-wing political parties on two key dimensions of political disagreement: the economic dimension and the moral dimension. Even so, the leftward shift in public opinion over the past quarter-century has not been accompanied by a corresponding improvement in the electoral prospects of left-wing parties. Simply, left-wing parties are doing no better today, and they may even be doing worse, than they used to. In the face of mass opinion change, right-wing parties have proven to be remarkably resilient, both in their level of support in the electorate and in their ability to form and lead governments.

This chapter has proposed a straightforward explanation that leaves little reason to expect that left-wing gains in mass opinion on economic and moral issues would translate into corresponding gains at the ballot box. Elites on the left – and indeed political parties on the left – bundle their positions on economic and moral issues into a coherent left-wing package.[23] But this packaging of political preferences is not typical of the public as a whole. It is not typical, even, of political activists as a whole. Rather, it is a peculiarity of elites and near-elites on the political left. Left-wing parties present a coherent ideological front to a fragmented electorate. Many of the voters who agree with left-wing parties on the economic dimension disagree with them on social issues. And many who agree with left-wing parties on the social issues disagree with them on the economic dimension. Indeed, there are far more people who agree with the left on one of these dimensions than who agree on both dimensions. It is the multidimensionalism of public opinion at the individual level that is consequential for understanding the behaviour of individuals in a ballot box.

Multidimensionality, of course, affects the right no less than the left. On the right, however, there is far less consensus at the elite level about the connection between economic and moral issues. Indeed, right-wing elites appear to be as divided as the public as a whole when it comes to economic and moral issues. Fiscal conservatives are not social conservatives, and social conservatives are not fiscal conservatives. Thus, where the divisions on the left cut between the masses and the elite, the divisions on the right cut between social conservatives, on the one hand, and fiscal conservatives on the other. To be sure, one consequence of this asymmetry is that right-wing parties are more vulnerable than their left-wing counterparts to fragmentation. Social conservatives and fiscal conservatives are natural allies because of their common opposition to various facets of the left, but they are uneasy allies as a result of their lack of agreement on social and economic issues. This alliance works, provided that economic conservatives do not accord a high degree of salience to their moral opinions, and moral conservatives to their economic opinions. Another consequence, however, is that the lines of disagreement on the right are more likely to play themselves out before an election, when elites craft policy positions, rather than during elections, when elites present their policies to the electorate. This disagreement at the elite level may well generate centralizing pressures that simply do not exist at the elite level on the left. Fiscal conservatives are likely to push for moderate positions on the social dimension; social conservative for moderate positions on the economic dimension. From this standpoint, the electoral prospects of the left and right look somewhat different from the big picture of cross-time opinion change might suggest. The patterns of public opinion at the aggregate level tell us very little about the patterns of opinion at the individual level. And individuals, not aggregates, cast ballots.

NOTES

1 David Apter, *The Politics of Modernization* (Chicago: University of Chicago Press, 1965); Daniel Bell, *The Coming of Post-Industrial Society: A Venture in Social Forecasting* (New York: Basic Books, 1973); Samuel Huntington, "Postindustrial Politics: How Benign Will It Be?," *Comparative Politics* 6, no. 2 (1974): 163–91.

2 Ronald Inglehart, "The Silent Revolution in Europe: Intergenerational Change in Post-Industrial Societies," *American Political Science Review* 65, no. 4 (1971): 991–1017; Inglehart, *Modernization and Postmodernization: Cultural, Economic, and Political Change in 43 Societies* (Princeton: Princeton University Press, 1997).

3 Scott Flanagan, "Changing Values in Advanced Industrial Societies," *Comparative Political Studies* 14 (1982): 403–44; Flanagan, "Changing Values in Advanced Industrial Societies: Towards a Resolution of the Values Debate," *American Political Science Review* 81 (1987): 1303–19; Neil Nevitte, *The Decline of Deference: Canadian Value-Change in Cross-National Perspective* (Peterborough: Broadview, 1996); Scott Flanagan and Aie-Rie Lee, "The New Politics, Culture Wars, and the Authoritarian-Libertarian Value Cleavage in Advanced Industrial Democracies," *Comparative Political Studies* 36 (2003): 235–70.

4 Ian Budge and Hans-Dieter Klingemann, *Mapping Policy Preferences: Estimates for Parties, Electors, and Governments 1945–1998* (Oxford: Oxford University Press, 2001); Hans-Dieter Klingemann, Andrea Volkens, Judith

Bara, Ian Budge, and Michael McDonald, *Mapping Policy Preferences II: Estimates for Parties, Electors, and Governments in Eastern Europe, European Union, and OECD 1990–2003* (Oxford: Oxford University Press, 2006); Wolfgang Müller and Kaare Strøm, *Coalition Governments in Western Europe* (Oxford: Oxford University Press, 2000).

5 These questions were not asked in earlier waves of the World Values Survey. There is also a question-wording change in the question about individual vs government responsibility. In 1990, the World Values Survey asked respondents to indicate their preferences on a ten-point scale, ranging from "Individuals should take more responsibility for providing for themselves," at the low extreme, to "The state should take more responsibility to ensure that everyone is provided for" at the high extreme. In 2000, the equivalent question in the WVS asked respondents to compare, on the same metric, "The government should take more responsibility to ensure that everyone is provided for," at the low end, to "People should take more responsibility to provide for themselves," at the high end. The change in the question wording, and the reversed non-random coding metric in which respondents often mistakenly treat "5" as the middle category, makes it difficult to compare the answers to this particular question across time.

6 Inglehart, *Modernization and Postmodernization*; Huntington, "Postindustrial Politics."

7 Budge and Klingemann, *Mapping Policy Preferences*, 21.

8 In both cases, the trend lines were estimated using random-effects regression suitable for cross-sectional time-series data. Even so, more technical models, and more detailed data, would be needed to examine more accurately the probability that these results occurred by chance alone.

9 Anders Widfeldt, "Sweden," *European Journal of Political Research* 42 (2003): 1091–101; Torii Aalberg, "Norway," *European Journal of Political Research* 41 (2002): 1047–56; Lars Bille, "Denmark," *European Journal of Political Research* 41 (2002): 941–6.

10 Donald Green, Bradley Palmquist, and Eric Schickler, *Partisan Hearts and Minds: Political Parties the Social Identities of Voters* (New Haven: Yale University Press, 2002).

11 Phillip Converse, "The Nature of Belief Systems in Mass Publics," in *Ideology and Discontent*, ed. David Apter (New York: Free Press, 1964), 254.

12 The necessity of this choice has the effect of suppressing the magnitudes of the coefficients for issue positions in models predicting vote choice.

13 Converse, "Nature of Belief Systems in Mass Publics," 24–7.

14 Ibid., 257.

15 Herbert Blumer, "Race Prejudice as a Sense of Group Threat," *Pacific Sociological Review* 1, no. 1 (1958): 3–7; Lauren McLaren, "Anti-Immigrant Prejudice in Europe: Contact, Threat Perception and Preferences for the Exclusion of Migrants," *Social Forces* 81, no. 3 (2003): 909–36.

16 Jennifer Hochschild, *What's Fair? American Beliefs about Distributive Justice* (Cambridge: Harvard University Press, 1981).

17 Norberto Bobbio, *Left and Right: The Significance of Political Distinction* (Chicago: University of Chicago Press, 1996); Alain Noel and Jean-Philippe Therien, *Left and Right in Global Politics* (New York: Cambridge University Press, 2008).

18 There is some reason to expect a possible connection between free-market support and animosity toward immigration. One possibility is that free-market support represents in some cases the veiled racism of sophisticated respondents. That is, some respondents may not express explicitly xenophobic comments because of social desirability pressures, but they may nonetheless manifest their prejudice more discreetly by opposing government benefits that disproportionately target citizens from different ethnic or racial backgrounds. Yet one problem with this line of argument in background analysis is that free-market support is not at all associated with animosity toward gays and lesbians. If some free-market supporters are, in effect, "closeted bigots," then we would expect to find some relationship between right-wing opinions about the free market and right-wing opinions about gays and lesbians. The evidence from background analyses, however, suggests no such relationship.

A second possibility is that free-market supporters oppose immigration because they believe – as many Europeans do – that immigrants draw disproportionately from the welfare state. In other words, free-market supporters do not oppose the welfare state because they dislike immigrants, but they oppose immigration because they dislike the welfare state. Further analysis suggests that the latter of these explanations is more accurate in the European case. The background analysis in this case was conducted by predicting opinions about immigration using an ordinal probit model that included among the covariates the answers of respondents to the following question: "Most people who come to live here work and pay taxes. They also use health and welfare services. On balance, do you think people who come here take out more than they put in or put in more than they take out?" Supporters and opponents of the free market are about. equally likely to answer that immigrants "take out more than they put in." The view that immigrants draw heavily from the welfare state is in turn associated with considerably less favourable opinions about immigration.

Yet when an additional item is added to the model to tap the interaction between free-market support, on the one hand, and opinions about welfare usage among immigrants, on the other, an analysis of the interaction effect indicates that the statistical relationship between opinions about immigrants' welfare usage and opinions about immigration is conditional on higher levels of free-market support. That is, the view that immigrants draw heavily on the welfare state underlies opposition to immigration only among those who oppose the welfare state in the first place. Thus, the link between free-market support and right-leaning opinions about immigration may well be conditional on the extent to which immigrants draw – or are perceived by free-market supporters to draw – more heavily than other citizens on welfare state resources.

19 Christopher Cochrane, "The Asymmetrical Structure of Left/Right Disagreement: Left-Wing Coherence and Right-Wing Fragmentation in Comparative Party Policy," *Party Politics* 19, no. 1 (2013): 104–21.

20 John R. Zaller, *The Nature and Origins of Mass Opinion* (New York: Cambridge University Press, 1992).

21 McLaren, "Anti-Immigrant Prejudice in Europe."

22 These statistics appear to indicate that the models predict more effectively the structure of opinion among politically engaged left-wingers than among politically engaged right-wingers, which is consistent with the hypotheses that this chapter puts forward. In CFA, a lower and less significant Chi-square statistic (χ^2) is a sign of better model fit. Even so, the Chi-square test statistic is also affected by the number of observations in the model, and there are more observations on the right than there are on the left. Thus, comparing these figures of model fit is not an appropriate way to compare the left and the right.

23 Cochrane, "Left-Wing Coherence and Right-Wing Fragmentation."

3 Canadian Populism in the Era of the United Right

JAMES FARNEY

A democratic deficit – which has as its symptoms declining voter turnout, levels of public trust, and general satisfaction with democratic government – has been widespread throughout the developed world since the 1970s. Three conditions are usually seen to underlie this malaise. The first is the reduction in the autonomy of elected governments. Economic globalization limits the autonomy of the state in the economy, especially during times of economic uncertainty. In some settings, the increased role of judicial review can limit the power of governments to act. The sheer complexity of the issues governments face also limits their ability to solve many problems. A second set of changes threatens the ability of parties to be attached to the electorate: a decline in partisan identification and membership, which is accompanied by a general sense that political parties do not offer voters genuine alternatives. Finally, party organizations have developed in a way that gives professionalized party elites great power while reducing party activists to little more than election workers and potential financial donors.[1]

The populist call to return government to the people is one important response to these patterns. Populism's central message, that "the people" need to be freed from political exploitation by "the elite," is amenable to both left- and right-wing interpretations, but left populists, who desire to use the state to protect people from big business and market fluctuations, have been less successful than their right-wing counterparts over the past generation. For populists of the right, the people are the hard-working members of the middle class who are set upon by special interest groups that have captured the welfare state. Those who do well in the existing system – civil servants, journalists, judges, established political parties, progressive social movement activists, and other unworthy public funding claimants – are all portrayed as being united in defence of the existing, unsatisfactory, system. The newest populist wave began in the in the late 1970s and 1980s in both North American and Europe. It targeted the welfare state (the major focus in North America), called for restrictions on immigration and multicultur-alism (the European focus), and/or for social conservative legislation in defence of the traditional family. Parties articulating this vision found their strongest support not in voters who would usually be consid-ered lower class, but amongst middle-class people who saw their eco-nomic standing and social status threatened by globalizing economies, demographic change (especially mass immigration), and government involvement in education and family life.[2] Right populists appealed to these voters with their promise to make the state smaller and less intrusive (which meshed well with neoliberalism's goals) and to give ordinary people more ways to say no to government action imposed on them by bureaucratic elites, politicians, and judicial decisions. This negative populism includes mechanisms like recall referendums and balanced budget legislation, but its most visible manifestation was in a political rhetoric generally hostile to elites and special interests. Provincial politicians, most notably Ralph Klein in Alberta and Mike Harris in Ontario, specialized in this formula in the 1990s.

At the same time, these parties promised to re-engage and re-energize democratic life – what one might call positive populism. This aspect of right populism was more visible in the Reform Party than in its pro-vincial analogues. Reform called for significant changes in Canadian political institutions (Senate reform, greater use of referendums and recall, relaxed party discipline, greater transparency, and some deliber-ative democracy measures) to ensure that the people could have more direct influence on political life. It also argued for government to have a smaller role in the economy and more autonomy for Canada's prov-inces. For many of its supporters, this set of commitments offered an attractive solution to what they saw as a troubling democratic deficit caused by the barriers political institutions put between the popular will and political outcomes.[3]

The Reform Party put a robust articulation of right populism front and centre in Canadian political life when, in 1993, it won fifty-two federal seats. Its success undercut the Progressive Conservatives and created a situation where neither Canadian party of the right could realisti-cally challenge the federal Liberals. Efforts to rectify this situation led to the transformation of the Reform Party into the Canadian Alliance

(CA) in 2000 and then to a merger between Progressive Conservatives (PCs) and the CA in 2003 that created the Conservative Party of Canada (CPC). Each step in this transformation saw Reform's original populism diluted as the party transformed itself into an unequivocally right-wing entity.[4] The new party emphasizes vote winning and the formation of a minimum winning coalition over ideological consistency, producing strong parallels to the old Progressive Conservative party. When conservative ideology does influence the CPC, it is usually of the neoliberal sort.[5] Occasionally, the party will tip its hat to its socially conservative supporters[6] or take a foreign policy position that is clearly nationalistic,[7] but these influences are usually seen to be much less important than the neoliberal element in the party or simple electoral calculation.

In this chapter, what is at issue is whether and how populism remains a significant force in any part of the Conservative Party of Canada and the provincial parties that share its right-populist heritage. What we find in all cases are remnants of populism in features of party organization, fundraising structure, and the kinds of electoral appeals deployed by the leadership. All have retained the basic "negative" orientation of reaching out to those Canadians who feel that their contributions and problems are overlooked by elites or "special interests." Most parties of the right, but especially the federal Conservatives, have become adept at integrating these populist appeals with conservatism in a way that, rather than seeming radical and challenging (as the Reform Party often did), seems commonsensical and moderate to enough Canadians to form a government. Programmatically, however, populism's influence has been much more limited. It can be seen in the federal party's pursuit of Senate reform and the Accountability Act, as well as its decisions on the long-form census and on law and order, as well as in a number of provincial initiatives. These reforms are relatively minor, however, and cannot be expected to significantly alleviate concerns with citizen disengagement so central to the sentiments that produced populism in the first place. In short, positive populism – even at the rhetorical level – seems not to have survived the unification of the Canadian right.

Populism in the Federal Conservative Party of Canada

Canadian political parties have always been noteworthy for their extremely strong leaders,[8] consistently high levels of party discipline, franchise approach to the selection of party personnel,[9] and brokerage or coalitional strategy electoral strategy.[10] Most are organized in a cadre fashion,[11] where there is little substantial organization outside of Parliament Hill. This results in parties that are highly centralized and frequently criticized for giving only a minimal role in making policy to ordinary members or even backbench MPs. Especially when in government, both the Liberals and Conservatives have a tendency to let the grassroots of their respective parties wither as their leadership focuses on the party in Parliament.

Given a combination of strong regionalism, parliamentary institutions, a first-past-the-post electoral system, and minimal class identity, there are incredibly strong pressures for convergence on this party model. It has been partially resisted by the New Democratic Party (NDP) and other third parties that accept that following a different organizational model will shut them out of government. At the same time, Canada's dominant model does produce grassroots dissatisfaction, so creating openings for the emergence of regionally based third parties that routinely threaten the survival of one or another of the existing major parties. The Conservatives have been particularly vulnerable to this threat, as majority Conservative governments have historically been followed by that party's implosion.[12] The last occasion when the party system suffered such a shock was 1993, when the Reform Party and Bloc Québécois destroyed the Progressive Conservatives on the Prairies and in Quebec.

Like several other third parties before it, the Reform Party challenged this organizational norm. In 1993, when it elected a substantial number of MPs for the first time, its members refused many of the traditional benefits of being MPs (like pensions and business-class airline seats), Preston Manning sat on the party's backbenches, it made an effort to be non-confrontational during Question Period, and caucus discipline was relaxed so that MPs could act as delegates for their constituents.[13] These innovations did not long survive the pressures of the Westminster system. Relaxed party discipline soon proved unworkable, as it prevented the party from presenting a coherent position to the media. Reform MPs also were soon accepting perks that come with being parliamentarians. When it came to operating in a Westminster setting, populist preferences had given way to political imperatives.

There were more enduring populist features in the party's organization outside Parliament. It barred formal ties to external or intermediary organizations, instead emphasizing vertical linkages between individual members and the leader. There were no youth or women's wings, and regional or provincial groups were unable to gain much independence. As Faron Ellis points out, the party was founded with the national organization and the local branch as the only legitimate organizational units, "both of which focussed on mass membership recruitment and the development of candidates and leaders from within their own ranks."[14] Fundraising depended entirely on members' subscriptions and voluntary contributions.

At the centre of Reform's populist organizational model was the policy convention. After its founding at a "non-partisan" convention in Vancouver, the new party's constitution, leadership, and core policy commitments were created at a 1987 convention followed by policy conventions in 1989, 1992, and 1997. Riding associations were given the opportunity to suggest policy recommendations they wished the party to adopt and to select delegates to take part in other parts of the process. These recommendations were discussed at regional or provincial meetings and then forwarded to a national agenda committee, which crafted the agenda for the national convention. On the face of it, this should have provided ordinary members with substantial involvement in policymaking. Certainly, it was an important part of Reform's appeal for much of its membership.

However, as Ellis also points out, this structure resulted in "the leadership's near absolute control of policy and strategy" – a pattern widely evident in other populist parties.[15] Preston Manning would not always dictate policy – for example, he shifted his position on the Charlottetown Accord in the face of opposition from his advisors and caucus. The leader, however, was undoubtedly more dominant than usual, even compared to those of other Canadian parties. As much as in other parties, the leader's office of advisors eclipsed caucus members. There was substantial leader control of ridings, motivated by Manning's need to control radical, especially racist, groups that tried to take over certain constituencies. This resulted in a process of nomination vetting by the national office in the early 1990s that was as strict as that in any established party. The building up of a national membership list and the focus on raising money by garnering small donations from many individuals, rather than focusing on large donations from a relatively few individuals or businesses, further enhanced the national office's leverage. It gave the leader a powerful tool for forming a direct relationship with members that no one else in the party had. As for the populist elements in the party's conventions, in practice the leadership exercised tight control of the national agenda committee and of the convention process. This resulted in a close monitoring of what policy proposals would see the light of day and a degree of leeway in translating formal resolutions into caucus and leadership priorities that was as great as in more established Canadian parties.[16]

There is a strong organizational legacy from Reform in the contemporary Conservative Party, all of it reinforcing the centralization of power in the leader's office, as Flanagan explores at more depth in chapter 5. The retention of a national membership list, accompanied by sophisticated fundraising strategies focused on small donations, is now buttressed by campaign finance laws limiting the size of donations to political parties. The close monitoring of candidate selection and substantial attention to candidate training reflects similar concerns about retaining party coherence and discipline. The party continues to hold policy conventions, which are, ostensibly, the pinnacle of extensive grassroots involvement but, even more so than in the Reform Party, are tightly scripted by the leader's office. Other aspects of party organization that were designed to give ordinary Canadians direct input into party decision-making had withered almost as soon as the Reform Party won a substantial number of parliamentary seats.

Does this mean that the Conservative Party of Canada has given up entirely on appealing to populist sentiment? No, it does not. We find recurrent evidence that the party's leadership concerns itself with retaining the loyalty of populist voters and members. Most such voters are willing to support the Conservatives because they are also fiscal or moral conservatives, but the party leadership seems to recognize that more than this is required to retain their enthusiasm and active support. They have done so by putting forward a series of policy proposals that embody a populist suspicion of experts and elites and a desire to enhance the ability of ordinary people to be involved in politics. Some of these initiatives can be seen as overlapping with conservative commitments, and none can be described as central to the government's agenda, but the party has still been willing to run considerable political risks to maintain its populist credentials by moving these proposals forward.

The newly elected government's very first piece of legislation, the 2006 Federal Accountability Act, can be seen as the most important instance where populism influenced government policy in the direction one might expect from the literature on the democratic deficit. This legislation further tightened the rules on political contributions, created new mechanisms for auditing within departments, increased the scope of the Access to Information Act, and forbade senior public officials from acting as lobbyists for five years after they left government. It also created a number of new parliamentary officers with oversight responsibilities: a commissioner of lobbying, a parliamentary budget officer, a public sector integrity commissioner, a procurement ombudsman, and a conflict of interest and ethics commissioner for the House of Commons. Although it enacted many of the recommendations of the Gomery Commission, the Act powerfully embodies the populist sense that politicians and senior bureaucrats cannot – if left to their own devices – be trusted to behave in the public's interest.

Though it falls short of Reform's demands for a "Triple E" Senate (Equal provincial representation, Effective, and Elected), the CPC has also been dogged in its pursuit of a limited form of Senate reform. Three bills (S-4 in 2006, C-19 in 2007, and S-7 in 2009) were introduced during Harper's minority governments to place limits on senators' terms. Each of these bills died on the order paper, but the measure was reintroduced in October 2011, only to be delayed again after the government referred the question of the constitutionality of its proposed changes to the Supreme Court. Harper has argued that limiting senators' terms does not require a constitutional amendment, thus allowing him to move forward on the issue without the support of provincial governments (which would be impossible to acquire). The government has sought to achieve an elected Senate by making it clear to the provinces that it will appoint to the Senate people who win provincially organized Senate elections – a mechanism that only Alberta has taken advantage of.[17] None of these reforms seem designed to change the Senate's role – the idea of representing provinces equally in it or making it a politically effective counterweight to the House of Commons has disappeared from the Conservative lexicon. Nevertheless, they arm the government with the capacity to assure populist supporters that they have taken significant steps.

The Conservatives have tried to introduce changes on a number of other democratic reform issues. The ending of the per vote public subsidy to political parties had brought on the prorogation controversy in 2008 but passed in the fall of 2011. During that same year the Fair Representation Act passed, adding thirty new seats to the House. Both of these measures fit with populist impulses but also clearly give a substantial partisan advantage to the Conservatives, making it difficult to ascribe the changes primarily to populist beliefs.

On a number of other issues, the Conservatives have maintained a stance that is sometimes described as conservative but is better understood as an implication of the populist distrust of elites. Their most consistent commitment of this sort has been to scrapping the long-gun registry in the face of opposition from, amongst other organizations, the Canadian Association of Police Chiefs. Similarly, the party's reforms to the criminal justice system – designed to make it tough on crime – have been tied to a denial that crime rates are falling in Canada (in the face of all available evidence) and the concerns that the tougher sentencing the government has brought in will do little to reduce crime. While cuts to arts funding hurt the party in Quebec in the 2008 election, the cuts were clearly supported by English-Canadian populists. Perhaps the most striking occasion where the government's actions embodied populist distrust of elites was in its willingness to trigger extensive opposition when it cancelled the long-form census.

Populism in Provincial Politics

Populism, of both left and right varieties, has long been strongest in Canada's western provinces. Federally, the NDP has historically done its best in British Columbia, Saskatchewan, and Manitoba, while Alberta has an equally long history of supporting right-populist parties like Social Credit and Reform federally and being a one-party state run by one version or another of conservative populism provincially. What has been striking, since the emergence of contemporary right populism around 1980, has been how successful conservatives have been at attracting Western Canadian populists. Reform successfully attracted many of the NDPs western populist supporters in 1993, and provincially the competitive party systems of BC, Saskatchewan, and Manitoba have all seen a powerful convergence where both the relevant right wing party and the provincial NDP have become significantly neoliberal in their economic policies and populist in their rhetoric.

Despite the strength of populism on both the left and the right, British Columbia provides the sole example of substantial democratic reforms instigated by a right-populist government in Canada. Most notably, the Liberal government of Gordon Campbell combined a deliberative democratic Citizens' Assembly process with two referendums (in 2005 and 2009) to examine the province's electoral system.[18] While the initiative did not pass the 60 per cent threshold that the government had set for its implementation in either referendum, it did nevertheless set a national example for other reconsiderations of Canada's first-past-the-post electoral system. In particular, its use of a randomly selected Citizens' Assembly, whose members had no previous links to partisan organizations, who were randomly selected, and who engaged in an extensive popular consultation before coming to their recommendation, was as grassroots a consultation as a populist could desire. While in opposition, the Campbell Liberals claimed that BC's requirement that any constitutional amendment pass a referendum before being approved by the province (a measure introduced by a NDP government in BC, but also in force in Alberta and Saskatchewan) should be applied to the Nisga'a Treaty. This claim was set aside in the *Campbell* decision, but the Campbell government did attempt to hold a referendum outlining principles for future treaty negotiations in 2002 (response rates were so low, and opposition so strong, that it was widely seen as a failed experiment).

The most striking aspect of the relationship between direct democracy and the BC Liberals, however, is the extent to which the province's recall and referendum legislation was used by opponents of the government. This legislation had been passed by the NDP government in 1991, after receiving majority approval in a referendum initiated by the previous Social Credit government. It contains provisions for groups of citizens to trigger a recall vote directed at sitting MLAs and for province-wide referendums on policy. The party also faced occasional challenges from opponents using the province's recall legislation, which allows voters in a riding to trigger a referendum on whether or not to recall their MLA between elections. It was a referendum on the Campbell government's decision to merge the provincial sales tax with the federal sales tax that was to reveal the power of such legislation. BC's version of the Harmonized Sales Tax (HST) was implemented in 2010 and, while arguably more efficient and progressive than the previously combined PST/GST tax structure, resulted in most British Columbians paying more sales tax. In the face of strong opposition to what he saw as a central policy – most notably a successful campaign to trigger a referendum on the topic – Campbell resigned as premier in March 2011. The HST itself was overturned after the province-wide referendum held during June and July 2011. That a referendum forced an otherwise successful provincial premier out of office and overturned a federal-provincial agreement on taxation is unprecedented in Canada and reveals something of the unpredictable power of direct democracy.

These important differences aside, BC's provincial Liberals (who are no longer associated with the federal party) offer a conventional right-populist approach to government, one that has attracted more committed populists than the left-populism promoted by its NDP rival but has not significantly opened up the party structure to its members.[19] Its emphasis has been, in a provincial party system polarized on right-left lines, to clearly position itself as the free-market party and to emphasize its pro-business identity. To that end, the party has stressed balanced budgets, reduced income and business taxes, limited rights of organized labour, significant public-sector layoffs and wage freezes, and privatized Crown corporations.[20] The Liberals have managed this while out-organizing other parties – notably BC Reform – that tried to attract the province's conservative populists after the previous right-wing party, Social Credit, fragmented in the early 1990s.

Alberta has a long history of government by parties that combine conservative and populist appeals. The provincial Progressive Conservative party, the archetype of this blend, now finds itself challenged in its ownership of that terrain by a new party, the Wildrose. Though Wildrose did less well in the 2011 provincial election than many had expected, perhaps because it was also identified with social conservatism, it has continued to pose a strong challenge to the Progressive Conservatives. Danielle Smith, the Wildrose Party's leader, has been clear about the centrality of neoliberalism in the party's platform but has also talked about making government more accountable and transparent. The PC premier, Alison Redford, is significantly more centrist on economic matters than Smith or previous PC premiers like Ralph Klein but also has an "anti-establishment" approach in running against what she has portrayed as the out-of-touch legacy of the unpopular former premier, Ed Stelmach.[21] The two parties are competing over the correct mix of populism and neoliberal fiscal policy.[22] Despite the centrality of populism to Alberta politics, however, it is important to note that PCs have been far more interested in creating a business-friendly environment and managing oil booms than they have been introducing any form of democratic reform during their forty years in office.

As in British Columbia, both of Saskatchewan's two major parties can lay claim to a populist heritage. The disappearance of the provincial PCs after a series of scandals in the early 1990s led to the formation of a new right-wing party, the Saskatchewan Party, in 1997. Although formed from a merger between remaining PC MLAs and some Liberal MLAs, its early character is perhaps best described as being a provincial equivalent to the Reform Party. The party's first leader, Elwin Hermanson, had been a Reform Party MP. The party's electoral success was concentrated in rural areas that had also supported Reform federally and was motivated by a similar sense that its supporters were not being taken into account when political decisions were made. The party's program initially centred on privatization, tax reduction, and toughening approaches to crime. This approach quickly allowed the party to become the official opposition but also meant that its appeal was limited to the rural parts of the province. Forming government would mean winning at least a few seats in either Saskatoon or Regina, and it was with that goal in mind that the party selected the more moderate Brad Wall as leader in 2004. The party quickly implemented a policy convention process, which culminated in a February 2005 convention. Like Reform and the federal Conservatives, this exercise generated significant grassroots involvement but culminated in a moderated policy platform in keeping with the desires of the party's leadership, who were operating very much with an eye to electability.[23] Under Wall, the party also professionalized and centralized its organization.[24] With both parties relatively committed to a neoliberal economic agenda, an important part of the 2007 campaign was how well each party could appeal to popular desire for change and for democratic reform. While the NDP's commitments (fixed election dates, a citizens' assembly on electoral reform, and lower voting age) was more extensive than the Saskatchewan Party's (who kept their promise to introduce fixed election date legislation), the latter convinced voters that it was the more likely to listen to them. Four years, and an unprecedented economic boom later, the party won a landslide on a record of (very moderate) democratic reform, extensive infrastructure and program spending, the attraction of substantial business investment, and the sense that it had put Saskatchewan back on the path to growth.

In Manitoba, right populists have been less successful than in the other Prairie provinces. Under Gary Doer and Greg Selinger, the NDP has dominated both the political centre and a good part of populist sentiment in the province. From the NDP victory in 1999 until 2006 or so, the Progressive Conservatives were also plagued by internal divisions, infighting, and an inability to fundraise that limited their ability to compete.[25]

In the rest of Canada, populism has been a less powerful current in provincial politics, but there are indications that it is growing. In Quebec, the surges in electoral support for the Action démocratique du Québec (ADQ) in the 1990s and early 2000s were derived in part from an anti-establishment right-wing populism. Andrea Lawlor and Éric Bélanger, and Brian Tanguay (in chapters 15 and 16 in this volume, respectively), point to dissatisfaction with existing alternatives and an electoral appeal very much centred on the party leader. In Ontario, a province where robust right populism has been limited essentially to Mike Harris's 1996 "Common Sense Revolution" and rejected by a sizeable part of the provincial PCs before and after Harris's leadership, the 2010 municipal election in Toronto came as a shock.[26] Rob Ford won the mayoralty on a classic right-populist platform: an opposition to public sector service provision, the promotion of the "little person's" interests (especially those of drivers), a celebration of anti-intellectualism, budget proposals focused mostly on eliminating "waste" (vaguely defined), and his distrust of expert advice.

Importantly, the most significant set of democratic reforms that address populist concerns – those to do with electoral reform – have not been closely linked to right-populist governments. Seven provinces (two led by right-populist governments), the Northwest Territories, and the Harper Conservatives have all introduced fixed election dates. BC, Ontario, and Prince Edward Island have all had Citizens' Assemblies and referendums considering some alternative to the current first-past-the-post system. That none of these electoral reform initiatives have succeeded matters less, for our purposes, than the simple fact that they were considered to start with, often because electoral reform seemed to offer an institutional mechanism to address citizen disengagement with Canadian democracy. While the Citizens' Assembly format is a very populist mechanism, it is worth noting that, of the governments that initiated such reviews, only the BC Liberals can be considered right populists.

Conclusion

What, then, are we to say of right-wing populism in Canada a decade after the Reform Party left the national stage? In many ways, the breadth of populism's influence since then has been surprisingly extensive. Few in the 1990s would have foreseen the rise of the ADQ in Quebec or the mayoral victory of Rob Ford in Toronto. The Saskatchewan Party's success and the continuing centrality of right populism in Alberta would have been more easily foreseen, but here, too, the extent to which some populist nostrums became centrist might have been surprising.

Nationally, unification with the Progressive Conservatives brought many who had gotten their political start with Reform into government, along with a considerable amount of their anti-establishment sentiment and rhetoric – their commitment to speaking for people who drink Tim Hortons rather than Starbucks.

Conservative electoral success and the widespread use of the rhetoric of "negative" populism are important changes, but they are only a part of the program that excited populists in the 1980s and 1990s. Together, they may offer a smaller, less intrusive state, but they do little to offer the population more direct input into the actions of governance – the goal of positive populism. Programmatic evidence of this latter sort of populism has been limited to a few, mostly symbolic, changes. To some extent, this lack of policy influence can be attributed to the need to moderate all ideological commitments if one is to form a government. As other chapters in this volume have shown, however, the neoliberal part of conservative principles has weathered this transformation with more success. While the Harper government has been more moderate than it is sometimes made out to be, it clearly pursues a free-market approach to governance. A similar pattern is evident in other successful right-populist governments (helped, in Alberta and Saskatchewan, by luckily timed natural resource booms). Similarly, the need for moderation has sometimes – but certainly not always – caused political parties to curb negative populist rhetoric.

Indeed, aside from a limited form of Senate reform, the federal Accountability Act, and BC's attempt at electoral reform, it is difficult to find deliberate and substantive action by any government with a populist heritage addressing concerns with the democratic deficit offering new and significant ways for ordinary Canadians to get involved in politics. Ironically, the area in which current Canadian conservatism's populist influence is most visible is in the ways that it encouraged the centralization of power in the party leader's office and the professionalization of party organization generally. While this has undoubtedly made Canada's right-wing parties more effective campaigning machines, it is a style of party organization that decreases grassroots participation and is usually seen to be an important factor contributing to citizen disengagement.

If we return to the three causes of general disengagement we began this chapter with, right populists most successfully moved political dialogue and economic policy further right, providing valuable allies for the reduction in the autonomy of the state in the market as they seek to free citizens from government oversight. Right populists have not implemented significant reforms to re-engage the mass public in politics or to convince the public that its participation in politics is meaningful. As to the third concern – that the professionalized party organization has actually devalued citizen involvement in the political process – the innovations introduced by Canadian populists have clearly exacerbated this trend. In short, the long-term legacy of the Reform Party, and of the type of populism it articulated, has been the worsening of the conditions that produced that dissatisfaction in the first place.

NOTES

1 See Grant Amyot, "The Waning of Political Parties," in *Canadian Politics in Transition*, 3rd ed., ed. Alain-G. Gagnon and A. Brian Tanguay, 496–509 (Peterborough: Broadview, 2007); and Elisabeth Gidengail, Richard Nadeau, Neil Nevitte, and André Blais, "Citizens," in *Auditing Canadian Democracy*, ed. William Cross, 93–118 (Vancouver: UBC Press, 2010), for useful overviews of this problem in Canada.

2 Classic comparative studies include Herbert Kitsheldt's *The Radical Right in Western Europe* (Ann Arbor: University of Michigan Press, 1995); and Hans George Betz's *Radical Right-Wing Populism in Western Europe* (New York: St Martin's, 1994). David Laycock, *The New Right and Democracy in Canada: Understanding Reform and the Canadian Alliance* (Don Mills: Oxford University Press, 2001); and Trevor Harrison, *Of Passionate Intensity: Right-Wing Populism and the Reform Party of Canada* (Toronto: University of Toronto Press, 1995), are excellent introductions to the ideology in Canada.

3 On Reform Party voters, see Faron Ellis, *The Limits of Participation: Members and Leaders in Canada's Reform Party* (Calgary: University of Calgary Press, 2005).

4 Tom Flanagan's *Waiting for the Wave: The Reform Party and Canada's Conservative Movement*, 2nd ed. (Montreal and Kingston: McGill-Queen's University Press, 2009), very usefully explores the tensions between populism and conservatism inside the Reform Party from the perspective of someone who wanted the party to become more conservative. Preston Manning's *Think Big: My Adventures in Life and Democracy* (Toronto: McClelland and Stewart, 2002), defends his populist vision. Bob Plamondon, *Full Circle: Death and Resurrection in Canadian Conservative*

Politics (Toronto: Key Porter Books, 2006), is a good overview of the unification process between Canada's right-wing parties.

5 See Patten, chapter 4 of this volume.

6 See Malloy's chapter 10 in this volume, and my *Social Conservatives and Party Politics in Canada and the United States* (Toronto: University of Toronto Press, 2012).

7 See Bloomfield and Nossal, chapter 8 in this volume.

8 William Cross, *Political Parties* (Vancouver: UBC Press, 2004), 29.

9 R.K. Carty, "The Politics of Tecumseh Corners: Canadian Political Parties as Franchise Organizations," *Canadian Journal of Political Science* 34 (December 2002): 723.

10 Harold Clarke, Jane Jenson, Larry Leduc, and Jon Pammett, *Absent Mandate: Interpreting Change in Canadian Elections* (Toronto: Gage, 1991).

11 Steven B. Wolinetz, "Cycles and Brokerage: Canadian Parties as Mobilizers of Interest," in *Canadian Parties in Transition*, 3rd ed., ed. Alain-G. Gagnon and A. Brian Tanguay, 179–97 (Peterborough: Broadview, 2007).

12 Richard Johnson, "Polarized Pluralism in the Canadian Party System," *Canadian Journal of Political Science* 41 (December 2008): 815.

13 Faron Ellis, *The Limits of Participation: Members and Leaders in Canada's Reform Party* (Calgary: University of Calgary Press, 2005), 149.

14 Ibid., xx.

15 Ibid., xxi.

16 The Reform Party also experimented with mechanisms like focus groups and telephone plebiscites to keep its MPs more abreast of opinion in their ridings. As tools for MPs, this never got beyond the experimental stage during the Reform Party's existence and seem to have been entirely dropped by its successor parties. As tools employed by the leader's office, alternatively, they have seen substantially more success.

17 It is worth pointing out that Harper holds the record for most Senate appointments – eighteen – in a single day when, having prorogued Parliament in the face of a confidence motion he was expected to lose, he filled every vacant Senate seat. See "Wallin, Duffy among 18 Named to Fill Senate Seats," CBC News, 22 December 2008, http://www.cbc.ca/news/canada/story/2008/12/22/senate-harper.html. Some have argued that such behaviour suggests a lack of commitment by Harper to actual reform, others that it is simply too early to tell.

18 On this process, see Dennis Pilon, "Democracy, BC-Style," in *British Columbia Politics and Government*, ed. Michael Howlett, Dennis Pilon, and Tracey Summerville, 87–109 (Toronto: Emond Montgomery, 2010).

19 Lynda Erickson, "Electoral Behaviour in British Columbia," in Howlett, Pilon, and Summerville, *British Columbia Politics and Government*, 136.

20 Stephen Phillips, "Party Politics in British Columbia: The Persistence of Polarization," in Howlett, Pilon, and Summerville, *British Columbia Politics and Government*, 116–24.

21 See CBC's coverage of Redford's victory in the PC leadership race on 28 September 2011 at http://www.cbc.ca/news/canada/calgary/story/2011/09/28/edmonton-redford-profile.html.

22 On the centrality of populism to Alberta's political culture, as well as the relatively moderate form of conservatism held by most voters in the province, see Stewart and Sayers in chapter 13 of this volume, as well as their "Is This the End of the Tory Dynasty? The Wildrose Alliance in Alberta Politics," University of Calgary School of Public Policy Working Paper 4, no. 6, 2011.

23 Raymond Blake, "The Saskatchewan Party and the Politics of Branding," in *Saskatchewan Politics: Crowding the Centre*, ed. Howard Leeson (Regina: Canadian Plains Research Centre, 2008), 174–5.

24 Ibid., 176.

25 Kelly Saunders, "Manitoba's Progressive Conservative Party: A 'Great Renewal' or Continued Disarray?," in *Manitoba Politics and Government: Issues, Institutions, Traditions*, ed. Paul G. Thomas and Curtis Brown (Winnipeg: University of Manitoba Press, 2010), 111–14.

26 This is not to say that a sizeable proportion of Ontario Tories could not be described as right populists – many clearly can be – but that it is a smaller proportion than in most other provinces and one that has never, in a sustained way, managed to dominate the political landscape.

4 The Triumph of Neoliberalism within Partisan Conservatism in Canada

STEVE PATTEN

Introduction

Political parties are spaces of ideological debate and struggle. They tend to represent a range of partially conflicting ideological perspectives. Over the past forty years at least four political and ideological forces have competed to define Canadian conservatism. A market-oriented liberalism has been championed by advocates of free enterprise, small government, and low taxes. A more progressive red toryism has been advanced by those who support socially active government and are willing to tame the free market by allowing social concerns and politics to trump economic logic. There has also been a variety of socially conservative ideological agendas in support of traditional social structures, relationships, and morality. Finally, conservative populists have drawn on right-wing ideological commitments to frame a politics of the common people in opposition to elites who are perceived as a threat to the social or economic interests of ordinary Canadians.

In the mid-1970s, Robert Stanfield led a Progressive Conservative Party defined primarily by a blend of red tory ideological commitments and market liberalism. By the early 1980s, however, partisan activists inspired by the examples of Margaret Thatcher and Ronald Reagan were actively reviving classic free enterprise liberalism – neoliberalism – in a bid to marginalize red toryism. Over the next quarter century these activists had considerable success advancing neoliberal conservatism through a series of policy debates, leadership contests, experiments with new political parties, and, most recently, the reunification of conservatives within the new Conservative Party of Canada.

This chapter tells the story of the triumph of neoliberalism within partisan conservatism in Canada. No effort is made to explore the social, political, economic, and international forces that have shaped neoliberalism's evolution and ascendance as the defining common sense of early twenty-first-century governance. But the historical narrative offered here emphasizes the importance of understanding the relationship between the processes of neoliberalization within and beyond partisan conservatism. Centrally important to the subsequent analysis is the argument that the success and character of Canadian neoliberalism and their implications for politics and governance have been shaped by the efforts of ideologically motivated party activists to redefine the character of partisan conservatism by marginalizing red toryism, partially containing socially conservative influences, and privileging the market orientation of neoliberalism.

Neoliberalism and Neoliberalization: Understanding an Ideology, State Form, and Rationality of Governance

Neoliberalism is a political ideology, a set of individualistic and market-oriented values, assumptions, and beliefs that shape how adherents approach politics and the challenges of policy and governance. It informs policy frameworks that aim to achieve economic competitiveness by rolling back the state and reining in expenditures. Its roots are in economic analysis and economistic social science theories that challenged the legitimacy of Keynesian liberalism, social democracy, and the post-war welfare state beginning in the 1960s and 1970s. At that time monetarism, supply-side economics, public choice theory, and the return to neoclassical economic analysis all contributed to the consolidation of neoliberalism as a re-strengthened free market orientation within conservatism.

Monetarist perspectives on the value of money and the problem of inflation underpinned neoliberalism's strong critique of deficit financing. Supply-side economics contributed a critique of Keynesian-inspired demand management, arguing that economic growth is best achieved through lowering input costs of production by cutting taxes on businesses and the wealthy investor class. Neoclassical economic analysis argued that an extensive program of privatization and deregulation would reduce the extent to which the state was crowding out private investment and creating cost rigidities that would vanish as market forces were encouraged to function freely. Public choice theory provided neoliberalism with an analytic framework for distrusting government and collective action by social interests. The argument that self-interested rent-seeking was over-politicizing public policy and creating "demand overload" informed neoliberalism's depiction of big welfare state government as dominated by a new class of social engineers whose agenda threatens individual liberty and the free market.

At the core of neoliberalism are three tenets. First, embrace free enterprise and markets as essential to both economic competitiveness and achieving individual and social well-being. Where the state's role cannot be wholly transferred to private market actors, efforts should be made to create public markets. The goal is to achieve the "ascendance of the market *over* the state and *inside* the state."[1] Second, shrink the state and limit our conception of the public sphere by rolling back government programs, cutting spending, deregulating, and offloading. The goal is to reduce the reach of the state and limit public expenditure through a process of "fiscalization" that demands that policy is assessed, first and foremost, according to its consequences for the state's fiscal position.[2] Third, privilege individualism, freedom of choice, and self-reliance. Citizens are appealed to as property owners, entrepreneurs, and taxpayers, while the legitimacy of collective social projects is questioned, and organized social interests are rejected as self-interested "special interests."

As neoliberal ideological commitments and policy frameworks became increasingly pervasive during the 1990s, scholars of neoliberalism noted how the reshaping of social relations and institutions was entrenching neoliberal perspectives on governance as a guiding common sense. It became increasingly common to interpret neoliberalism not only as an ideology, but as a state form, or even as a set of organized practices and rationalities – a "governmentality" or mode of governance – through which we discursively constitute the nature of rule, our individual subjectivities and political identities.[3] While noting considerable variation in the timing of neoliberalism's ascendance and the specificity of its institutionalization as a state form and rationality of governance, Peck and Tickell outline an influential conceptualization of neoliberalization as a process of neoliberalism taking hold as a governing paradigm, and then experiencing "*internal* shifts in its institutional form, its political rationality, and its economic and social consequences."[4] The process begins with a period of "proto-neoliberalism," when ideologues are experimenting with this new ideological orientation, pushing political boundaries, and launching neoliberal political projects. Once neoliberal policy commitments begin to take hold as a policy framework, there is a period of "rollback neoliberalism" during which the institutions and policies of the post-war welfare state are replaced and a neoliberal market logic is established as the hegemonic mode of governance.

It is clear, however, that the neoliberalization process does not stop there. Peck and Tickell identify a third period – "roll-out neoliberalism" – during which the neoliberal rationality of governance is further normalized and technically embedded in a wider range of social, political, and policy institutions. But others see roll-out neoliberalism as more complex and contradictory. After several years of often aggressive market-oriented policy changes, neoliberal state forms tend to generate social and economic contradictions, illogics, and political reactions that require containment and redirection. As a result, roll-out neoliberalism is a period of discursive adjustment and policy learning with two very different tracks. There are policies that deepen neoliberal marketization while containing and marginalizing those who have been dispossessed and sought to challenge neoliberalism. But there have also been socially interventionist and ameliorative policies that introduce non-market (non-neoliberal) logics to stabilize and enhance the legitimacy of what is otherwise a neoliberal state form.[5]

Neoliberalism and Partisan Conservatism in Canada

The process of neoliberalization in Canada has been advanced and shaped by international forces, economic conditions, and a range of domestic political actors. The ideological triumph of neoliberalism within partisan conservatism has both contributed to and been shaped by the broader process of neoliberalization. It is, therefore, essential that our study of neoliberal partisan struggles take seriously the relationship between the processes of neoliberalization within and beyond partisan conservatism. As such, the narrative to follow organizes the story of neoliberalism within partisan conservatism in relation to the three periods of neoliberalization.

Proto-Neoliberalism and the Ascendance of Neoliberal Ideology in the Progressive Conservative Party

Under the leadership of John Diefenbaker (1956–67) and Robert Stanfield (1967–76) the Progressive Conservative Party had been defined by a blend of progressive red toryism and market-oriented liberalism.[6] The party never rejected its long tradition of supporting market liberal principles, but, at the height of the post-war welfare state, Canada's Progressive Conservatives were willing to be "progressive" and "activist" supporters of a mixed economy and the use of state power to serve social interests.[7] The Progressive Conservative Party stood apart from parties of the ideological left but did not pose a fundamental challenge to the policies of welfare capitalism.[8] In an essay on conservative principles, Robert Stanfield gave pride of place to free enterprise, but also to social order and social action by the state; he explained that a decent civilized society responds to social concerns regarding poverty and the plight of the less fortunate.[9]

There were "genuine intraparty ideological differences" at play at the 1976 leadership convention that selected Joe Clark to replace Stanfield.[10] While party activists remained confident that ideological difference could be reconciled, a more market-oriented and small-state form of conservatism was growing in prominence.[11] Conservatives were aware of how Margaret Thatcher was busy transforming the British Conservative Party in light of the Hayekian ideas of the Institute of Economic Affairs. Moreover, outside the partisan arena, neoliberal ideas were being championed by the National Citizens Coalition (founded in 1967) and the Fraser Institute (founded in 1974). These were the early days of proto-neoliberalism; neoliberal governing projects were taking shape on the ideological right of the Progressive Conservative Party.

Through the 1979 election, his short time as prime minister, and into the early 1980s, Joe Clark remained a conservative moderate, balancing the red tory willingness to accept state activism with his party's market liberal desire to generally limit the size of government. His ideological orientation was largely consistent with Stanfield's. Although Clark called for the privatization of Petro-Canada, opposed the nationalist neo-interventionism of the Trudeau Liberals, and took other market-oriented policy positions, he showed no interest in embracing the free-market conservatism of Thatcher and Reagan. Not unsurprisingly, the more committed neoliberal ideologues responded by organizing to force Clark from his position at the helm of the party. This new wave of neoliberal enthusiasts believed that deposing Clark was an opportunity to select a leader who would turn the party to the ideological right. But the party remained divided. Robert Stanfield returned briefly to public life to make a speech warning conservatives off the neoliberal market enthusiasm of the Reagan Republicans: "This exaggerated claim for the marketplace, and this denigration of government ... are not in the Conservative tradition."[12] Stanfield urged his party to avoid the neoliberal prescriptions of the new right and reminded conservatives that their "party has always accepted that state intervention may be necessary to achieve national objectives or fulfil social responsibilities that transcend the values of the market."[13]

The leadership issue came to a head at a party convention in 1983, when one-third of party members voted in favour of a motion calling on Joe Clark to step down and call a convention to select a new leader. Clark called a leadership convention but then announced he would stand again for the position. Going into the 1983 PC leadership convention, the neoliberal right had the momentum and was defining the debate, although never actually winning a clear majority of delegates over to their ideological world view. The slate of candidates included an array of new-right voices – including free-market champions Michael Wilson and Peter Pocklington and the new-right populist John Gamble. Former Toronto mayor David Crombie campaigned as the conscience of the party's red tory progressive tradition. Joe Clark stood as the moderate tory representative of the status quo. The two major challengers to Clark – John Crosbie and Brian Mulroney – offered right-wing messages aimed at appealing to the new wave of neoliberalism but avoided policy that might define their candidacy as extreme or narrowly neoliberal.

Mulroney had been identified as a "progressive" or "Stanfield Conservative" on the left of the party during his unsuccessful 1976 bid for the leadership.[14] In 1983 he stood opposed to continental free trade and was purposefully vague on many issues of importance to neoliberals. For his part, Crosbie campaigned as a supporter of free markets and free trade but was also clear that he "wouldn't cut a dollar from any social program."[15] For many neoliberal ideologues, however, the primary goal was simply to replace Joe Clark with a more electorally attractive leader who displayed some openness to neoliberal ideas. Sensing the mood in the party, both Crosbie and Mulroney embraced the rhetoric and symbolism (and, obviously, some of the platform) of the neoliberal right. But it was the slick and bilingual Mulroney who appeared most capable of defeating the governing Liberals. This attracted leading neoliberal activists to prominent roles on Mulroney's campaign team and helped create the impression that his assumption of the Progressive Conservative leadership was closely tied to the rise of neoliberalism within the party.

Brian Mulroney's landslide win in the 1984 general election has been regularly depicted as a defining moment in the neoliberal (or neoconservative) revolution of the early 1980s. In retrospect, however, this characterization is not particularly accurate. The first Mulroney government was slow to act on policy initiatives that appealed to those with strong neoliberal ideological orientations. Shortly after the 1984 election, Mulroney's finance minister, Michael Wilson, released a document defining the government's priorities in neoliberal terms as deficit reduction, deregulation, and privatization. Wilson even suggested that ending the universality of social programs might make a useful contribution to reducing the deficit.[16] This was controversial with the red tory wing of the PC party, and public reaction was quite negative. In the end, Mulroney's cautious pragmatism won out, and he declared universality in existing social programs to be a "sacred trust" that his government would never undermine.[17] Indeed, during his first term in office (1984–8) Mulroney's social policy agenda focused on little more than limiting social spending; it was "a strategy of containment rather than neo-conservative dismantlement."[18] In this era of proto-neoliberalism Mulroney was "strong on rhetorical formulation" but "weak on consistency and follow-through."[19]

Stephen Harper was among those who came early to the conclusion that Mulroney had not delivered on the neoliberal promise of his leadership campaign. Harper had hoped the Mulroney landslide of 1984 would bring the politics of Thatcher and Reagan to Canada.[20] By 1986 he was actively reading the works of influential neoconservative and neoliberal thinkers and strategizing on how to build a "Blue Tory network" of grassroots conservatives interested in an ideologically purer Progressive Conservative Party.[21] But before that effort amounted to anything of significance, Harper was introduced to Preston Manning and soon got on board with the project to launch the Reform Party of Canada as a new and more conservative option to the PC Party. By the time of the Reform Party's founding convention in 1987, Harper was emerging as a key thinker in the Reform movement. He delivered a major speech outlining a neoliberal populist critique of the welfare state and justifying neoliberalism's rollback agenda: "The welfare state has placed unprecedented power in the centralizing hands of the federal bureaucracy, both in terms of its new reaches into Canadian life and its insistence on standardizing all policies and practices on a national scale. The welfare state has witnessed the phenomenon of greedy pressure-group politics reaching unprecedented depths. The vested interests of the welfare state operate in the guts of government decision-making machinery. Thus, their networks have been highly successful in achieving constant growth for their programs and bureaucracies."[22]

In ideological terms, the Reform Party represented a clearer and deeper commitment to neoliberalism, an absolute rejection of red toryism, and a partisan space for expressing the values of socially conservative traditionalism. Social conservatism had been a marginal ideological influence in the PC Party. A group of socially conservative MPs had established an informal "family caucus" in the mid-1980s, but this was more an expression of weakness than strength. Social conservatism would be more visible with the rise of Reform, even if the party's main contribution to the Canadian political landscape was, in the end, to deepen the process of neoliberalization.

Rollback Neoliberalism, Partisan Politics,
and the Entrenchment of Canada's Neoliberal Project

Ironically, the launch of the Reform Party coincided with negotiations towards the Canada-U.S. Free Trade Agreement, and the Mulroney government's more assertive moves towards the neoliberal right. Between 1988 and 1993 the PC government made cuts to a range of Keynesian-era social policies. Family Allowances were terminated, the universality of Old Age Security was abolished, ceilings were placed on funds transferred to selected provinces under the Canada Assistance Plan, and federal contributions to Unemployment Insurance were ended.[23] The rationale was that government must respond to the imperatives of a mounting fiscal crisis and new challenges associated with economic competitiveness in an era of globalization. The fact that this reasoning echoed arguments advanced by leading think tanks of the ideological right, the editorial pages of major newspapers, and the Canadian business community merely demonstrated the extent to which a neoliberal logic of governance was ascendant.

Of course, Mulroney-era social policy cuts did not satisfy the Reform Party's taste for welfare-state retrenchment. Nor did it speak to the socially conservative populism that was so central to the party's ideological identity.[24] Populism is the political defence of the interests, values, and lifestyles of the common people against the rule of powerful, yet unrepresentative special interests.[25] Emerging, as it did, at a moment of heightened social-movement activism, when a number of social groups – including women, ethnocultural and racialized minorities,

queers, and Aboriginal peoples – were embracing a progressive identitarian politics and calling for meaningful political recognition and
the extension of social rights, Reform's populism is best understood
as a reaction against late twentieth-century new social movements and
their politics of cultural recognition.[26] The party's populism spoke to
social conservative anxiety regarding the nature and extent of social
change and, simultaneously, to neoliberal concerns about a new class
of social and state interests that were contributing to demand overload
and unchecked spending.

The 1993 general election saw the Progressive Conservatives reduced
to just two seats in Parliament and Reform thrust to prominence
with a caucus of fifty-two MPs. The new Liberal government of Jean
Chrétien was elected on promises that amounted to resisting neoliberal trends: repudiating central features of the North American Free
Trade Agreement (NAFTA), state spending to stimulate job creation,
and an overhaul of Canada's social security system. But over the course
of its first sixteen months in power, the government redefined itself
in keeping with neoliberal ideas. Social security reform was set aside,
continental free trade was embraced, and one policy goal was elevated
above all others: slaying the deficit. With this goal in mind, the Liberals'
1995 budget introduced cost-cutting measures and "irrevocable" structural changes to government.[27] These included bringing federal funding for health, post-secondary education, welfare, and social services
under one dramatically smaller transfer program called the Canada
Health and Social Transfer and initiating dramatic cuts in the size of
the Canadian public service. It was a defining moment in the process
of neoliberalization. The federal role in the Canadian welfare state was
transformed by the logic of "fiscalization," and the politics of retrenchment and rollback neoliberalism were now dominant.[28]

Similar developments were occurring provincially. In Alberta the
1993 election of Ralph Klein was followed by dramatic cuts in provincial program spending, a significant downsizing of the provincial
public service, privatization of retail liquor sales, and the introduction of a flat-rate provincial income tax. In 1995 Mike Harris led the
Ontario PC Party to power with his "Common Sense Revolution,"
a policy platform calling for a dramatic 30 per cent cut to the provincial income tax rate, a 22.6 per cent reduction in social assistance
rates, a commitment to balancing the provincial budget within five
years, and a promise of massive job creation by removing regulatory
barriers to investment and business confidence.[29] In addition to their

contribution to the neoliberalization of governance, party activists from Alberta and Ontario helped redefine partisan conservatism at the national level.

After the 1993 electoral debacle, Jean Charest replaced Kim Campbell as PC leader and established a process to revitalize the party and involve rank-and-file party members in setting policy. The committee that guided this process and drafted the PCs' 1997 election platform was led by Ontario-based activists with ties to Mike Harris. Not surprisingly, the result was a policy agenda marked by a discursive and substantive commitment to neoliberal ideals. Policy documents called for a new "culture of opportunity" to replace Canada's "welfare state."[30] Proposals called for "experimentation with different approaches to management and financing" of health care – implying greater leeway for private health insurance and for-profit delivery.[31] The privatization agenda also included the possible privatization of CBC-TV.[32] Although the final platform was not as aggressive as internal policy documents, it retained neoliberal promises regarding tax cuts, deregulation, and the further removal of trade barriers.[33]

The 1997 federal election left partisan conservatives deeply frustrated. The Reform Party made important gains, adding eight members to its parliamentary caucus. But it was now clear that vote-splitting on the right would doom conservatives to perpetual opposition status. Neoliberals within the PC Party were disappointed that they had failed to outdo Reform with their ideologically decisive platform, and red tories felt the party had given up too much by allowing neoliberal ideologues to draft the party's platform.

Roll-out Neoliberalism and the Project of Uniting
the Right under a Single Neoliberal Conservative Party

Soon after being re-elected, the Chrétien Liberals achieved a balanced federal budget and turned to charting a post-deficit policy agenda. After years of neoliberal-inspired welfare state retrenchment, there was interest in a "Third Way" agenda of social reinvestment. Commitments to neoliberal marketization remained a powerful determinant of federal policy, but there was openness to investing in social capital and delivering ameliorative policies that would help Canadians adapt and succeed in the competitive economy of the twenty-first century. The high-water mark of rollback neoliberalism was passing as Canada transitioned to roll-out neoliberalism.

On the partisan right, change was afoot. In April 1998, Jean Charest stepped down as federal PC leader to seek the leadership of the Quebec Liberal Party. A month later, Preston Manning launched an initiative to build a united conservative partisan alternative to the governing Liberals. But when the PC Party selected Joe Clark to once again lead their party, hope of building a new united party vanished. Clark believed Reform's neoliberal and socially conservative views were too extreme; his agenda involved pulling the PCs back from the neoliberal right.

Of course, many long-time Progressive Conservatives disagreed with Clark. Tony Clement, then an Ontario provincial Cabinet minister, lead a group of Ontario PCs to meet with Clark and discuss the possibility of formal cooperation with the Reform Party. Clark alienated Clement and other right-wing conservatives by dismissing them as an "insignificant group" within his party.[34] One neoliberal political pundit wrote that Joe Clark's decision to reject any form of cooperation with Reform "marked the end of the federal Tories' 25-year flirtation with the ideological Right."[35] Many conservative supporters of the neoliberal governing agendas of Ralph Klein and Mike Harris abandoned their federal party to support Preston Manning's United Alternative initiative. Clement joined the Steering Committee, and Harris's campaign manager, Tom Long, agreed to co-chair the January 2000 founding convention of the Canadian Alliance. Long used his role at the new party's convention to lash out at Clark's red toryism, declaring that Clark was not a "true conservative" and had "no meaningful record of accomplishments on promoting the things conservatives really care about."[36] While the Canadian Alliance was meant to unite the right, division within partisan conservatism seemed as deep as ever.

The campaign to lead the Canadian Alliance pitted the Reform's Manning against two candidates from provincial wings of the PC Party. Tom Long entered the race as the strategist and policy leader who oversaw Mike Harris's successful 1995 and 1999 election campaigns. Stockwell Day came from Alberta, where he had served as a prominent minister in the government of Premier Ralph Klein. Day had earned his neoliberal credentials by overseeing budget cuts and the introduction of the flat-rate income tax, but he was also a social conservative, and he made effective use of evangelical Christian networks to rally support and win the leadership race.[37]

Stockwell Day performed poorly in the 2000 federal election and soon become a lightning rod for criticism. A group of about a dozen

Canadian Alliance MPs broke ranks and established the Democratic Reform Caucus (DRC), an independent parliamentary coalition that worked to force Day from the leadership while actively cooperating with Clark's PCs. The DRC example heightened enthusiasm for uniting the right, but with Day and Clark refusing to cooperate it was evident that a merger would have to await new and willing party leaders. When Stephen Harper took over from Day in 2002, pro-merger partisans were only a touch more optimistic. Harper claimed to support uniting the right but refused to cooperate with the red tory Clark. Then hope seemed lost in 2003 when Peter MacKay was selected to replace Clark after a convention-floor promise to never enter into merger negotiations. But, to the surprise of most, Harper and MacKay soon authorized negotiations and, on 15 October 2003, they announced an agreement to merge their parties to form a new national party of conservatism: the Conservative Party of Canada.

Perhaps exposing the extent of Reform/Alliance influence over the new party, Harper won the Conservative leadership with a decisive first-ballot victory. Unsuccessful in the 2004 general election, the Conservatives held their founding policy convention in Montreal in March 2005. The policy resolutions and debates at that convention revealed much about the relative influence of various conservative ideological voices.[38] Most striking was the absence of red tory voices. But equally significant to many long-time Reformers were decisions that involved dropping commitments to mechanisms of direct democracy and expunging policy documents of populist rhetorical attacks on the power of minority special interests. Moral traditionalism was downplayed, but there was still considerable evidence of the vitality of social conservatism in the new Conservative Party. Even though Harper made a point of stating unequivocally in his keynote speech that he would not introduce abortion legislation of any kind, a significant minority of delegates (45%) were uncomfortable with ducking the abortion debate. The social conservatives' presence at the convention was evidenced by Campaign Life encouraging its members to become delegates and then hosting a delegate briefing room to organize voting in favour of socially conservative resolutions. While not dominating policy debates, they were well-organized and obviously committed to remaining a force in the new party.

The clearest ideological message to be taken from these policy discussions was the decisively neoliberal orientation of the new Conservative Party. With very little debate, delegates passed a resolution committing the party to creating opportunities for for-profit delivery of health-care services. Delegates also took a stand against the "statist interventionism" of the Liberal government's popular national child-care agenda, committed a Conservative government to aggressive debt repayment, and voted in favour of constitutionally entrenched protection for property rights. The pro-market orientation of these policy commitments was significantly to the right of the more mainstream neoliberal policies of then–prime minister Paul Martin. It was clear the Harper Conservatives wanted nothing to do with the social investment agenda of the federal Liberals.

In early 2006, with the governing Liberals plagued by ongoing revelations associated with the sponsorship scandal, Stephen Harper was elected Canada's twenty-second prime minister. Since he came to office, Harper's actions have been guided by his neoliberal ideology and a keen sense of strategic pragmatism. Harper is, at times, aggressively partisan, but he understands when limited concessions are necessary to ensure electoral success – and his goal is not simply to win successive elections, but to have the new Conservative Party replace the Liberals as Canada's natural governing party. Still, in recent years a number of political pundits have raised doubts about Harper's conservative credentials. Gerry Nicholls, a former colleague of Harper's at the National Citizens' Coalition, now criticizes Harper for becoming too focused on partisan advantage and abandoning principled conservatism in favour of a "deliberate strategy of diluting conservative principles and moving the party to the left."[39] *Globe and Mail* columnist Margaret Wente concurs, arguing that instead of moving the country to the right, Harper has moved his party to the left, racking up deficits, expanding the size of government, quashing the foreign takeover of the Potash Corporation of Saskatchewan, and refusing to recriminalize abortion or repeal gay marriage.[40]

No policy decision did more to raise questions about Harper's neoliberal credentials than the 2009 decision to launch a massive stimulus package and allow the government of Canada to assume significant deficits. The national editor of *Maclean's*, Andrew Coyne, depicted the 2009 federal budget as a retreat from conservative principles – the "end of conservatism."[41] It is certainly true that, as a result of spending on infrastructure, the military, and correctional services, Harper has failed to deliver on his commitment to smaller government.[42] Still, it is wrong to suggest that Harper is a failure as a neoliberal. Critics like Nicholls pine for the Stephen Harper of the mid-1990s. But that was the era of rollback neoliberalism, when the public mindset was still being shifted in neoliberal directions. It took aggressive action by neoliberals to shift Canada's governing paradigm. A decade later, many policies and programs have been neoliberalized, and neoliberalism is now mainstream common sense in the Canadian party system. In the 2008 federal election, New Democratic Pary leader Jack Layton – a social liberal who rejected so much of the Harper Conservatives' agenda – was as firm as Harper on the principle that the federal government should not run a deficit. Even during the period of Liberal social reinvestment before Harper's election, social policy was being shaped by the Department of Finance and "fiscalized" political calculations.

There is, moreover, considerable evidence that the Harper Conservatives remain particularly committed to neoliberal conservatism. The government's steadfast refusal to shift its position on state action in response to climate change, its aggressive drive to be a partner in trans-Pacific free trade, its continued commitment to corporate tax cuts, and its repeated use of targeted tax breaks rather than government programs or spending to address social needs reveal the extent of their neoliberal orientation. It was estimated that tax cuts brought in by the Conservatives before the 2011 election would "result in foregone federal revenues of $220 billion between 2007 and 2013."[43] This willingness to forego potential revenue has contributed to the emergence of a "structural deficit" that Canada's Parliamentary Budget Office says will continue to grow.[44] Where the government has been less aggressively conservative has been on moral issues and social conservatism. Harper understands the politics of social conservatism and in recent years has developed a deeper faith in the Christian gospel and chosen to worship in an evangelical church. Still, his message to social conservatives has been to "let things happen incrementally when the times are right."[45] Until then, that wing of the party is partially pacified with a law-and-order agenda and isolated initiatives such as establishing the Office of Religious Freedom that speak directly – if insufficiently – to their instincts and preferences. What about the future? With deficit financing delegitimized by three decades of neoliberalization, political parties unwilling to consider more than trivial tax increases, and now a significant revenue dilemma, it was clear by 2013 that another period of neoliberal cuts and restructuring similar to the 1990s may be as likely as action on social conservative issues if the Harper Conservatives continue to govern.

Conclusion

A variety of social forces, institutional dynamics, and political economic conditions have shaped the process of neoliberalization in Canada. But an important part of the story of neoliberalism has been the struggles of partisan ideologues to take control of and redefine partisan conservatism. From deposing Joe Clark in 1983, through the founding of the Reform Party, Manning's United Alternative initiative, various leadership races and exercises in drafting party policy and campaign platforms, to reuniting Canadian conservatives in the Conservative Party of Canada, free market–oriented activists have worked to sideline red toryism and partially contain socially conservative ideological impulses. For Stephen Harper and many of the protagonists in this struggle, the goal has always been to bring their own version of the Thatcher/Reagan revolution to Canada. Loyalty to ideas has often been more important than loyalty to party. Indeed, from 1987 to 2003 partisan conservatism splintered as the Reform/Alliance campaigned against the Progressive Conservatives.

Today the ideological face of partisan conservatism is quite unlike the blend of red tory ideological commitments and milder market liberal influences that shaped the PCs in the era of Robert Stanfield. Indeed, when Stanfield sensed the growing influence of a more market-oriented neoliberal conservatism he warned conservatives off this path. But many activists, particularly young ideologues like Stephen Harper, were not persuaded. Today, many of these same activists, and a new generation who came to partisan politics in the context of neoliberalism, are leaders in the Conservative Party. Neoliberalism is now triumphant, and there are few signs of this changing anytime soon.

NOTES

1 Janine Brodie, "Meso-Discourses, State Forms and the Gendering of Liberal-Democratic Citizenship," *Citizenship Studies* 1, no. 2 (1997): 235.
2 Timothy Lewis, *In the Long Run We're All Dead: The Canadian Turn to Fiscal Restraint* (Vancouver: University of British Columbia Press, 2004).
3 Wendy Larner, "Neo-liberalism: Policy, Ideology, Governmentality," *Studies in Political Economy* 63 (2000): 5–25.
4 Jamie Peck and Adam Tickell, "Neoliberalizing Space," *Antipode* 34, no. 3 (2002): 384.

5   Peter Graefe, "Roll-out Neoliberalism and the Social Economy" (paper prepared for the Annual Meeting of the Canadian Political Science Association, University of Western Ontario, London, 2 June 2005).

6   William Christian and Colin Campbell, *Political Parties and Ideologies in Canada*, 3rd ed. (Toronto: McGraw-Hill Ryerson, 1990).

7   George C. Perlin, *The Tory Syndrome: Leadership Politics in the Progressive Conservative Party* (Montreal and Kingston: McGill-Queen's University Press, 1980), 182–3, 186.

8   Duncan Cameron, "Political Discourse in the Eighties," in *Canadian Parties in Transition: Discourse, Organization, and Representation*, ed. Alain-G. Gagnon and A. Brian Tanguay (Toronto: Nelson Canada, 1989), 67.

9   Robert L. Stanfield, "Conservative Principles and Philosophy," in *Politics: Canada*, ed. Paul Fox and Graham White, 376–81 (Toronto: McGraw-Hill Ryerson, 1987).

10 Robert Krause and Lawrence Leduc, "Voting Behaviour and Electoral Strategies in the Progressive Conservative Leadership Convention of 1976," *Canadian Journal of Political Science* 12, no. 1 (1979): 121.

11 Perlin, *Tory Syndrome*, 174, 184.

12 Christian and Campbell, *Political Parties and Ideologies in Canada*, 104.

13 Patrick Martin, Allan Gregg, and George Perlin, *Contenders: The Tory Quest for Power* (Scarborough: Prentice-Hall Canada, 1983), 155.

14 Krause and Leduc, "Voting Behaviour and Electoral Strategies"; Perlin, *Tory Syndrome*.

15 Martin, Gregg, and Perlin, *Contenders*, 114.

16 Neil Bradford, *Commissioning Ideas: Canadian National Policy Innovation in Comparative Perspective* (Toronto: Oxford University Press, 1998), 118.

17 Christian and Campbell, *Political Parties and Ideologies in Canada*, 157–8.

18 Michael J. Prince, "From Health and Welfare to Stealth and Farewell: Federal Social Policy, 1980–2000," in *How Ottawa Spends 1999–2000: Shape Shifting; Canadian Governance toward the 21st Century*, ed. Leslie A. Pal (Toronto: Oxford University Press, 1999), 156.

19 Reg Whitaker, "The Chrétien Legacy," in *The Chrétien Legacy: Politics and Public Policy in Canada*, ed. Lois Harder and Steve Patten (Montreal and Kingston: McGill-Queen's University Press, 2006), 7.

20 Tom Flanagan, *Waiting for the Wave: The Reform Party and Preston Manning* (Toronto: Stoddart, 1995), 60.

21 Bob Plamondon, *Full Circle: Death and Resurrection in Canadian Conservative Politics* (Toronto: Key Porter Books, 2006), 88, 90; William Johnson, *Stephen Harper and the Future of Canada* (Toronto: McClelland & Stewart, 2005), 44.

22 Stephen Harper, cited in "Act of Faith," *BC Reports*, ed. Terry O'Neill (Vancouver: British Columbia Report Books, 1991), 44.

23 James J. Rice and Michael J. Prince, "Lowering the Safety Net and Weakening the Bonds of Nationhood: Social Policy in the Mulroney Years," in *How Ottawa Spends 1993–1994: A More Democratic Canada …?*, ed. Susan D. Phillips, 381–416 (Ottawa: Carleton University Press, 1993).

24 Steve Patten, "Preston Manning's Populism: Constructing the Common Sense of the Common People," *Studies in Political Economy* 50 (1996): 95–132.

25 Paul Taggart, *Populism* (Buckingham: Open University Press, 2000).

26 Carol Johnson, Steve Patten, and Hans-Georg Betz, "Identitarian Politics and Populism in Canada and the Antipodes," in *Movements of Exclusion: Radical Right-Wing Populism in the Western World*, ed. Jens Rydgren (New York: Nova Science Publishers, 2005), 86.

27 Paul Martin, *Budget Speech* (Ottawa: Department of Supply and Services Canada, 1995), 6.

28 Prince, "From Health and Welfare to Stealth and Farewell," 157.

29 Thomas Walkom, "The Harris Government: Restoration or Revolution?," in *Government and Politics of Ontario*, ed. Jens Rydgren, 5th ed. (Toronto: University of Toronto Press, 1997), 403.

30 Policy Advisory Committee of the Progressive Conservative Party of Canada, *Perspectives '96: Designing a Blueprint for Canadians* (Ottawa: Progressive Conservative Party of Canada, 1996), section 1.

31 Ibid., 53.

32 Ibid., 86.

33 Progressive Conservative Party of Canada, *Let the Future Begin: Jean Charest's Plan for Canada's Next Century* (Ottawa: Progressive Conservative Party of Canada, 1997), 4.

34 Ibid., 142.

35 Andrew Coyne, "Clark Has United the Right," *National Post*, 6 October 1999.

36 Author's observations of the founding convention of the Canadian Alliance in Ottawa, 29 January 2000.

37 Plamondon, *Full Circle*, 200.

38 Steve Patten, "Red Tory Voice Missing in New Conservatives," *Edmonton Journal*, 26 March 2005.

39 Gerry Nicholls, "Selling Out True Conservatism," *National Post*, 27 April 2007.

40 Margaret Wente, "Actually, He's Moved the Party to the Left: It's Known as 'Finding the Sweet Spot,'" *Globe and Mail*, 25 January 2011.

41 Andrew Coyne, "The Right in Full Retreat," *Maclean's*, February 2009.
42 Amy Minsky, "Government Grows under Harper," *Edmonton Journal*, 7 February 2011.
43 Les Whittington, "Tax Cuts Drive Harper's Right-Wing Agenda," *Toronto Star*, 19 January 2011.
44 Russell Barnett and Chris Matier, *Estimating Potential GDP and the Government's Structural Budget Balance* (Ottawa: Office of the Parliamentary Budget Officer, 2010).
45 Lloyd Mackey, *The Pilgrimage of Stephen Harper* (Toronto: ECW, 2005), 62.

PART TWO

The Conservative Party of Canada

5 Something Blue: The Harper Conservatives as Garrison Party

TOM FLANAGAN

Something old
Something new
Something borrowed
Something blue.

The organization of the Conservative Party of Canada has inherited traits from both of its predecessor parties, the Progressive Conservatives and Reform/Canadian Alliance. It also has some novel features stemming from the personality of Stephen Harper, the founder and only leader so far of the Conservative Party; his experience with Reform Party and Canadian Alliance populism; and the all-pervasive state of "permanent campaign" that has existed in Canadian federal politics since 2004. The result is a unique configuration of organizational features amounting to a virtual fusion of political party and campaign team. This powerful and effective organizational model helped the Conservative Party bring the Liberals down to minority status in 2004, win Conservative minority governments in 2006 and 2008, and elect a Conservative majority in 2011. Only the future can say whether the Conservatives will continue with this model of organization after Stephen Harper retires and whether other parties may choose to imitate it.

The Populist Impulse

Stephen Harper's political development was moulded in the crucible of Preston Manning's populism, and one can still see the effects today, both positive and negative – i.e., in Harper's retention of some aspects of populism as well as his deliberate rejection of others. But it must also be noted that Manning's version of populism allowed ample scope for him to exercise personal control over the party through manipulation of decision-making processes, furnishing additional lessons for Harper.

Manning deliberately cast the Reform Party as a neo-populist revival, imitating such Western predecessors as the Progressive Party, the United Farmers, and Social Credit.[1] This meant adoption of direct-democratic policies such as referendum, initiative, and recall, as well as a quasi-delegate theory of the MP's role, according to which the elected member was supposed to vote according to "the consensus of the constituency," at least on controversial moral issues. Manning's populism also involved a novel approach to party organization. In comparison to other Canadian parties of the late 1980s, Reform exhibited a number of specific characteristics, all of which could be interpreted as populist:

- Reform put great emphasis on formal party membership. Of course, other parties also sold memberships, but Reform kept all membership records in a centrally controlled database held in the national party office in Calgary.[2] The national party employed direct mail to persuade members to renew annually and also pushed constituency associations to conduct membership renewal drives through face-to-face or telephone contact. In comparison, other parties of that era were more likely to have membership lists controlled by provincial wings and/or riddled with out-of-date data. The Reform approach produced a membership list that was much more efficient for grass-roots fundraising, as discussed in the next point. Its approach was closest to that of the New Democratic Party, which also put emphasis on formal membership; but the NDP was legally a federation of provincial parties, whereas Reform had a unitary structure.
- The Reform Party was open to receiving corporate and high-end personal contributions, but in practice the party's populist character meant it had little appeal to big corporations and wealthy donors. Reform, therefore, became almost entirely reliant on small donations. Partly this was done face-to-face through the legendary Colonel Sanders Kentucky Fried Chicken bucket passed at every Reform public meeting. Larger amounts of money were raised through direct mail based on the nationally controlled database. John Laschinger had made direct mail an important part of Progressive Conservative fundraising in the 1970s, but the PCs under Brian Mulroney also continued to raise large amounts of

money from the corporate world.[3] Reform resembled the NDP in reliance on small donations but lacked the NDP's ability to draw large contributions from organized labour in election years. Reform was almost entirely reliant on grassroots fundraising and pushed direct mail even harder than the PCs had and also started to use telephone solicitation – first at the constituency level, later under control of the national party. Thus, out of necessity Reform took the PC heritage of grassroots fundraising and made it even more productive – in effect, the lifeline of the party.

- The first Reform Party constitution put control of all party affairs in the hands of an "Executive Council." This was not a National Council, advisory to the leader, as was typical of other parties, but a full-fledged management body. The leader was a member of the Executive Council but had no independent authority over party affairs. For example, only Reform's Executive Council, and not the leader, could veto a constituency association's choice of candidate.[4] Also, there was no Reform Fund, appointed by the leader and independent of Executive Council, to conduct fundraising and manage the party's financial affairs. Rather, the constitution provided for a Finance Committee chaired by the vice-president (finance) of the Executive Council to manage all the party's financial business.[5]

- The constitution did not provide for any intermediate bodies between the constituency associations and the Executive Council – no regional or provincial councils, no special-interest associations for youth, women, seniors, First Nations, ethnic groups, etc. It was the ultimate flat organization. A couple of attempts to create local area councils from the bottom up failed badly. One of my first memories upon going to work for the party in May 1991 was getting caught in a fight between the Executive Council and the Winnipeg Area Council, which ended with dissolution of the local council and numerous resignations and expulsions from the party.

- Another populist provision of the Reform Party constitution was approval of important decisions by membership referendum. Section 8 provided for non-binding membership polls as well as binding referendums (with a two-thirds decision rule) that could be initiated either by the Executive Council or by a petition signed by 15 per cent of the membership.[6] The party actually held three referendums – one in 1991 to authorize expansion east of the Manitoba border, and two in 1999–2000 as part of the transformation of Reform through the United Alternative into the Canadian

Alliance.[7] There was also a Canadian Alliance party referendum in 2003 to approve its merger with the Progressive Conservatives.[8]

- Election of the leader by membership ballot would have been a logical procedure for the Reform Party, but that was still a relatively new and experimental idea when the party was founded in 1987.[9] Hence the party's constitution provided for, and Preston Manning was elected by, a delegated convention. However, leadership election through membership voting was adopted when Reform transformed itself into the Canadian Alliance in 2000, and that method was used to select Stockwell Day in 2000 and Stephen Harper in 2002.

- The "Statement of Principles" adopted at Reform's founding meeting in Winnipeg in October 1987 asserted, "We affirm that political parties should be guided by stated *values and principles* which are shared by their members and rooted in the political beliefs of Canadians."[10] Guided by this principle, Reformers treated their policy manual, or Blue Book, almost as Holy Writ. Once adopted at an assembly, wording could be changed only at a subsequent assembly, and enormous energy went into debates over wording. Interim policies could be adopted by the Executive Council but had to be presented to the biennial assembly at the next opportunity.[11] The leader, MPs, and candidates always insisted that they, like all other members of the party, were bound by the Blue Book. In other words, the leader of the Reform Party did not have the freedom historically exercised by the leaders of the Liberal and Conservative parties to adjust policy for the needs of campaigning and governing. Not all populist parties have shared this creedal approach to politics; many have been ideologically vague, leaving doctrine in the hands of a charismatic leader. In a sense, Manning's version of populism was closer to the ideological politics of the NDP and other parties in the social democratic tradition.

Reform was more populist – in the sense of having a flat organization combined with membership control of business – than the other parties with which it competed in the 1990s. The true situation, however, was far more complex than the triumph of populism, for behind the scenes Preston Manning (with Stephen Harper taking mental notes) exercised a remarkable level of control over the Reform Party. He used his prestige as the founder and only leader of the party to structure decision-making processes and control the agenda for discussion.

To make Reform populist and leader-centred at the same time required acrobatic talents that Manning possessed but that Stockwell Day did not have, so it is not surprising that the Canadian Alliance was quickly faced with disintegration after Day became leader.

Manning exercised control and maintained coherence in the party through the following mechanisms:

- He drafted key documents, such as the "Statement of Principles" embedded in the Blue Book.
- In effect, he chose the officers of the Executive Council. The party's constitution provided for at-large election of members of Executive Council, after which they were to choose their own chair and other officers.[12] But this election took place at a council meeting in which Manning led a discussion of responsibilities and then recommended names for the various positions. Dissenters on council were isolated and, if necessary, expelled, as happened to the Winnipeg group. Later Manning used similar methods in caucus and ended up expelling more members than any other national leader I can remember.[13]
- Manning managed the organization through "chosen instruments," whom he supported unconditionally. Cliff Fryers became his indispensable chief organizer, assisted by Rick Anderson and Gordon Shaw. Titles and job assignments sometimes shifted, but these three formed a stable core around Manning, supplemented at various times by others.
- Working with Chief Policy Officer Stephen Harper, Manning provided careful guidance to policy development. Grassroots members were indeed asked to submit policy resolutions for consideration at assemblies, but Manning and Harper would edit and consolidate the resolutions, as well as introduce their own to fill voids that they perceived. They would also intervene at crucial points to provide leadership if floor discussions seemed to be going askew. The Blue Book was democratic in the sense that its provisions were all approved by majority vote at assemblies, but once approved, it was binding and in that sense served as a form of control over members.
- Manning took a personal hand in wording all important resolutions, such as the questions that went to membership in the three referendums, or the non-binding poll questions that members often received with their *Reformer* newsletters and fundraising solicitations.

Especially in his early years of leadership, Manning often described the Reform Party as a populist movement expressing "the common sense of the common people." Yet his real view as expressed in private was more nuanced. I often heard him say, "The function of the political party is to mediate between expert and public opinion."[14]

I argued in *Waiting for the Wave* that Manning's behind-the-scenes leadership was an essential complement to his populism. As William Riker showed in his classic *Liberalism against Populism*, populism is intellectually incoherent.[15] There is no such thing as "the will of the people." Following Riker, my view is that what exists in reality is a large number of people with divergent preferences. For democratic decision-making, everything depends on the processes by which those preferences are revealed and aggregated. The same set of preferences can often give rise to very different decisions, depending on how those preferences are weighed and counted. Agenda control – the formulation of questions for decision and the structuring of processes for making decisions – is the key to managing populist movements.

When I was working for Manning, we had some interesting arguments on this issue. He seemed to believe that the will of the people was something real, not just an artefact of the decision-making processes. On the other hand, he had an intuitive flair for agenda control. Even as he spoke about "the common sense of the common people," "the consensus of the constituency," "the will of the people," and other populist shibboleths, he was masterfully managing consultative and decision-making processes within the party to give him the results he was aiming at. He could also be a very competent rhetorician; at least in certain settings, he could persuade listeners with his long, carefully reasoned speeches. But his real mastery was not in rhetoric but in what Riker called heresthetic – the art of dividing, of setting up alternatives for decision-making.[16]

During Stephen Harper's invaluable apprenticeship to Manning as chief policy officer of the Reform Party, he learned how to manage a populist movement. He used to grumble privately about Manning's manipulations, but he was absorbing the lessons. Indeed, he ultimately ended up with a view of leadership far more aggressive than Manning's, after he saw the Canadian Alliance experience of how populism could get out of control.

Under the leadership of Stockwell Day, who lacked Manning's manipulative abilities, populism dissolved into factionalism, and the Alliance seemed on the verge of tearing itself apart. Harper saved the Alliance by winning the leadership race in March 2002, but he now had to deal with a National Council, most of whose members owed nothing to him and some of whom, including the president, George Richardson, and a few other members, were quite suspicious. The president's philosophy seemed to be that his job was to protect the party and its constitution from the leader. Matters came to a head in fall 2002 when, as Harper's chief of staff and acting on his orders, I fired George Richardson's son Adam as a regional organizer in Atlantic Canada. The firing precipitated an all-out power struggle on council that lasted for about four months until Harper was able to put together a coalition to depose Richardson and take control under the presidency of (now Senator) Don Plett.[17]

Little got into the media about this power struggle, but it was a draining, time-and-energy-consuming experience for Harper. It convinced him that he, as party leader, should never again be subject to a governing council and led, I believe, to many features of the constitution adopted by the Conservative Party of Canada after the 2003 merger. This desire to exercise unhampered control over the party was also congenial to Harper's basic personality, which is dominant and controlling in all matters in which he is personally involved.

Harper's Revision

Regardless of what Bob Plamondon says in *Full Circle*,[18] the merger of the Canadian Alliance and the Progressive Conservatives was Stephen Harper's project. He conceived the idea, raised it first in public, and hounded Peter MacKay for months until the deal was consummated. The merger was done on the basis of an interim constitution, and approval of the final version was put off until the March 2005 convention in Montreal, which meant that Harper had a great deal of influence over its drafting once he won the leadership of the new party. As the Conservative Party's only leader to date, he has exercised at least as much sway over it as Preston Manning did over the Reform Party in its early years.

With respect to populism, the Conservative Party bears some important resemblances to the Reform Party but even more important differences. Let us look first at the similarities.

• Grassroots fundraising is still paramount. Of course, all parties have had to renounce high-end personal contributions, as well as corporate and union donations, as a result of Jean Chrétien's Bill C-24 (2003), but Harper turned the screw even further by using the

Accountability Act (2006) to reduce the limit for personal contributions from $5,000 to $1,000 (adjusted for inflation). In effect, he imposed a populist model of grassroots fundraising upon all parties (though highly tempered by the public-support provisions of C-24). Under the new regime, the Conservatives raise far more money than any other party, partly because of the earlier Reform experience in grassroots fundraising, and partly because of technological advances. The key to Conservative success is the unification of fundraising with mass voter identification, using a custom-designed database (Constituent Information Management System, or CIMS) that integrates all these forms of information. It is populism with a technological edge.[19] External observers often wrongly assert that the key to raising money is cultivating small single-interest groups, such as gun-owners or prolife campaigners, but in fact frequent contact with a large number of potential donors is much more important than cultivation of small groups.

- The national organization is still flat, consisting only of the Electoral District Associations and the national-level entities (National Council, Conservative Fund, and National Office). With one exception, there are still no regional or provincial layers of organization. The one exception is a provincial Conservative organization, which Harper finally acceded to after years of resisting demands from Quebec. The organization, however, is quite weak. Unlike the Quebec wing of the Liberal Party of Canada, it does not have its own budget, director, and council. There is still no Conservative youth wing, women's organization, or commissions for special interests.

- The Conservative Party projects a populist image of simple, common tastes, as Harper openly displays his love of hockey and curling. Adviser Patrick Muttart expressed this memorably by the way he tried to brand the parties in the 2005–6 campaign: Liberals drink latte at Starbucks, while Conservatives go to Tim Hortons for coffee.[20] (Of course, he said this to a group of latte-sipping Conservative campaign workers, but we have known since Plato that politics is more about image than reality.)

The differences from the Reform era are more profound:

- The financial side of the party, including both budgetary management and fundraising, has been taken away from council and given to the Conservative Fund Canada. Although this was the practice of the former Progressive Conservative Party, the new Conservative Party has not simply resurrected the older approach. The Progressive Conservative Fund was a large body with dozens of members, recruited mainly for their ability to contribute to corporate and high-end personal fundraising, which relies heavily on networking. The Conservative Fund, in contrast, has only a handful of members, all of whom are appointed by the leader, subject to the ratification of council.[21] In practice the fund has been dominated by the chairman, (now Senator) Irving Gerstein. The 2005 Montreal convention saw a floor fight over this arrangement, which some saw as giving too much unchecked power to the leader.[22] In the end, a compromise was negotiated, according to which the Conservative Fund makes a quarterly report and also presents its annual budget to National Council for purposes of information but is not controlled by or accountable to the council.[23] At the 2008 Winnipeg convention, there was an unsuccessful attempt to make national councillors members of the Conservative Fund.[24] The reality is that the leader controls the party through the fund, especially its chairman, and through the national director of the party, who reports in budgetary and fundraising matters to the fund, especially to its chairman.

- The Reform Party's "Executive Council" has been replaced with a "National Council," as indeed had already happened in the Canadian Alliance. The significance of the name change is that council is no longer a true executive body, responsible for running the party. As described above, the party is run largely by staff accountable to the national director, the chairman of the Conservative Fund, and the leader. The council is now more of a governance than an executive body. It approves the appointments of the national director and the Conservative Fund, receives regular reports from these authorities, and comments on the annual budget proposal. Its most important area of independent activity concerns membership and electoral district associations (EDAs). It establishes rules for membership, monitors the status of constituency associations, sets rules and deadlines for nomination contests, and arbitrates the disputes that frequently arise at the grassroots level in all parties.[25] But unlike the Reform Executive Council, it does not have a formal role in establishing party policy (except indirectly through the conventions that it helps organize), conducting communications, raising money, or planning election campaigns.

- Like the Reform Party, the Conservative Party of Canada has a policy book approved by membership delegates at national conventions. Called the "Policy Declaration," it was first adopted in Montreal in March 2005 and amended in Winnipeg in November 2008.[26] Like Reform's Blue Book, it is a mixture of general principles and specific policies, but it has nowhere near the same hold over members' imaginations. It is available on line but not in pamphlet form for members to carry around and distribute. I joined the Reform Party in 1990 after a graduate student gave me the Blue Book to read, but I doubt that would happen today. Members no longer regard the Policy Declaration as sacred writ. Both in government and in opposition, the leader has been accorded wide latitude to develop policy for strategic purposes. Items from the Policy Declaration often appear in one way or another in campaign platforms, but no one expects perfect correspondence. In other words, the leader is free to develop or alter policy for political purposes. In that respect, the Conservative Party is very much like the "old-line parties" that Manning and Reformers used to criticize. As an example, the 2008 Conservative national convention voted to repeal section 13 of the Canadian Human Rights Act, which gave the Canadian Human Rights Commission jurisdiction in certain free speech disputes. Harper and the Conservative government never campaigned on that resolution, that it was put into practice through a private member's bill in 2012.

Permanent Campaign

This tendency towards centralized control of the Conservative Party stemming from Harper's personality as well as his experience of Reform-style populism has been reinforced by the emergence in Canada of the permanent campaign, in which political parties seem at all times to be as much preoccupied with campaigning as with government and opposition.[27] The permanent campaign is a trend that first emerged in the United States with Jimmy Carter, intensified under Bill Clinton and George Bush, and is now going worldwide.[28] Harper's Conservatives have become permanent-campaign over-achievers, perhaps as a result of the extraordinary amount of Canadian campaigning in the early years of the twenty-first century, as shown in table 5.1:

Table 5.1. Canadian National Political Campaigns, 2000–9

Date	Winner
National Election Campaigns	
2000	Liberals
2004	Liberals
2005–6	Conservatives
2008	Conservatives
Leadership Campaigns	
2000 (Canadian Alliance)	Stockwell Day
2001–2 (Canadian Alliance)	Stephen Harper
2003 (NDP)	Jack Layton
2003 (Greens)	Jim Harris
2003 (Progressive Conservatives)	Peter MacKay
2003 (Liberals)	Paul Martin
2004 (Conservatives)	Stephen Harper
2004 (Greens)	Jim Harris
2006 (Greens)	Elizabeth May
2006 (Liberals)	Stéphane Dion
2009 (Liberals)	Michael Ignatieff

In fact, campaigning has been even more prevalent than the bare facts of the table indicate, for there was a persistent sense that the minority governments elected in 2004, 2006, and 2008 were liable to be defeated at any time. Thus federal parties had to maintain non-stop election readiness from early 2004, when Paul Martin became Liberal prime minister and indicated he would soon be asking for an election, until the 2011 election resulted in a majority government. These years have deeply affected Canadian government and political culture. After so many years of continuous campaigning, federal politicians are like child soldiers in a war-torn African country: all they know how to do is to fire their AK-47s.

Political campaigning has many resemblances to the military campaigning of warfare, one of which is the importance of unified command

and discipline. The permanent campaign environment has thus led to centralizing innovations in Conservative Party organization. Perhaps the most important of these is the creation of a permanent position of campaign manager reporting directly to the leader. The older pattern for Canadian parties, when elections happened only every four or five years, was to appoint a campaign committee a year or so before an election was expected. There might also be a separate committee or task force to prepare the platform, as Paul Martin and Chaviva Hošek did with the Liberal Red Book to prepare for the 1993 election.

In the Conservative model, however, everything is centralized. There is no campaign committee. The platform is developed by the leader's policy advisers, who report directly to him. Other aspects of the campaign are prepared under the direction of the manager, who again reports directly to the leader. Fundraising is carried out by direct-mail and telemarketing contractors working with the national director and chairman of the Conservative Fund. Because there is no need to network with corporate and high-end individual donors, there is no semi-independent corps of well-connected fundraisers who might exert their own influence on the structure of the campaign.

In this situation of always being prepared for political warfare, message discipline is naturally carried to great lengths. Loose lips sink political ships. Conservative staffers and operatives almost never talk to the press and would risk loss of employment if they did. MPs religiously follow official talking points. Even – maybe I should say especially – ministers are carefully controlled through the Prime Minister's Office. Discipline is far stricter than it ever was in the former Reform and Progressive Conservative parties. Preston Manning expelled numerous caucus members, and Brian Mulroney had to endure defections to the Bloc Québécois, but Harper's Conservative followers have internalized an ethic of obedience and self-censorship to the point where public punishment is rarely needed. I have no explanation for how Harper's Conservatives have so thoroughly transcended the indiscipline and disorganization that George Perlin called the "Tory Syndrome," but it is a development of great importance.[29]

Policy development within the party also has had to take second place. The 2005 Montreal convention was all about policy because it was necessary to have a policy manual for electoral purposes, to deflect opponents' charges that Harper was pursuing a "hidden agenda." But after that, national conventions were repeatedly postponed because of electoral exigencies. When one was finally held three and a half years later in Winnipeg, there was some discussion of policy, to be sure, but it was a secondary feature of the event. Election readiness has largely replaced policy development as the party emphasizes fundraising, campaign training, and building grassroots teams for signage, door-knocking, and phone-banking.

Just as chronic warfare produces a garrison state, permanent campaigning has caused the Conservative Party to merge with the campaign team, producing a garrison party. The party is today, for all intents and purposes, a campaign organization focused on being ready for and winning the next election, whenever it may come.

Conclusion

Certain populist aspects remain in the current Conservative model of organization, especially reliance on grassroots fundraising and a flat organization with no intermediate structures between the national office and the EDAs. But these populist relics don't confer membership control over the party leadership; in fact, they work in the opposite direction. The national office and Conservative Fund control the grassroots fundraising, which tends to give the national party fiscal leverage over the EDAs. And the absence of intermediate structures means there are no points of refuge in which opposition to the leadership could coalesce.

By any standard, the party is highly centralized. The leader appoints the Conservative Fund, which oversees all the party's business affairs. The leader appoints the campaign manager, who reports directly to him rather than to a campaign committee. There is an official policy manual, but the leader is free to adopt virtually any policy he wishes for strategic purposes. In any case, the party is focused on election readiness rather than policy development. Message discipline is carefully enforced at all levels, and a high level of secrecy surrounds internal deliberations. The overall atmosphere is almost military, as befits an era of permanent campaign.

The biggest question for the future is whether this "garrison party" will survive the specific circumstances of the present, i.e., the leadership of Stephen Harper and the need for constant election readiness in a period of minority government. In fact, all signs in the months after the 2011 election pointed to continuation of the permanent campaign model. There was little goodwill and cooperation between government and opposition parties in the House of Commons, as all sides seemed preoccupied with getting ready for the 2015 election (which, for the NDP, Liberals, and BQ, also involved finding new leaders).

The Conservative fusion of political party and campaign team has been extraordinarily effective in doing what all the pundits thought was impossible – overthrowing the Liberal dynasty and installing a Conservative government. The Liberals have already started to follow the Conservative example in several respects, e.g., revising their constitution to assert national control over membership rules and grassroots fundraising, enforcing more effective message discipline, and running negative ads between writ periods. If, as seems likely, the era of permanent campaign and its arms race logic continues, the Conservative organizational model will persist and be imitated by other parties trying to survive in the Darwinian world of electoral competition. And yet the garrison party model is not without its own internal problems. In all parties, some members are happy with non-stop electoral activity, but others see the party as an organization for representing their views and developing policy. Members of this latter type may turn away from the party if it becomes nothing but an electoral machine. Thus, it is possible that too long a period of constant election readiness may exhaust a party and undercut its effectiveness even in purely electoral terms. At the moment, however, this remains just a theoretical possibility. The Conservative Party, which has developed the permanent campaign model in Canada, seems highly effective – indeed, more effective than any other party – in retaining and activating its core supporters.

NOTES

1 Tom Flanagan, *Waiting for the Wave: The Reform Party and the Conservative Movement*, rev. ed. (Montreal and Kingston: McGill-Queen's University Press, 2009), 20–37.
2 Tom Flanagan, "Database Party: The 2002 Leadership Campaign for the Canadian Alliance," *Canadian Parliamentary Review* 26 (Spring 2003): 8–11.
3 John Laschinger and Geoffrey Stevens, *Leaders and Lesser Mortals* (Toronto: Key Porter Books, 1992), 168–70.
4 Reform Party of Canada, Constitution, 1987, s. 4(d). http://contentdm. ucalgary.ca/cdm4/document.php?CISOROOT=/reform&CISOPTR=237.

5 Ibid., s. 5(g).

6 Ibid., s. 8.

7 Preston Manning, *The New Canada* (Toronto: Macmillan Canada, 1992), 288; Manning, *Think Big: My Adventures in Life and Democracy* (Toronto: McClelland and Stewart, 2002), 284–8, 296–8.

8 Bob Plamondon, *Full Circle: Death and Resurrection in Canadian Conservative Politics* (Toronto: Key Porter Books, 2006), 336.

9 William Cross, "Direct Election of Provincial Party Leaders in Canada, 1985–1995: The End of the Leadership Convention?," *Canadian Journal of Political Science* 29 (1996): 295–315.

10 Reform Party of Canada, *Platform & Statement of Principles of the Reform Party of Canada*, 1988, 26, http://contentdm.ucalgary.ca/cdm4/document. php?CISOROOT=/reform&CISOPTR=197.

11 Reform Party of Canada, Constitution, s. 5(f).

12 Ibid., s. 5(b) and 5(c).

13 Tom Flanagan, "Man Overboard: Jake Hoeppner's Ouster Makes It Five and Counting," *Globe and Mail*, 12 August 1999.

14 Flanagan, *Waiting for the Wave*, 25. Although he attributed that saying to Vaçlav Havel, for whom he had tremendous respect, I could never find the source in Havel's writings, even after much searching.

15 William H. Riker, *Liberalism against Populism: A Confrontation between the Theory of Democracy and Theory of Social Choice* (1982; Prospect Heights, IL: Waveland, 1988).

16 William H. Riker, *The Art of Political Manipulation* (New Haven: Yale University Press, 1986), ix.

17 Flanagan, *Harper's Team*, 81.

18 Plamondon, *Full Circle*, 287.

19 Tom Flanagan and Harold J. Jansen, "Election Campaigns under Canada's Party Finance Laws," in *The Canadian Federal Election of 2008*, ed. Jon H. Pammett and Christopher Dornan, 194–204 (Toronto: Dundurn, 2009).

20 Flanagan, *Harper's Team*, 224.

21 Conservative Party of Canada, Constitution, s. 9.8, http://www.conservative.ca/media/2012/06/Sept2011-Constitution-E.pdf.

22 Flanagan, *Harper's Team*, 204–6.

23 Conservative Constitution, ss. 9.2 and 9.3.

24 Kady O'Malley, "CPC ConventionWatch 2008: And Now, the Policy Plenary Session We've Been Not-So-Patiently Waiting For ... ," *Maclean's*, 15 November 2009, http://www2.macleans.ca/tag/cpc-conventionwatch-2008/.

25 Conservative Constitution, ss. 8.7.1 and 8.7.2.

26 Conservative Party of Canada, *Policy Declaration*, 2011. http://www.
conservative.ca/media/2012/07/20120705-CPC-PolicyDec-E.pdf.

27 Tom Flanagan, "Political Communication and the Permanent Campaign,"
in *How Canadians Communicate IV*, ed. David Taras and Christopher
Waddell, 129–48 (Edmonton: Alberta University Press, 2012).

28 Norman Ornstein and Thomas Mann, eds., *The Permanent Campaign and
Its Future* (Washington: American Enterprise Institute and the Brookings
Institution, 2000); Corey Cook, "The Contemporary Presidency: The
Permanence of 'The Permanent Campaign'; George W. Bush's Public
Presidency," *Presidential Studies Quarterly* 32 (2002): 753–64; Catherine
Needham, "Brand Leaders: Clinton, Blair and the Limitations of the
Permanent Campaign," *Political Studies* 53 (2005): 343–61; Peter van
Onselen and Wayne Errington, "The Democratic State as a Marketing Tool:
The Permanent Campaign in Australia," *Commonwealth & Comparative
Politics* 45 (2007): 78–94.

29 George Perlin, *The Tory Syndrome: Leadership Politics in the Progressive
Conservative Party* (Montreal and Kingston: McGill-Queen's University
Press, 1980).

6 Immigration, Citizenship, and Canada's New Conservative Party

INDER MARWAH, TRIADAFILOS
TRIADAFILOPOULOS, AND STEPHEN WHITE

Since its inception in 2003, and particularly since forming government in 2006, the Conservative Party has made a concerted effort to draw support from new Canadians. Its aggressive courting of the "ethnic vote" stands in marked contrast to positions taken by its predecessors, the Reform Party and Canadian Alliance. Unlike conservative parties in Europe, the United States, and Australia, Canada's new Conservatives have supported the maintenance of a relatively expansive program of mass immigration. They have also abandoned their predecessors' rejection of multiculturalism and, under the current minister of citizenship, immigration and multiculturalism, Jason Kenney, implemented an aggressive ethnic "outreach" strategy aimed at peeling immigrant support away from their principal competitor, the Liberal Party of Canada.

At the same time, however, the Conservatives have pursued policies aimed at appealing to their conservative base. With regard to citizenship, new rules have been introduced making it harder for naturalized citizens to pass Canadian nationality on to their children while residing outside of Canada.[1] A review of citizenship policy also promised to further toughen rules on naturalization while extending the state's ability to revoke nationality. In one official's words, citizenship would become "harder to get and easier to lose."[2] Changes to refugee policy have also been introduced to crack down on "bogus" claimants. While citizenship policy has provided the Conservatives with a forum for developing themes relating to patriotism and core Canadian values, their positions on refugee policy have nicely complemented their "tough on crime" credentials.[3]

This situation is the result of structural factors peculiar to Canada that pull Canadian political parties towards a relatively liberal and expansionary consensus on immigration policy. We argue that the combination of immigrant settlement patterns, citizenship laws, and Canada's single member plurality (SMP) electoral system create a context in which appeals to immigrant voters are required of any party with aspirations to national power. We illustrate this point through a brief appraisal of the Reform Party's experience with the immigration issue, from the party's first days in the late 1980s to its transformation into the Canadian Alliance and subsequent merger with the Progressive Conservative party in 2003. On the other hand, efforts to maintain support among grassroots conservative voters account for a countervailing push to the right. The resulting balancing act marks a peculiarly Canadian solution to a more basic "populist's paradox" confronting right-of-centre parties interested in preserving their conservative base while expanding support among "ethnic" and other voters.[4] The Conservative Party's marked shifts away from Reform's positions on immigration respond to precisely this populist's paradox. We review the Conservative Party's positions on immigration since winning office in 2006 to illustrate this point, emphasizing the Tories' balancing of consensus politics and ethnic outreach on the one hand, and subtle restrictiveness in citizenship and refugee policy on the other. We conclude with a discussion of the Conservative Party's use of social issues and "values" to craft a message aimed at bridging support among new Canadians and traditional conservative voters. While critics maintain that the Conservatives' strategy is little more than a cynical vote grab, in the broader context of centre-right political parties – which typically make opposition to immigration (and immigrants more generally) a core part of their ideological and electoral repertoire – it marks a distinctive and noteworthy approach that has led Canadian conservatives to explore what they have in common with immigrant voters.[5]

Settlement, Citizenship, and Institutions: Structuring Canada's Immigration Consensus

Whereas immigration policy is a source of intense political contestation in most countries, generating divisions across and within parties, in Canada it has been shaped by a solid cross-party political consensus at the federal level.[6] All of Canada's political parties agree that annual admissions should be relatively high (at approximately 250,000 immigrants per year). The parties also agree that immigrants contribute positively to Canada's social and economic well-being. In contrast to other countries, official multiculturalism continues to enjoy the support of Canadian governments, regardless of their ideological orientation.[7] Canada is unique among major immigration countries in the degree to which immigration policy is de-politicized, and immigration itself is enthusiastically embraced by federal political parties.[8] Quebec's provincial politics since 2007 may be a partial exception to this pattern, but this has not had a discernable impact on Quebec voices in federal policy debates over immigration.[9]

One might reasonably point out that this consensus is due to Canadian political parties' more general rejection of divisive ideological positions in favour of "brokerage politics." Major federal parties are widely seen to have eschewed unambiguous and consistent policy stances, because their primary goal is to maximize electoral support rather than take principled positions.[10] Even if this model were to still apply, however, we are left with the question of why the consensus on immigration in Canada is as liberal as it is. One need only look to Great Britain for an example of a consensus that tilts towards restriction.[11] Recall, too, that an important part of the present Conservative Party's root structure lies in the Reform Party and Canadian Alliance, which maintained distinctive positions on a bevy of other issues, from "family values," to the federal–provincial division of power and taxation.

We maintain that Canada's immigration policy consensus is based on a distinctive intersection of immigration settlement patterns, citizenship rules, and political institutions – particularly Canada's electoral system. Canadian parties are drawn to relatively open positions on immigration policy because the interplay of these structures ensures that immigrants are able to express their interests and have them acknowledged in a politically meaningful way.

Settlement

Canada receives approximately 250,000 immigrants per year, and most settle in regions that no major party can ignore. More than half of all newcomers settle in Ontario, with close to three-quarters of them ultimately residing in the Greater Toronto Area (GTA).[12] As a result, approximately 47 per cent of Toronto's population is foreign born, and more than 28 per cent of Ontarians are foreign born (see table 6.1). Other large cities, most notably Vancouver, receive most of the immigrants who do not settle in Ontario. Approximately 40 per cent of Vancouver's

Table 6.1. Percentage of Population Foreign Born, 1991–2006

	1991	1996	2001	2006
Canada	16.1	17.4	18.4	19.8
Ontario	23.7	25.6	26.8	28.3
Toronto Census Metropolitan Area	38.0	41.9	43.7	47.3
British Columbia	22.3	24.5	26.1	27.5
Vancouver Census Metropolitan Area	30.1	34.9	37.5	39.6

Source: Canadian Census (1991–2006)

population is foreign born, and nearly 28 per cent of British Columbians are foreign born. The overall proportion of Canadians who are foreign born is considerably lower outside of these regions.

Immigration is not only changing Canada's demographic complexion; it is also changing its political dynamics at the constituency level, especially in Ontario and British Columbia. Table 6.2 shows the demographic breakdown of constituencies in the 1997 and 2006 Canadian elections. The table divides federal electoral constituencies into three categories: those in which the share of residents who are foreign born is similar to, or less than, the national share of residents who are foreign born (fewer than 20% foreign born); those in which the proportion of foreign-born residents is large enough to potentially play a very important role in the outcome of elections in those local constituencies (20%–40% foreign born); and finally, those in which foreign-born residents constitute a large minority of residents, sharing an effective veto over the election outcome in the riding (more than 40% foreign born).

In Ontario and British Columbia, more than half of all federal constituencies in 2006 comprised more than 20 per cent foreign-born residents, and foreign-born residents constituted at least 40 per cent of the population in more than one-quarter of Ontario's and British Columbia's constituencies. These included constituencies in the Toronto and Vancouver areas, but also cities in Ontario such as Ottawa, London, Windsor, Kitchener-Waterloo, and Hamilton. In contrast, in the Prairie provinces and Quebec nearly three-quarters of all constituencies had proportions of foreign-born residents that were smaller than the national average,

Table 6.2. Percentage of Immigrants in Federal Ridings by Region, 2006 (1997)

%	BC	Prairies	Ontario	Quebec	Atlantic
			Region		
< 20	44 (50)	73 (75)	43 (46)	74 (82)	100 (100)
20–40	25 (33)	27 (25)	28 (29)	17 (13)	0 (0)
> 40	31 (17)	0 (0)	29 (24)	8 (5)	0 (0)

Source: Elections Canada and Canadian Census (1996 and 2006)

Table 6.3. Percentage of Federal Seats in Ontario, BC, Toronto, and Vancouver CMAs, 1997–2008

	1997–2003	2004–8
Ontario	34.2	34.4
Toronto Census Metropolitan Area	14.0	15.3
British Columbia	11.3	11.7
Vancouver Census Metropolitan Area	5.0	5.3

Source: Elections Canada

and there were no federal constituencies in the Atlantic provinces with more than 20 per cent foreign born. The regional pattern was similar in 1997, although the number of British Columbia constituencies that comprised more than 40 per cent foreign-born residents grew considerably between 1997 and 2006.

As noted already, this shift was most pronounced in Greater Toronto and Greater Vancouver. This is crucially important politically, as these two urban regions hold more than one-fifth of all federal seats (see table 6.3). In sum, immigrants are concentrated in politically important urban regions. Given the large number of seats in these areas, especially in the GTA, immigrants are a potentially important constituency for any party competing for national office. Indeed, the Liberal Party's dominance of GTA ridings – based in large part on the overwhelming support of new Canadian voters – helped it win majority governments in 1997 and 2000, despite capturing only 38 and 41 per cent of the popular vote, respectively, in those elections.[13]

Citizenship

Canada's liberal citizenship regime converts immigrants' latent political potential into power by granting newcomers access to political rights via rapid naturalization. In contrast to those of many other immigration-receiving states, Canada's naturalization rules are relatively uncomplicated, and policy is geared towards facilitating immigrants' political integration. Irene Bloemraad maintains that Canada's official policy of multiculturalism plays an important role in this regard, by formalizing ties between immigrant groups and the state and signalling the state's acceptance of diversity in a manner that resonates with newcomers.[14] Will Kymlicka has noted that Canada's high naturalization rate might also be a consequence of the type of immigrants Canada receives: typically well educated and highly skilled.[15]

Figure 6.1. Support for Greater Restrictions on Immigration among Foreign-Born and Native-Born Canadians, 1988–2006 (% "Canada should admit fewer immigrants")

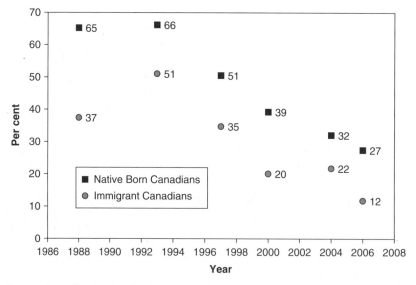

Source: Canadian Election Studies (1988–2006)

Whatever the reasons, there is no gainsaying that immigrants in Canada naturalize more quickly and at a higher rate than in other "immigrant countries." In Canada, 84 per cent of eligible immigrants become naturalized citizens, compared to 75 per cent in Australia, 56 per cent in the United Kingdom, and only 40 per cent in the United States.[16] Enfranchised immigrants have also demonstrated that they are able and willing to use their political rights. Turnout rates among immigrant voters are identical to those of Canadian-born voters.[17] Moreover, immigrant voters are *more* likely than other Canadians to pay attention to election-related news on the radio, television, and newspapers; watch leaders' debates; and seek electoral information on the Internet.[18]

Immigrants' political activity may be driven in part by their distinctive interests. As figure 6.1 makes clear, foreign-born and native-born Canadians differ in the degree to which they support immigration; the former prefer the maintenance of robust annual admissions, while the latter opt for tighter restrictions. While the proportion of native-born

Figure 6.2. Support for Greater Restrictions on Immigration by Percentage of Foreign Born in Federal Constituency

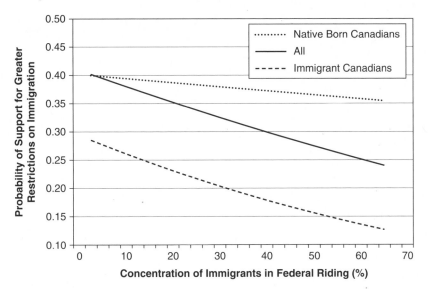

Source: Canadian Election Study (2000)

citizens holding more restrictive views has declined considerably since the early 1990s, it is still more than twice that of foreign-born Canadians.

Immigrant settlement patterns can have a dramatic effect on how federal parties' positions on immigration resonate with voters in some electoral constituencies. Evidence from the 2000 Canadian Election Study indicates that residents in federal ridings with higher concentrations of immigrants are less receptive to restrictions on immigration than those living in ridings with lower concentrations of immigrants (see figure 6.2).[19] This pattern is due almost entirely to the distinctively pro-immigration opinions of foreign-born residents in constituencies with higher concentrations of immigrants. The attitudes of native born Canadians appear to be largely unaffected by the composition of their local constituencies.

Electoral System

Canada's electoral system gives parties very strong incentives to avoid anti-immigrant policies and messages when immigrant settlement is geographically concentrated. In an SMP system, finishing second in a constituency holds no rewards in parliamentary representation: each federal election in Canada consists of winner-take-all contests in each federal constituency. At the same time, because candidates need only to win a plurality of votes in their constituencies, the SMP system can transform even modest differences in the popular vote between parties into significant differences in seats won. This makes an immigrant-friendly approach quite rational in ridings with high percentages of new Canadians. Given Ontario's and British Columbia's share of Canada's federal ridings (142 of 308), the concentration of immigrant voters in those two provinces, and their positions on immigration-related questions, populist anti-immigrant positions make little sense for any party interested in national winning office. To alienate large numbers of immigrant voters in dozens of federal ridings would almost certainly mean surrendering those ridings to other parties. Given all this, we should *expect* Canadian political parties (especially major parties) to move to the political centre, limiting the politicization of immigration policy-making and competing for the votes of immigrant voters by advancing immigrant-friendly positions and policies.

Ontario's importance is especially pronounced for conservative parties that have historically fared poorly in Quebec, which holds seventy-five federal seats. The Reform Party's opposition to official bilingualism and to Quebec's "special status" eliminated any possibility of support from the province. While Stephen Harper's Conservatives made tenuous inroads into Quebec in the mid-2000s, this rapidly deteriorated when the prime minister demonized the Bloc Québécois in late 2008, following Gilles Duceppe's agreement to support the potential Liberal-NDP coalition government. The waning of Quebec as a source of growth has made Ontario all the more important.

Straying from the Centre: The Reform Party and Immigration

As a rule, then, Canadian political parties have supported relatively open immigration policies with high numbers of annual admissions. This has been true of the Liberals as well as the Progressive Conservatives who, under Prime Minister Brian Mulroney, introduced the policy of setting annual admissions targets at approximately 250,000 per year, regardless of whether the economy was doing well or in a slump, and entrenched multiculturalism in statute through the passage of the 1988 Multiculturalism Act.[20] The exception to this rule of Canadian immigration politics was the Reform Party of Canada.

Reform rose to political prominence in the early 1990s, riding a wave of populist sentiment in the West.[21] The party fostered a maverick image based on its willingness to tackle controversial issues that the major parties refused to address, including parliamentary reform, opposition to the Meech Lake Accord (specifically, to the distinct-society clause for Quebec), a rejection of the "two nations" view of Canadian identity in favour of an unhyphenated national identity, opposition to official bilingualism and multiculturalism, and immigration reform.[22]

Immigration featured prominently in almost all of the Reform Party's official policy blueprints, early news releases, and electoral materials.[23] Party literature in the late 1980s echoed many of the concerns and rhetoric typical of far-right populist parties in Western Europe: not only were too many immigrants, both legal and illegal, entering the country, they were also the wrong *kind* of immigrant. The party was also drawing support from those with radically anti-immigrant sentiments. Doug Collins, a Reform Party nominee in Vancouver, publicly expressed an interest in returning to "the immigration policies of the fifties and sixties, when quotas were imposed on non-whites."[24] Collins's statements were quickly disavowed and his candidacy withdrawn while the party instituted rigorous vetting to avoid similar embarrassment in the future, but there is little doubt that his views did represent one current

of thought amongst Reform Party activists. A chief Reform Party organizer in Alberta maintained the party's commitment "to 'righting the
balance' in immigration," suggesting, "It should be geared more to
Europe – 50-50 between Europe and the Third World."[25] This attempt
at "righting the balance" was most explicitly laid out in the Reform
Party's electoral materials and Blue Books from 1988 and 1990, in which
the party stipulated that immigration policy should not "be explicitly
designed to radically or suddenly alter the ethnic makeup of Canada,
as it increasingly seems to be."[26]

From the early 1990s onwards, the Reform Party became a significant political force in Canadian politics, surpassing the Progressive
Conservative Party as Canada's primary federal party of the right.
Reform won fifty-two seats in the 1993 federal election (capturing just
under 19% of the popular vote), falling just two seats short of the Bloc
Québécois' fifty-four, and only narrowly missing becoming the official
opposition party.[27] Both the Liberal and Conservative parties' immigration policies became more restrictive during this period, in part because
of high unemployment and recurrent economic instability, but also
because Reform was politicizing the issue.[28]

This "swing to the right" was particularly pronounced in the Liberals'
immigration policies in the early to mid-1990s. In 1994, the Liberal government lowered its annual admission target, announced its intention
to increase the number of European immigrants admitted, and refo-
cused Canada's immigration program away from family reunification
and towards the independent/economic class.[29] Reacting to the Reform
Party's "law and order" platform, Liberal Immigration Minister Sergio
Marchi announced that the Liberals would carefully vet applications to
screen out applicants with criminal records.[30]

While scholars interested in the role of parties in Canadian immigration policy have correctly noted that the Reform Party pushed the
Liberal Party rightward during the 1990s, they have largely overlooked
the more interesting pull to the centre that Reform experienced during this period.[31] As Reform developed into a national party, its leaders
sought to distance the party from its earlier views on immigration and
multiculturalism, and particularly from framing immigration policy in
cultural terms. Tom Flanagan maintains that Stephen Harper regarded
the Reform Party's stance on immigration and multiculturalism as
deeply problematic as early as 1991. At the 1991 Saskatoon Assembly,
where membership ratified the party leadership's decision to compete
nationally, Harper insisted that all immigration policy be framed in

economic terms, as a "culturally phrased policy would be politically too dangerous – it would be too easy for the other parties to attack as veiled racism."[32]

Harper's pessimism was warranted: one of the central impediments to the Reform Party's national ambitions was the widely held view of Reformers as anti-immigrant, anti-French, and generally intolerant.[33] Reform's rivals, and the Liberal Party in particular, never tired of reminding voters of the party's early positions on immigration and multiculturalism, making Preston Manning's efforts to shake off accusations of intolerance all the more difficult.[34]

The Populist's Paradox

The Reform Party's shift to a "national strategy" presented a distinct set of challenges for a populist party whose appeal lay in its willingness to voice the demands of "ordinary" Canadians. As Tom Flanagan notes, the party's commitment to grassroots organization attracted members who held views not represented by mainstream parties.[35] The Reform Party became a de facto protest party, a repository for disaffected groups and individuals who saw an opportunity to address their narrow and often polarizing concerns – regarding immigration, bilingualism, and multiculturalism, among others.[36] In the late 1980s and early 1990s, this proved to be highly effective, particularly with a Western base that felt abandoned by Brian Mulroney's Progressive Conservatives.

Herein lay the populist's paradox: positions and rhetoric that galvanized a Western electorate that felt alienated from the old-line parties conflicted with the development of a more moderate orientation meant to appeal to a broader Canadian populace, including new Canadians.[37] Reform's development into a national party required that it ditch, or significantly moderate, many of the policies that had attracted its base, and yet much of this populist base saw the party's movement towards a more centrist position as abandoning its original principles.

Recognizing the party's limitations, Preston Manning had, by the late 1990s, initiated the processes of "uniting the right" that would bring an end to the Reform Party and see it reborn as the Canadian Alliance. The decision to pursue the United Alternative created significant internal tensions; some party members and Western media voices accused Reform of "becoming what it used to shun, a top-down political party in which its members are expected to toe the line."[38] As the Reform

Party moved onto the national stage and aimed to make gains as a viable federal party, these tensions became increasingly pronounced.[39]

This populist's paradox was perhaps best exemplified in Preston Manning's defeat in the 2000 leadership contest for the newly formed Canadian Alliance party. While Manning's election platform focused on his credentials and experience as leader of the Reform Party, Stockwell Day returned to the populist rhetoric of its past and won. Day recklessly drew on the immigration issue that Manning had sought to downplay, confidently asserting that he would "not be frightened by the forces of political correctness when it [came] to the issue of illegal immigration."[40]

This strategy would quickly threaten the new party's raison d'être: winning office. Only a few short months after his successful leadership bid, Day and his Alliance compatriots were being portrayed as "racists, bigots and people ... hostile to immigration [who] deny the reality of the Holocaust."[41] The party was also accused of harbouring a "'hidden agenda' on immigration," being "against the Chinese" and exhibiting "racist tendenc[ies]."[42] These were precisely the attacks that Manning's efforts aimed to avoid. The Alliance's failure to improve on Reform's results in Ontario ultimately prompted its dissolution and merger with the Progressive Conservatives in 2003 as the new Conservative Party of Canada.

Shifting Grounds: The New Canadian Conservatism

The new Conservative Party quickly set about reconfiguring its approach to immigration, multiculturalism, and cultural diversity. From its inception, the party has responded to the Reform Party's limitations on the national stage by falling into line with the centrist consensus on immigration and multiculturalism. Yet rather than simply reasserting the positions of Mulroney's Progressive Conservatives, Stephen Harper has reached out to ethnic voters in a way that affirmed his party's distinctively conservative orientation on key social issues. Tom Flanagan recalls a meeting in December 2004, during which Harper expressed his intention to use same-sex marriage to draw ethnic voters away from the Liberals: "He said that he wanted to do some advertising directed at ethnic communities and he wanted to use same-sex marriage as the wedge issue to try and peel them away from the Liberals, and he said this was going to be the beginning of a long-term strategy to make inroads into ethnic communities. I remember him saying he thought he might lose some supporters

Table 6.4. Social Attitudes by Place of Birth, 2006 (%)

	Place of Birth		
	Canada	Europe	Outside Europe
Oppose same-sex marriage	47	59	77
Believe it should be "very easy" or "quite easy" for women to get an abortion	65	67	55
Agree "society would be better off if women stayed at home with their children"	18	25	28

Source: Canadian Election Study (2006)

within the party, but he thought that was a loss that had to be borne because of the greater gain."[43] By January 2005, the Conservative Party ran print ads "in every ethnic publication we could find ... that would be the beginning of Harper's attempt to target ethnic voters."[44]

There is survey evidence giving credence to this kind of pitch. Data from recent Canadian Election Studies consistently show that visible minorities and immigrants tend to be more conservative than non-visible minority and non-immigrant Canadians on a number of contentious social issues.[45] The attitudes of immigrants from non-European countries are particularly striking. The 2006 Canadian Election Study, for example, shows that on the issues of same-sex marriage, abortion, and the role of women in society, immigrants from outside Europe are more likely than other Canadians to hold socially conservative positions (see table 6.4).

This attention to detail and planning vis-à-vis new Canadian voters signalled an important shift in the Conservatives' approach to immigration and multiculturalism. The Liberal Party's success in attracting immigrant voters depended less on specific matters of policy than on maintaining a continued presence and contact with immigrant communities. Flanagan suggests that this was a great failing of the Reform Party, one that the Conservative party worked diligently to rectify by appointing Jason Kenney as secretary of state for multiculturalism and Canadian identity in 2007 and minister for immigration, citizenship, and multiculturalism after the 2008 election. Kenney and the PMO formed an "ethnic outreach team" in 2007, tasked with explicitly targeting socially and fiscally conservative immigrant groups whose values were deemed amenable to those of the Conservative Party.

The outreach team's strategy has been "multi-pronged," and its tactics have included "targeted mailings, one-on-one meetings at 'major ethnic events' and the creation of large databases of immigrants and new Canadians."[46] Kenney has earned a reputation for personally reaching out to new Canadians, partly through attending a bevy of community events.[47] The Conservatives' outreach strategy has also encouraged MPs to "work beyond their traditional base, even if it meant 'look[ing] outside [their] normal comfort zone.'" The fact that this strategy has been framed inside the party by an emphasis on traditional family values and the small business propensities of immigrants has obviously helped MPs effect this change.[48]

Knowing that many newcomer participants in Canadian politics pay close attention to immigration issues, Stephen Harper has also made public statements directed at redressing historic wrongs committed against minorities in Canada. In an important symbolic move, he issued a public apology to Canada's Chinese community in 2006 for the Head Tax – thus responding to a request that previous Liberal governments had studiously avoided. In 2008, Harper apologized to the Sikh community for the *Komagata Maru* incident of 1914 – again meeting a longstanding demand. Apologies were also extended to signal contrition over the turning away of refugees fleeing Nazi Germany aboard the *St Louis* in 1939 and the internment of Italians during the Second World War. Harper has lauded Canada's diversity and multicultural approach to social integration as "preserving and strengthening the cultural diversity that makes us strong."[49] The new Conservative Party has also turned away from Reform's calls to curb immigration numbers, setting immigration targets for 2007 that were among the most aggressive in over a decade. In total, the new Conservatives have consciously crafted immigration policies and a public image that – in contrast with the Reform Party – aim to draw the support of new Canadians. At the same time, the Conservatives have tried to distinguish themselves in the field of immigration to maintain the support of their Reform-era base. Harper's conservatism has consciously aimed at avoiding the alienation that Mulroney produced in Westerners and in more traditional voters of the right. Thus, while clearly shifting closer to Liberal and Progressive Conservative positions on immigration and multiculturalism, the new Conservative Party has also initiated policy changes to appeal to traditional conservative voters.

The Conservatives have also used citizenship policy to develop what they would argue is a thicker sense of Canadian identity in ways that would appeal to significant parts of their conservative base. On 17 April 2009, Jason Kenney announced a new law amending Canada's Citizenship Act.[50] Prominent among these amendments is the limitation of "citizenship by descent to one generation born outside Canada."[51] The new law recognizes children born outside of Canada as Canadian only if one parent was born in Canada or immigrated to Canada and acquired Canadian citizenship through naturalization. The law is, in the words of Citizenship and Immigration Canada, intended to "protect the value of Canadian citizenship for the future."[52]

The Conservatives' citizenship reform also marks a response to the backlash against dual citizenship catalysed by the evacuation of Canadian citizens from Lebanon in the summer of 2006. Some commentators at the time suggested that too many Canadian citizens in Lebanon and elsewhere took advantage of their nationality to extract material benefits from Canada without giving enough back in return – whether in the form of taxes or simple allegiance and devotion to Canada.[53] The new law checked this in part by tying citizenship more concretely to physical presence in Canada.

Conservative approaches to citizenship policy have also featured reassertions of membership and identity based on what are thought to be unifying symbols and distinctively Canadian values as Conservatives understand them. In a 2009 speech entitled "Good Citizenship: The Duty to Integrate,"[54] Kenney described the "song, sari and samosa" multiculturalism of the 1970s as outdated; Canada's new immigration, citizenship, and multiculturalism programs should "focus on integration, on the successful and rapid integration of newcomers to Canadian society, and on a deepening understanding of the values, symbols and institutions that are rooted in our history."[55] The new citizenship guide, released by CIC in November 2009, reflects the minister's view of citizenship as grounded in Canadian traditions and cultural values. The older citizenship guide informed newcomers of contemporary conditions in Canada (general facts about the economy, political institutions, regional variations, First Nations communities, English-French heritage, etc.), providing the grounds for a basic civic and political literacy. The new citizenship guide, conversely, emphasizes Canada's military history and cultural iconography, commits a full section to Canadian traditions and symbols, and de-emphasizes the Charter and public policies aimed at the recognition of diversity. The shift in emphasis, from civic to cultural values, points towards a thicker view of Canadian cultural traditions as the grounds of political membership.[56]

The Conservatives have also borrowed from the playbook of European right-wing parties in tying citizenship acquisition via naturalization to a specific interpretation of civic virtues. In December 2011, Minister Kenney announced that Muslim women would "be banned from wearing face coverings such as burka and niqab veils when swearing the oath of citizenship."[57]

Refugee policy has also been used to burnish the Conservatives' "law and order" credentials. Recent changes to the rules on "in-land" refugee claimants are meant to underscore the Harper government's opposition to "human smugglers" and unscrupulous queue-jumpers abusing Canada's generosity.[58] While restrictions on asylum seeking are certainly not new – Liberal and Progressive Conservative governments were similarly intent on imposing tighter controls on asylum-seekers in the 1980s and 1990s – the Conservatives have been careful to make their intentions clear through an aggressive PR campaign headed by Minister Kenney and Minister of Public Safety Vic Toews.[59] While there may be a case to be made for reforming Canada's refugee determination system, the government's highly publicized intent to root out immigration cheaters and inject "common sense" into Canada's refugee policies clearly appeals to conservative voters. Kenney's efforts have also elicited approval in wider circles. Political commentator John Ibbitson lauded the Tories' moves to speed up the removal of asylum seekers "whose claims aren't valid."[60]

The Conservatives campaigned aggressively for the votes of new Canadians during the campaign leading up to the federal election of 2 May 2011. Stephen Harper and Jason Kenney attended religious ceremonies, donned "ethnic" attire in numerous meet-and-greet sessions, granted interviews to the "ethnic press," and promised repeatedly to maintain an expansive immigration policy, while cracking down on "human smugglers" and "queue-jumpers." During the English-language leaders' debate, Harper forcefully rejected criticisms of official multiculturalism by the Bloc Québécois leader Gilles Duceppe, arguing, "What Canadians need to understand about multiculturalism is that people who make the hard decision to … come here … first and foremost want to belong to this country … They also at the same time will change our country. And we show through multiculturalism our willingness to accommodate their differences, so they are more comfortable. That's why we're so successful integrating people as a country. I think we're probably the most successful country in the world in that regard."[61]

The election saw the Conservatives secure a majority government in part through their success in Ontario, where they captured 73 of the province's 106 federal seats, including 32 of 47 seats in the Greater Toronto Area, where immigrants make up 50 per cent of the total population.[62] They managed to do this while maintaining their grip on Western Canada, thus forming a strikingly new electoral coalition. Whether the "immigrant vote" actually helped the Conservatives achieve their breakthrough in Ontario has yet to be definitively proven. Nevertheless, there is no doubting that the party tailored its campaign to compete for the votes of new Canadians without losing sight of its traditional base of support in the West.

Conclusion: A Value-Based Consensus?

The Conservative Party's positions on immigration and citizenship policy are driven by structurally determined need to reach out to ethnic voters. At the same time, the party displays strategies aimed at maintaining a base of support among core conservative voters. While the former has led the party to embrace longstanding consensus positions on immigration and multiculturalism policies, the latter has prompted efforts to use citizenship and refugee policies to underscore the party's conservative credentials. This is the Conservative solution to what we term the populist's paradox.

Regardless of how well it succeeds, the Conservatives have arrived at a *plausible* response to what is fast becoming a more general challenge among right-of-centre parties in countries of immigration. Reporting on Arizona's controversial immigration law, for example, the *New York Times* observed, "Republican lawmakers and candidates are increasingly divided over illegal immigration – torn between the need to attract Latino support, especially at the ballot box, and rallying party members who support tougher action."[63] This debate within the Republican Party has intensified in the wake of presidential candidate Mitt Romney's loss in the 2012 election.[64] Similarly, the German Christian Democratic Union has acknowledged the growing importance of naturalized voters of Turkish origin in what is an extremely competitive party system but have yet to form a workable strategy for reaching out to these potential supporters.[65]

Although critics of the Conservative Party see its ethnic outreach strategy as a crass and cynical vote grab, what is more interesting to us is the party's efforts to devise a conservative ideology that includes immigrants and builds on their perceived ideological predispositions. The Conservatives have attempted to build bridges to immigrant communities by appealing to *shared* conservative values on issues such as same-sex marriage and the importance of free enterprise. As the strategic blueprint outlining the Conservatives' 2007 outreach program states, there is "growing anecdotal evidence that New Canadian values are more aligned with the values of the Conservative Party of Canada."[66] By appealing to the socially and fiscally conservative values that the party perceives in immigrant communities, the Conservatives have sought to form common political ground joining new and native-born Canadians. Stephen Harper has made it clear that the Conservative Party's "goal is to make small-*c* conservatives into big-*C* Conservatives."[67]

As we have noted, the Conservative Party of Canada has come to this position by necessity. As winning national office in Canada means capturing at least some of the support of new Canadians, Canadian conservatism has had to adapt, bending itself to appeal to ethnically diverse (sub)urban voters without losing the support of its conservative base.[68] This is a distinctive and extremely interesting experiment that is likely to rouse the interest of conservative politicians in other countries where immigrants and ethnic minorities are also gaining electoral clout. The Conservative Party of Canada's answer to the populist's paradox may thus be of use to other conservative parties seeking to remain competitive in political contexts transformed by immigration.

NOTES

1 Inder Marwah and Triadafilos Triadafilopoulos, *Europeanizing Canada's Citizenship Regime?*, Canada-Europe Transatlantic Dialogue: Policy Commentary, May 2009, http://canada-europe-dialogue. ca/?s=inder+marwah.

2 Overheard at the 12th National Metropolis Conference, Montreal, March 2010. The official asked to remain anonymous.

3 The Conservatives have also pursued a radical expansion of Canada's Temporary Foreign Worker (TFW) program to satisfy employers. See Office of the Auditor General of Canada, "Selecting Foreign Workers under the Immigration Program," in *Report of the Auditor General of Canada to the House of Commons* (Fall 2009), http://www.oag-bvg.gc.ca/internet/docs/ parl_oag_200911_02_e.pdf. Given that employers' influence on immigration policy is typically pursued through client, rather than electoral, politics, we do not explore TFW policy further in this chapter. For a classic

statement on the influence of client politics on immigration policymaking, see Gary Freeman, "Modes of Immigration Politics in Liberal Democratic Societies," *International Migration Review* 29, no. 4 (1995): 881–902.

4 Tim Bale, "Turning Round the Telescope: Centre-Right Parties and Immigration and Integration Policy in Europe," *Journal of European Public Policy* 15, no. 3 (2008): 315–30.

5 Terri Givens and Adam Luedtke, "European Immigration Policies in Comparative Perspective: Issue Salience, Partisanship and Immigrants' Rights," *Comparative European Politics* 3, no. 1 (2005): 1–22.

6 Triadafilos Triadafilopoulos and Andrej Zaslove, "Influencing Migration Policy from Inside: Political Parties," in *Dialogues on Migration Policy*, ed. Marco Giugni and Florence Passy, 171–92 (Lanham, MD: Lexington Books, 2006); Martin A. Schain, "The Politics of Immigration in France, Britain and the United States: A Transatlantic Comparison," in *Immigration and the Transformation of Europe*, ed. Craig A. Parsons and Timothy M. Smeeding, 362–92 (Cambridge: Cambridge University Press, 2006); Jerome H. Black and Bruce M. Hicks, "Electoral Politics and Immigration in Canada: How Does Immigration Matter?," *Journal of International Migration and Integration* 9 (2008): 242. It is worth noting that a similar consensus among Quebec's parties was upset in 2007, when the Action démocratique du Québec campaigned against the policy of reasonable accommodation for religious minorities. Since the 2007 election, both the Parti Québécois and the Liberal Party of Quebec have sought to tap into voter discontent on immigrant integration and identity. Thus a new, rather less liberal, cross-party consensus has emerged in Quebec. See Yasmeen Abu-Laban and Baha Abu-Laban, "Reasonable Accommodation in a Global Village," *Policy Options* (September 2007): 28–33; Tim Nieguth and Aurélie Lacassagne, "Contesting the Nation: Reasonable Accommodation in Rural Quebec," *Canadian Political Science Review* 3, no. 1 (2009): 1–16; Gada Mahrouse, "'Reasonable Accommodation' in Québec: The Limits of Participation and Dialogue," *Race & Class* 52, no. 1 (2010): 85–96.

7 Christian Joppke, "The Retreat of Multiculturalism in the Liberal State: Theory and Policy," *British Journal of Sociology* 55, no. 2 (2004): 237–57; Keith Banting and Will Kymlicka, "Canadian Multiculturalism: Global Anxieties and Local Debates," *British Journal of Canadian Studies* 23, no. 1 (2010): 43–72.

8 Jerome Black and Bruce Hicks note that when immigration is broached during campaigns, parties have tended to support liberal positions, sometimes engaging in outbidding. See Black and Hicks, "Electoral Politics and

Immigration in Canada," 255, 258. We can think of no other country where this is true.

9 Media-inflamed stories of what were characterized as excessive accommodations of religious minorities led to important shifts in public pronouncements of the Parti Québécois and, especially, the Action démocratique du Québec, pointing to the risks to Quebec values posed by the cultural and religious values espoused within some minority communities. The Bouchard-Taylor report emanating from that debate played down differences in approaches to immigration between Quebec and the rest of Canada, though there are still important differences in the cross-party consensus within that province and elsewhere. This was evident in the cross-party support for a 2010 ban on full-face-covering dress by women providing or seeking provincial government services. So far, however, this shift on immigration or minority policies has not affected the provincial consensus about the importance of encouraging immigration and the economic value it represents.

10 Robert MacGregor Dawson, *The Government of Canada* (Toronto: University of Toronto Press, 1948), 508; Janine M. Brodie and Jane Jenson, "Piercing the Smokescreen: Brokerage Politics and Class Politics," in *Canadian Parties in Transition: Discourse, Organization and Representation*, ed. Alain-G. Gagnon and A. Brian Tanguay, 52–72 (Scarborough: Nelson, 1991); Richard Johnston, "The Ideological Structure of Opinion on Policy," in *Party Democracy in Canada: The Politics of National Party Conventions*, ed. George Perlin, 54–70 (Scarborough: Prentice Hall, 1988).

11 Jeanette Money, "No Vacancy: The Political Geography of Immigration Control in Advanced Industrial Countries," *International Organization* 51, no. 4 (1997): 685–720.

12 For data, see Citizenship and Immigration Canada, *Facts and Figures: Immigration Overview, Permanent and Temporary Residents 2008*, http://www.cic.gc.ca/english/pdf/research-stats/facts2008.pdf. Ontario's share of immigrant admissions dropped in 2010; it remains to be seen whether this trend persists.

13 André Blais, "Accounting for the Electoral Success of the Liberal Party in Canada," *Canadian Journal of Political Science* 38, no. 4 (2005): 821–40; Linda Gerber, "The Visible Minority Immigrant, and Bilingual Composition of Ridings and Party Support in the Canadian Federal Election of 2004," *Canadian Ethnic Studies* 38, no. 1 (2006): 65–82; Antoine Bilodeau and Mebs Kanji, "The New Immigrant Voter, 1965–2004: The Emergence of a New Liberal Partisan?," in *Perspectives on the Canadian Voter: Puzzles of Influence and Choice*, ed. Laura Stephenson and Cameron Anderson, 65–85

(Vancouver: UBC Press, 2010); Allison Harell, "Revisiting the 'Ethnic' Vote: Liberal Allegiance and Vote Choice among Racialized Minorities in Canada" (paper presented at the Political Parties and Elections in Canada Workshop, Memorial University, St John's, 25–6 October 2010).

14 Irene Bloemraad, "Becoming a Citizen in the United States and Canada: Structured Mobilization and Immigrant Political Incorporation," *Social Forces* 85, no. 2 (2006): 667–96; Bloemraad, *Becoming a Citizen: Incorporating Immigrants and Refugees in the United States and Canada* (Cambridge: Harvard University Press, 2006), 51.

15 Will Kymlicka, "The Uncertain Future of Multiculturalism," *Canadian Diversity* 4, no. 1 (2005): 82–5.

16 Kelly Tran, Stan Kustec, and Tina Chui, "Becoming Canadian: Intent, Process and Outcome," *Canadian Social Trends* 76 (Spring 2005): 8–13.

17 Ailsa Henderson, "Ideal Citizens? Immigrant Voting Patterns in Canadian Elections," *Canadian Issues /Thèmes canadiens* (Summer 2005): 57–60.

18 Antoine Bilodeau and Mebs Kanji, "Political Engagement among Immigrants in Four Anglo-Democracies," *Electoral Insight*, December 2006, http://www.elections.ca/res/eim/article_search/article.asp?id=149&lang=e&frmPageSize=10.

19 André Blais, Elisabeth Gidengil, Richard Nadeau, and Neil Nevitte, "Canadian Election Survey," 2000 (computer file) ICPSR 03969-v1 (Toronto: York University, Institute for Social Research [producer], 2000; Ann Arbor, MI: Inter-University Consortium for Political and Social Research [distributor], 2004). Data from the 2000 Canadian Election Study were provided by the Institute for Social Research (ISR), York University. The survey was funded by the Social Sciences and Humanities Research Council (SSHRC). Neither the original collectors of these data, SSHRC, nor ISR bears any responsibility for the analyses or interpretations presented here. Estimates are derived from binary logit analyses with standard errors corrected for clustering at the constituency level. The relationship between support for immigration and concentration of immigrants at the constituency level is significant at $p = 0.000$ among all respondents, $p = .030$ when the analysis is restricted to immigrant respondents, and $p = .430$ when the analysis is restricted to native-born respondents.

20 Jack W.P. Veugelers, "State–Society Relations in the Making of Canadian Immigration Policy during the Mulroney Era," *Canadian Review of Sociology and Anthropology* 37, no. 1 (2000): 95–110.

21 David Laycock argues, "Like European parties of the new and/or extreme right, Canada's Reform party was far more prepared than its mainstream predecessors and rivals to raise the issue of immigration." See David

Laycock, *The New Right and Democracy in Canada: Understanding Reform and the Canadian Alliance* (Don Mills: Oxford University Press, 2002), 144.

22 For a detailed examination of Canadian conservatives' alienation from all major parties (and particularly from Brian Mulroney's Progressive Conservatives) during this period, see Tom Flanagan, *Waiting for the Wave: The Reform Party and the Conservative Movement* (Montreal and Kingston: McGill-Queen's University Press, 2009), 40–6.

23 The Reform Party's 1988 electoral platform stipulated, "There is perhaps no area of public policy where the views of Canadians have been more systematically ignored than the area of immigration. Despite the cries of 'racism' and the invocation of legal fictions, political change can occur … Immigration abuse must be ended, and not just by legalizing it." Reform Party of Canada, "'The West Wants In!,'" Election Platform of the Reform Party of Canada, 1988, 25.

24 Thomas Walkom, "Running a Campaign on Race," *Globe and Mail*, 31 October 1988.

25 Ibid.

26 *Platform and Statement of Principles of the Reform Party of Canada*, Calgary, 1988, 23.

27 Faron Ellis, *The Limits of Participation: Members and Leaders in Canada's Reform Party* (Calgary: University of Calgary Press, 2005), 146.

28 Yasmeen Abu-Laban, "Welcome/STAY OUT: The Contradictions of Canadian Integration and Immigration Policies at the Millennium," *Canadian Ethnic Studies* 30, no. 3 (1998): 190–211; Estanislao Oziewicz, "Coalition Attacks Proposed Immigration Policy: Labour, Church, Refugee Groups Contend Legislation Caters to Reform Party," *Globe and Mail*, 23 June 1992; Ross Howard and Lila Sarick, "Immigration Proposals Aimed at Serious Crime: Government Accused of Pandering to Reform Critics in Moving to Limit Appeals against Deportation," *Globe and Mail*, 18 June 1994.

29 Lila Sarick, "Canada Falls Short of Immigration Target: Economic Factors, Tougher Regulations Main Reasons for Decline, Experts Say," *Globe and Mail*, 21 September 1994; Sarick, "Immigration from Europe a Priority, Marchi Says: Minister to Revive Independent Class," *Globe and Mail*, 13 September 1994; Sarick, "Family Immigration Faces Change: Marchi under Pressure to Restrict Reunification of Relatives," *Globe and Mail*, 24 October 1994.

30 Howard and Sarick, "Immigration Proposals"; Edward Greenspon, "Reform Backs Immigration Cuts: MP Says Party Was 'Catalyst' for Debate That Led to Ottawa's Move," *Globe and Mail*, 31 October 1994.

31 Abu-Laban, "Welcome/STAY OUT," 190–211.

32 Authors' telephone interview with Tom Flanagan, 14 November 2008; see also Flanagan, *Waiting for the Wave*, 66–72.

33 Reform Party supporters were significantly more conservative, particularly on social issues, than any other party's supporters, including the Progressive Conservatives. See Flanagan, *Waiting for the Wave*, 41, 148.

34 Miro Cernetig, "Reform Party Sees Radicals as Problem: Image a Factor in National Drive," *Globe and Mail*, 4 April 1991. For more on the challenges the Reform Party faced with greater media scrutiny, see Flanagan, *Waiting for the Wave*, 89–98.

35 Authors' interview with Tom Flanagan.

36 Ibid.

37 Laycock, *New Right*, 13.

38 Robert Matas, "The Pundits Aren't Welcoming the Chinese Boat People and They Say Suspended Reformer Jack Hoeppner Is What the Party Is All About," *Globe and Mail*, 30 July 1999.

39 Tom Flanagan argues that the central tension running through, and frequently dividing, the Reform Party was "the internal tension between populism and conservatism that has marked the party's history" (*Waiting for the Wave*, 60). While Preston Manning had always envisioned the RP as a non-ideological party, defined by its populism, the membership attracted to the party was clearly aligned with the right. Throughout *Waiting for the Wave*, Flanagan describes the persistence of this tension – between Manning's attempts to moderate the party's conservatism and other members' desire to strengthen it.

40 "The Candidates Speak: Stockwell Day," *Globe and Mail*, 24 June 2000.

41 Shawn McCarthy, "Day Talks Tougher on Crime: Law-and-Order Stand a Hit with Audiences," *Globe and Mail*, 15 November 2000.

42 Robert Matas, "'Scurrilous' Ads Enrage Alliance: Liberals Using Chinese-Language Media to Paint Portrait of Rival Party as 'Scary' and Racist," *Globe and Mail*, 24 November 2000; Rod Mickleburgh, "Alliance Fundraiser Fired for Comments Chinese Voter Fraud. Remark 'Racist': Grits," *Globe and Mail*, 17 November 2000.

43 Authors' interview with Tom Flanagan.

44 Ibid. Also see Heather Mallick, "Everywhere You Look, Irony's in the Fire," *Globe and Mail*, 19 February 2005.

45 See André Blais, "Accounting for the Electoral Success of the Liberal Party in Canada," *Canadian Journal of Political Science* 38, no. 4 (2005): 832; and John Ibbitson and Joe Friesen, "Conservative Immigrants Boost Tory Fortunes," *Globe and Mail*, 4 October 2010.

46 Daniel Leblanc, "Tories Target Specific Ethnic Voters," *Globe and Mail*, 16 October 2007.

47 Ibbitson and Friesen, "Conservative Immigrants Boost Tory Fortunes."

48 Ibid.

49 Rod Mickleburgh, "Harper Defends Canadian Diversity: PM Rejects Calls to Curb Immigration, Calls Open Society 'Our Greatest Strength,'" *Globe and Mail*, 20 June 2006.

50 Citizenship and Immigration Canada, "Minister Kenney Announces New Citizenship Law," news release,17 April 2009, http://www.cic.gc.ca/english/department/media/releases/2009/2009-04-17.asp.

51 Citizenship and Immigration Canada, "Changes to Citizenship Rules as of April 2009," http://www.cic.gc.ca/english/citizenship/rules_2009.asp.

52 Ibid.

53 Rudyard Griffiths, *Who We Are: A Citizen's Manifesto* (Vancouver: Douglas & McIntyre, 2009), 160–1.

54 Citizenship and Immigration Canada, "Speaking Notes for the Honourable Jason Kenney, P.C., M.P. Minister of Citizenship, Immigration and Multiculturalism 'Good Citizenship: The Duty to Integrate' at Huron University College's Canadian Leaders Speakers' Series," 18 March 2009, http://www.cic.gc.ca/english/department/media/speeches/2009/2009-03-18.asp.

55 Ibid.

56 A revised version of the new guide was released in March 2011. It features extended coverage of the War of 1812 and mentions Canada's acceptance of same-sex marriage – a point that was neglected in the 2009 volume (courtesy of an "oversight," in Jason Kenney's words). See John Ibbitson, "War and Wedlock Get More Ink in Latest Citizenship Guide," *Globe and Mail*, 15 March 2011.

57 "Niqabs, Burkas Must be Removed During Citizenship Ceremonies: Jason Kenney," *National Post*, 11 December 2011, http://news.nationalpost.com/2011/12/12/niqabs-burkas-must-be-removed-during-citizenship-ceremonies-jason-kenney/.

58 Protecting Canada's Immigration System Act, 2012 (Bill C-31), http://laws-lois.justice.gc.ca/eng/AnnualStatutes/2012_17/page-1.html; Citizenship and Immigration Canada, "Opening Remarks for the Honourable Jason Kenney, P.C., M.P. Minister of Citizenship, Immigration and Multiculturalism, Balanced Refugee Reform, The Canadian Club Winnipeg, Manitoba," 8 April 2010.

59 Christopher G. Anderson, *Canadian Liberalism and the Politics of Border Control: 1867–1967* (Vancouver: UBC Press, 2013), 198.

60 John Ibbitson, "Tories Can Point to Immigration Policy as Their One Well-Executed Legacy Issue," *Globe and Mail*, 1 November 2012.

61 Haroon Siddiqui, "Siddiqui: On Multiculturalism, Harper's Got It Right," *Toronto Star*, 16 April 2011.

62 Kenyon Wallace, "Liberals Crushed in GTA," *Toronto Star*, 3 May 2011.
63 Jennifer Steinhauer, "Arizona Law Reveals Split within G.O.P.," *New York Times*, 22 May 2010.
64 Carl Hulse, "Republicans Face Struggle over Party's Direction," *New York Times*, 7 November 2012.
65 Sara Clara de Fonseca, "New Citizens – New Candidates? Candidate Selection and the Mobilization of Immigrant Voters in German Elections," *The Political Representation of Immigrants and Minorities: Voters, Parties and Parliaments in Liberal Democracies*, ed. Karen Bird, Thomas Saalfeld, and Andreas M. Wüst, 109–27 (New York: Routledge, 2011); Margarete van Ackeren, "Potenzielle Wähler: CDU entdeckt im Wahlkampf ihr Herz für Zuwanderer," Focus Online, 20 November 2012, http://www.focus.de/politik/deutschland/tid-28198/partei-will-sympathischer-werden-potenzielle-waehler-cdu-entdeckt-im-wahlkampf-ihr-herz-fuer-zuwanderer_aid_864656.html; "Partei will „sympathischer" werden: Potenzielle Wähler: CDU entdeckt im Wahlkampf ihr Herz für Zuwanderer," Focus Online, http://www.focus.de/politik/deutschland/tid-28198/partei-will-sympathischer-werden-potenzielle-waehler-cdu-entdeckt-im-wahlkampf-ihr-herz-fuer-zuwanderer_aid_864656.html.
66 "Tories Target Specific Ethnic Voters."
67 Stephen Chase, "Transcript: Prime Minister Stephen Harper on International Trade, Politics and Immigration," *Globe and Mail*, 9 November 2012, http://m.theglobeandmail.com/news/politics/transcript-prime-minister-stephen-harper-on-international-trade-politics-and-immigration/article5173326/?service=mobile.
68 John Ibbitson and Steve Chase, "Minister of the Crown or Party Operative?," *Globe and Mail*, 5 March 2011.

7 Fiscal Frugality and Party Politics

JOHN FRENDREIS AND RAYMOND TATALOVICH

Here we compare fiscal policy in Canada and the United States, posing three questions. First, is there a conservative belief system that values balanced budgets as the hallmark of good government in these two countries? Second, are political parties on the right more sympathetic to balanced budgets, and does their policy record while in government reflect that?[1] Third, if there are differences in the fiscal records over time, can they be explained primarily by differences in which party has been in control of government, by the principles guiding parties of the right, or by the circumstances in which each government has operated?

The balanced budget ethos was grounded in the Scottish Enlightenment. David Hume harshly criticized indebtedness as a financial burden transferred to future generations.[2] Adam Smith praised frugality, condemned prodigality, and believed that "great nations are never impoverished by private, though they sometimes are by public prodigality and misconduct."[3] Smith's laissez-faire economics advocated a limited governmental role in the private economy, and his analogy between private budgeting and governmental fiscal frugality became a powerful influence in Britain during the second half of the nineteenth century, and in the United States throughout that century. In Canada, as we shall see, the dominance of such views was much less clear-cut.

It seems reasonable to argue that political parties on the right would be more sympathetic to balanced budgets, on the grounds of being more suspicious of state intervention than parties on the left, and more inclined to the view that high taxation impinges excessively on the free market. However, in North America as well as in Europe, conservative parties have at times stood for strengthening the hand of national governments in regulating economic affairs and providing social services, in part as a reflection of a "tory" commitment to maintaining solidarity and preventing destitution, in part because of a tendency to lower taxes without reducing spending commitments made by governments of the centre and left. We also recognize that some rightist governments rhetorically committed to balancing budgets left office with higher deficits than their centrist or leftist alternatives. Ronald Reagan campaigned for balancing the budget but bequeathed the largest deficits of the post-war era. Cross-national comparisons in Europe and North America for 1965–81 led David Cameron to conclude that right-leaning governments were more likely to run deficits than left-leaning governments.[4] What does the history of rhetoric and record, particularly in the decades since the Second World War, tell us about differences between Canada and the United States?

Nineteenth-Century and Early Twentieth-Century United States

Lewis Kimmel surveyed budgetary and fiscal policy in the United States from 1789 to 1958 and concluded, "Throughout the greater part of our history, peacetime budget and fiscal policy was predicated on the belief that the federal budget should be balanced annually."[5] James Buchanan and Richard Wagner characterize this norm as the "fiscal constitution" and argue that it prevailed until the economic theories of John Maynard Keynes began to take hold.[6]

From 1801 until 1860 – the period when the Jeffersonians (renamed Democrats, beginning with Jackson) dominated American politics – the federal budget showed surpluses in forty-one years. The Jeffersonians disliked banks in general and the debt in particular, and they were determined to pay off the national debt (which for all practical purposes occurred in the mid-1830s under President Andrew Jackson). The following four decades displayed mixed results, in large part because of the Civil War and not because of partisan or ideological shifts. In 1860 the public debt (or the accumulation of yearly deficits) stood at $64.8 million, but five years of massive deficit spending to fund the war increased it to $2.7 billion by 1865. For almost thirty years thereafter, the federal government ran budget surpluses but then showed deficits during 1894–9. From the turn of the century until 1930, budgetary surpluses were overwhelmingly the norm, regardless of party.

The Great Depression and the costs associated with U.S. involvement in the Second World War produced massive deficits for the entire 1931–46 period, increasing the national debt from $16.2 billion to $271.0

billion. At the very least in the early stages of the Depression, however, the balanced budget ethos remained influential. One week after his inauguration, President Franklin D. Roosevelt spoke about the evils of deficits and warned the nation, "Too often in recent history liberal governments have been wrecked on the roots of loose fiscal policy. We must avoid this danger."[7] Roosevelt quickly learned that he could not finance his ambitious program of "relief, recovery, and reform" within the strictures of a balanced budget, and the federal government accrued deficits every year into the 1940s, though it is not clear that this was a shift motivated by a systemic shift away from the "fiscal constitution."

The Canadian Pre-war Record

It is doubtful that any such a "fiscal constitution" restrained the Canadian government during the nineteenth and early twentieth centuries. Savoie asserts that "the ideology of balanced budgets had prevailed in most political parties,"[8] but Gillespie disagrees, arguing that the goals of nation-building and attracting immigrants that were so paramount to the new dominion government led to an acquiescence to deficits. In particular, interest in reducing emigration to the United States induced governments to establish tax rates lower than in the United States.[9] And yet, as Lewis points out, there were high costs associated with building a vast infrastructure of canals and railroads in a country with only a fraction of the population south of the border.[10] This prompted the dominion government to rely on British capital markets, and as Gillespie points out it, was able to obtain lower interest rates than the United States.[11] All this reduced the power of the idea of balancing budgets.

From 1868 to 1900, a period in which Conservative Party rule was the norm, all but three years showed deficits. From 1901 until 1920, when both Liberals and Conservatives held national office, only five of twenty budgets showed surpluses. In the following decade of largely Liberal Party rule, every budget during 1921–30 showed a surplus. Then, deficits were recorded every year from 1931 to 1946, in large measure because of the severity of the Depression and the enormous costs associated with Canadian involvement in the Second World War.[12]

Savoie argues that the Depression did not "shake the conviction that budgets should be balanced," and Lewis agrees.[13] In 1930 newly elected Conservative Prime Minister R.B. Bennett proposed stringent economy measures and then even more serious economies the following year when the cost of relief produced a deficit for 1931. The Liberals under W.L. Mackenzie King were returned to power in 1935, whereupon Finance Minister Charles Dunning told Parliament that it was "the declared purpose of the government to end in the shortest practicable time the era of recurring deficits."[14] The seriousness of the economic downturn produced a "crisis" in fiscal policy in 1938, with intense Cabinet debate and concerns voiced that Dunning might resign if he was forced to accept too large a deficit.[15]

Over the entire period from 1868 to 1946, the Canadian federal government recorded sixty years of deficits, and only nineteen years of surpluses. The American record over the same period shows forty-four years of surpluses and thirty-five years of deficits. Neither of these policy records shows much association between the fiscal outcome and the political party in power. At the very end of this period, however, signs of a shift in thinking were evident, particularly in Canada.

Shifting Frameworks during and after the Second World War

In some Western governments, the hardship associated with the Great Depression opened policymakers to the ideas developed by Keynes at Cambridge, particularly seminal work offering policy prescriptions to combat high unemployment. In Canada the first budget to reflect Keynesian thinking was adopted in 1939, under Prime Minister Mackenzie King.[16] By 1945, still under King, a consensus over Keynesian ideas had developed, fully evident in a government White Paper presented to Parliament.[17] This did not lead to government deficits – the first appearing only in the mid-1950s – in part no doubt because of post-war prosperity (see figure 7.1). Robert Campbell also argues that "the intrinsic value of a balanced budget was not displaced from the policy agenda, and there was often a tension between revenue goals (a balanced budget) and economic goals (the shaping of economic conditions)."[18] He believes, in fact, that Keynesianism "was never fully applied and played a less important role than other types of policy," though others, like Wolfe and Lewis,[19] argue that Keynesian ideas were in fact dominant during these years.

In the United States, Keynesianism influenced Congress to enact the Employment Act of 1946, which committed the federal government to economic stewardship. This built upon the social policy record of the Roosevelt administrations before and during the war, which marked the beginnings of the modestly scaled American

Figure 7.1. U.S. and Canadian Annual Budget Surpluses/Deficits as
Percentage of Total Economy (GNP for Canada and GDP for United States)

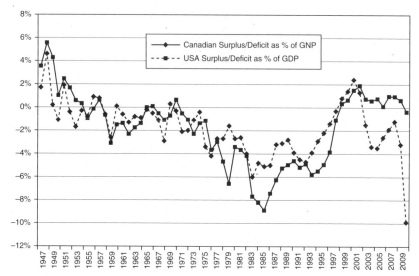

welfare state. And yet, while there was a symbolic commitment to full employment in the 1946 statute, it did not mandate that deficits be used to guarantee jobs for all Americans desiring to work. More than in Canada, there was substantial ambivalence and disagreement about the extent to which Keynesian frameworks had merit.[20] That said, there were more years of federal budget deficits in the United States than in Canada between 1947 and 1959 (six, compared to two).

From 1960 through to the early 1970s, there seemed a stronger adherence to Keynesian views on both sides of the border. There was also a similar record in budget outcomes, with deficits outnumbering surpluses (balanced budgets or moderate surpluses reported only three times in Canada and twice in the United States).

The rise of inflationary pressures in the late 1960s in both countries raised questions about the efficacy of Keynesian policy prescriptions, and those doubts were magnified by the stagflation (inflation with unemployment) of the 1970s. The intellectual challenge to Keynesianism came from monetarism, which argued that a stable money supply would stabilize the inflation rate, and later supply-side economics, which favoured tax cuts to stimulate production and investment. Such ideas spread as more policy-makers and close observers in the 1970s began to see deficits as "structural" rather than cyclically related to the business cycle.[21] Lewis agrees fully with that assessment.[22]

The monetarist critique of Keynesianism influenced President Richard Nixon in 1969 to pursue a "gradualist" economic game plan in hopes of reducing inflationary pressures without rekindling an economic slow-down and rising unemployment, though eventually Nixon resorted to wage and price controls in 1971–2.[23] It would not be until 1980, with the election of Ronald Reagan, that there was a full rhetorical abandonment of Keynesian policy tools in the U.S. federal administration. The focus on tax cuts to reflect supply-side fiscal and monetary policy, however, was not matched by corresponding reductions in spending, so that the most dramatic turn away from Keynesianism was also accompanied by unprecedented deficits. Those deficits were overcome in the mid- and late 1990s, without a turn away from monetarist and supply-side policy. Deficits returned in the early years of the new century through a com-bination of major cuts in taxation and increased military expenditures, compounded by the economic crisis of the late 2000s.

Monetarism in Canada emerged forcibly in the mid-1970s, when the Bank of Canada began to severely tighten monetary policy and gen-erate higher interest rates.[24] McBride dates the end of Keynesianism to 1975, when Canada shifted to anti-inflationary monetary policies.[25] But a more nuanced analysis of budget speeches led Timothy Lewis to argue that Keynesian ideas about deficit finance "endured from 1975 to 1984 roughly to the extent they had a hold from 1945 to 1974."[26] There was a shift, to be sure, but the Liberals under Prime Minister Pierre Trudeau refused to abandon their unemployment goals entirely while confronting inflation.[27]

Although the anti-deficit rhetoric of the Mulroney government first elected in 1984 did not translate into radically altered budgeting, the Progressive Conservative assault on the idea of deficits undoubtedly paved the way for more decisive action.[28] The end of Keynesianism and the wholesale commitment to balanced budgets and debt reduction came when the Liberals regained power in 1993. As Lewis points out, the "objective" reality of inflation did not bring about an immediate shift in Canadian fiscal policy until there had been a fundamental realign-ment in the mindset of politicians and their constituents to the view that deficits were harmful and balanced budgets beneficial. That shift was not enough to prevent the return of significant deficits in the late 2000s, driven primarily by economic crisis, though also by tax reductions.

Figure 7.1 compares the federal budget surplus or deficit as a percentage of GNP (Canada) or GDP (United States) across the post-war period.[29] There are strong parallels between the two countries until 2001. Both nations had annual surpluses after the Second World War, but this fiscal soundness lasted longer in Canada. The extended period of "fiscal stress" from roughly 1979 through 1999 showed both countries generating large annual deficits relative to national income, but the situation was markedly worse in Canada than in the United States. The situation was then reversed in the early 2000s, with Canadian surpluses contrasting sharply with American deficits. Overall, across the whole post-war period, the Canadian federal budget showed surpluses twenty-three times, compared to only twelve times in the United States.

National Debts

The accumulated national debt is also a marker of government track records in managing fiscal and monetary policy, providing an additional measure of cross-national differences and the influence of party control. Since the majority of U.S. states have long had balanced budget requirements, whereas only recently, beginning in 1995, have seven Canadian provinces adopted such laws of varying effectiveness, their presence may at least temper the level of their de facto deficits. Thus, by leaving aside those deficits accumulated at the provincial or state level, our measures would underestimate total debt loads in Canada particularly, which would end up being higher than their American counterparts for most periods until the most recent decade.[30] We pursue this option primarily because the growing international concern over sovereign debt has focused on the credit-worthiness of national governments.[31]

Figure 7.2 shows the national debt as a percentage of the total worth of the Canadian (GNP) and American (GDP) economies. At the end of the Second World War, total federal debt in Canada equalled the size of the Canadian economy and, in the United States, 120 per cent of the gross domestic product. Sustained economic growth on both sides of the border, and a significant number of budgetary surpluses, reduced total indebtedness until the early 1970s, when recessionary cycles began to disrupt the trend. The reduction in debt to this point was more pronounced in Canada, in part because important areas of increasing expenditure were under provincial jurisdiction, whereas the federal government had access to a wider range of tax powers.

Figure 7.2. Canadian and U.S. National Debt as Percentage of Total Economy (GNP for Canada and GDP for United States)

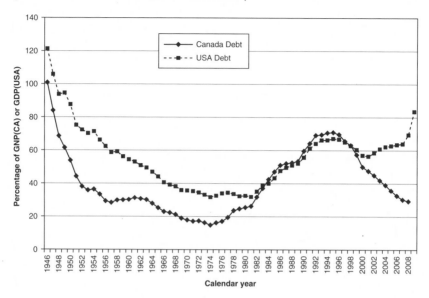

Sustained deficits of the early 1980s increased the total federal debt in both countries, with strikingly similar trend lines through the end of the 1990s. Beginning in 2001, however, trends in total national debt sharply diverge, and during fiscal year 2009 the federal debts approximated 30 per cent of GNP in Canada and 80 per cent of GDP in the United States. This gap derives in part from the Canadian government's comprehensive resolve during the 1990s and early 2000s to confront the deficit. As Dodge argues, the Canadian government had tried to address the problem of rising debt-to-GDP ratios beginning in the mid-1980s, but it was not until February 1995 "that the Government of Canada was perceived to have established an objective for fiscal policy that was specific enough to provide a basis for achieving a reduction in deficits to zero and setting the economy on a path that would reduce the debt-to-GDP ratio."[32] There seemed no similar concertedness in the United States, especially in the 1980s and the 2000s, when there was more resolve directed at tax reduction than at expenditure containment – a disconnection amplified by rapidly expanding military expenses and steeply rising costs associated with federal "entitlement" programs.

Political Parties, Deficits, Debts

The question of how influential the party of government is in shaping budget outcomes is greatly complicated by institutional differences between Canada and the United States. In Canada, most governments can expect easy parliamentary approval of their budgets, particularly when the governing party controls a majority of seats in Parliament or when the opposition parties are not in agreement with one another. The groundwork on formulating the federal budget is done by the . Department of Finance (previously, the Treasury Board), operating entirely under the direction of the finance minister and the prime minister.[33] In the United States, the "executive budget" is merely the starting point of the process, and what gets enacted by Congress can be quite different from what the administration originally proposed. Thus, attributing the U.S. federal budget to the party of the presidential administration must be more qualified than identifying a Canadian federal budget outcome with the party in power, particularly when the president's party is not in control of both houses of Congress. Democrats have controlled the presidency for twenty-six years (see table 7.1), and of those they controlled both houses of Congress for eighteen. Republicans held the White House for thirty-six years, but in those years held both houses for only six.

With such caution in mind, we attribute the performance for each fiscal year to the administration or government that prepared the budget during the *previous* calendar year. As an example, the federal budget for fiscal year 2001 (which covered 1 October 2000 to 30 September 2001) was introduced to Congress by President Bill Clinton in February 2000 (his last year in office).

In the United States, nine of the twelve federal budget surpluses are attributed to Democratic Presidents Truman, Johnson, and Clinton, though all but one were achieved without control of both Congressional chambers. The worst string of federal deficits can be attributed to Republicans Ronald Reagan (whose party never controlled both houses) and George W. Bush (with Republican control of Congress during half of his eight years). Although Reagan promised to balance the federal budget by the end of his first term, his support for income tax cuts and increased defence spending, without commensurate reductions in domestic expenditures, began a period of large deficits that reached 6 per cent of gross domestic product. Reagan was influenced by "supply-side" economists, who argued that cutting income taxes would

Table 7.1. Summary Statistics

Party in control	Time period (fiscal years)	Number of fiscal years	Average yearly change in revenues in constant dollars (%)	Average yearly change in outlays in constant dollars (%)	Average surplus (or deficit) as percentage of GDP (U.S.) or GNP (Canada)
All Canada	1948–2009	62	4.7	4.9	−1.76
All Liberal		42	5.4	5.6	−0.90
All Progressive Conservative/ Conservative		20	3.3	3.3	−3.58
Liberal	1948–57	10	2.7	5.6	1.54
Progressive Conservative	1958–63	6	3.3	1.9	−1.78
Liberal	1964–79	16	8.3	8.5	−1.70
Progressive Conservative	1980	1	14.0	9.7	−3.40
Liberal	1981–4	4	−0.8	−2.3	−5.94
Progressive Conservative	1985–94	10	3.4	4.1	−5.87
Liberal	1995–2006	12	5.9	4.4	−0.19
Conservative	2007–9	3	−0.5	1.6	0.41
All U.S.	1948–2009	62	2.9	4.0	−1.80
All Democratic		26	6.2	6.0	−0.55
All Republican		36	0.5	2.5	−2.71
Democratic	1948–53	6	9.3	14.0	0.60
Republican	1954–61	8	0.4	−0.4	−0.40
Democratic	1962–9	8	6.0	5.4	−0.90
Republican	1970–7	8	0.9	2.8	−2.00
Democratic	1978–81	4	4.5	3.9	−2.40
Republican	1982–93	12	1.7	2.3	−4.30
Democratic	1994–2001	8	5.0	1.5	−0.10
Republican	2002–9	8	−1.5	5.6	−3.40

spur enough investments and productivity to increase overall revenue. Instead the revenue stream was reduced while the rate of expenditures was barely slowed.

Unlike President Reagan, the administration of George W. Bush inherited a surplus. However, within a couple of years, this was turned into a deficit, in part because of additional tax cuts and in part because of the escalating costs of foreign military engagements. During Bush's second term, there was some reduction in the deficit, until the economic crisis of 2008 moved Republicans (for a time, while still in office) and Democrats, to enact major stimulus measures that drove the federal budget into unprecedented deficit levels. In its Fiscal Year 2011 Budget Message, the Obama administration forecasted deficits in fiscal years 2010 and 2011 of 10.6 per cent and 8.3 per cent of GDP, with smaller but substantial deficits predicted for the remainder of the decade.[34]

In Canada, the Liberal Party held power at the federal level for roughly forty-three years. Twenty of the twenty-three federal budgetary surpluses can be attributed to the Liberal governments under W.L Mackenzie King, Louis St Laurent, Lester B. Pearson, and Pierre Elliott Trudeau (during the 1960s), as well as Jean Chrétien and Paul Martin at the end of the 1990s and beginning of the twenty-first century. The worst federal deficit, reaching about 9 per cent of GNP, can be attributed to Progressive Conservative Prime Minister Brian Mulroney, whose tenure overlapped President Reagan's.

Concern about rising government deficits had been growing since the mid-1970s but escalated during the 1980s, particularly because high interest rates were dramatically increasing the cost of servicing government indebtedness. Both the Progressive Conservatives and the Liberals made deficit reduction a major theme during the 1984 elections, which yielded a majority of seats for the PCs. The new minister of finance, Michael Wilson, said that "the growing public debt has become a severe handicap to economic progress and the most serious obstacle to economic growth."[35] However, even if the Mulroney government said deficit reduction would be achieved through expenditure cuts rather than major tax increases, the government presided over a significantly increased deficit. Mulroney and his Progressive Conservative Party were re-elected in 1988 and, once again, promised to bring the deficit under control. However, its budgeting was grounded in overly optimistic economic forecasts, and it enacted no measures that seriously curtailed expenditures.[36] Savoie blames the Mulroney government's lack of "political will" for its failure to make deeper spending cuts.[37]

It was under the Liberal governments led by Jean Chrétien and Paul Martin that the deficit was successfully tackled. By that time, as Lewis points out, "for the first time deficit reduction had become a top priority of Canadians."[38] Starting when the Liberals gained office in 1993, Finance Minister Paul Martin, with full support from Prime Minister Chrétien, orchestrated a determined policy to balance the budget and reduce federal indebtedness, effected to some extent by radically containing social policy transfers to the provinces. Former Bank of Canada governor Dodge argues that the Liberals were able to do this because they were not seen by the public as "black-hearted accountants." "They were perceived to believe in government," and "cleaning up the nation's balance sheet to maintain social programs over the long run was a credible message that reflected Canadian values."[39] Timothy Lewis argues that the convergence of economic and political forces created the conditions under which the Liberals could end the last vestiges of Keynesianism and embrace deficit reduction.[40] First, there was a fundamental shift in public opinion, due to widespread economic insecurity, that questioned whether the state had become overly burdensome on Canadians. And political elites, aware that Canada had the worst economic growth rate of any G-7 nation during the early 1990s and a national debt equalling 70 per cent of GDP, embraced neoliberalism to better position Canada to compete in a global economy. Reducing the debt-to-GDP ratio became the Liberals' top fiscal priority.

The paradox, then, is that the 1980s saw a major revival of concern about deficit spending that propelled into office national rightist parties that prioritized an attack on the deficit as well as on inflation. In both Canada and the United States, those parties then presided over the most substantial deficits of the post-war period (until 2010 in the U.S. case). A significant portion of this deficit can be attributed to social program spending programs installed in earlier decades, with costs escalating in part because of changing demographics but whose popularity (often strongest among conservative voters) made them politically costly to change. But some part of the deficit increases arose from reduced taxation, particularly in the United States, reflecting a commitment to supply-side economics, and to some extent a growing popular resentment of tax increases during a time when most people's take-home income was stable or declining. The causes of growing deficits, therefore, are complex, but the broad outcome of this analysis suggests that neither right-wing party control of government nor the rhetorical commitment to deficit reduction of those parties' leaders has produced much real reduction.

An Overview of the Difference That Party Makes

To explore the impact of having conservative parties in power, we draw together data on deficits and on annual changes in revenue and expenditure from 1948 to 2009 (see table 7.1). These include the average size of the deficits for Liberals and Conservatives in Canada and for Democrats and Republicans in the United States.

In the aftermath of the Second World War, expenditure changes outpaced revenue changes under the Liberals (1948–57) and the Democrats (1948–53). In the later 1950s and early 1960s, revenue increases were greater than or equal to expenditure changes in both countries – under Republican President Dwight D. Eisenhower and Democratic Presidents John F. Kennedy and Lyndon B. Johnson and in Canada under Progressive Conservative Prime Minister John Diefenbaker and Liberal Lester B. Pearson. In the 1970s and 1980s, the pattern became more volatile in both countries and more differentiated by party. In general, expenditure changes have consistently outstripped revenue changes under Republicans and Conservatives, whereas revenue changes have exceeded expenditure changes under Democrats and the Liberals.

These summary statistics indicate that of the four governing parties, the best fiscal guardian has been the Democratic Party, followed by the Liberal Party, then the Republican Party, and lastly the Conservatives (and Progressive Conservatives). On average, all governed with deficits, but the Conservatives' deficits averaged 2.7 per cent of GNP more than those of their opponents. Republicans outdid Democrats by 2.2 per cent. In sum, deficit management was superior under parties of the left or centre compared with parties of the right, although this portrait may change radically for the United States over the next ten years.

Now consider the average annual percentage changes in "real" revenue and outlays (measured in constant dollars). Over the entire post-war period, both Canada and the United States show a greater average increase in outlays than revenues, although the gap between revenue changes and outlays is much smaller for Canada. In Canada, Conservatives spent and took in about 2 per cent less than the Liberals. In the United States, however, the data clearly indicate that Republicans were much more determined to hold the revenue line steady with little or no growth. Their average spending increase was 3.5 per cent lower than the Democrats', but their average revenue increase was 5.7 per cent less. This gives credence to the Cameron argument, with GOP revenue growth in the United States one-fifth the size of expenditure growth.

Conclusion and Implications

Thus, to the question of whether "fiscal frugality" lies at the heart of Canadian or American conservatism, the answer must be that it does rhetorically, but not in practice. The history of fiscal outcomes for the last six decades shows clearly that Liberal governments in Canada have shown greater fiscal frugality in deficit financing than the Progressive Conservatives, just as Democrats have out-performed Republicans in the United States.

With respect to whether there has been an overall shift towards deficit reluctance – a shift to what was once called the "fiscal constitution" in the United States – the evidence seems to indicate that there indeed has been. Before the Great Depression, American policymakers were pressed hard to balance federal budgets annually, though Canadian politicians faced pressures that mitigated that commitment. Both countries saw at least a partial embrace of Keynesian economics by the end of the Second World War and a parallel departure into recurrent red ink over a period of close to half a century. While this was happening, and particularly from the 1980s on, an anti-tax sentiment was articulated with increasing forcefulness by the Republicans, and to some extent by the Progressive Conservatives, up to the point of a reconfigured Conservative party in the early 2000s. The advent of supply-side economics provided President Ronald Reagan and the Republican Party with a rationale for cutting taxes that goes beyond simply appealing to public dislike of taxation. Such arguments were powerful within the Progressive Conservative Party under Prime Minister Mulroney but became even more powerful under the leadership of a reconfigured Conservative Party under Stephen Harper. These arguments were also highly influential on currents within the Democratic and Liberal Parties.

The governments in power at the end of the twentieth century display both familiar and unfamiliar patterns. From fiscal year 1993 through 1998 there was a steady decline in the size of deficits under the Liberals, who ultimately achieved budgetary surpluses in fiscal years 2000 and 2001, then deficits returned for three years, after which fiscal years 2005–8 showed surpluses. Since the Conservatives took power after the January 2006 elections, arguably the surpluses of their early tenure were a legacy from the Liberals. But the Conservatives soon established new fiscal priorities. In his budget speech of 2 May 2006, Finance Minister James M. Flaherty said, "Nowhere are we more focused than in the area of tax relief. For years, Ottawa has been over-taxing Canadians."[41] That budget included $20 billion of tax relief for Canadians, including a cut in the GST from 7 to 6 per cent (later cut to 5%) as well as other tax breaks for corporations and small businesses. The minority Harper government called for new elections in October 2008, which returned Prime Minister Harper to power with more Conservative MPs but not a majority. A month later, the National Convention of the Conservative Party adopted a "policy declaration" that endorsed "balanced budget legislation," and prioritized "pay[ing] down the mortgage."[42]

Although the 2007 budget showed a surplus, as did fiscal year 2008, they were followed by the return of deficit spending. The small ($5.8 billion) deficit of 2009 ballooned to $53.8 billion in 2010 and $49.2 billion in 2011, primarily because the Great Recession prompted the Harper government to announce in its 2009 budget speech a Canada Economic Action Plan that would provide $62 billion of fiscal stimulus over two years through more tax cuts and increased expenditures. That would cause a "temporary" budget deficit, but Finance Minister Flaherty anticipated a return to surplus by fiscal year 2013. The Great Recession also hit the United States particularly hard, and the commitment to an aggressive $860 billion stimulus package (initially bipartisan) compounded the deficits of the previous Bush administration to produce an unprecedented level of deficits. There is no doubt that the Obama administration's fiscal record will weaken the overall case that Democrats have been better managers of the economy, though whether in the longer term the Republicans' rhetorical commitment to sound fiscal management will be reflected in actual stewardship will take some time to discern.

As the Great Recession recedes, policy debate in both Canada and the United States has turned from weathering the economic downturn to balancing the federal budgets. The prospects do not look good in the United States. The partisan divide is still accurately captured by competing 2011 plans, and the budget impasse continues, as of March 2013. Divided control of the U.S. government requires bipartisan support for a plan to be adopted, and the gap then and now between Democratic and Republican approaches is vast. As originally proposed, the 2011

House plan included both a large tax cut (amounting to about US$1 trillion over a decade) coupled with a much larger spending reduction of about $5.8 trillion. The Obama plan yielded about the same amount of reductions but was based upon much smaller cuts of about $3 trillion and a tax increase of about $1 trillion. The philosophical differences between the two plans are stark, and the chief prospect for achieving a lasting budgetary solution rested originally upon the slim hope that a bipartisan "Group of Six" in the U.S. Senate could broker an agreement that combined cuts in both defence and entitlement programs, as well as an increase in taxes.[43] Achieving this, however, would have required both Democrats and Republicans to jointly adopt a plan that rejects policy and philosophical positions of several decades' duration. That was not to be, as the "Group of Six" failed to reach agreement, and the partisan budgetary standoff continues into 2013.

The prospects may seem brighter in Canada, only because the deficits are so much more manageable than U.S. indebtedness. In his March 2009 budget speech Finance Minister Flaherty anticipated a surplus of $700 million for fiscal year 2013, but that date was postponed to 2016 in Flaherty's March 2011 budget speech. Then Prime Minister Harper pledged during the spring 2011 election to eliminate the federal deficit by 2014–15, a year earlier than his government had previously declared.[44] The odds of achieving budgetary balance are no certainty, however, given the Harper government's firm advocacy of tax relief, first rationalized as fiscal stimulus during the Great Recession but continued afterwards. The 2011 budget speech called low taxes the "foundation" for "protecting and creating jobs now" and "for long-term growth." Obviously balancing the budget is a lesser priority than cutting taxes for the Harper government. Thus, consistent with historical patterns, Harper's rhetorical approach to fiscal policy is to eschew revenue increases and rely exclusively on spending reductions, a strategy Liberals see as unrealistic. The political verdict on the Conservatives, now the majority government, awaits fiscal year 2016 and the next round of parliamentary elections.

NOTES

1 David R. Cameron, "The Expansion of the Public Economy: A Comparative Analysis," *American Political Science Review* 72 (December 1978): 1243–61; also see Douglas A. Hibbs, Jr, "On the Political Economy of Long-Run

Trends in Strike Activity," *British Journal of Political Science* 8, no. 2 (1978): 153–75.

2 See his essay "Of Public Credit," in *David Hume, Selected Essays*, ed. Stephen Copley and Andrew Edgar (Oxford: Oxford University Press, 1998), 205.

3 Adam Smith, *An Inquiry into the Nature and Causes of the Wealth of Nations* (Chicago: Encyclopaedia Britannica, 1952), book 2, 148 and 150; book 5, 413. Smith devotes an entire chapter to "Of Public Debts" in book 5.

4 David R. Cameron, "Does Government Cause Inflation? Taxes, Spending and Deficits," in *The Politics of Inflation and Economic Stagnation*, ed. Leon N. Lindberg and Charles S. Maier (Washington: Brookings Institution, 1985), 259–60.

5 Lewis H. Kimmel, *Federal Budget and Fiscal Policy, 1789–1958* (Washington: Brookings Institution, 1959), 301.

6 James M. Buchanan and Richard E. Wagner, *Democracy in Deficit: The Political Legacy of Lord Keynes* (New York: Academic, 1977), 21. Also see Jesse Burkhead, "The Balanced Budget," *Quarterly Journal of Economics* 68 (May 1954): 191–216.

7 Kimmel, *Federal Budget and Fiscal Policy*, 176.

8 Donald J. Savoie, *The Politics of Public Spending in Canada* (Toronto: University of Toronto Press, 1990), 15.

9 W. Irwin Gillespie, *Tax, Borrow and Spend: Financing Federal Spending in Canada, 1867–1990* (Ottawa: Carleton University Press, 1991), 51.

10 Timothy Lewis, *In the Long Run We're All Dead: The Canadian Turn to Fiscal Restraint* (Vancouver: UBC Press, 2003), 23.

11 Gillespie, *Tax, Borrow and Spend*, 54. However, there is scant evidence from primary sources on this point.

12 Gillespie, *Tax, Borrow and Spend*, appendix B, table 8-1.

13 Savoie, *Politics of Public Spending in Canada*, 15; Lewis, *In the Long Run We're All Dead*, 29.

14 Robert B. Bryce, *Maturing in Hard Times: Canada's Department of Finance through the Great Depression* (Montreal and Kingston: McGill-Queen's University Press, 1986), 113.

15 Ibid., 115–19.

16 Ibid., 120.

17 Canada, Department of Reconstruction and Supply, *Employment and Income with Special Reference to the Initial Period of Reconstruction* (Ottawa: King's Printer, 1945), 21. Cited in Savoie, *Politics of Public Spending in Canada*, 14.

18 Robert M. Campbell, *Grand Illusions: The Politics of the Keynesian Experience in Canada 1945–1975* (Peterborough: Broadview, 1987), 190, 206.

19 See David Wolfe, "The Politics of the Deficit," in *The Politics of Economic Policy*, ed. G. Bruce Doern (Toronto: University of Toronto Press, 1985), 128–9; also Lewis, *In the Long Run We're All Dead*, 82.

20 For a discussion of how timid the Employment Act of 1946 was, and why, see Stephen K. Bailey, *Congress Makes a Law* (New York: Columbia University Press, 1950).

21 A similar discussion of the critical change in the mid-1970s is found in Wolfe, "Politics of the Deficit," especially 113–20.

22 Lewis, *In the Long Run We're All Dead*, 67.

23 Chris J. Dolan, John Frendreis, and Raymond Tatalovich, *The Presidency and Economic Policy* (Lanham: Rowman & Littlefield, 2008), 178–80.

24 David A. Dodge, "Reflections on the Role of Fiscal Policy: The Doug Purvis Memorial Lecture," *Canadian Public Policy* 24 (September 1998): 281–2.

25 Stephen McBride, *Not Working: State, Unemployment and Neo-Conservatism in Canada* (Toronto: University of Toronto Press, 1992), 15–16.

26 Lewis, *In the Long Run We're All Dead*, 82.

27 Ibid., 46.

28 Ibid., 113.

29 GNP is used for Canada rather than GDP because of the lack of comparable GDP data before 1961. A comparison of Canadian GNP and GDP from 1961 to 2008 shows that GDP averages 102.5 per cent of GNP for that period. A re-analysis of the data reported in this chapter incorporating an adjustment of this size yields results virtually identical to those reported in figures 7.1 and 7.2 and table 7.1. Budget and GNP/GDP data are taken from Gillespie, *Tax, Borrow and Spend*, tables B-1 and C-1; from tables 379-0012, 380-001, 380-0030, and 383-0008, Statistics Canada; and from Historical Tables 1.1, 1.2, and 1.3, *Economic Report of the President* (USA).

30 David Perry, "What Price Canadian? Taxation and Debt Compared," in *Canada and the United States: Differences that Count*, 3rd ed., ed. David M. Thomas and Barbara Boyle Torrey (Peterborough: Broadview, 2008), 207–8.

31 Ronald D. Kneebone, "Deficits and Debt in Canada: Some Lessons from Recent History," *Canadian Public Policy* 20 (June 1994): 152–64.

32 David Dodge, "The Interaction between Monetary and Fiscal Policies," *Canadian Public Policy* 28 (June 2002): 193–4.

33 An extensive discussion of the budgetary process is found in Donald J. Savoie, *The Politics of Public Spending in Canada*, chapters 3–5. Also see Gerard Veilleux and Donald J. Savoie, "Kafka's Castle: The Treasury Board of Canada Revisited," *Canadian Public Administration* 31 (Winter 1988): 517–38; A.W. Johnson, "The Treasury Board of Canada and the Machinery of Government of the 1970s," *Canadian Journal of Political Science* 4 (September 1971): 346–66, esp. 358–9.

34 See table S-1, "Budget Totals," 146, http://www.whitehouse.gov/omb/budget/fy2011/assets/tables.pdf.

35 Michael Wilson, *A New Direction for Canada: An Agenda for Economic Renewal* (Ottawa: Department of Finance, 1984), 9.

36 "Wilson Gambles on Good Times," *Financial Post*, 15 February 1988.

37 Savoie, *Politics of Public Spending in Canada*, 332.

38 Lewis, *In the Long Run We're All Dead*, 169.

39 Dodge, "Reflections on the Role of Fiscal Policy," 282.

40 Lewis, *In the Long Run We're All Dead*, 147–8, 164–6.

41 James M. Flaherty, minister of finance, "The Budget Speech 2006,"2 May 2006, Department of Finance, http://www.fin.gc.ca/budget06/speech/speech-eng.asp.

42 Conservative Party of Canada, Policy Declaration, As amended by the delegates to the National Convention on November 15, 2008, As consolidated by the National Policy Committee and approved by the National Council, 6, http://www.conservative.ca/media/2012/07/20120705-CPC-PolicyDec-E.pdf.

43 Eugene Lang, "Why U.S. Can't Beat Its Deficit," *Ottawa Citizen*, 15 April 2011; Jackie Calmes, "'Gang of Six' in the Senate Seeking a Plan on Debt," *New York Times*, 17 April 2011.

44 "Canada's Conservatives 'Aim to End Deficit Early,'" BBC News online, 8 April 2011.

8 A Conservative Foreign Policy? Canada and Australia Compared

ALAN BLOOMFIELD AND KIM RICHARD NOSSAL

Soon after the 2 May 2011 general election in which the Conservatives secured a majority, Stephen Harper articulated his government's approach to foreign policy. Speaking to the Conservative Party's 2011 convention on 13 June, Harper asserted that, unlike his predecessors, his government was intent on pursuing Canada's national interests. Its purpose "is no longer just to go along and get along with everyone else's agenda. It is no longer to please every dictator with a vote at the United Nations." Rather, "we know where our interests lie, and who our friends are. And we take strong, principled positions in our dealings with other nations – whether popular or not ... and that is what the world can count on from Canada!"[1]

Soon after, Harper expanded on his approach to foreign policy with Kenneth Whyte, the editor of *Maclean's*.[2] As Roland Paris has aptly observed, in this interview Harper persistently articulated a Manichean vision of global politics: "a struggle between good and bad, and of moral clarity as the greatest asset and most reliable guide to foreign policy."[3] Harper claimed, "We take stands that we think reflect our own interests but our own interests in a way that reflects the interests of the wider community of nations, or particularly the wider interests of those nations with whom we share values and interests." He also stressed the importance of military capabilities, noting that "when you're in a dangerous world and countries are from time to time called upon to do things to deal with those dangers, if you don't have the capacity to act you are not taken seriously." While trade, peacekeeping, and development assistance were not unimportant, Harper suggested, "the real defining moments for the country and for the world are those big conflicts where everything's at stake and where you take a side and show you can contribute to the right side."[4]

Some argued that this represented the advent of the "Harper Doctrine";[5] others were more sceptical.[6] On one matter, however, commentators agreed: the new "muscularity" in Canadian foreign policy was deemed to be a distinctive aspect of Conservative foreign policy. But in this chapter, we seek to answer what may at first blush seem to be a deceptively simple question: has Stephen Harper in fact pursued a particularly *conservative* approach to Canadian foreign policy?

To answer this question the chapter proceeds in three steps. First, we examine what the theoretical characteristics of a "conservative foreign policy" might be. Second, to illustrate the particular nature of a conservative foreign policy in a Canadian context, we compare the foreign policy of the Conservative government of Stephen Harper with the approach of the conservative government of another non-hegemonic middle power that is also a close ally of the United States and whose parliamentary system of government is very similar to Canada's – Australia under John Howard's Liberal/National Coalition between 1996 and 2007. We argue that while Howard's foreign policy was clearly marked by conservatism, it also exhibited a healthy dose of pragmatism. In Canada a similar but reversed dynamic was at work: from 2006 to 2011, Harper's foreign policy was mostly pragmatic and only occasionally principled. Finally, we suggest that this pragmatic tendency was only partially the result of the minority governments produced by the 2006 and 2008 elections. Rather, we suggest that foreign policy must also be seen in the context of Harper's broader domestic political goals, and thus it is unlikely to be substantially affected by the achievement of a majority in the general election of 2 May 2011.

Defining a Conservative Foreign Policy

To assess foreign policy under the Howard and Harper governments, we must begin by outlining what constitutes a *conservative* foreign policy. We begin with American reflections, not only because the American literature is voluminous, but also because there is also a considerable heterogeneity within it regarding the meaning of conservatism.[7] The two most prominent recent conservative traditions in U.S. foreign policy debates include the neoconservatives, who enjoyed ascendency during the first, strategically crucial term of George W. Bush's presidency (2001–5); and their opponents from within the conservative camp, who have been variously described as "traditional" conservatives, "the Newest Right," the "revived Old Right" and/or "paleoconservatives."[8]

Almost two decades ago Jeane J. Kirkpatrick outlined the traditionalist position, arguing that a conservative foreign policy should be characterized by a respect for history, a respect for individual freedoms, a suspicion of overly large government, and patriotism. She suggested that a conservative expects the future to look not very different from the past and is sceptical of utopian claims that humankind can rid itself of the scourge of war: conservatism, she noted, "accepts the human capacity for evil as well as for good; for indifference as well as for empathy; for selfishness as well as generosity."[9] George F. Will has also advocated this brief recipe for a traditional-conservative approach to U.S. foreign policy: "Preserve US sovereignty and freedom of action by marginalizing the United Nations. Reserve military interventions for reasons of US national security, not altruism. Avoid peacekeeping operations that compromise the military's war-fighting proficiencies. Beware of the political hubris inherent in the intensely unconservative project of 'nation-building.'"[10]

Brian C. Schmidt and Michael C. Williams note that the debates about the 2003 invasion of Iraq became a contest between the neoconservatives and the traditionalists (or realists, as they called them). While traditional conservatives may have been "pessimistic about the prospects for a dramatic improvement in the condition of international politics ... they are nevertheless cautious about the use of military force." Moreover, the traditionalists were "fierce critics of the tendency of the United States to engage in moralistic foreign policy crusades to remake the world in its own image."[11] Perhaps the key feature of the realist-conservative approach to foreign policy is the emphasis on *prudence* in the exercise of power; to paraphrase Michael Oakeshott, just keeping the ship of state afloat in the stormy waters of international politics is challenge enough without deliberately rocking the boat.[12]

Francis Fukuyama points to a 1996 *Foreign Affairs* article by William Kristol and Robert Kagan as a key moment in the evolution of the neoconservative approach to U.S. foreign policy.[13] Kristol and Kagan argued that post–Cold War America should capitalize on its enormous power-advantage over its rivals and practise "benevolent global hegemony," by "resisting, and where possible, undermining dictators and hostile ideologies; ... supporting American interests and liberal democratic principles; and ... providing assistance to those struggling against the more extreme manifestations of human evil."[14] In the introduction to their follow-up 2000 book entitled *Present Dangers*, they also argued that American power should be used to promote regime change.[15]

In 2003, William Kristol's father, Irving Kristol, outlined four "theses" that to him encapsulated what a (neo)conservative foreign policy should look like. The first was patriotism, described as a "natural and healthy sentiment." The second thesis argued that "international institutions … should be regarded with the deepest suspicion." To this extent neoconservatism differs little from the traditional/realist position described above – but Kristol's third thesis widens the gulf. He felt that leaders of states should "distinguish friends from enemies," a view that Stefan Halper and Jonathan Clarke have argued equates in practice to an aggressive moralism "derived from the religious conviction that the human condition is defined as a choice between good and evil."[16] Kristol's fourth thesis flows naturally from his third: "large nations [like the United States] inevitably have ideological interests in addition to more material concerns," which they *should* actively pursue.[17] In effect the "neocons," John J. Mearsheimer argues, "divide the world into good and bad states … [in which] the democracies are the white hats."[18]

Even before the invasion of Iraq, Samuel P. Huntington was characterizing neoconservatism as "doctrinal conservatism."[19] Huntington argued that this form of conservatism differed considerably from "classic conservatism," which he felt had at most only sought, Disraeli-like, to manage change and render it "safe." Others have characterized neoconservatism as "crusading," "democratic imperialism," "Wilsonianism with teeth," and "imperial universalism."[20] For his part, Roger Scruton claimed that it is not "true" conservatism at all, which involves pursuing "the national interest, but leav[ing] others to their fate."[21] Ilan Peleg went further, claiming it was "one of the most revolutionary, nonconservative movements in the history of American foreign policy."[22] Jennifer Welsh, however, ultimately concluded that because the neoconservatives were acting to preserve the existing global order (i.e., by reinforcing U.S. hegemony), they remained essentially conservative in *intent*, despite their radical methods.[23]

By contrast with the extensive American debate about foreign policy conservatism, there is very little comparable discussion in other English-speaking countries. The best non-American articulation of foreign policy conservatism is by Jennifer Welsh, who extrapolated from conservative writers in the British tradition – David Hume, Edmund Burke, Michael Oakeshott, and Roger Scruton – to explore what conservatism means in the foreign policy context.[24]

Welsh argues that a conservative foreign policy is characterized by three core concepts or "tendencies": an attachment to a particular political *order* that is "assumed rather than accounted for" and needs to be entrenched, legitimized, and given longevity; a *scepticism* about progressivist assumptions about humankind's perfectibility and an embrace of "prudential" politics; and, finally, a veneration of *tradition*, including established institutions and practices.[25]

We add a fourth "tendency" – the pursuit of the "national interest." From an international relations theory perspective we suggest that conservative leaders tend towards a *realist* position, accepting that international politics is conducted in conditions of anarchy, and that they are less inclined to pursue multilateral solutions to foreign challenges or to promote or rely on international law and institutions. Needless to say, these four aspects of conservatism in foreign policy also feature in discussions of American foreign policy conservatism, although differences between the British and American varieties of conservatism nevertheless remain.[26]

With these four characteristics in mind, we turn now to a consideration of the extent to which we see these four characteristics in the foreign policies of John Howard and Stephen Harper.

Australia: The Howard Coalition Government

The Liberal-National Coalition under John Howard was elected in 1996 and was re-elected in the next three elections (1998, 2001, and 2004). In a political culture where overt conservatism has historically not worn well – it is no coincidence that Australia's conservative party is named the Liberal Party – there can be little doubt of Howard's conservatism. He has been described as "the most conservative leader the Liberal Party ever had" and a "Burkean conservative."[27] As Howard himself put it in 2006, "I have often described myself ... as somebody who is an economic liberal and a social conservative. I see no incompatibility between the two."[28] Michael Wesley believes that John Howard's policymaking in all spheres was motivated unashamedly by *values*, and obviously conservative ones. But he tells us that Howard also had an "acute understanding of how power works and an intense pragmatism about what should and can be achieved in politics ... [He was] both pragmatically flexible and dogmatically self-assured."[29]

At the core of Howard's world view was the belief that "states represent moral communities that identify with or are separated from other moral communities based on the values that they hold."[30] He accordingly strengthened ties, both economic and strategic, with culturally similar countries like Britain and especially the United States, because, in his view, "it is common values that in the end bind us together more tightly than anything else."[31] The corollary was that Australia's relations with states like China would never be particularly close; instead, Howard claimed, "societies that have different cultures and different histories can ... work together ... [only] if they understand those differences and [if] they focus less on what divides them and more on what brings them together ... like trade."[32] It has been argued that "the spheres of values and interests respectively, became increasingly blurred" as the Howard era progressed; Carol Johnson also notes Howard repeatedly offered "clash-of-values-based" explanations, similar to those George W. Bush favoured, when discussing the "War on Terror."[33] Thus, for example, Howard argued that Australia is an "offshoot of Western civilisation" and that its *jihadi* enemies "hate our freedoms and our way of life."[34]

It can therefore be suggested that Howard's approach to relations with other states was roughly analogous to the process by which individuals pick friends, enemies, and "acquaintances" according to whether they share similar worldviews. The argument should not, however, be taken too far: for example, both Howard and his foreign minister, Alexander Downer, publicly refuted Huntington's "clash of civilizations" thesis.[35] Nevertheless, this clearly illustrates the Coalition's commitment to one of the conservative values identified by Welsh, namely, traditionalism: Howard preferred to work with Australia's traditional, geographically distant yet culturally close allies like the United States, in long-lived alliances like the Australia, New Zealand, United States (ANZUS) Security Treaty of 1951. He was less enthusiastic about new and untested multilateral forums or potential new partners in Asia. His dogged pursuit of a Free Trade Agreement (FTA) with the United States is further evidence of these inclinations: the trade minister, Mark Vaile, even called the FTA "the commercial equivalent of the ANZUS treaty."[36]

Howard's foreign policy also demonstrated commitment to the conservative preference for order, especially when it came to supporting the strategic status quo in Asia whereby the United States remained the hegemonic power. In March 1996 Howard backed the United States in its dispute with China over Taiwan, earning a stiff rebuke from Beijing. Unsurprisingly, Downer was soon announcing that "enhancing links with the United States at all levels is something this government sees as vitally important."[37] The 2000 defence White Paper outlined an aggressive restructuring of the Australian Defence Force (ADF) and a plan for a substantial increase in the ability to use force in pursuit of policy objectives.[38] Spending would rise by 3 per cent in real terms each year for a decade, to ensure that Australia could deploy and sustain two brigades overseas simultaneously.[39] Australia's strategic goals were expressed in sweeping terms: unilaterally protecting Australia from direct attack, maintaining preponderance in the "arc of instability" to the immediate north, and "uphold[ing] global security" in partnership with the United States.[40] Subsequently Howard actively supported the "Global War on Terror" in both Afghanistan and Iraq; and in 2003 Australia led the Regional Assistance Mission to Solomon Islands (RAMSI) to stabilize that country.[41]

We also see evidence of the sort of scepticism of international institutions that tends to be a hallmark of conservative foreign policy. Despite its success working with the UN in East Timor in 1999, the Howard government's relationship with it became increasingly frosty thereafter.[42] When a UN report criticized Australia's handling of Aboriginal issues in 2000, the report was categorically rejected and Australia's ties with the world body were formally reviewed. Then, before the invasion of Iraq, Howard testily noted that "the United Nations should have done something about Iraq's non-compliance [with weapons inspections] a long time ago."[43] In early 2003 Howard categorically stated that Australia's relationship with the United States was significantly more important than its ties to the UN, while Downer mused in mid-2003 that "increasingly, multilateralism is a synonym for ineffective and unfocused policy involving internationalism of the lowest common denominator."[44] Later, as conditions in Iraq deteriorated and criticism mounted at home, Howard tried to deflect some of the blame onto the UN by calling it "paralyzed" in the face of serious international crises.[45] Later, Canberra pointedly reduced its involvement in UN committees. It should be noted, however, that Howard was not opposed to international institutions per se: his government *did* strongly support the International Criminal Court, and after 2005 Australia actively sought entry into expanding regional institutions, like the East Asia Summit.[46]

It is generally accepted, therefore, that Howard was no radical ideologue. For example, Liberal Senator George Brandis observed that, once in power, Howard proved to be "a bundle of contradictions," and Robyn Hollander writes that "his conservatism was far from complete and he eschewed [some] elements of conservative dogma."[47] We argue that Howard was an instinctive politician with a good "feel" for what would and wouldn't "fly" with the Australian electorate. Two types of pragmatism in particular were notable: he readily accepted, consistent with the tenets of realism, that Australia should pursue its national interests prudently, given the constraints that flow from being a middle power; and he was always aware of what it took to get elected.

A clear realist streak ran through Howard's foreign policy. While pursuing "the national interest" is not the sole preserve of conservative governments, they are arguably more *preoccupied* with doing so than other governments, and they usually prefer to work bilaterally or even unilaterally rather than multilaterally. Howard's government was no exception to this general rule, and its first foreign affairs White Paper (not coincidentally entitled "In the National Interest") explicitly committed the government to "the hard-headed pursuit of the interests which lie at the core of foreign and trade policy: the security of the Australian nation and the jobs and standards of living of the Australian people." Without entirely dismissing multilateralism, it asserted bluntly that bilateral relationships were the "basic building block" of foreign policy efforts.[48] A second White Paper released a month before the Iraq war reiterated these principles.[49] In taking what Shirley Scott has called a "hard-headed pro-industry stand ... designed to protect Australian jobs," Howard also secured very significant exemptions in Australia's favour in the Kyoto Protocol; nevertheless, he ultimately refused in 2002 to ratify or implement its provisions.[50]

Howard's realist-like pragmatism can also be seen in the lead-up to the U.S.-led invasion of Iraq in 2003. The decision to contribute Australian forces to the invasion was clearly motivated by a scepticism of the UN and by Howard's traditionalist and order-seeking instincts in supporting American hegemony. But we can also see realist-like calculations of Australia's long-term strategic interests in this decision: put simply, in supporting the United States in Iraq, Australia "paid the premium" on the "strategic insurance" that ANZUS represents. Indeed, in addressing Parliament on the eve of the invasion, Howard stated bluntly, "Our alliance with the United States is unapologetically a factor in the decision we have taken. The crucial long-term value of the United States alliance should always be a factor in any national security decision taken by Australia."[51]

Yet the fact that Australia made a limited commitment to the invasion – a squadron of F-18s, several special forces units, a small naval flotilla – reinforces our contention that Howard took a *prudential* approach to Iraq. In particular, no substantial infantry force for combat or occupation was deployed; the most that the United States could squeeze out of Howard later in the Iraq campaign when it was under real pressure from the insurgency was a single battalion (approximately 450 troops) to protect Japanese engineers in a relatively quiet part of Iraq.[52] Surely, if Howard had really believed the neoconservative line about the importance of spreading democratic values in the Middle East, Australia would have been much more heavily involved. Yet, as the neocon project began to falter, Howard limited Australia's exposure. He clearly harboured doubts about how much Australia could do, given its size; yet he could also repeatedly deny that Australia had "cut and run."[53] In this way, Howard gained strategic/political kudos for a military commitment that was actually quite limited.

But we do not wish to overstate the case. Howard was well aware that his decision on Iraq was an unpopular one and, at a press conference following the address to Parliament quoted above, he showed considerable political courage by delivering a plea that echoed Burke's 1774 speech to the electors of Bristol: he acknowledged "not all will agree with me" but he maintained that the government had taken a decision that it genuinely believed was in the medium- and longer-term interests of this country:[54] "I say to people who disagree – have your beef with the Government, have your beef with me, do not have your beef with the men and women of the Australian Defence Force … Let none of your rancour go in their direction, let it come, as it should in a great democracy, in the direction of those who have taken the decision."[55]

When necessary, however, Howard adopted the sort of flexibility that an electorally successful politician must at times show. Derek McDougall and Kingsley Edney argue that Howard was a pragmatist, because he tried to *lead* public opinion in "deliberative" contexts when lengthy debate was possible, but in "crises" he was more inclined to *follow* public opinion.[56] This is what essentially occurred in relations with Indonesia.

In the early stages of the East Timor crisis, Howard and Downer played a cautious game, emphasizing the importance of not undermining Indonesia's integrity, and their first intervention in mid-1998 urged only that some measure of autonomy be considered for East Timor.[57] But as public opinion in Australia increasingly condemned the continuing violence, in December 1998 Howard suggested to President B.J. Habibie that an autonomy agreement could include provisions for a referendum on full independence, a move that is often credited with precipitating Habibie's shock announcement in January 1999 that such a referendum would be held before the end of that year.[58] The August 1999 "yes" vote for independence precipitated even more violence, and by mid-September Australia was leading an armed intervention into East Timor. While relations with Indonesia sank to their lowest ebb in decades, Howard had undoubtedly pleased his domestic audience.[59] Howard adopted a similarly populist approach when an Australian citizen, Schapelle Corby, was indicted in Bali for drug smuggling in 2004: the prime minister publicly cast doubt upon the version of events offered by Indonesia's public prosecutors. Likewise, when Indonesian authorities arrested another group of Australians on heroin-smuggling charges in 2005, Howard criticized the possibility that the "Bali Nine" would receive the death penalty.[60]

In sum, we find that Howard's foreign policymaking clearly demonstrates the influence of conservative thought. He valued strong links with traditional allies. He took concrete steps to support the current international order (characterized by U.S. hegemony). He was sceptical of international institutions. And he unashamedly pursued the national interest. But he could also be prudentially flexible, as he showed when he skilfully backed the United States (but not too heavily) in Iraq, and in his dealings with Indonesia he was often prepared to play to the domestic audience. For these reasons we conclude that Howard's foreign policymaking was usually principled but occasionally pragmatic.

Canada: The Harper Conservative Government

During the 2005–6 election campaign, the Liberal Party of Canada ran a series of attack ads aimed at Stephen Harper and the Conservatives. One English-language ad reminded viewers of an article in the *Washington Times* that claimed that "Canada may elect the most pro-American leader in the Western world. Harper is pro-Iraq, anti-Kyoto and socially conservative. Bush's best new friend is the poster boy for his ideal foreign leader. A Harper victory will put a smile on George W. Bush's face." The ad concluded, "Well, at least somebody will be happy, eh?"[61] A French-language ad contained even more pointed reminders of Harper's conservative dispositions.[62]

Such ads sought to portray Harper as a right-wing neoconservative, linked to a U.S. president who was deeply unpopular in Canada. And the portrayal of Harper was not historically inaccurate. In the fifteen years prior to becoming prime minister he accumulated many unambiguously conservative positions, *pace* Johnson, who suggests that Harper was always a moderate, and Kirton, who argues that Harper had "fully absorbed the Progressive Conservative tradition."[63]

Harper was on the record as opposing spousal benefits for same-sex couples and same-sex marriage, and he opposed the establishment of the Canadian Firearms Registry. The Liberal claim that Harper opposed the legal entrenchment of abortion rights was technically correct but was somewhat disingenuous: Harper actually said he would not alter the legal vacuum created by the Supreme Court in 1988.[64]

More pertinently, Harper also expressed himself on a number of foreign policy issues before he became prime minister. Writing in the *Wall Street Journal* in March 2003, he claimed Chrétien's decision to keep Canada outside the coalition of the willing was "a serious mistake," noting that the Canadian Alliance supported the U.S. and British position because "we share their concerns, their worries about the future if Iraq is left unattended to, and their fundamental vision of civilization and human values. Disarming Iraq is necessary for the long-term security of the world, and for the collective interests of our historic allies and therefore manifestly in the national interest of Canada."[65] Harper waxed even more lyrically on this matter when he addressed a "Friends of America" rally held in Toronto in April 2003: "Thank you for saying to our friends in … America, you are our ally, our neighbour, and our best friend in the whole wide world. And when your brave men and women give their lives for freedom and democracy we are not neutral. We do not stand on the sidelines; we're for the disarmament of Saddam and the liberation of the people of Iraq."[66]

Likewise, after Paul Martin's Liberal government announced in February 2005 that Canada would not take part in the U.S. ballistic missile defence system, Harper indicated that the Conservatives favoured doing so.[67] He also unambiguously opposed the Kyoto Protocol, claiming that the Liberal government could not implement the targets it had embraced.[68] And in 2003 he expressed Howard-like scepticism about the UN, claiming that "the time has come to recognize that the US will continue to exercise unprecedented power in a world where international rules are still unreliable and where security and advancing of the free democratic order still depend significantly on the possession and use of military might."[69]

In short, the picture the Liberals painted of Harper in early 2006 was not wholly inaccurate. And in his various positions we can see all the elements of what we think are characteristics of a conservative approach to foreign policy: a preference for order (i.e., support for the hegemonic role of the United States); scepticism of international institutions, especially the UN; traditionalism, in that he emphasized that

Canada shared values similar to those of Britain and the United States; and a determination to pursue the national interest (especially when it came to scrapping Kyoto). At times in 2003 Harper even sounded like a neoconservative vis-à-vis the Middle East. But his stances on these and other issues while he was in opposition proved to be an inaccurate guide to how the Conservative government would behave after it assumed office in February 2006.

Even before he became prime minister, Harper had already changed his earlier support for the mission in Iraq, reflecting not only the deterioration of the situation in Iraq itself but also a recognition of the widespread support that the Chrétien government's decision not to join the "coalition of the willing" had generated in Canada. Likewise, he quietly backed away from his promise to reopen the matter of participating in ballistic missile defence, a pragmatic response to the ongoing unpopularity of BMD in Canada, and to the fact that the United States did not need Canada to participate in order to make the system operational.

On the mission in Afghanistan, Harper also departed from his pre-election stance. Upon becoming prime minister he was still a strong and enthusiastic supporter of the mission: his first overseas trip was to visit the troops in Kandahar, and his speech revealed much about the mixture of motives that had taken Canada there. He emphasized that it was in Canada's national security interest to ensure that Afghanistan would never again be an "incubator" of terrorism, reminding his troops that Canadians had died on 9/11 too and that Al-Qaeda had recently identified Canada as a "legitimate" target. He also emphasized how important it was for Canada to lead, alongside its NATO allies, in global politics. Finally, he spoke about the humanitarian mission and importance of "standing up for Canadian values," and he borrowed from the Howard playbook by promising that "Canadians do not cut and run."[70]

However, as it became clear from polls that Canadian public opinion was not being persuaded, the government's line shifted. Mentions of the national interest, both long-term (i.e., supporting allies) and short-term (i.e., defeating terrorism) became briefer, and more emphasis was placed on achieving humanitarian goals. This, on the face of it, seems a rather strange tack for a conservative to take, given that it is reminiscent of the sort of "internationalist" approach usually associated more with progressive parties.[71]

On the other hand, Harper's shift to emphasizing humanitarianism could also be explained as an effort to bring policy narratives about Afghanistan more closely in line with the public's understanding of what "Canada stands for" internationally. Scholars like Don Munton have argued that "internationalism became the watchword of Canadian foreign policy" in the post–Second World War era, while Munton and Tom Keating have mused that internationalism is "central to Canadian foreign policy. If not quite the official 'religion,' it is certainly much revered."[72] In other words, it could be argued that electoral pragmatism drove the shift. Indeed, the essential malleability of Harper's position on Afghanistan can perhaps best be seen by what happened next: when the prime minister realized that humanitarian justifications were also failing to move public opinion, he essentially gave up on the mission and attempted to largely remove it from the political agenda. In March 2008 he negotiated a bipartisan deal with the opposition Liberals, securing a parliamentary resolution committing the government to remove Canadian troops from Afghanistan before the end of 2011, regardless of the situation "on the ground."

When Barack Obama announced his "Afghan surge" in late 2009 and asked for allies to increase their commitments, Harper was conspicuously silent. And when pressed about the future of Canada's role in Afghanistan, Harper reiterated his intention to withdraw all military forces by 2011, promising in January 2010 that "we will not be undertaking any activities that require any kind of military presence, other than the odd guard guarding an embassy."[73] In March 2010, U.S. Secretary of State Hillary Rodham Clinton visited Canada and openly pressed the Harper government to change its mind, noting that the United States "would love Canada to stay in this fight with us." But the best she could get was a guarded commitment that Canada may continue in a "development role," while the foreign minister, Lawrence Cannon, immediately reiterated that "there will be no military mission post-2011."[74] Indeed, in April 2010 the Prime Minister's Office began to put out the idea that for about two years Harper had been having "deep doubts" about the prospects for nation-building in that country.[75] For much of 2010, Harper steadfastly rebuffed all efforts to change his position; only after Canada's allies began applying serious pressure – and the Liberal opposition also began pushing for a continued military role after 2011– did the prime minister eventually bend, agreeing in November 2010 to embrace a training mission until 2014.

On climate change, Harper also altered policy direction. In opposition he had been keenly aware that the commitment to reduce greenhouse gas (GHG) emissions to 6 per cent below 1990 levels was a figure that had been pulled out of thin air by Chrétien: Canada's population-growth profile, given its large annual immigrant intake, makes it *structurally* impossible to reach such goals, and so, not surprisingly, between 1997 and 2006 Canada's GHG emissions steadily grew (despite the Chrétien government's ratification of the protocol in 2002).[76] Prior to 2006, Harper regularly claimed the Liberal position was at best fanciful and at worst disingenuous, and promised that he would renegotiate Canada's Kyoto commitments.[77] Yet a remarkable transformation came over the Conservatives once they were in government and found that truth-telling attracted criticism from a public that had become used to taking their government's Kyoto commitments at face value. So, rather than adopt the principled and unwavering anti-Kyoto stance that John Howard stuck to right until his defeat in the 2007 election, Harper took a more nuanced tack. While it remained steadfastly opposed to Kyoto – finally withdrawing from the protocol in December 2011 – the Harper government nonetheless adopted an emissions-reduction targeting approach similar to one the prime minister had spent so many years ridiculing. Indeed, the so-called 20/20 target introduced in 2007 – reducing Canada's GHG emissions to 20 per cent below 2006 levels by 2020 – was as unlikely to be achievable as Chrétien's commitments.[78] To be sure, the government further refined its position in 2010 to make it less politically assailable: the Conservatives decided to take advantage of Barack Obama's huge popularity in Canada by simply aligning its own emissions target with the target set by the Obama administration: 17 per cent below 2005 levels by 2020.[79] Clearly, Harper's position on climate change policy was driven largely by a desire to at least *seem* engaged with such matters. So, while it can certainly be argued that the Conservative government has not done much to reduce GHG emissions – Ottawa remains strongly committed to the Alberta oil sands, for example – Harper nevertheless abandoned the sort of principled stance against emissions-reduction efforts that Howard stuck to doggedly for a decade.

There is one area of foreign policy, however, where we see no change at all in Harper's approach before and after becoming prime minister: policy towards Israel. Some aspects of Canadian Middle Eastern policy, like support for a two-state solution, have not formally altered. Yet the "basic premise" from which Canada viewed the Israeli-Palestinian dispute changed significantly.[80] For example, after Hamas won the Palestinian Legislative Council elections in 2006, the newly elected Harper limited contacts with the Palestinian Authority. Canada also unequivocally backed the Israelis in their war against Hezbollah in mid-2006, and in December 2008 as fighting erupted in Gaza, Lawrence Cannon reiterated that "Israel has a clear right to defend itself ... first and foremost, those rocket attacks [by Hamas] must stop."[81]

Support for Israel reached new rhetorical heights in February 2010 when Peter Kent, Harper's minister of state for foreign affairs, claimed that "an attack on Israel would be considered an attack on Canada." This was an extraordinary statement, given that no treaty in force between the two countries requires anything remotely like that reaction. But Harper had said something similar in May 2008: "Our government believes that those who threaten Israel also threaten Canada, because, as the last war showed, hate-fuelled bigotry against some is ultimately a threat to us all, and must be resisted wherever it may lurk ... In this ongoing battle, Canada stands firmly side-by-side with the State of Israel, our friend and ally in the democratic family of nations."[82]

Such rhetorical commitments were also backed up with concrete policy action. For example, Stéphane Paquin and Annie Chaloux have noted that Canada's voting patterns on Middle East matters generally have shifted to align Canada with the United States.[83] And Harper's ministers have rarely missed an opportunity to underscore where Canada stands, as John Baird, the minister of foreign affairs, and Jim Flaherty, the minister of finance, did in February 2012, when they engaged in what Jeffrey Simpson called "aggressive in-your-face lecturing" of the leadership of the Palestinian Authority for having sought UN membership.[84] While Harper faced considerable criticism for his Middle Eastern policy, he has stood firm in his view that principles drive his policy, noting, "There are, after all, a lot more votes – a lot more – in being anti-Israeli than in taking a stand."[85]

On only one international issue can we discern an electorally risky example of a principled *neoconservative* foreign policy position. In January 2010, the Harper government formally announced that as host of the G8 summit, it was planning to launch a maternal health initiative.[86] However, in March it was revealed that family planning and abortion services would not be included, and criticism erupted. Harper soon abandoned the family planning exclusion but stood firm on excluding abortion. Yet doing so incurred the ire of the Obama administration: at a meeting of G8 foreign ministers, Hillary Rodham Clinton claimed that "maternal health ... includes contraception and family planning and access to safe, legal abortion," and Britain's foreign secretary, David Milliband, concurred.[87] Harper countered by claiming that he "wanted to make sure our funds are used to save the lives of women and children and are used on the many, many things that are available to us and do not divide the Canadian population."[88] But criticism continued on the basis that Harper was "pandering" to the government's conservative base.[89]

Analysis

In comparing Canadian and Australian foreign policy we do see parallels. In both countries conservative principles guided foreign policymaking, although both Howard and Harper showed a willingness to act pragmatically too. However, we reiterate that Howard seemed to follow principle more often than he was forced to play to public opinion, while Harper's foreign policymaking showed the opposite trend. One explanation for the difference is that Howard enjoyed a firm majority in the lower house of Parliament throughout his tenure (and, indeed, from 2004 to 2007, the conservative coalition controlled the upper house too, a rarity in Australian history). In contrast, Harper-led minority governments before May 2011 lived with the regular threat of being toppled by no-confidence motions, including one such "scare" only six weeks after the October 2008 federal election. The precarious nature of Harper's tenure must go some way to explaining why he could not follow his (conservative) heart as readily as Howard could. Indeed, after finally securing a majority in 2011, Harper admitted that for the previous five years he had been virtually obsessed with preparing for unexpected elections.[90]

However, we also propose an additional, longer-term electoral explanation for Harper's pragmatism. Put simply, he has made no secret of his desire to have the Conservatives displace the Liberals as Canada's "natural governing party."[91] As he stated on 17 September 2008, a month before the general election: "My long-term goal is to make the Conservatives the natural governing party of the country. And I'm a realist. You do that in two ways ... One thing you do is you pull the conservatives, to pull the party, to the centre of politics. But what you also have to do, if you're really serious about making transformations, is you have to pull the centre of the political spectrum toward conservatism."[92] Indeed as early as 2004, the Conservative "war room" was likening their task to the Punic Wars: just as Rome had weakened, then destroyed, Carthage in three wars, so the Conservatives would take three elections to weaken and then destroy the Liberal Party.[93] To be sure, it took a "fourth Punic War" – the election of 2 May 2011 – to secure a Conservative majority. And it is too early to tell whether the exceedingly weak state of the Liberals will be permanent or whether Harper has been able to make the Conservatives the natural governing party of Canada.[94]

Nevertheless, we suggest that foreign policy played a crucial role in Harper's longer-term strategy. Between 2006 and 2011, it can be argued that the Conservative government framed virtually all major foreign policy issues in terms of domestic politics and the expected impact that foreign policy stances were likely to have. "Principled" foreign policy positions might have been embraced, but only as long as they did not run the risk of alienating important groups of voters. Thus, for example, Harper's China policy in the first years in power was all about not cosying up to dictators; the prime minister's decision to welcome the Dalai Lama to Canada or to pointedly snub China by refusing to attend the 2008 Beijing Olympics – and join in the celebration of this recognition of the country's standing in global affairs – was designed to show Canadians that the Conservatives were capable of being "tough on China." However, when it became apparent that Canadians of Chinese extraction – a key demographic targeted by Conservative strategists – were not impressed by the Olympic snub, the Harper government changed course, improving relations to the point that by 2011, John Baird, the foreign minister, could – incredibly – describe the People's Republic of China as "an important ally."[95] By the time that the prime minister visited China a second time in February 2012, the visit was entirely devoid of the "toughness" of his early years in power, notwithstanding that his hosts – spooked by the rumblings of dissent seeping in from the Arab Spring and mindful of the potential for instability inherent in the upcoming leadership transition – were carrying out the hardest crackdown on dissidents since Tiananmen Square.[96]

But the case of China is not unusual: in nearly every foreign policy issue faced by the Harper government – the case of the child soldier Omar Khadr, the issue of Arctic sovereignty, the agreement to allow the government of Quebec to send its own representative to UNESCO, the dispute with the United Arab Emirates over landing rights that cost Canada its staging base at Camp Mirage, the willingness to allow a Canadian to take command of the NATO bombing of Libya in 2011, or the open castigation of the Sinhalese-dominated government of Sri Lanka – electoral politics not only loomed large, but trumped virtually all other strategic considerations. The only case where the demands of domestic politics were clearly subordinated to systemic strategic imperatives – and only at the very last minute – was Harper's complete reversal on the issue of a total military withdrawal from Afghanistan by 2011. Had it not been for the crushing pressure on Canada from other NATO allies (aided and abetted by the dramatic reversal of Liberal policy on the issue, which eventually forced the Conservative government's hand), domestic political considerations – the tepid support for the mission on the part of Canadians – would have triumphed, and the only Canadian military presence in Afghanistan after 2011 would indeed have been the "odd guard guarding an embassy."

The obvious efforts of the Harper Conservatives to align their foreign policy positions with the views of Canadians – rather than to embrace a narrow ideological foreign policy agenda – leads us to agree with Jeffrey Simpson, who has argued that the Conservatives did not secure their majority in 2011 because Canadians have become more conservative. The prime minister might have asserted to the 2011 party convention that "Conservative values are Canadian values. Canadian values are conservative values. They always were. And Canadians are going back to the party that most closely reflects who they really are: the Conservative Party, which is Canada's party." But in Simpson's view, however, that "stands reality on its head." Rather, another dynamic was at work: "The Conservatives became more traditionally Canadian or, to put matters another way, have learned that Conservatives had to evolve from something much more ideological into something more malleable. Having learned that lesson, the Conservatives became the country's dominant political party, not so much because the country changed, although it has in a few ways, but because the party changed to fit the country."[97]

The conclusion that Harper has shaped his government's foreign policy as part of a broader strategy to "fit the country" can be confirmed by looking at foreign and defence policy since the Conservatives gained a majority in 2011. To be sure, some argued in the immediate aftermath of that election that Harper, girded with a majority government, would unleash a more ideologically driven foreign policy. But there is little evidence of this. There were some policy initiatives that were clearly conservative, such as the restoration of the word *Royal* to the name of Canada's air force and navy in August 2011. The severing of diplomatic relations with Iran in September 2012 was an example of a hard and muscular foreign policy move, but it was, by all accounts,[98] not driven by any particularly *conservative* ideology.

Rather, it is clear that the Conservative government continued to pursue the kind of foreign policy that we saw during the two minority governments from 2006 to 2011. In other words, even with a majority, foreign policy decisions continued to be framed primarily for domestic political and electoral purposes, as was the case with the prime minister's caution over the intervention in Mali in 2013. Positions continued to be taken with particular target groups of voters in mind. "Principles" continued to be invoked, especially in the case of Israel. But principles were also happily set aside when there were good political reasons to downplay them and tread a more pragmatic path, as was the case with the continued improvement of relations with China.

In short, like Howard in Australia, Harper seems driven by both principles and pragmatism. But unlike Howard, whose foreign policy was propelled by a mixture of both domestic/electoral politics and broader foreign policy considerations, Harper's foreign policy seems guided primarily by domestic politics and the larger, though entirely parochial, project of making the Conservatives the natural governing party of Canada. It therefore seems reasonable to assume that his inherently cautious disposition will continue to incline him away from a radical, "principled" revamp of Canada's foreign policy stance.

NOTES

1 Stephen Harper, "Prime Minister Stephen Harper's 2011 Convention Speech," Ottawa, 16 June 2011, http://www.conservative.ca/?p=110.
2 Kenneth Whyte, "In Conversation: Stephen Harper," *Maclean's*, 5 July 2011, http://www2.macleans.ca/2011/07/05/how-he-sees-canada%E2%80%99s-role-in-the-world-and-where-he-wants-to-take-the-country-2/.
3 Roland Paris, "What Is Stephen Harper Afraid Of?," *Embassy*, 20 July 2011, http://embassymag.ca/page/printpage/paris-07-20-2011.
4 Whyte, "In Conversation."
5 John Ibbitson, "The Harper Doctrine: Conservative Foreign Policy in Black and White," *Globe and Mail*, 12 June 2011, http://www.theglobeandmail.com/news/politics/ottawa-notebook/the-harper-doctrine-conservative-foreign-policy-in-black-and-white/article2057886/.

6 Brian Stewart, "The New Harper Doctrine in Foreign Relations," CBC News, 16 June 2011,http://www.cbc.ca/news/canada/story/2011/06/16/f-vp-stewart.html. Peter McKenna, "Harper's 'Doctrine' Is Same Old Same Old," *Winnipeg Free Press*, 13 July 2011, http://www.winnipegfreepress.com/opinion/westview/harpers-doctrine-is-same-old-same-old-125471768.html.

7 Patrick Allitt, *The Conservatives: Ideas and Personalities throughout American History* (New Haven: Yale University Press, 2009).

8 Russell Kirk, *The Politics of Prudence* (Wilmington: ISI Books, 1993); Nancy S. Love, "Anti-, Neo-, Post-, and Proto-: Conservative Hybrids, Ironic Reversals, and Global Terror(ism)," *New Political Science* 31, no. 4 (2009): 443–59; Joseph Scotchie, *Revolt from the Heartland: The Struggle for an Authentic Conservatism* (Brunswick: Transaction Publishers, 2002).

9 Jeane F. Kirkpatrick, "Defining a Conservative Foreign Policy," Heritage Foundation, 25 February 1993, http://www.policyarchive.org/handle/10207/bitstreams/12661.pdf.

10 George F. Will, "A Questionable Kind of Conservatism," *Washington Post*, 24 July 2003.

11 Brian C. Schmidt and Michael C. William, "The Bush Doctrine and the Iraq War: Neoconservatives versus Realists," *Security Studies* 17, no. 2 (2008): 191–220.

12 As Oakeshott put it, "In political activity, men sail a boundless and bottomless sea; there is neither harbour for shelter nor floor for anchorage, neither starting place nor appointed destination. The enterprise is to keep afloat on an even keel." Michael Oakeshott, *Rationalism in Politics, and Other Essays* (New York: Basic Books, 1962), 127.

13 Francis Fukuyama, *After the Neocons: America at the Crossroads* (London: Profile Books, 2006), 40–2.

14 William Kristol and Robert Kagan, "Toward a Neo-Reaganite Foreign Policy," *Foreign Affairs* 75, no. 4 (1996): 18–32.

15 William Kristol and Robert Kagan, "Introduction: National Interest and Global Responsibility," in *Present Dangers: Crisis and Opportunity in American Foreign and Defense Policy*, ed. Kristol and Kagan, 17–22 (San Francisco: Encounter Books, 2000).

16 Irving Kristol, "The Neoconservative Persuasion," *Weekly Standard* 8, no. 47 (2003), http://www.weeklystandard.com/Content/Public/Articles/000/000/003/000tzmlw.asp; Stefan A. Halper and Jonathan Clarke, *America Alone: The Neo-Conservatives and the Global Order* (New York: Cambridge University Press, 2005), 11.

17 Kristol, "Neoconservative Persuasion."

18 John J. Mearsheimer, "Hans Morgenthau and the Iraq War: Realism versus Neoconservatism," Open Democracy, 18 May 2005, http://www.open democracy.net/democracy-americanpower/morgenthau_2522.jsp.

19 Samuel P. Huntington, "Robust Nationalism," *National Interest* 58 (Winter 1999–2000): 31–40.

20 Walter A. McDougall, *Promised Land, Crusader State* (Boston: Houghton Mifflin, 1997); Ivo H. Daalder, and James M. Lindsay, *America Unbound: The Bush Revolution in Foreign Policy* (Washington: Brookings Institution, 2003); Ilan Peleg, *The Legacy of George W. Bush's Foreign Policy: Moving beyond Neoconservatism* (Boulder: Westview, 2009), 66; Mearsheimer, "Hans Morgenthau and the Iraq War."

21 Roger Scruton, "An Englishman Looks at American Conservatism in the New Century," (address to the Howard Center, Chicago, 1 May 2004), http://www.profam.org/Special/thc_scruton_0405s.htm.

22 Peleg, *Legacy of George W. Bush's Foreign Policy.*

23 Jennifer M. Welsh, "'I' Is for Ideology: Conservatism in International Affairs," *Global Society* 17, no. 2 (2003): 181–3.

24 Oakeshott, *Rationalism in Politics.*

25 Welsh, "'I' Is for Ideology," 169–74.

26 Louis Hartz, *The Liberal Tradition in America: An Interpretation of American Political Thought since the Revolution* (New York: Harcourt, Brace, 1955); Hartz, *The Founding of New Societies: Studies in the History of the United States, Latin America, South Africa, Canada, and Australia* (New York: Harcourt, Brace, 1964); Arthur Aughey, Greta Jones, and W.T.M. Riches, *The Conservative Political Tradition in Britain and the United States* (Rutherford: Fairleigh Dickinson University Press, 1992).

27 Waleed Aly, *What's Right? The Future of Conservatism in Australia*, Quarterly Essay 37 (Melbourne: Black, 2010); Michael Wesley, *The Howard Paradox: Australian Diplomacy in Asia, 1996–2006* (Sydney: ABC Books, 2007), 39.

28 Quoted in Robyn Hollander, "John Howard, Economic Liberalism, Social Conservatism, and Australian Federalism," *Australian Journal of Politics and History* 54, no. 1 (2008): 97.

29 Wesley, *Howard Paradox*, 34–5.

30 Ibid., 35.

31 Cited in Allan Gyngell and Michael Wesley, *Making Australian Foreign Policy* (Cambridge: Cambridge University Press, 2007), 278.

32 John Howard, "Australia's International Relations: Ready for the Future" (speech, Menzies Research Centre, Canberra, 22 August 2001).

33 Gary Smith and David Lowe, "Howard, Downer and the Liberals'
    Realist Tradition," *Australian Journal of Politics and History* 51, no. 3
    (2005): 460.
34 Carol Johnson, "John Howard's 'Values' and Australian Identity,"
    Australian Journal of Political Science 42, no. 2 (2007): 200–2.
35 Robert Garran, *True Believer: John Howard, George Bush and the American
    Alliance* (Sydney: Allen & Unwin, 2004), 52; Colin Brown, "Problems in
    Australian Foreign Policy: January–June 1996," *Australian Journal of Politics
    and History* 42, no. 3 (1996): 333.
36 Ann Capling, *All the Way with the USA: Australia, the US and Free Trade*
    (Sydney: University of New South Wales Press, 2005), 53–4.
37 Brown, "Problems in Australian Foreign Policy," 339.
38 Alan Bloomfield and Kim Richard Nossal, "Towards an Explicative
    Understanding of Strategic Culture: The Cases of Australia and Canada,"
    Contemporary Security Policy 28, no. 2 (2007): 286–307.
39 Kim Richard Nossal, "Looking Enviously Down Under? The Australian
    Experience and Canadian Foreign Policy," *Canada among Nations 2005: Split
    Images*, ed. Andrew F. Cooper and Dane Rowlands, 79–92 (Montreal and
    Kingston: McGill-Queen's University Press, 2005).
40 Australia Department of Defence, *Defence 2000: Our Future Defence Force*
    (Canberra: National Capital Printing, 2000).
41 Elsie Wainright, "Responding to State Failure: The Case of Australia and
    the Solomon Islands," *Australian Journal of International Affairs* 57, no. 3
    (2003): 485–98.
42 Australia Department of Defence, *Defence 2000: Our Future Defence Force*.
43 David McCraw, "The Howard Government's Foreign Policy: Really
    Realist?," *Australian Journal of Political Science* 43, no. 3 (2008): 465–80.
44 Thomas Watkins, "Clark and Howard to Talk to Iraq," *Dominion Post*,
    17 February 2003; Alexander Downer, "Security in an Unstable World"
    (speech, National Press Club, 26 June 2003).
45 "Iraq War Allies Rebuff UN Chief," BBC News, 16 September 2004.
46 McCraw, "Howard Government's Foreign Policy," 473–4; Smith and Lowe,
    "Howard, Downer and the Liberals' Realist Tradition," 468.
47 Quoted in Rae Wear, "The Howard Years: An Evaluation," *Australian
    Journal of Politics and History* 55, no. 3 (2009): 349; Hollander, "John
    Howard, Economic Liberalism, Social Conservatism, and Australian
    Federalism," 98.
48 Australia Department of Foreign Affairs and Trade, *In the National Interest:
    Australia's Foreign and Trade Policy White Paper* (Canberra: National Capital
    Printing, 1997) 4; David Goldsworthy, "An Overview," in *The National*

Interest in an Global Era: Australia in World Affairs, 1996–2000, ed. James Cotton and John Ravenhill, 10-30 (Melbourne: Oxford University Press, 2001); Nossal, "Looking Enviously Down Under?"

49 Australia Department of Foreign Affairs and Trade, *Advancing the National Interest* (Canberra: National Capital Printing, 2003).

50 Shirley Scott, "Issues in Australian Foreign Policy, July–December 1997," *Australian Journal of Politics and History* 44, no. 2 (1998): 226.

51 Australia, *Commonwealth Parliamentary Debates*, House of Representatives, 18 March 2003, 12507.

52 "Howard Sends More Troops to Iraq," *Age*, 22 February 2005.

53 "Howard's Iraq Speech," *Sydney Morning Herald*, 30 March 2004.

54 Murray Goot, "Public Opinion and the Democratic Deficit: Australia and the War against Iraq," *Australian Humanities Review* 29 (May–June 2003), http://www.australianhumanitiesreview.org/archive/Issue-May-2003/goot.html.

55 John Howard, "Transcript of the Prime Minister, the Hon John Howard MP, Press Conference, Parliament House, Canberra," 18 March 2003, http://parlinfo.aph.gov.au/parlInfo/download/media/pressrel/WVT86/upload_binary/wvt864.pdf.

56 Derek McDougall and Kingsley Edney, "Howard's Way? Public Opinion as an Influence on Australia's Engagement with Asia, 1996–2007," *Australian Journal of International Affairs* 64, no. 2 (2010): 206.

57 Alexander Downer, cablegram to Jakarta, 23 June 1998, National Archives of Australia, A9737, CS: 92/051651, part 17, 1998.

58 Don Greenleas and Robert Garran, *Deliverance: The Inside Story of East Timor's Fight for Freedom* (Crows Nest, NSW: Allen & Unwin, 2002), 85.

59 James Cotton and John Ravenhill, eds., *The National Interest in a Global Era: Australia in World Affairs, 1996–2000* (Melbourne: Oxford University Press, 2001), 4: Smith and Lowe, "Howard, Downer and the Liberals' Realist Tradition," 464; McDougall and Edney, "Howard's Way?," 214–15.

60 McDougall and Edney, "Howard's Way?," 216.

61 Liberal Party of Canada, 2006, campaign ads, YouTube, http://www.youtube.com/watch?v=OE-JGcQ76yg&feature=related.

62 After noting that there would be pros and cons ("des pours and des contres") if Harper won, the French-language ad claimed that Harper was "*contre* l'accord de Kyoto; *pour* le guerre en Irak; *contre* les droit des femmes au libre-choix; *pour* la présence de l'armée dans toute nos villes; *contre* les mariages entre conjoints de même sexe; *pour* le programme américain de bouclier antimissile; *contre* le bannissement des armes de poing" (Liberal Party of Canada, 2006).

63 William Johnson, *Stephen Harper and the Future of Canada* (Toronto: McClelland & Stewart, 2005); John Kirton, "Harper's 'Made in Canada' Global Leadership," in *Canada among Nations 2006: Minorities and Priorities*, ed. Andrew F. Cooper and Dane Rowlands, 34–57 (Montreal and Kingston: McGill-Queen's University Press, 2006), 30.

64 "No Plans to Change Abortion Laws: Harper," CBC News, 1 June 2004, http://www.cbc.ca/canada/story/2004/06/01/harpabort040601.html.

65 Stephen Harper and Stockwell Day, "Canadians Stand with You," *Wall Street Journal*, 28 March 2003.

66 "'Friends of America' Rally in Toronto," CBC News, 4 April 2003, http://www.cbc.ca/news/canada/story/2003/04/04/usrally_030404.html.

67 Ann Denholm Crosby, "The New Conservative Government and Missile Defence," in Cooper and Rowlands, *Canada among Nations 2006*, 164.

68 "Conservative Government Would Scrap Kyoto: Harper," *CBC News*, 9 June 2004, http://www.cbc.ca/news/story/2004/06/09/elxnharp-kyoto040609.html.

69 Stephen Harper, "Priorities and Challenges for Canadians" (speech to the Institute for Research on Public Policy, Toronto, 21 May 2003).

70 Stephen Harper, "Address by the Prime Minister to the Canadian Armed Forces in Afghanistan, Kandahar, Afghanistan," 13 March 2006, http://www.pm.gc.ca/eng/media.asp?category=2&id=1056.

71 Kim Richard Nossal, Stéphane Roussel, and Stéphane Paquin, *International Policy and Politics in Canada* (Toronto: Pearson, 2011), 143.

72 Don Munton, "Whither Internationalism?," *International Journal* 58, no. 1 (2002–3): 156; Don Munton and Tom Keating, "Internationalism and the Canadian Public," *Canadian Journal of Political Science* 34, no. 3 (2001): 517.

73 David Akin, "Afghan Role to Be 'Strictly Civilian': PM," Canwest News Service, 7 January 2010.

74 "Canada Firm on Afghan Exit Date," CBC News, 30 March 2010, http://www.cbc.ca/news/world/story/2010/03/30/afghanistan-clinton-cannon.html.

75 Clark Campbell, "Harper-Karzai Rift Reveals PM's Deep Doubts about Afghanistan," *Globe and Mail*, 7 April 2010.

76 Jeffrey Simpson, Mark Jaccard, and Nic Rivers, *Hot Air: Meeting Canada's Climate Change Challenge* (Toronto: McClelland & Stewart, 2007).

77 "Conservative Government Would Scrap Kyoto: Harper," CBC News, 9 June 2004, http://www.cbc.ca/news/story/2004/06/09/elxnharp-kyoto040609.html.

78 For an assessment, see Matthew Bramley, *Analysis of the Government of Canada's April 2007 Greenhouse Gas Policy Announcement*, Pembina Institute, 28 May 2007, pubs.pembina.org/reports/Reg_framework_comments.pdf.

79 Environment Canada, "A Climate Change Plan for the Purposes of the *Kyoto Protocol Implementation Act* – May 2010," http://www.climatechange.gc.ca/default.asp?lang=En&n=145D6FE5-1; Canada's Action on Climate Change (May 2010), 3.

80 Marie-Joëlle Zahar, "Talking One Talk, Walking Another: Norm Entrepreneurship and Canada's Foreign Policy in the Middle East," in *Canada and the Middle East in Theory and Practice*, ed. Paul Heinbecker and Bessma Momani, 45–72 (Waterloo: Wilfrid Laurier University Press, 2007); Patrick Martin, "Canada and the Middle East," in *Canada among Nations 2009–2010: As Others See Us*, ed. Fen Osler Hampson and Paul Heinbecker, 195–201 (Montreal and Kingston: McGill-Queen's University Press, 2010).

81 "Palestinians in Canada Condemn Israeli Attacks in Gaza," CBC News, 28 December 2008, http://www.cbc.ca/news/canada/story/2008/12/28/gaza-canada.html.

82 Steven Chase, "'An Attack on Israel Would Be Considered an Attack on Canada,'" *Globe and Mail*, 16 February 2010.

83 Stéphane Paquin and Annie Chaloux, "Comment vit-on aux marges de l'Empire? Les relations Canada-États-Unis et la nature de la relation trans-atlantique," *Études internationales* 40, no. 2 (June 2009): 201–21.

84 Jeffrey Simpson, "Truculent Moralizing for a Domestic Audience," *Globe and Mail*, 4 February 2012.

85 Mark Kennedy and Meagan Fitzpatrick, "Harper Says Canada Will Stand by Israel," *Montreal Gazette*, 8 November 2010, http://www.montrealgazette.com/life/Harper+says+Canada+will+stand+Israel/3794920/story.html.

86 Stephen Harper, "Canada's G8 Priorities," 26 January 2010, Ottawa, http://www.pm.gc.ca/eng/media.asp?id=3093.

87 Campbell Clark, "Clinton's Tough Diplomacy Stings Ottawa," *Globe and Mail*, 30 March 2010.

88 Meagan Fitzpatrick and Richard Foot, "Harper Defends Maternal Health Project Funding Minus Abortions for Third World Countries," *Vancouver Sun*, 27 April 2010.

89 Clark, "Clinton's Tough Diplomacy Stings Ottawa."

90 Harper told *Maclean's*, "Every three months [between 2006 and 2011] we've had the plan for the government and every three months we've had the plan for the election … every single three months … we've had the

threat of an election, and we've always taken it seriously," in Whyte, "In Conversation."

91 Leon D. Epstein, "A Comparative Study of Canadian Parties," *American Political Science Review* 58, no. 1 (1964): 46–59; Kenneth R. Carty, "Political Turbulence in a Dominant Party System," *Political Science and Politics* 39, no. 4 (2006) 825–7; Adam Chapnick, "Peace, Order and Good Government: The 'Conservative' Tradition in Canadian Foreign Policy," *International Journal* 60, no. 3 (2005): 637.

92 Paul Wells, "Harper's Canadian Revolution," *Maclean's*, 17 September 2008, http://www.macleans.ca/canada/national/article.jsp?cont ent=20080917_106770_106770.

93 Tom Flanagan, *Harper's Team: Behind the Scenes in the Conservative Rise to Power*, 2nd rev. (Montreal and Kingston: McGill-Queen's University Press, 2009), 190–2; Michael D. Behiels, "Stephen Harper's Rise to Power: Will His 'New' Conservative Party Become Canada's 'Natural Governing Party' of the Twenty-First Century?," *American Review of Canadian Studies* 40, no. 1 (2010): 132.

94 Greg Weston, "How the Liberal Meltdown Gave Stephen Harper His Majority," CBC News, 3 May 2011, http://www.cbc.ca/news/politics/ canadavotes2011/story/2011/05/03/cv-election-vp-weston.html.

95 Campbell Clark, "Calling China an 'Important Ally,' Baird Turns Cold Shoulder to Fugitive," *Globe and Mail*, 18 July 2011.

96 "Unrest in China: A Dangerous Year," *Economist*, 28 January 2012.

97 Jeffrey Simpson, "It's the Conservatives Who Changed to Fit Canada," *Globe and Mail*, 25 July 2011.

98 Daniel Schwartz, "Why Canada Severed Relations with Iran," CBC News, 8 September 2012.

9 Women, Feminism, and the Harper Conservatives

KAREN BIRD AND ANDREA ROWE

Introduction

The Harper Conservative Party has a complex relationship with women. Feminists are wary of the party and its leader and concerned about hard-won equality rights during a Conservative majority government. This transformed party has been able to secure its governing status whilst maintaining what is, on the whole, a markedly anti-feminist position on women's issues. And yet the party has to pay some heed to a persistent gap between the proportion of women and men supporting it. It has increased, modestly, the proportion of female candidates it presents to the electorate. It has also proposed and enacted policy that party leaders believe will appeal to women with traditional attitudes towards family and gender, marshalling the language of choice rather than evoking the explicit language of traditional family values. This outreach has not been as concerted as that directed at ethnic minority voters, but the party appears to have recognized that it needed to minimize the gender gap that plagued its predecessors, the Canadian Alliance and Reform Party.

In short, Conservatives have not ignored women as a constituency, or the interests of women as they see them. There is, however, a crucial distinction between the kind of gender consciousness that this reflects and the perspectives on issues adopted by feminists and supported by many other women. Conservatives have not been at all afraid to accentuate this distinction and to make clear their opposition to feminist policy preferences. This stands in some contrast to a number of right and centre-right governments in Europe, which have taken some steps towards a more feminist-friendly agenda.

Mind the Gap! Women's Support for the Harper Conservatives

The question of women's relationship to the Conservative Party can be viewed from the perspective of women themselves, as voters, civic actors, and members of organized movements. The question can also be viewed through the words and deeds of the party. What is the party's receptiveness to and demonstrated concern for women, and what frameworks are used to advance its policy preferences? We begin with an examination of women's responses to the Conservative Party at the ballot box.

Survey evidence from the Canadian Election Studies shows that the proportion of women supporting the Reform Party and the Canadian Alliance was persistently about 11 per cent less than the proportion of men, for voters outside Quebec. The gender gap remained at roughly this level from 1993 through 2000, despite increases in overall popular support for these parties.[1] This is not out of line with findings in other countries, where new right parties generally find less support among women than men.[2] Figure 9.1 shows that the new Conservative Party closed the gap in its first electoral outing in 2004 but that a moderate gender differential (between 4% and 6%) returned in elections in 2006 and 2008. In 2011, the gap was all but eliminated, with 41.9 per cent of women reporting that they voted for the Conservative Party, compared to 43.5 per cent of men (again for voters outside Quebec).

CES researchers have concluded that the gender gap in support for Reform, Alliance, and the new Conservative Party is due principally to differences in the values and beliefs held by women and men, though it also reflects differences in individual background and current situation. Women tend to hold less conservative views on law and order, the role of the state, social issues like abortion and gay marriage, and feminism itself. This reduces the likelihood that any party clearly representing right-wing options on those issues will ever eliminate the gender gap completely, though it does not preclude solidifying support among those who do hold to conservative values or occupy centrist or ambivalent positions on such issues. What about situational factors? Conservatives are more likely to find support among voters who have less than a university education, who are married, and who are comparatively religious. Since women tend to be more religious than men, the gender gap would have been even wider, had it not been for the vote of religious women. The party's strategic and instrumentalist

Figure 9.1. The Gender Gap in Conservative Support (Votes outside of Quebec)

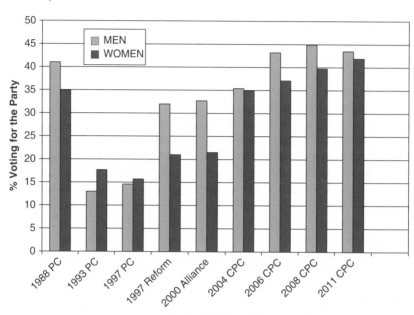

Election Year and Party

approach to increasing its vote share among such women is suggested by Tom Flanagan: "That's the kind of women you work on, because they ought to be Conservative."[3]

Standing for Women? The Conservative Record on Descriptive Representation

Another strategic possibility for the Conservatives would be to increase the number of women running for the party and winning legislative seats. What does the record show about the demographics of candidacies and caucus members?

We recognize that the "descriptive" representation of women does not necessarily translate into the representation of women's interests.[4] Hanna Pitkin argued that an over-emphasis upon the composition of

political bodies prevents a proper focus upon the activity of representation.[5] It is, in her view, more important to focus on what representatives do than on who they are. Still, many democratic theorists insist
that descriptive representation does matter. They argue, first and foremost, that reasons of fairness and justice demand that men should not
be privileged over women in their access to elected office.[6] And they
argue that there is a connection between descriptive and substantive
representation: that women, when present in politics, are more likely to
act for women than men.[7]

The overall picture of women's numerical representation in the
Canadian Parliament is less than rosy. From just under 10 per cent in
1984, the figure grew to the very low 20s through all of the first decade
of the new millennium, rising to a comparatively modest 25 per cent
in the 2011 election.[8] Canada has failed to keep pace with improvements
in women's access to parliaments around the world. Between 1997 and
2011, Canada fell steadily behind other countries (from sixteenth to
forty-sixth place) on the Inter-Parliamentary Union's index of women's
representation in national parliaments. With the latest election, Canada
improved to thirty-eighth position.[9]

Closer analysis indicates that the presence of women in the Canadian
House of Commons depends largely on the electoral fortunes of the
New Democratic Party. This became especially clear in the 2011 election,
where the increase in women's standing came almost entirely from the
NDP's electoral success. Of the party's 104 seats, 40 are held by women,
and this group counts for more than half of the 76 seats held by women
in this Parliament. This success reflects the party's formal commitment
to ensuring that at least half of all candidates come from designated
groups, including women. With two consecutive female leaders –
Audrey McLaughlin from 1989 to 1995, and Alexa McDonough from
1995 to 2003 – the NDP also has the strongest record for party leadership by women.

In the Conservative Party, women comprise only 17 per cent of the
caucus. This is largely a reflection of the limited number of women running as candidates (see figure 9.2). In 2004, 11.7 per cent of Conservative
Party candidates were women (compared to 24.3 per cent among Liberal
candidates, 31.3 per cent among the NDP, and 24 per cent among the
Bloc). In 2006, 12.8 per cent of CPC candidates were women. Since
then, there seems to have been somewhat more attention to this issue,
during a period when all parties were addressing the issue of female

candidacies. In 2008, the party ran female candidates in 20.5 per cent of ridings; and in 2011, 22.1 per cent. This record still lagged significantly behind the Liberals (36.8% in 2008; 29.2% in 2011) and the NDP (33.8% in 2008; 40.2% in 2011).

The Progressive Conservative Party did establish mechanisms to encourage women to run for office. Both Joe Clark and Brian Mulroney promoted women within the party and government.[10] This was a period of burgeoning activism for PC women. The party's women's bureau organized women's caucuses in major cities, emphasizing the development of political skills, networking, and access to power for women. The party also operated the Ellen Fairclough fund to help women

Figure 9.2. Female Candidates by Party

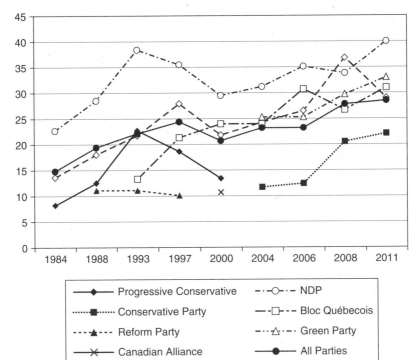

candidates. Women – some of them influenced by feminism – were well represented in powerful Cabinet positions during those years, including Flora MacDonald, Barbara McDougall, Pat Carney, and Kim Campbell. Campbell, of course, served briefly in 1992 as Canada's first female prime minister.

However, like Reform and Alliance, the Conservatives have firmly rejected quotas and other forms of affirmative action aimed at encouraging women to become candidates. This is framed in terms of avoiding artificial mechanisms that would rely on any criteria other than merit. In 2004, when asked what measures he would take to promote the nomination of women, Stephen Harper replied that he would leave the matter to the local riding associations and noted furthermore that women in his party were successful as a result of their own hard work.[11] Cabinet minister Bev Oda, speaking to the issue on the floor of the House of Commons, argued that "women deserve the same opportunity to earn a seat in the House, not through special dispensation, but on merit."[12] The party has also spurned the creation of any official women's caucus, apparently abiding by the Reform/Alliance principle that such structures create unnecessary "special interests." The resistance to assertive measures to enhance the status of women within the party and government is reflected in Prime Minister Harper's Cabinet appointments. Over the course of Harper's time in government, only two women – Leona Aglukkaq (Health) and Diane Finley (Citizenship and Immigration) – have headed high-profile ministries. This trend continued with the appointment of Cabinet members following the 2011 election. Of the twenty-seven ministerial posts, only six of those (22%) were awarded to women, while three additional women were awarded more junior positions as ministers of state. The most prestigious posts such as the roles of minister of foreign affairs and minister of national defence continue to be held by men.

Acting for Women? The Conservative Record on Substantive Representation

The Conservatives' campaigning and policy record suggests an often subtle targeting of women who are part of traditional families, or who are for other reasons drawn to an agenda that provides benefits to such families and prioritizes law and order. They are avoiding the language of "traditional family values" and staying far away from the most explosive hot button issues. They are instead deploying the language of "choice" to shift away from policy options favoured by feminists.

Family Policies

Conservative Party election platforms have included a great deal of language on the importance of the family unit. A typical passage states that the "family unit is essential to the well-being of individuals and society … Therefore government legislation and programs should support and respect the role of the Canadian family."[13] The party's commitment to the protection of the family undergirds a wide range of policies from tax reform to child-care allowances to youth criminal justice reform.

One of the first policies introduced by the Conservative government was its "Choices in Childcare" legislation, which pointedly shifted federal policy away from decades of feminist advocacy on the issue in the direction of embracing a form of the free-market model. The Liberals had established funding just prior to the 2006 election to expand the number of child-care spaces across all provinces. Now the Conservative government was moving in a very different direction, replacing this program with a taxable benefit (in the amount of $100 per month per child under six) paid directly to families. The benefit is taxable in the hands of the spouse with the lowest income, such that the greatest benefit accrues to the family where one parent stays home to care for the children full time. The normative intent seems unmistakably to reward "traditional families."

The Conservatives' portrayal of this as in the interests of women was forcibly demonstrated by Rona Ambrose, chosen as the main Conservative interlocutor on the Liberal government's national child-care plan. She argued that "working women want to make their own choices. We do not need old white guys telling us what to do." She went on to claim that the Liberal plan was "unfair to working women and to women who would like to make choices of their own. For myself as a young working woman, I find this policy particularly offensive because it discriminates against me. It discriminates against my opportunity to make choices as a young working woman."[14]

The Conservatives have also proposed tax incentives to encourage non-professional caregivers (again, typically women) to look after senior citizens at home. The implementation of "income splitting" rules also offers a tax break to traditional families where one spouse (again, typically the woman) earns little or no income. Though now dropped as a policy commitment, the party strongly signalled its opposition to same-sex marriage while the issue had a high media profile, and in its first minority government introduced a bill to reinstate the heterosexual definition of marriage. This too signalled the party's allegiance to traditional family norms. While not a specifically gendered issue, the Conservatives' law-and-order agenda is laced with references to family, with frequent reference paid to "laws to protect children and the elderly" from predators. Since 2006, the government has introduced a number of bills relating to child sex offences, age of consent, child pornography, Internet luring, and trafficking in children.

Of all of the Conservatives' explicitly family-oriented policies, the only one that would have had feminist supporters was its decision in 2006 to exempt midwifery services from the Goods and Services Tax.[15] However, many Conservative women would have also supported this as giving women more choices and control over their maternal health.

Abortion

Much like same-sex marriage, abortion has been an issue requiring deft handling by the Prime Minister's Office. There is little doubt that much of the party's caucus, and important elements of Stephen Harper's inner circle, would like to see more controls on women's access to abortion. However, it made little sense for the government to address such a divisive issue while it held minority status, and it may well be strategically difficult for any Conservative government to move too dramatically on the issue.[16] The party's 2005 policy convention approved a resolution that the government would not support any legislation to regulate. Harper has also expressed his personal preference to avoid the issue: "I've been clear throughout my entire political career. I don't intend to open the abortion issue. I haven't in the past. I'm not going to in the future. Yes, there will be people in the Conservative Party who wish I would and there are some in the Liberal Party who also wish I would. But I have not done that in my entire political career, don't intend to start now. We have a lot of challenges in front of the country … That has to be the focus of government. And I simply have no intention of ever making that a focus, the abortion question a focus of my political career."[17]

Nevertheless, the Conservatives have not closed the matter. The government's maternal health initiative introduced at the 2010 G8 Summit

explicitly excluded support for abortion access in the aid it was propos-
ing for women in developing nations. Federal funding for International
Planned Parenthood also came into question throughout 2010. In
2009, Canada had given the organization $6 million in unrestricted
funds, but this commitment was not renewed in 2010.[18] As of 2011,
unrestricted grants to the organization were cancelled and replaced
with project-based funding under the Muskoka Initiative.[19] In 2011,
the IPPF received a $6 million grant to cover a three-year period, for
work in Afghanistan, Bangladesh, Mali, Sudan, and Tanzania, all countries in which abortion is illegal unless the mother's life is at risk.[20]
These funds represent a $4 million annual reduction in contributions to
the organization and a loss of $12 million over three years.[21]

Most notably, Harper has been unable or perhaps unwilling to prevent his backbenchers from introducing (in the form of private member's bills) proposals to regulate abortion on Canadian soil. Several
such motions have been introduced since 2011. Bill C-150 (put forward
by Conservative MP Rod Bruinooge) was presented as a measure
to prohibit anyone from coercing a woman into having an abortion.
M-312 (a motion introduced by Conservative backbencher Stephen
Woodworth) sought to establish a parliamentary committee to study
parts of the Criminal Code that establish when a fetus becomes a legal
person. Another motion (M-408 from Conservative Mark Warawa), targeting abortion based on the sex of a fetus, was set to be debated at the
end of March 2013. Each of these proposals has failed, but the pattern
demonstrates the continued importance of the abortion issue within
the party. More than a problem of reining in recalcitrant backbenchers,
the votes reveal genuine tensions within the party on whether abortion should continue to be a focus. They also suggest a dual-prong
strategy: on the one hand reminding pro-life voters which of the federal parties is closest to their position; on the other rearticulating the
abortion issue in ways that might gain allegiance among conservative
women.[22]

Status of Women and Women's Organizations

Further evidence of the Conservatives' gender-conscious but anti-
feminist approach to policy can be seen in changes made to the Status
of Women Canada, and funding for women's organizations. During
their first term of government, the Conservatives changed the mandate
of the Status of Women so that it would henceforth "facilitate women's

participation in Canadian society by addressing their economic, social and cultural situation through Canadian organizations," rather than pursue its previous mission to "advance equality for women by addressing women's economic, social, political and legal situation."[23] Removal of the term *equality* signalled clearly that the Status of Women would no longer privilege feminist organizations or policy objectives. The elimination of the phrase *political and legal* also shifted the focus decidedly away from advocacy. Not surprisingly, these changes were applauded by the conservative women's organization REAL Women of Canada.[24]

Afterward, the Conservatives announced that the 2007/8 budget allocation for the Status of Women Canada would increase from $8 million to $20 million. The increase was motivated in part to send a relatively low-cost signal that it was concerned about women. More importantly, though, it was a vehicle for shifting the agency's focus to support for social services rather than advocacy. The agency's grants program was restructured to provide support for non-governmental organizations offering services in three areas: ending violence against women and girls, especially those in remote, Aboriginal, or immigrant communities; improving women's and girls' economic security and prosperity; and encouraging women and girls in leadership and decision-making roles. Grant guidelines stipulate that projects must provide concrete outcomes, demonstrate value for money, and report back to government with measurable results. The emphasis on investing resources "where there is a clear potential to make a real difference in women's lives" implicitly downplays advocacy. Funding for the highly respected Canadian Research Institute for the Advancement of Women and several other prominent advocacy groups has been denied.[25]

Women's Equality Rights

There can be no doubt that the Conservatives are broadly unsympathetic to state programs aiming at pay equity, though they have not sought directly to effect major changes in the federal statute governing pay equity for federal public sector employees. What they have successfully effected, through the 2009 budget, is a prohibition on government employees turning to the courts to obtain settlements in pay-equity cases. Instead, they require female workers to achieve wage parity with their male colleagues exclusively through collective bargaining.[26] The opposition criticized the measure, arguing that it denied pay equity as a fundamental right, while the government maintained that leaving equity to the courts only delayed justice for women.

Across our full review of Conservative legislative initiatives from 2006 through 2012, we found only one measure that explicitly and unequivocally promoted women's equality rights. Bill C-3, an Act to Promote Gender Equality in Indian Registration, was a measure tabled in response to a BC appeal court's finding in *McIvor v. Canada* that the Indian Act discriminated against women's right to Indian status registration. The court had ordered the federal government to correct this discrimination by amending the act. This was also a case of clear and explicit discrimination, which made it easier for the government to approve than the kinds of measures that speak to indirect or systemic discrimination.

Overall, there is a clear anti-feminist direction throughout the Conservative policy initiatives, discussed above. Much of the party's focus is on raising the value and prestige of work that women do in the home, and undercutting advocacy that it portrays as limiting women's choices. At the same time, the party advances an agenda that calls for a reduction in the role of government and for an increased reliance on the free market as an arbiter of social as well as economic claims.

Conservative Parties Elsewhere

Harper's Conservatives stand somewhat apart from conservative parties in other industrialized democracies. Consider the Conservative Party of Britain under David Cameron, who has voiced his clear intent and put in place solid measures to increase women's representation in the party and in Parliament. In his acceptance speech after being selected party leader, he pointed out that "9 out of 10 Conservative MPs, like me, are white men," and then asserted that "we need to change the scandalous under-representation of women in the Conservative party, and we'll do that."[27] He then pushed forward reforms in candidate selection procedures, which translated into almost triple their number of female MPs, from seventeen in 2005 to forty-eight in 2010. This is still only 16 per cent of the caucus (compared to 17 per cent women in the Canadian Conservative caucus), but the rhetorical commitment and the actual shift in numbers are significant.

The British Conservatives have also been much more willing than the CPC to take feminist-friendly positions on a range of women's issues.

In speeches made by Conservative MPs in their capacity as either minister or shadow minister for women and equalities (in Britain), or status of women (in Canada), there is markedly greater attention among the former to women's equality rights.[28] For example, Conservative Eleanor Laing (Britain's shadow minister for women and equalities, 2004–7) has called for measures to increase the number of female MPs, for reform to end discrimination against women in rules of succession to the Crown, for pension reforms to assist women, for increases in paternity and maternity leave pay for working families, for measures to address the gender pay gap and sexual discrimination in the workplace, and for tougher penalties against sex trafficking and domestic violence.

There was also considerably greater attention to women's equality rights within France's recent UMP (conservative) government. The most significant piece of pro-feminist legislation to have been introduced under Prime Minister François Fillon is the law of 27 January 2011 concerning the representation of women and men on boards of directors and professional societies. This law imposes a quota of a minimum of 40 per cent women on the boards of large companies. France has, since 2000, had both a constitutional provision and legislation concerning parity for men and women in politics. The law requires that fully 50 per cent of candidates for elected office must be women and, though the process of application and the penalties for noncompliance differ across the type of election, it is clear that the measures have had significant effect.[29] In 2008, the Fillon government laid the groundwork for the 2011 measure by amending the constitutional principle of parity so that it applied not only to "electoral mandates and elective functions," but also to "professional and social responsibilities." The government also strengthened the rules on parity in elections, by increasing the financial penalties to be levied against noncompliant parties. The adoption and gradual extension of parity is especially noteworthy, given that it has required the reconceptualization of a pillar of French republican values, regarding the indivisibility of the republic and non-division of citizens by any category.

Other measures approved under France's conservative government include the law of 27 May 2008 on workplace discrimination, which included sexual discrimination (and sexual harassment), and the law of 9 July 2010 on violence against women.[30] Pension legislation of 9 November 2010 penalizes companies that fail to develop an action plan for pension equality between women and men. Some of these statutes have equivalents in Canadian law enacted years ago, but it is hard to imagine the current Conservative government of Canada moving as assertively as the French in areas not yet covered adequately by legislation.

Conclusion and a Look Forward

In discussing the responsiveness of the Harper Conservative government to women, we have been careful to point out that while the party has shown increasing signs of gender consciousness, it remains firmly anti-feminist in its policy directions. The comparative assessment presented above, while certainly not exhaustive, shows that there is a remarkable difference between the CPC and conservative parties in at least some other countries.

How can a party that resists the rhetoric of gender equality (let alone the promotion or guarantee of gender equality) win a majority government in a Canada where most gender equity goals have majority support? How has it been able to turn away feminist policy claims in the face of evidence of an economic and political gender gap that remains persistently large, and in some areas growing?

One possibility is that selected elements of a women's equality agenda have been lobbied for behind the scenes but operating within the conventions of party behaviour to ensure that disagreements are not noticeable to outsiders. We know that pressure from women within parties matters, and that change can emerge dramatically once members become persuaded that it is in the best interests of the party to promote women's equality. During the Mulroney years, we know that there was internal pressure on issues like abortion and the rights of sexual minorities, even if the success of such advocacy was uneven. However, there have been no hints of such intra-party pressure under Harper's leadership. There certainly have been signs of dissent on the party's morally conservative right flank, on the issues of abortion and gay marriage, but nothing equivalent making the case for gender-related advances.

Another possibility is that most Canadians agree more with the Conservative Party's leadership than with feminist advocates for full gender equity. In fact, evidence from the World Values Study shows that Canadians rank very high in support for gender equality. Canada scores fourth among sixty-one countries on this dimension, coming just behind Finland, Sweden, and Germany, and ahead of Norway, Spain, New Zealand, the United States, and Australia.[31]

That leaves open the question of whether most Canadians consider women's equality to be an important issue or believe that all that can be achieved politically has been achieved. It may well be these sentiments, rather than a principled rejection of equity, that create openings for Conservatives to marginalize advocacy on gender. The ideological commitment that towers over others in the Conservative Party of Canada is a commitment to the free market, coupled with a suspicion of government's capacity to address social and economic problems. It is entirely possible that this principled stance attracts some Canadians, including women, who believe in gender equality but have become swayed by arguments that state-sponsored solutions will not work.

We believe another factor is also at play. The anti-feminist distinctiveness of the Canadian Conservative Party may be rooted partly in Canadian-European contrasts on multiculturalism and immigration. The crucial difference between Canadian and European conservative parties appears to lie less in ideas about women's equality and more in the degree to and ways in which feminist rhetoric is engaged in advancing a set of ideas about multiculturalism and immigration. Across much of Western Europe, moderate and right-wing parties appear to have adopted gender equality as an ideational device in order to draw critical attention to what are asserted to be the cultural practices of non-Western immigrants. The emergence and stunning popularity of leaders like Marine Le Pen of France's National Front also suggests that a more feminine touch can broaden the appeal of the far right and amplify the argument that the right supports women.[32] A very different dynamic appears to be at work in Canada. Here, the new right has shifted in the opposite direction, deftly repositioning itself as a credible advocate of immigration and multiculturalism. The rhetoric of gender equality is not such a crucial device in this Canadian Conservative Party project, as it is for conservatives leading the "multiculturalism backlash" in Europe.[33]

In some respects, the differences in gender equality rhetoric in this context are not so stark. In its revised study guide for Canadian citizenship, the Conservative government did not shy away from strong condemnation of "barbaric cultural practices that tolerate spousal abuse, 'honour killings,' female genital mutilation, forced marriage or other gender-based violence."[34] But on more politically sensitive issues such as the veil, it is rare to hear the Conservative government evoke ideas of gender equality. For example, in justifying new rules banning Muslim women from wearing facial coverings when swearing the oath of citizenship, Minister Jason Kenney's remarks focused on the need for openness as a precaution against potential identity fraud in the ceremonial procedure.[35] Similarly, the government has addressed the issue of polygamy primarily as a problem of fraudulent immigration applications (such as a wife posing as a sister or cousin), thereby justifying the need for tougher enforcement in the overall immigration and refugee framework. This is a discursive approach notably different from that taken in Quebec, France, or even Britain, where the emphasis has been more squarely on gender equality and women's rights.

In conclusion, we see the Conservative party in Canada as drawing a new coalition of support that pivots upon multiculturalism, socially conservative values, and personal choice. The Conservatives believe that women must be a part of this coalition and have put considerable effort into attracting those with more traditional attitudes towards family and gender. At the same time, the party has written off feminists and introduced changes that significantly erode the capacity for feminist advocacy in public policy. How far women's equality will suffer as a result remains to be seen.

NOTES

1 Elisabeth Gidengil, André Blais, Joanna Everitt, Patrick Fournier, and Neil Nevitte, *Dominance and Decline: Making Sense of Recent Canadian Elections* (North York: University of Toronto Press, 2012).

2 Ronald Inglehart and Pippa Norris, "The Developmental Theory of the Gender Gap in Women's and Men's Voting Behavior in Global Perspective," *International Review of Political Science* 21, no. 4 (2000): 441–63.

3 Quoted in Erin Anderssen, "Can Harper Align Venus with Mars?," *Globe and Mail*, 28 March 2008, http://www.twca.ca/wp-content/uploads/2013/02/Can_Harper_align_Venus_with_Mars.pdf.

4 Sarah Childs, "The Complicated Relationship between Sex, Gender and the Substantive Representation of Women," *European Journal of Women's Studies* 13, no. 1 (2006): 7–21; Karen Celis and Sarah Childs, "Introduction: The Descriptive and Substantive Representation of Women; New Directions," *Parliamentary Affairs* 61, no. 3 (2008): 419–25.

5 Hanna Pitkin, *The Concept of Representation* (Berkeley: University of California Press, 1972).

6 Anne Phillips, *The Politics of Presence* (Oxford: Clarendon, 1995).
7 "Should Blacks Represent Blacks and Women Represent Women? A Contingent 'Yes,'" *Journal of Politics* 61 (1999): 628–57.
8 Julie Cool, *Women in Parliament*, publication no. 05-62E, Library of Parliament, 2010, http://www.parl.gc.ca/content/lop/researchpublications/prb0562-e.htm.
9 Inter-Parliamentary Union, "Women in National Parliaments," 31 May 2011, http://www.ipu.org/wmn-e/classif.htm.
10 Lisa Young and William Cross, "Women and Conservative Parties in Canada and the United States," in *Conservative Parties and Right-Wing Politics in North America: Reaping the Benefits of an Ideological Victory?*, ed. Rainer-Olaf Schultze, Roland Sturm, and Dagmar Eberle (Opladen: Leske and Budrich, 2003), 215; Sydney Sharpe, *The Gilded Ghetto: Women and Political Power in Canada* (Toronto: Harper Collins, 1994), 111–27.
11 Nikki Macdonald, "Women beneath the Electoral Barrier," Electoral Insight, January 2005, http://www.elections.ca/res/eim/article_search/article.asp?id=125&lang=e&frmPageSize=.
12 Bev Oda (minister of Canadian heritage and status of women), "Status of Women," *House of Commons Debates (Hansard)*, 134 (17 April 2007).
13 Conservative Party of Canada, *Stand Up for Canada, Federal Election Platform*, 2006, http://www.cbc.ca/canadavotes2006/leadersparties/pdf/conservative_platform20060113.pdf.
14 Rona Ambrose (Edmonton – Spruce Grove, CPC), "Child Care Funding," *House of Commons Debates (Hansard)*, 1245 (15 February 2005).
15 Ministry of Finance, "Canada's New Government Proposes Tax Exemption for Midwifery Services," 2006, http://www.fin.gc.ca/n06/06-090-eng.asp.
16 Even with a majority government, Brian Mulroney was unable to pass legislation limiting access to abortion. Thomas Flanagan, *Game Theory and Canadian Politics* (Toronto: University of Toronto Press, 1998), 120–39.
17 Paul Wells, "What Does 'No Debate on Abortion' Mean?," *Maclean's*, 18 March 2010.
18 International Planned Parenthood Federation, *Financial Statements 2010*, 30 http://ippf.org/sites/default/files/ippf_financial_statements_2010.pdf.
19 International Planned Parenthood Federation, *Financial Statements 2011*, 27, http://ippf.org/resource/Financial-Statements-2011. Canadian International Development Agency, "Call for Proposals: Muskoka Initiative Partnership Program – Closed," http://www.acdi-cida.gc.ca/acdi-cida/acdi-cida.nsf/eng/ANN-111145457-Q7E.

20 Canadian International Development Agency, "Disclosure of Grants over $25,000.00," http://www.acdi-cida.gc.ca/acdi-cida/contributions.nsf/Eng/C7B5BB3ABBD7A9ED85257A0F005FF0AC

21 "Planned Parenthood's Canadian Funding Renewed," CBC, 22 September 2011, http://www.cbc.ca/news/politics/story/2011/09/22/pol-planned-parenthood-funding.html.

22 Prime Minister Harper has reportedly instructed Cabinet to vote against these motions, and sought to reduce the openings to such measures by his backbenchers. See "Conservative Backbenchers Warned Not to Dredge Up Controversial Bills or Issues in Majority Government," *Hill Times*, 2 June 2011. Nevertheless, each motion has received support from within the front benches. For example, eight Cabinet ministers and two ministers of state voted in favour of M-312. These included notably Jason Kenney (minister of citizenship and immigration) and Rona Ambrose (minister for status of women). The motion on sex-selective abortion is an exception, where the party effectively prevented the issue from reaching the parliamentary floor. The party's control over its backbench in this instance is consistent with the Conservative government's effort to position itself as a credible advocate of immigration and multiculturalism. As we discuss below, the government has been manifestly reluctant to deploy a gender equality discourse in this policy domain.

23 "Tories to Cut Off Funding for Women's Lobby Groups," CBC, 5 October 2006, http://www.cbc.ca/canada/story/2006/10/04/tory-funding.html#.

24 REAL Women of Canada, "Government Increases Funding for the Status of Women," Newsletter 27, no. 2 (2008), http://www.realwomenofcanada.ca/wp-content/uploads/2013/02/REALity-March-April-2008.pdf.

25 "National Women's Group Calls for Investigation into Funding Decisions by Helena Guergis as Minister of Status of Women Canada," Canadian Research Institute for the Advancement of Women, 27 April 2010, http://www.criaw-icref.ca/latest/press-releases.

26 Aaron Wherry, "Is This the Quiet End to Pay Equity?" *Maclean's*, 21 February 2009, http://www2.macleans.ca/2009/02/21/is-this-the-quiet-end-to-pay-equity/.

27 Rosie Campbell, Sarah Childs, and Joni Lovenduski, "Women's Equality Guarantees and the Conservative Party," *Political Quarterly* 77, no. 1 (2006): 18.

28 This analysis is based on our review of parliamentary speeches of these Conservative MPs, on any issue involving the topic of women.

The selection of items was facilitated by keyword searches using search engines of the respective parliamentary websites. The members examined in Britain were Eleanor Laing and Theresa May, and in Canada, Rona Ambrose, Helena Guergis, Bev Oda, Josée Verner, and Lynne Yelich.

29 For example, at the municipal level, where candidates run via party lists and where noncompliance makes a list ineligible, the percentage of female councillors increased from 25.7 (pre-parity) to 47.5 in 2001, to full parity (50 per cent) in 2008. At the national level, where candidates compete in single member districts, and where noncompliant parties are penalized by a reduction in their public subsidy, the effects have been less pronounced. The gender distribution in the National Assembly grew from 10.9 per cent women in 1997 to merely 12.2 per cent in 2002, and to 18.5 per cent in 2007.

30 This legislation conforms to new European directives on this matter.

31 Ronald Inglehart and Pippa Norris, "Modernization and Gender Equality: A Response to Adams and Orloff," *Politics & Gender* 1, no. 3 (2005): 482–92; The World Values Survey gender-equality scale includes five items tapping into ideas about women's role in politics, the workforce, education, and the family. Respondents are asked about their level of agreement or disagreement with the following statements. "On the whole, men make better political leaders than women do." "When jobs are scare, men should have more right to a job than women." "A university education is more important for a boy than a girl." "Do you think that a woman has to have children in order to be fulfilled or is this not necessary?" "If a woman wants to have a child as a single parent but she doesn't want to have a stable relationship with a man, do you approve or disapprove?" On the combined 100-point scale of attitudinal support for gender equality, Canadian respondents overall score around 85.

32 Russell Shorto, "The Kinder, Gentler Extremist," *New York Times Magazine*, 1 May 2011.

33 Anne Phillips and Sawitri Saharso, "Guest Editorial: The Rights of Women and the Crisis of Multiculturalism," *Ethnicities* 8, no. 3 (2008): 291–301.

34 In addition to this language, the revised study guide for Canadian citizenship, *Discover Canada*, also includes a discussion of women's right to vote and the history of the women's suffrage movement in Canada.

35 In his remarks as he announced the new law, Minister Kenney explained, "I have received complaints from members of Parliament, from citizens,

from judges of the citizenship court that it is hard to ensure that individuals whose faces are covered are actually reciting the oath. Requiring that all candidates show their faces while reciting the oath allows judges and everyone present to share in the ceremony, to ensure that all citizenship candidates are in fact, reciting the oath as required by our law."

10 The Relationship between the Conservative Party of Canada and Evangelicals and Social Conservatives[1]

JONATHAN MALLOY

The relationship between the post-2003 Conservative Party of Canada and socially conservative evangelical Christians has attracted significant interest in scholarly and other circles. Scholars have long noted the intertwining of religion, social conservatism, and other elements in the earlier Reform Party and its successor, the Canadian Alliance.[2] Studies of recent elections, while not always in full agreement, find a strong preference among evangelicals for the Conservative party.[3] In general, and unlike the Liberal and Progressive Conservative parties, Reform/Alliance and the post-2003 Conservatives have demonstrated both a clear affinity with these groups and an understanding of how to cultivate and apparently maintain their support. But while journalists and activists have speculated about a semi-hidden social conservative agenda in the Harper government, there is limited scholarship that looks directly at the relationship.[4] I have argued elsewhere that the unusual political window of same-sex marriage in the mid-2000s was a prime motivator for evangelicals and social conservatives to turn to the Conservative Party.[5] But this does not fully explain why or how the party has reciprocated.

This chapter focuses on this new development in the relationship between religion and Canadian politics. I explore how Conservative leader Stephen Harper and his Reform and Alliance predecessors, Preston Manning and Stockwell Day, have managed their relationship with evangelical Christians and social conservatives (two distinct but overlapping categories that are explained below). The study concentrates on party leaders and top-down processes because of the dominant role of leaders in Canadian parties and especially in these parties.[6] Using the literature on Reform and the Alliance as well as more recent evidence from the Harper government, the paper analyses the strategies used by Manning, Day, and Harper to attract, but also to manage and control, evangelicals and social conservatives as part of an overall conservative coalition. These strategies include careful messages to target groups, relying on "democratic" populist-style options rather than firm policy stances, tight control of party platforms, and an expanded focus on "family" issues. While the Conservatives have shown a willingness to promote more narrow social conservative ideals as well, the relationship is best understood in this broader and carefully managed context.

The chapter begins with a brief review of religion and Canadian party politics and a discussion of the overlapping but distinct categories of evangelicals and social conservatives. It then looks at the experience of Preston Manning and the Reform Party, analysing Manning's attempts to keep socially conservative evangelicals within a larger conservative movement, and how this differed from Stockwell Day's more outspoken cultivation of these groups. We then turn to the Conservative Party and how Stephen Harper has also focused on social conservatives and evangelicals as part of a larger conservative coalition strategy. Research for the chapter draws from the academic and other literature on the Reform, Canadian Alliance, and Conservative parties and their leaders, interviews and consultations with current Harper government officials, and contemporary press reports.

Religion and Canadian Party Politics

Religion has generally been seen in recent decades as being of diminishing significance in Canadian politics and indeed in politics more generally.[7] While Catholic-Protestant sectarian struggles characterized much of nineteenth- and early twentieth-century Canadian history, and the Catholic Church played an especially important roles in Quebec, the rapid secularization of Canadian society since the 1960s and the dwindling of overt religious discourse and issues suggested a reduced importance for religion in contemporary Canadian politics. The Co-operative Commonwealth Federation/New Democratic Party, founded on an explicit "social gospel" with minister-politicians like Tommy Douglas, J.S. Woodsworth, and Stanley Knowles, gradually moved away (though never entirely) from its religious roots, and the gradual demise of the religiously inclined Social Credit party both federally and provincially also suggested a growing irrelevance for religion in Canadian politics. While religious issues remained (e.g., controversies over Catholic school funding in Ontario in 1985), they were sporadic and increasingly marginal, especially as a partisan issue.[8]

But this apparent decline in the importance of religion was challenged by the rise of the Reform Party in the 1990s. Not only was Reform leader Preston Manning outspoken about his religious beliefs, but evidence suggested a strong three-way correlation among evangelical Christian beliefs, socially conservative attitudes on abortion and gay rights, and support for the Reform Party.[9] While Reform did not prioritize opposition to abortion and gay rights in its platform or official rhetoric, it clearly attracted support from religious conservatives holding such attitudes.[10] This religious dimension to party politics and voting carried over to the Canadian Alliance under the even more outspokenly religious Stockwell Day and has been maintained and even increased under the reunited Conservative Party of Stephen Harper.[11] Gidengil, Fournier, Everitt, Nevitte, and Blais report that while "fundamentalist Christians" already preferred the Canadian Alliance in 2000 and the Conservatives in 2004, the 2006 and 2008 elections saw even more dramatic increases in "fundamentalist" support for the Conservatives.[12] This correlates with social conservative attitudes; Kay, Perrella, and Brown find significant relationships among conservative Protestant denominations, traditional positions on abortion and gay rights, and support for the Conservative Party.[13]

This evangelical and social conservative tilt towards the Conservative Party not only challenges past assumptions about the declining importance of religion in Canadian politics, but also institutionalist arguments in the comparative literature that religious conservatives in Westminster parliamentary democracies avoid entanglements with any one party because of the relatively closed, winner-take-all nature of these systems.[14] In such systems, power is concentrated in party leaders, leaving few openings for intra-party factions and challenges, and legislative agendas are controlled by governing parties (along with other party leaders in minority Parliaments). In contrast, the more porous American system provides numerous openings and institutional levers for evangelical and social conservative activism. The link between the Conservatives and evangelicals and social conservatives also goes against the traditional understandings of Canadian brokerage politics that suggest the two major parties avoid and downplay divisive ideological stances in their pursuit of electoral majorities and/or national unity.[15] While the Reform and Alliance parties are widely seen as having been more ideological than brokerage parties, the post-2003 Conservative Party, too, continues to take socially conservative positions on abortion and same-sex marriage – unlike its equivocal PC predecessor – and, as we have seen, appears to be rewarded by electoral support from these groups. Whether or not we accept that the Conservative Party of Canada is "essentially the same party" as the historic Progressive Conservatives, it is worth investigating its distinctive relationship with evangelicals and other social conservatives.[16]

Evangelicals versus Social Conservatives

This chapter focuses broadly on both evangelicals and social conservatives, two groups with considerable overlap but also some differences. This overlap is a key difficulty facing research in the field, with researchers using different categories like *evangelical, social or moral conservatives, Christian Right, born-again Christians, conservative Protestants, fundamentalists*, etc., which are similar but not interchangeable.

Social conservative can have a variety of definitions, but there is wide agreement that the term refers to traditional and moralistic attitudes towards reproductive rights, sexual orientation, and sexuality generally, as well as to support for a high degree of state regulation of "morality."[17] Social conservatism was re-energized politically in the 1960s and 1970s, in part as a response to changes in state policy.[18] The social movement arising from such responses "accepts that the personal has become politicized and seeks to use political means to promote traditionalist notions of correct sexual behaviour and family structure."[19] Most social conservatives, but not all, are religious, and not all who are would describe themselves as evangelical.

Precisely defining *evangelical Christians* is a difficult task, for it involves using careful theological distinctions to describe groups and individuals that may or may not identify as evangelical or accept others as evangelical. In general, evangelicals are committed to spreading the Word of God with the goal of individual conversion. Historically the category has encompassed a broad ideological range on issues related to social justice and public morality. They remain diverse on economic, social, and foreign policy issues, but studies consistently find evangelicals to be strongly opposed to abortion and same-sex marriage and to hold social conservative views on other issues of sexuality and reproduction.[20] Studies suggest somewhere between 9 and 15 per cent of Canadians are evangelical.[21] For the purposes of this chapter, evangelicals and social conservatives remain conceptually distinct but are highly overlapping categories with a shared "moral" agenda. Further, the moral agenda of social conservatism, which is often (mistakenly) conflated with evangelicalism, has created a political common ground with other religious groups (most notably conservative Roman Catholics, but also some Jews, Muslims, Sikhs, and Hindus) from whom evangelicals are often religiously estranged. This chapter will generally refer broadly to evangelicals and social conservatives as a single grouping, though the latter sections will note areas in which the Conservatives approach evangelicals beyond their social conservative dimensions, especially in foreign policy.

Evangelical and social conservative activism has notably increased in Canada since the 1990s, especially on the issue of same-sex marriage.[22] However, these groups and activist networks vary considerably, both in their level of organization and sophistication and in their approach to party and electoral politics. Some groups like the Evangelical Fellowship of Canada and Focus on the Family Canada are nominally non-partisan; other groups, like those associated with activists Charles McVety and Tristan Emmanuel, have run candidates for Conservative nominations.[23] Alberta social conservative activist Craig Chandler even ran for the Progressive Conservative leadership in 2003. But this partisan engagement is often ephemeral and episodic. Some groups themselves come and go, attracting publicity through their charismatic leaders but with their actual influence and effectiveness difficult to track.[24]

Until the 2000s, social conservatives and evangelicals had no obvious single home in a major national party. Farney notes the marginal relevance of social conservatives in the Progressive Conservative Party in the 1970s and 1980s, arguing that the party's leaders consistently rejected taking firm partisan stances on abortion and same-sex rights.[25] And while we saw above that social conservatives and evangelicals were drawn to Reform in the 1990s, a significant number remained Liberal supporters. One academic study by Hoover reported that in 1996, 22 per cent of "Christian Right sympathizers" favoured the Reform Party in 1996, while a surprising 52 per cent favoured the Liberal Party.[26] Hutchinson and Hiemstra also find significant evangelical support for the Liberal party in the 1990s and early 2000s.[27]

But significant shifts have occurred since. Part of this is a result of the emergence of a new Conservative Party, but Hutchinson and Hiemstra (senior employees of the Evangelical Fellowship of Canada) argue that the Liberals actively drove their own evangelical supporters away from the party in the early 2000s.[28] This occurred not necessarily through a rejection of the social conservative agenda but through key messages directly disparaging evangelicals. When Stockwell Day's creationist beliefs were mocked in the 2000 election, Hutchinson and Hiemstra note "While Evangelicals hold various views on Creation, most understood this as an attempt to denigrate their faith."[29] They also note a Liberal 2004 poll that asked voters, "Would you be more or less likely to vote for the Conservatives if you knew they had been taken over by evangelical Christians?" These writers argue that these messages were taken by evangelicals to mean that they did not belong in the Liberal Party. Regardless, neither the Liberals nor the historic Progressive Conservative parties appears to have placed a priority on mobilizing evangelicals and social conservatives.

Preston Manning and the Reform Party

The Reform Party under Preston Manning represented a very different approach. As we will see in the following section, Manning did not necessarily directly cultivate evangelical and social conservative supporters or explicitly promote their agenda. Rather, he used his position as party leader to attract these supporters but also carefully manage the relationship between them and the party, a role that has been emulated even more successfully by Stephen Harper.

Dominance by the party leader is a characteristic of Canadian parties, with leaders exercising considerable control over their parliamentary caucuses and party machinery. Both Preston Manning and Stephen Harper (less so, Stockwell Day) stand out as dominating figures in the Reform and Conservative parties respectively. Manning was "the driving force" behind Reform who insisted on "directing all aspects of the party"; Harper demonstrates a similar tight control of the Conservative Party.[30] For example, while evangelicals and social conservatives have made organized attempts to control nomination meetings in the Conservative Party, these have been sporadic and largely unsuccessful.[31] On other occasions, the control exercised by Manning and Harper has been evident in the strategies they have deployed to attract, retain, and control social conservatives and evangelicals as activists and supporters.

Manning's own religious faith and social conservatism have often been cited as shaping the agenda of the Reform Party.[32] But the scholarly literature presents a more complex picture. Writing in 1995, Trevor Harrison states that "except for Manning and [MP Deborah] Grey, the values of moral conservatism are not readily found in the highest echelons of the party."[33] Similarly, scholar and party operative Tom Flanagan discusses the nuanced relationship between evangelicalism and party operations in his reflections on the early 1990s Reform organization. Writing in 1995, he wrote that it was a misconception to think Preston Manning's "political philosophy is directly derived from his religious convictions" and that "I can report that religion never played a role in considering the merits of policy positions."[34] Yet Flanagan immediately goes on to say, "However, Manning does have an increasing tendency to surround himself with evangelical Christians, not for policy reasons but because a common approach to religion encourages rapport and loyalty."[35]

In an analysis of how Manning's faith influences his broad political philosophy, David Laycock notes that Manning believes that "Christian teachings warn against the creation or continuation of invidious distinctions between people."[36] This, argues Laycock, underlay Manning and Reform's opposition to social citizenship ideas that promoted group rights and a redistributive state, in a way that appealed simultaneously to fiscal conservatives, social conservatives, and libertarians. Indeed, Manning's suspicion of group identities extended even to appealing to his own evangelical constituency; in his 2002 memoirs, he writes that "appealing for votes on the basis of religious faith is ultimately bad politics and bad public policy, conducive to creating permanent and divisive cleavages among the electorate that can destroy the unity of a party and even a country."[37] Like his father's "gospel of individualism," Manning's religious beliefs fit naturally with his broader views of state and society, well beyond social conservative issues of sexuality.[38] He was identified with social conservatives and evangelicals and wanted their support but did not allow himself to be limited to this constituency alone.

Instead, Manning managed Reform's evangelicals and social conservatives through "careful but clear remarks" signalling his own views and affinity with them.[39] Social conservative issues were also managed through the party's direct democracy agenda, at least in its initial years. Tom Flanagan writes that Manning's "theory of representation was designed to prevent Reform from becoming identified as a socially conservative party" by emphasizing referendums and decisions by individual MPs on such issues.[40] Harrison also notes how the party relied, at least in its early years, on gaining appeal on difficult issues through "a vagueness further obfuscated by populist calls to 'let the people decide.'"[41] This evasiveness, says Ellis, "served Manning and the party well" prior to its 1993 breakthrough.[42]

However, tensions grew as the party competed for national office. Ellis notes that by the mid-1990s Manning was "heading in opposite directions" from party members by not prioritizing opposition to gay rights and seemingly ignoring grassroots opinion on this and other issues.[43] In 1996 Manning had to deal with a dispute between caucus members over anti-gay remarks, and social conservatism remained a simmering issue in the party, supplanting earlier problems with racist and anti-immigration elements.[44] In 2000 Manning lost the new Canadian Alliance leadership to fellow evangelical Stockwell Day, who relied heavily on membership recruitment through churches and social conservative organizations. Under Day's leadership, "the Alliance could be a more outspoken partisan standard-bearer of the Christian fundamentalist campaign against modern secular society than Manning had allowed Reform to become."[45] But lacking Manning's "careful but clear" approach, Day became fodder for criticism and mockery in the 2000 election and soon afterward faced a caucus revolt, notably led by fellow evangelicals and Manning loyalists Chuck Strahl and Deborah Grey, and an eventual defeat at the hands of Stephen Harper.[46] The Day-Manning struggle clearly reveals the internal divisions *among* evangelicals and social conservatives in the party, and Day's outspoken cultivation of these groups versus Manning's more cautious strategy.

Stephen Harper and the Conservative Party

Unlike Preston Manning, Stephen Harper has said little about his personal religious beliefs and in his early career appeared to have had little interest in an evangelical/social conservative agenda. Tom Flanagan classified him as a non-evangelical in 1995, and Trevor Harrison wrote in 1995 that Harper was one of "a number of influential people connected with the party [who] appear genuinely uninterested in the conservative moral agenda."[47] Journalists have examined Harper's churchgoing and rare statements about religion but can do little more than speculate and conjecture about his private beliefs.[48] It is similarly difficult to track systematically the religious beliefs of other Conservative elites. Attempts to categorize legislators' religious beliefs with any precision is difficult, but there is clearly a significant group of evangelical Conservative MPs in Parliament.[49] Harper's government includes some senior evangelical staffers, including until recently a senior policy advisor who was formerly the president of Focus on the Family Canada, and another who was the former director of the evangelical Laurentian Leadership Centre, part of Trinity Western University (both were also former Manning staffers).[50]

In his stated visions for the Conservative party, Stephen Harper has repeatedly stressed the need for different elements of conservatism to come together, though not always in a consistent formula. In the 1990s, writing with Tom Flanagan, Harper stressed the idea of a "three sisters" approach that brought together Ontario Tories, prairie populists, and Quebec nationalists (more recently, Flanagan suggests ethnic minorities as an additional grouping).[51] In a 2003 speech, Harper cited *Alberta Report* founder Ted Byfield's distinction between economic "neo-cons" and social conservative "theo-cons," arguing that both were essential pillars of a successful conservative party.[52] Like Preston Manning (and unlike Stockwell Day), Harper takes a careful approach that sees social conservatives as one element of a larger conservative coalition. For some, this is essentially a return to the old Progressive Conservative brokerage strategy.[53] But Harper's Conservatives have been much more explicit in their cultivation of evangelical and social conservative support than the Progressive Conservatives ever were. And while more circumspect than Preston Manning, Harper follows much of the earlier pattern set by the Reform leader.

Manning devoted an entire chapter of his 1992 autobiography to his religious beliefs, but Harper has been far more selective in communicating "careful but clear" signals to evangelicals and social conservatives, especially in publicly available speeches.[54] While he concluded his 2006 election victory speech with "God bless Canada," Harper has generally been much more guarded in references to religion. His most noted remarks have been in private gatherings such as the 2003 Civitas speech (the "theo-con" reference above) and a 2009 speech at the Manning Networking Conference where he said "that his version of conservatism is summed up 'in three Fs: freedom, family and faith'" and that "faith in all its forms teaches … that there is a right and wrong beyond mere opinion or desire."[55] Such remarks are vague and open to various interpretations, and copies of these speeches are difficult to find.[56]

While guarded in his messages to the grassroots, Harper has espoused elements of Manning's other technique of relying on democratic instruments to deal with social conservative concerns. The most notable example is same-sex marriage. Campaigning in 2004, Harper promised to hold a free parliamentary vote on the issue (which Paul Martin did in 2005), and in the 2006 election Harper promised to hold another free vote on whether to reopen the issue. When this vote was defeated in late 2006, he argued that Parliament had spoken and the issue would not be revisited. However, as Ellis and Woolstencroft note, this approach risked "a populist trap" in which Harper could not disavow comments by MPs and candidates who suggested that Parliament revisit other issues like abortion, or that the Charter's notwithstanding clause be used to uphold laws at risk of being ruled unconstitutional.[57]

To avoid this trap, Harper has been even more controlling than Manning of party priorities. At the party's 2005 policy convention, Harper made clear that abortion was not on his agenda, regardless of what delegates said – a position that was "antithetical to Harper's Reform roots."[58] Ellis and Woolstencroft argue that Harper "effectively eliminated most of the social conservative and populist hot button issues that allowed their opponents to label the Conservatives as extreme and accuse them of harbouring hidden agendas."[59] Harper's determination to avoid divisive social conservative issues is also seen in his management of off-message candidates and MPs. His 2004 campaign was damaged by the musings of MPs like Cheryl Gallant and Randy White and other anti-gay candidates (Tom Flanagan calls White's comments "enormously damaging").[60] Harper strongly disavowed such comments, and his office tightened its monitoring of candidates during election campaigns.

The Conservatives in Power

As a governing party, Harper's Conservatives face a more complex environment than that faced by Manning and Reform in opposition. The Harper Conservatives are noted for their extensive use of direct mail and advertising to specific groups, allowing careful messaging and mobilizing of discrete groups, including social conservatives and evangelicals.[61] They also maintain regular connections to conservative groups through key ministers like Jason Kenney.[62] The full extent of this political outreach activity is difficult to document. But we can look at the concrete policies and initiatives by the Harper government and what they reveal about the mix of strategies and approaches directed at evangelicals and social conservatives. There are echoes here of Manning's key strategies of "careful but clear" remarks and the language of direct democracy. Harper has also subsumed issue positions related to a "moral" agenda under a larger "family" agenda that appeals to other types of conservatives and at the same time has delivered on policy commitments that signal the government's support of social conservative stances. Such activity is in some ways consistent with traditional brokerage party behaviour. Yet the Conservatives under Harper have also chosen to support social conservatives in more controversial areas and at times appear to deliberately polarize, rather than broker, contentious issues like censorship, sexual orientation, and abortion.

The accession to power in some ways made caucus management easier for the Conservative party, by drawing a distinction between government priorities and statements or actions by backbench MPs. For example, a number of Conservative MPs have introduced private member's bills and motions related to abortion, such as Rod Bruinooge's 2010 "Roxanne's Law" that proposed additional penalties for coercing women to have an abortion. The Harper government joined pro-choice groups in opposing Bruinooge's bill, affirming its commitment to not reopen abortion laws, and Harper himself, along with his Cabinet, voted with pro-choice MPs to defeat the bill in December 2010. Harper further pledged in the 2011 election to continue this policy and to oppose future abortion-related legislation by backbenchers. Later in 2011 another backbencher, Stephen Woodworth, proposed a motion to study the definition of human life, especially prior to birth.[63] When the motion was debated in April 2012, Harper called it "unfortunate" and said he would vote against it. Conservative whip Gordon O'Connor spoke strongly against the motion, saying, "I cannot understand why those who are adamantly opposed to abortion want to impose their belief on others by way of the Criminal Code."[64] However, when the vote was finally held in September 2012, ten ministers, including Minister of Status of Women Rona Ambrose, voted in favour of the motion, Ambrose explaining her vote as reflecting her concern about sex-selective abortion.[65] The Conservative caucus divided almost equally, with 83 of 163 Tory MPs favouring the motion.[66] In general, Conservative ministers, as opposed to backbenchers, have avoided controversial religious and social conservative statements, though there are still occasional lapses such the flustered response in 2009 of

Gary Goodyear, minister of science and technology, about whether he believed in evolution.[67]

When we examine actual government policies as opposed to back-bencher actions, the events and issues can still fit different interpretations. For example, in January 2012 controversy arose when government lawyers were reported to have argued against the legality of Canadian same-sex marriages for non-Canadians.[68] When questioned at a press conference, the prime minister claimed to be unaware of the issue; later that day, he announced a reversal of the government position and said it would support the legality of all same-sex marriages. The Conservatives blamed the previous Liberal government for leaving the issue ambiguous when same-sex marriage was legalized in 2005. Several questions can be asked here. Had the government deliberately tried to undermine same-sex marriage? Was it not aware of the arguments of its own lawyers? Had the minister of justice acted on his own, only to be refuted later by Harper? The incident provides evidence for those seeking to find a "hidden agenda"; yet Harper's swift reversal can also suggest the issue was unexpected and the legal arguments were not endorsed by him or his immediate circle.

At times the Conservative government has clearly delivered on certain discrete issues that please social conservatives.[69] In 2008 the Harper government raised the age of sexual consent from fourteen to sixteen (while retaining the age of consent for anal sex at eighteen). This pleased evangelical and social conservative activists at little political cost or controversy, since none of the opposition parties dared to stand against such a change. Another example of an action that pleased social conservatives at limited political cost may be the exclusion of references to sexual orientation in new 2009 Canadian citizenship guides, an act that gathered media attention but little widespread controversy.[70]

However, the larger Conservative strategy appears to emphasize broader brokerage issues, especially "family-friendly" policies that appeal strongly to social conservatives without polarizing others. According to a senior Conservative government official interviewed for this research, Harper government policymaking is strongly driven by "what can be sold to other groups as well?" (i.e., other parts of the conservative coalition).[71] This official and a second senior Conservative[72] both argued that very few evangelicals and social conservatives voted solely on issues of abortion or sexuality rights – however, as the first official put it, an evangelical is also likely to be "married, middle income, exurban/suburban, a parent, concerned about taxation," etc.

Government priorities were thus driven by a broad focus in which evangelicals themselves were not necessarily "the primary target." An example was the cancellation of the Court Challenges funding program, which the first official claimed "wasn't an evangelical thing; it was a small government thing."[73] Regardless of this claim, given the program's support for feminist and sexual-orientation Charter challenges, the cancellation clearly pleased social conservatives as well.

This approach gels with scholarly research such as Nevitte and Cochrane's distinction between "moral values" and "family values" among the Canadian public.[74] While "moral values" touch directly on abortion, divorce, prostitution, etc., "family values" refers to "whether children need a home with both a mother and father, perspectives on single parenting and outlooks toward women and children."[75] While Nevitte and Cochrane find a strong correlation between traditional attitudes on both measures, they remain distinct sets of views (most intriguingly, Nevitte and Cochrane find that Bloc Québécois supporters are the least traditional on "moral" issues and yet the *most* traditional on "family" values).[76] Conservative policies have been directed more at these "family" values, which, while still traditional, are less politically explosive than reproductive and sexual orientation rights. An example of adopting a policy with appeal much broader than "moral" conservatives is the cancellation of Paul Martin's national child-care program in favour of the Universal Child Care Benefit, a policy that could simultaneously please traditional "moral" social conservatives, larger "family" values voters, fiscal conservatives, and even provincial decentralists. Other policies like a new tax deduction for dependent children, tax credits for children's sports, and the 2011 election proposal for income-splitting on tax returns for families with children, are also part of this agenda.[77] The official quoted above also suggested the raising of the age of consent was popular with this broader "family" constituency, especially mothers, even if they did not share other social conservative views about sexuality.[78]

In addition to domestic "family" policies that range beyond "moral" social conservatism, evangelical concerns have been blended into Conservative foreign policy. Support for the state of Israel appeals to a range of party constituencies – evangelicals who support Israel out of theological convictions, others favouring closer ties to the United States and its global allies, and anti-internationalists – while offering the potential to lure some Jewish support from the Liberal Party. The government's cool initial relationship with China also fit such patterns, playing both to traditional anti-Communist elements and also religious activists concerned about religious rights for Christians and others in China. Interest in religious freedom abroad also led the Conservatives in the 2011 election to promise an Office of Religious Freedom within the Department of Foreign Affairs, a pledge that resonated both with certain minority ethnic communities and evangelical Christians in general. However, the office was not created until 2013, with a director drawn from a small conservative Christian college in Ottawa, and after controversy about its precise mandate and whether the government had sufficiently consulted with a full spectrum of religious groups.[79]

On the other hand, the Harper government has not always been successful at controlling outcomes and downplaying social conservative priorities. Some issues that were perhaps meant to be discreet, low-profile issues have instead become high-profile controversies. In some cases, such as the brief 2012 controversy over non-Canadian same-sex marriages, the government was quick to respond and reverse its views. But at other times, and in defiance of traditional party brokerage theory, the Conservatives have been willing to differentiate themselves from other parties and to clearly favour social conservative views. Three examples are the C-10 film tax credits, the cancellation of Pride Day funding, and the exclusion of abortion services from international maternal health funding.

In 2007 the government introduced Bill C-10, a large budget bill held over from previous parliamentary sessions that included provisions to deny tax credits to films with objectionable content, among other regulatory changes. Charles McVety, head of (among other organizations) the Canadian Family Action Coalition, claimed these proposals were the result of his lobbying efforts with senior Conservative officials.[80] Criticism arose from arts groups and the opposition. (Interestingly, other leading evangelical groups like the Evangelical Fellowship of Canada and Focus on the Family Canada remained silent on the issue, and some evangelicals even criticized McVety for focusing on such a narrow issue with its anti-intellectual and censorship overtones – again, demonstrating important distinctions *within* the evangelical movement.[81]) The government vowed to proceed with the bill (which was complex, with many other sections quite unrelated to the film tax credits), and in Senate committee hearings Conservative senators – interestingly – focused their efforts not on defending its provisions but establishing that McVety and his supporters had not actually met with government ministers.[82] According to the second official consulted for this study, the government was not even prepared for the controversy: "I don't think anyone in the government realized what was in that bill before it reached the Senate. The bill was inherited from the previous government and I can tell you we had no idea that the film tax credit measure was it in."[83] This claim is supported by the fact that the controversial provisions did not attract attention when the bill passed through the House of Commons. The bill was not passed before the 2008 election, and Harper pledged in the election to not reintroduce the controversial provisions. Nevertheless, by not immediately backing down and deleting or amending the proposals, the Conservatives allowed themselves to be portrayed as on one side of a polarizing social conservative agenda.

A second case of issue polarization is Pride funding. In July 2009 a Conservative backbencher, Brad Trost, criticized the funding of Pride Day events in Toronto and said the responsible minister, Diane Ablonczy, herself an evangelical Christian, had been disciplined for allowing it and for personally appearing in the Pride parade.[84] Trost said such funding was not government policy and that "most of the Prime Minister's Office were taken by surprise at this announcement."[85] By early 2010, the government changed its policies in a way that greatly reduced funding to such large urban events. While also appealing to small-government activists and spreading more money to Conservative-friendly rural areas and smaller cities, the policy may have been driven primarily by anti-Pride social conservative pressures.[86] Interestingly, Tom Flanagan has argued that this change was "atrocious political management" because it played excessively and visibly to the social conservative base.[87] In both the above cases, it is useful to note that the controversies were set in motion by actors outside the Conservative leadership – an evangelical activist and a government backbencher. The government thus did not necessarily seek out these polarizing and confrontational debates; but it also clearly allowed itself to be situated on the social conservative side of the issues, rather than searching for a traditional brokerage compromise like earlier Liberal and Progressive Conservative governments.

A third example of polarization is the Harper government's exclusion of abortion from extensive new funding for international maternal health development in early 2010. This attracted widespread domestic and international criticism, but the government refused to modify the exclusion. Again, though, it is not entirely clear that the government intended to make abortion such a wedge issue or expected the high level of controversy. According to a third senior official, the maternal health initiative was designed specifically to attract women voters and play well generally with the Conservatives' broader middle-class base, in the fashion of the "family" policies mentioned above. The official said, "I wouldn't have believed in a million years that it would become so visible and controversial."[88] Nevertheless, in this case the government directly placed the issue of excluding abortion on the agenda and was not afraid of proceeding whether or not it met controversy. In doing so, it again demonstrated its commitment to social conservatives rather than abandoning them in a brokerage-style compromise.

Overall, the Conservatives have tried to manage their evangelical and social conservative elements with a mix of Preston Manning's earlier approaches and a policy agenda that generally, but not always, avoids or downplays social conservative concerns. In line with Stephen Harper's stated visions for the party, the Conservative government approaches social conservatives as one part of a broader conservative base, preferring to pursue policies that are either discrete and relatively uncontroversial (like the age of consent, or the Office of Religious Freedom), or "family" policies that appeal broadly to a larger base and especially suburban, middle-class voters. And Harper has been consistent in not wanting to "reopen" abortion as a domestic issue, even if not all his ministers agree, and his quick 2012 reversal on same-sex marriage again suggests he has no interest in revisiting the issue.

But at other times the Harper Conservatives remain loyal to social conservatives on polarizing issues, even when their values may clash with this broader suburban base. The result is a somewhat puzzling pattern, with a mixed set of evidence that can be used to support different interpretations. Some may argue that the Conservative strategy is simply incremental, and that its lurching and seemingly contradictory actions reflect an indirect long-term strategy to shift Canadian public values in the direction of religiosity and moral regulation of sexuality and reproduction. But such "hidden agenda" arguments remain vague and speculative; again, evidence can be marshalled to suit a variety of interpretations. Overall, the relationship between the Conservative party in power and evangelicals and social conservatives remains nuanced, complex, and difficult to simplify.

Conclusion

This chapter has analysed how the Conservative Party under Stephen Harper, and before it the Reform Party under Preston Manning, has managed relationships with evangelicals and social conservatives.

Like Manning, Harper has used various strategies to manage evangelical and social conservative elements, signalling a personal commitment to these groups but in a more nuanced fashion than the outspoken Stockwell Day. With the discipline and opportunity of power, Harper's Conservatives have attempted to broker evangelicals and social conservatives into larger conservative coalitions and especially into a broader "family" agenda. But the Harper government has also shown a willingness at times to polarize rather than downplay key social conservative issues, seemingly in contravention of traditional brokerage strategy.

The indications from other Westminster systems would lead us to believe that evangelicals and social conservatives avoid putting all their eggs in one party basket. But in Canada there is a clear link between evangelical and social conservative groups and the Harper Conservatives, cultivated and managed by the party and its leader. This seems to arise in part from the peculiarities of Canadian conservatism, especially after the shock of the 1993 election, the legacy of the Reform Party and Preston Manning, and the particular leadership style and electoral strategy of Stephen Harper.

The implications of this are unclear. The post-2003 Conservative Party and indeed the entire Canadian party system since 1993 have posed difficult puzzles for scholars, since they do not entirely follow the patterns of the past and in some ways appear to be still evolving.[89] The relationship between the Harper Conservatives and evangelicals and social conservatives is particularly interesting. Does it signify a renewed significance for religion and religiously driven issues in Canadian politics, and an attempt to shape long-term values and policy agendas? Or is it a temporary legacy of the old Reform and Alliance currents in the post-2003 Conservative Party? Most of all, will the relationship strengthen or diminish in the future, especially in a post-Harper era?

NOTES

1 Earlier versions of this chapter were presented at the American Political Science Association and Association for Canadian Studies in the United States annual conferences. I thank the numerous people that have commented on various drafts, especially the editors of this volume. This research has been supported by a standard research grant from the Social Sciences and Humanities Research Council of Canada.

2 Trevor Harrison, *Of Passionate Intensity: Right-Wing Populism and the Reform Party of Canada* (Toronto: University of Toronto Press, 1995); Tom Flanagan, *Waiting for the Wave: The Reform Party and the Conservative Movement* (Montreal and Kingston: McGill-Queen's University Press, 2009) (first edition published in 1995 as *Waiting for the Wave: The Reform Party and Preston Manning*); David Laycock, *The New Right and Democracy in Canada: Understanding Reform and the Canadian Alliance* (Don Mills: Oxford University Press, 2002); Faron Ellis, *The Limits of Participation: Activists and Leaders in Canada's Reform Party* (Calgary: University of Calgary Press, 2005).

3 There is little published scholarly research on recent religious voting trends in Canada. However, see Barry J. Kay, Andrea M. Perrella, and Steven D. Brown, "The Religion Enigma: Theoretical Riddle or Classificational Artifact?" (paper prepared for the American Political Science Association Conference, September 2009, Toronto); Elisabeth Gidengil Patrick Fournier, Joanna Everitt, Neil Nevitte, and André Blais, "The Anatomy of a Liberal Defeat" (paper presented to the annual meetings of the Canadian Political Science Association, Ottawa, May 2009); Donald Hutchinson and Rick Hiemstra, "Canadian Evangelical Voting Trends by Region, 1996–2008," *Church and Faith Trends* 2, no. 3 (2009): 1–25; Darrell Bricker and Karen Gottfried, "The New Tectonics of Canadian Politics," *Policy Options* (October 2011): 22–6.

4 Marci McDonald, *The Armageddon Factor: The Rise of Christian Nationalism in Canada* (Toronto: Random House, 2010); Tom Warner, *Canada's Social Conservatives in the Age of Rights* (Toronto: Between the Lines, 2010).

5 Jonathan Malloy, "Canadian Evangelicals and Same-Sex Marriage," in *Faith, Politics and Sexual Diversity in Canada and the United States*, ed. David Rayside and Clyde Wilcox, 144–65 (Vancouver: University of British Columbia Press, 2011).

6 Kenneth R. Carty and William Cross, "Political Parties and the Practice of Brokerage Politics" in *Oxford Handbook of Canadian Politics*, ed. John C. Courtney and David E. Smith, 191–07 (Toronto: Oxford University Press, 2010).

7 Kenneth Wald and Clyde Wilcox, "Getting Religion: Has Political Science Rediscovered the Faith Factor?," *American Political Science Review* (November 2006): 523–9.

8 However, scholars have long expressed puzzlement over the apparent "paradox" that Catholics were more likely to vote Liberal but did not appear to significantly differ on issues. André Blais, "Accounting for the Electoral Success of the Liberal Party in Canada," *Canadian Journal*

of Political Science 38 (2005): 821–40; William P. Irvine, "Explaining the Religious Basis of the Canadian Partisan Identity: Success on the Third Try," *Canadian Journal of Political Science* 7, no. 3 (1974): 560–3; Richard Johnston, "The Reproduction of the Religious Cleavage in Canadian Elections," *Canadian Journal of Political Science* 18, no. 1 (1985): 99–113; Laura B. Stephenson, "The Catholic-Liberal Connection: A Test of Strength," in *Voting Behaviour in Canada*, ed. Cameron D. Anderson and Laura B. Stephenson (Vancouver: University of British Columbia Press, 2010).

  9 Preston Manning, *The New Canada* (Toronto: Macmillan, 1992); James Guth and Cleveland Fraser, "Religion and Partisanship in Canada," *Journal for the Scientific Study of Religion* 40, no. 1 (2001): 51–64; Michael Lusztig and J. Matthew Wilson, "A New Right? Moral Issues and Partisan Change in Canada," *Social Science Quarterly* 86, no. 1 (2005): 109–28.

10 Harrison, *Passionate Intensity*; Flanagan, *Waiting for the Wave*.

11 Trevor Harrison, *Requiem for a Lightweight: Stockwell Day and Image Politics* (Montreal: Black Rose, 2002).

12 Gidengil et al., "Anatomy of a Liberal Defeat." Information from at least one large commercial poll in the 2011 election suggests a further consolidation of conservative Protestant support for the Conservatives; see Bricker and Gottfried, "New Tectonics of Canadian Politics."

13 Kay, Perrella, and Brown, "Religion Enigma." Stephenson finds that opposition to same-sex marriage reduced Catholic support for the Liberals in 2004 and 2006 but cautions that this and other issues like the sponsorship scandal still "were mostly unable to overcome the tendency of Catholics to support the Liberals." Stephenson, "Catholic-Liberal Connection," 101.

14 Steve Bruce, *The Rise and Fall of the Christian Right* (London: Oxford University Press, 1988); Bruce, *Conservative Protestant Politics* (London: Oxford University Press, 1998); Christopher J. Soper, *Evangelical Christianity in the United States and Great Britain: Religious Beliefs, Political Choices* (Basingstoke: Macmillan, 2004).

15 Jane Jenson and Janine Brodie, *Crisis, Challenge and Change: Party and Class in Canada Revisited* (Ottawa: Carleton University Press, 1988). Carty and Cross, "Political Parties and the Practice of Brokerage Politics."

16 Carty and Cross, "Political Parties and the Practice of Brokerage Politics"; James Farney and Jonathan Malloy, "Ideology and Discipline in the Conservative Party of Canada," in *The Canadian Federal Election of 2011*, ed. Christopher Dornan and Jon Pammett, 247–70 (Toronto: Dundurn, 2012.)

17 Warner, *Canada's Social Conservatives in the Age of Rights*.

18 Ibid.

19 James Farney, "The Personal Is Not Political: The Progressive Conservative Response to Social Issues," *American Review of Canadian Studies* 39, no. 3 (2009): 243.

20 Dennis Hoover, Michael D. Martinez, Samuel Reimer, and Kenneth D. Wald, "Evangelicalism Meets the Continental Divide: Moral and Economic Conservatism in the United States and Canada," *Political Research Quarterly* 55, no. 2 (2002): 351–74; Sam Reimer, *Evangelicals and the Continental Divide: The Conservative Protestant Subculture in Canada and the United States* (Montreal and Kingston: McGill-Queen's University Press, 2003); Lydia Bean, Marco Gonzalez, and Jason Kaufman, "Why Doesn't Canada Have an American-Style Christian Right? A Comparative Framework for Analyzing the Political Effects of Evangelical Subcultural Identity," *Canadian Journal of Sociology* 33, no. 4 (2008), 899–943; Sam Reimer, "'Civility without Compromise': Evangelical Attitudes toward Same-Sex Issues in Comparative Context," in Rayside and Wilcox, *Faith, Politics and Sexual Diversity*, 71–86.

21 Hoover et al., "Evangelicalism Meets the Continental Divide," 351–74; Rick Hiemstra, "Counting Canadian Evangelicals," *Church and Faith Trends* 2, no. 3 (2007): 1–10; though see Kurt Bowen, *Christians in a Secular World* (Montreal and Kingston: McGill-Queen's University Press, 2005).

22 Malloy, "Canadian Evangelicals and Same-Sex Marriage."

23 Gloria Galloway, "Christian Activists Capturing Tory Races," *Globe and Mail*, 27 May 2005; Jim Wilkes, "'Religious Agenda' Fails to Toss Turner: No Challenger in Halton Riding; Tory MP to Be Acclaimed," *Toronto Star*, 22 August 2006.

24 Malloy, "Canadian Evangelicals and Same-Sex Marriage."

25 Farney, "Personal Is Not Political," 242–52.

26 Dennis Hoover, "The Christian Right under Old Glory and the Maple Leaf," in *Sojourners in the Wilderness: The Christian Right in Comparative Perspective*, ed. Corwin E. Smidt and James M. Penning, 193–215 (Lanham: Rowman and Littlefield, 1997); see also Bean, Gonzalez, and Kaufman, "Why Doesn't Canada Have an American-Style Christian Right?"

27 Hutchinson and Hiemstra, "Canadian Evangelical Voting Trends by Region, 1996–2008."

28 Ibid.

29 Ibid., 4.

30 Kenneth R. Carty, William Cross, and Lisa Young, *Rebuilding Canadian Party Politics* (Vancouver: University of British Columbia Press, 2000), 40; Flanagan, *Waiting for the Wave*; Tom Flanagan, *Harper's Team: Behind the Scenes in the Conservative Rise to Power*, 2nd ed. (Montreal and Kingston: McGill-Queen's University Press, 2009).

31 Galloway, "Christian Activists Capturing Tory Races"; Wilkes, "'Religious Agenda' Fails to Toss Turner."

32 Murray Dobbin, *Preston Manning and the Reform Party* (Toronto: James Lorimer, 1991).

33 Trevor Harrison, "Populist and Conservative Christian Evangelical Movements: A Comparison of Canada and the United States," in *Group Politics and Social Movements in Canada*, ed. Miriam Smith, 203–24 (Toronto: Broadview, 2007).

34 Flanagan, *Waiting for the Wave*, 4, 9.

35 Ibid.

36 Laycock, *New Right and Democracy in Canada*, 82.

37 Preston Manning, *Think Big! My Adventures in Life and Politics* (Toronto: McClelland and Stewart, 2002), 150.

38 Alvin Finkel, *The Social Credit Phenomenon in Alberta* (Toronto: University of Toronto Press, 1989).

39 Laycock, *New Right and Democracy in Canada*, 18.

40 Flanagan, *Waiting for the Wave*, 214.

41 Harrison, *Passionate Intensity*, 136.

42 Ellis, *Limits of Participation*, 67.

43 Ibid., 152–3.

44 Ibid., 151–2.

45 Laycock, *New Right and Democracy in Canada*, 19.

46 Deborah Grey, *Never Retreat, Never Explain, Never Apologize: My Life, My Politics* (Toronto: Key Porter Books, 2004).

47 Flanagan, *Waiting for the Wave*, 9; Harrison, *Passionate Intensity*, 210.

48 Colin Campbell, "The Church of Stephen Harper," *Maclean's*, 26 February 2006; McDonald, *Armageddon Factor*.

49 Warner, *Canada's Social Conservatives in the Age of Rights*; McDonald, *Armageddon Factor*.

50 Douglas Todd, "Evangelical Activists Promoted to Top Jobs by Stephen Harper," *Vancouver Sun*, 25 March 2009.

51 Flanagan, *Waiting for the Wave*, 201–2; Tom Flanagan, "The Emerging Conservative Coalition," *Policy Options* (June–July 2011): 104–8.

52 McDonald, *Armageddon Factor*.

53 Faron Ellis and Peter Woolstencroft, "A Change of Government, Not a Change of Country: The Conservatives and the 2006 Election," in *The Canadian Federal Election of 2006*, ed. Chris Dornan and Jon H. Pammett, 58–92 (Toronto: Dundurn, 2006).

54 Preston Manning, *The New Canada* (Macmillan: Toronto, 1992).

55 David Akin, "Spendthrift Consumers Caused Global Recession: Harper," *National Post*, 12 March 2009.

56 Alleged transcripts of the 2003 Civitas speech can be found online on sites critical of Harper. An audio record of the 2009 speech is available on a blog maintained by reporter David Akin; the above quotes are taken from a published Canwest News article by Akin.

57 Faron Ellis and Peter Woolstencroft, "New Conservatives, Old Realities: The 2004 Election Campaign," in *The Canadian Federal Election of 2004*, ed. Chris Dornan and Jon H. Pammett (Toronto: Dundurn, 2004), 92.

58 Ellis and Woolstencroft, "Change of Government," 64.

59 Ibid.

60 Flanagan, *Harper's Team*, 182.

61 Ibid.

62 McDonald, *Armageddon Factor*.

63 Gloria Galloway, "Tory MP's Call to Revisit Rights-of-Unborn Law Fuels Abortion Debate," *Globe and Mail*, 21 December 2011.

64 Gloria Galloway, "Harper Denounces 'Unfortunate' Bid to Reopen Abortion Debate," *Globe and Mail*, 26 April 2012.

65 Kim Mackrael, "Status of Women Minister Criticized after Voting for Woodworth Motion," *Globe and Mail*, 27 September 2012.

66 Mark Kennedy and Natalie Stechyson, "Harper's Tory MPs Divided over Abortion," *Vancouver Sun*, 26 September, 2012.

67 Anne McIlroy, "Science Minister Won't Confirm Belief in Evolution," *Globe and Mail*, 17 March 2009.

68 Kirk Makin, "Despite Legal About-Face, Harper Has 'No Intention' of Reopening Gay Marriage," *Globe and Mail*, 12 January 2012.

69 Warner, *Canada's Social Conservatives in the Age of Rights*.

70 Dean Beeby, "Minister Nixed Gay Rights Mention in Study Guide," *Globe and Mail*, 3 March 2010.

71 Confidential interview, 2010.

72 Confidential e-mail, 2010.

73 Confidential interview, 2010.

74 Neil Nevitte and Chris Cochrane, "Value Change and the Dynamics of the Canadian Partisan Landscape," in *Canadian Parties in Transition*, 3rd ed., ed. Alain-G. Gagnon and A. Brian Tanguay, 255–75 (Peterborough: Broadview, 2007).

75 Ibid., 258.

76 Ibid., 262.

77 Malloy and Farney, "Ideology and Discipline in the Conservative Party of Canada."

78 Confidential interview, 2010.

79 CBC News, "Christian College Dean to Head Religious Freedom Office," 19 February 2013, http://www.cbc.ca/news/politics/story/2013/02/19/pol-ambassdor-office-religious-freedom-announced.html.

80 Bill Curry and Gayle MacDonald, "Evangelist Takes Credit for Film Crackdown," *Globe and Mail*, 29 February 2008.

81 Omar El Akkad, "Tax-Credit Crackdown on Films Puts Spotlight on Evangelical Community," *Globe and Mail*, 4 March 2008.

82 Senate of Canada, *Proceedings of the Standing Senate Committee on Banking, Trade and Commerce*, no. 16, 16 April 2008.

83 Confidential e-mail, 2010.

84 David Akin, "Tourism Minister Loses Funding Program after Grant to Gay Pride Week," *National Post*, 7 July 2009.

85 John-Henry Westen, "Canadian Conservative MP: Party Funding of Gay Pride Parade Came as Shock to Most of Caucus," LifeSiteNews.com, 6 July 2009, http://www.lifesitenews.com/ldn/2009/jul/09070615.html.

86 Kevin Libin, "Grants and Drag Queens Don't Mix," *National Post*, 11 May 2010.

87 Ibid.

88 Confidential Interview, 2010.

89 Farney and Malloy, "Ideology and Discipline in the Conservative Party of Canada."

PART THREE

Provincial Conservatism

11 Provincial Conservatism

NELSON WISEMAN

Tory conservatism with its emphasis on tradition and contemporary neoconservatism with its emphasis on the free market contrast in their essentials. These two quite different credos have informed the character of provincial Conservative parties, whose ethos has always been more liberal than tory. Tory conservatism, however, has been a distinctive touch in these parties' outlooks and it has been more influential in some parts of the country than in others.[1] Tories see individuals as members of communities, while neoconservatives, like classical liberals, see communities as associations of individuals. Tories recognize groups, their status, rights, and obligations. Conservative leader Joe Clark used a communitarian tory formulation to describe Canada as a "community of communities." State-oriented, tories subscribe to a muscular and authoritative, if small, state. They view the good society as a hive, the harmonious blending of the interests of various groups and socio-economic classes. As classical conservatives, tories hark back to the wisdom of the ages to warn and encourage people to think and behave as did their forbears. They consider social institutions – the family, church, corporation, university, military, government – as hierarchically structured and properly so. Seeing people as innately imperfect, limited, and weak, tories treasure social order and are frightened by the potential chaos unleashed by revolutionary change.

In contrast, many neoconservatives adopt libertarian positions – the church of the self – on such matters. Classical liberalism, with its greater faith in personal than collective choices, marks all neoconservatives, even if many do not extend their notions of individual choice as far as this. Subscribing to a gospel of equal opportunities for all individuals, irrespective of their origins or status, neoconservatives, like tories and classical liberals, accept the acquisition of wealth by inheritance. Unlike the elitism associated with toryism, neoconservatism embraces middle-class ordinariness. In the neoconservative ken, society is composed of neither distinct competing groups nor cooperative classes; society is no more or less than the sum of its atomistic individuals. Seeing society as a market, neoconservatives are resolutely sceptical of state intrusions in the marketplace; they deem government a suspect but necessary instrument to maintain law and order as citizens compete with one another. Informed by neoclassical economics, neoconservatives tout globalized free markets and low taxes as economic elixirs. Both tories and neoconservatives tend to endorse state projection of military power as a symbol of national pride and might.[2]

This chapter uses regional and provincial prisms to enhance our understanding of Canadian conservatism and the balance between its tory and neoconservative inclinations. This is not to suggest the absence of a distinguishable national conservative tradition or to contend that Canadian conservatism is a mere amalgam of regional cases. If we zoom out our lens to look for touchstones of a national conservative tradition, we will find them. If we zoom in to discern distinctive provincial conservative traits, we will locate those too. This chapter undertakes the latter approach from a comparative historical perspective. It casts light on Canadian conservatism by tracing the tory communitarian and the more contemporary neoconservative imprints on provincial politics. Organized along regional lines, the chapter locates each region's founding conservative tradition, traces the evolution of conservative beliefs, and endeavours to determine the extent to which the provincial Conservative parties have aligned with conservative values, as well as how those values have evolved. The outlooks, policies, and fortunes of successful Conservative parties and leaders serve as indirect indicators of societal sentiments.

In the Atlantic provinces, the oldest part of English Canada, British immigrants keenly followed British politics and transplanted the Conservative and Tory marques from the mother country. In Quebec, a pre-liberal Catholic conservatism predates the British Conquest and the Enlightenment. In Ontario, decamped British Americans, the Loyalists, had left America's liberal revolution behind. Toryism and loyalism fit well together and members of the business elite, many of whom were Loyalists, constituted the nuclei of English Canada's early Conservative parties. In western Canada, settled long after the Loyalist influx, pioneer settlers from Ontario, Britain, and the United States brought with them progressive and populist ideas. In this region, liberal values stressing individual liberty, competitive markets, equality, and a circumscribed public sphere – the core of neoconservatism – became most vibrant.

Atlantic Canada

The founding conservatism of the Atlantic region comes from both its early pre-revolutionary American and post-revolutionary Loyalist settlers. In Nova Scotia, the dominant historical strand of political analysis identifies "tradition and conservatism" as driving forces, themes that echo throughout the region.[3] In all four provinces, there has been little in the way of ideological fissures between the dominant Conservative and Liberal parties. From their earliest origins, those parties have appeared as Tweedledum and Tweedledee, seen and seeing themselves as little more than Ins and Outs. Newfoundland stands apart from the Maritimes in its separation from the Canadian mainland and the absence of Loyalists. A similar physical separation nourished an inward-looking parochialism in Prince Edward Island, where a pastoral setting generated a romanticized illusion of an idyllic past and the valorization of the family farm.[4] In New Brunswick, with its large Acadian population, the Loyalists' anti-French prejudices drove the no less conservative Catholic Acadians to the Liberal Party.[5]

Touchstones of toryism – localism, tradition, caution, stability, social order, elitism, hierarchical religious and state institutions, and deference to authority – took root and survived in Atlantic Canada. A pervasive system of patronage and cradle-to-grave partisan loyalties, more pronounced than elsewhere in English Canada, cemented these norms. Atlantic Canadian toryism lacked the intensity of the liberal individualism so prominent in the United States and, later, in some parts of western Canada. The Atlantic region, unlike Lower and Upper Canada, experienced no rebellion in 1837–8. Personal, cellular, localized patronage and nepotism – marks of a traditional conservative political culture – were largely accepted in a regional setting of social stratification and cultural immobility.

Maritime political culture congealed by the 1850s against the backdrop of a stagnant population in a context of little immigration. Nascent Conservative and Liberal parties emerged, but blurred partisan lines generated a received image of ideological harmony. Changes of government signalled little more than changes in personnel and the beneficiaries of patronage. Governments, essentially compacts of personalities engaged in a form of elite accommodation, had Liberals and Conservatives, anglophones and francophones, Protestants and Catholics, at the Cabinet table. Nevertheless, Conservative parties, more strongly identified with entrenched elites, dominated the appointed upper chambers, the Legislative Councils, a lingering tory institution; Nova Scotia's survived until 1928. Undivided by principle, the parties have exchanged policy positions without apology – one opposing the other's policy whatever it is but not hesitant to adopt that policy when in office.

Partisan identities, like religion, proved familial and cross-generational, more commonly inherited in Atlantic Canada than in other regions. Electoral systems institutionalized religion's hold on politics. In the first half of the twentieth century in PEI, one could not predict which party would win office but one could predict with certainty the election of twenty-one Protestants and nine Catholics, because of party conventions about religious representation in individual constituencies. This led to the observation that the province had "four political parties: Liberal, Conservative, Catholic and Protestant."[6] Newfoundland's electoral law provided for the equal representation of Anglicans, Catholics, and "others" (United Church, Salvation Army, and Pentecostals) and, until 1974, New Brunswick's two-, three-, four-, and five-member multi-member ridings accommodated party tickets that balanced the representation of various religious and ethnic groups.[7]

Conservatism appeared shaken in 1920 with the election of some provincial labour and farmer candidates in Nova Scotia and New Brunswick, but this departure was muted and temporary compared to western developments. In 1921, the federal Progressive party won sixty-four seats west of Quebec but only one in the Maritimes, as the traditional parties retained their hegemony in the region. Associated with the Depression, the federal and provincial Conservative parties declined in Atlantic Canada, but its conservative political culture persisted: "The two dominant parties," observed Hugh Thorburn, "stand for traditions, principles, attitudes, and prejudices which resemble one another very closely."[8] To be sure, modernization has weakened cross-generational partisan durability, but it continued to be more pronounced in the Maritimes than elsewhere; in response to a question asking Nova Scotia Conservative convention delegates in the 1970s when they had become party members, one replied, "At conception."[9]

Long-serving leaders – four held Nova Scotia's premiership for sixty-six of the eighty-three years between 1884 and 1967 – point to another

tory trait, the father figure. In Newfoundland, Joey Smallwood operated a self-described "democratic dictatorship" in which he chose his
party's candidates.[10] In a sign of enduring tory elitism, New Brunswick's
Conservatives deferred selection of their leader to the party caucus
until the late 1960s, the last Canadian party to do so. As another indica-
tor of conservatism's persistence, no woman ran for office in PEI until
1966 and none was elected until 1970. In Newfoundland, party brands
came to mean little for political grandees; more have crossed the floor
in this province than in any other.[11]

Using surveys of public opinion measuring social values, Michael
Adams classified Canada's twelve "tribes" at the end of the millennium
and identified Atlantic Canadians as "traditionalists."[12] Their weekly
attendance at religious institutions is highest in the country and their
affiliation to fundamentalist Christian denominations is the lowest.[13]
Resilient attitudes regarding patronage surfaced in the 1990s when
party loyalists challenged the promise of Nova Scotia's premier to ter-
minate patronage. Atlantic Canadians continue to consider politicians
as "cash cows" and the pork barrel as the just reward of power.[14]

Robert Stanfield, Richard Hatfield, Dalton Camp, and David
MacDonald reflected the red in Atlantic Canadian toryism in the second half of the twentieth century. Stanfield had underscored the links
between his party and its British roots; he cited both Burke and the pio-
neering labour legislation of Britain's nineteenth-century Conservatives
as part of Canadian conservatism's legacy and justified restraint of
the individual in the interests of the community's welfare as a whole.
He proposed protection for the less secure, becoming the first major
Canadian political leader to endorse a guaranteed annual income.[15]
Hatfield wrested much of the Acadian vote from the Liberals after he
made French an official language in the 1980s and distanced himself,
as did Atlantic Canada, from the neoconservatism of the Reform party.
MacDonald went from having been a Conservative federal Cabinet
minister to cohabiting with the New Democratic Party leader and
becoming an NDP candidate.

The orientations of Stanfield, Hatfield, MacDonald, and Camp
and the old Conservative Party's British political pedigree are alien
to modern neoconservatism. Neoconservatism has been quietest in
Atlantic Canada, the region where the new federal Conservative party
has been weakest in English Canada. A 2002 survey revealed Atlantic
Canadians' continued relative deference to institutional authority:
an overwhelming majority (86%) of them was satisfied with the

Supreme Court's performance, in contrast to a minority of westerners.[16] Former Cabinet minister and Progressive Conservative senator Lowell Murray articulated his tory sensibility when, in 2003, he spurned the new federal Conservative party and its neoconservative agenda as spoiling "all the good arguments for the market economy by making a religion of it, pretending there are market criteria and market solutions to all of our social and economic problems." "Democratic politics must define the public interest and ensure it always prevails over more private ambition."[17] The meteoric rise and sudden demise of New Brunswick's Confederation of Regions party – a Maritime version of the anti-multicultural, anti-bilingual, and populist federal Reform/ Canadian Alliance party – and the subsequent success of Nova Scotia's NDP, laid bare the weak resonance of neoconservatism in the region. Newfoundland's Danny Williams, a self-made millionaire, attacked Stephen Harper's federal Conservatives as not reflective of his province's "red tory" leanings.[18]

Some more self-confident neoconservative voices have come from the region in recent years. New Brunswick's former premier, Frank McKenna, denounced dependence on Ottawa as "the opiate of this region" and characterized unemployment insurance, transfer payments, and welfare cheques as "a narcotic to which we have become addicted."[19] He and others seek to address what Stephen Harper had once derided as the region's "culture of defeatism." The Atlantic Institute for Market Studies, for example, expresses neoconservative sentiments; its founding president decries the welfare state as having produced a nation of takers rather than makers. AIMS promotes regional prosperity via fiscal prudence and spending restraint, and its studies depict federal equalization payments as a millstone.[20] Among the broader public, however, support for provincial Conservative parties appears unrelated to an appetite for such inclinations.

Quebec

Spun off from a monarchical, aristocratic, and absolutist *ancien régime*, French Canada shared social stratification, cultural immobility, and economic stagnation with Atlantic Canada. Distinctions between the two regions, however, tower over parallels. While the divisions between Atlantic Canada's Protestant and Catholic anglophones went hand-in-hand with partisanship, French Quebec's universally Catholic composition rendered the province a constituency naturally receptive to the classical conservatism of Joseph de Maistre. Thus, when representative government came, ultramontanisme proposed church primacy over state in policymaking. The church's glorification of agrarian virtues contributed to perpetuating conservative spiritual values amidst limited avenues of economic and social advancement for the Québécois.

Agrarianism prevailed throughout Canada but, in Quebec, little about it was "grit," as in Ontario, or populist and progressive, as in the West. The 1838 rebel *patriotes* and the liberalism of the Institut canadien represented a streak of liberal *rouge*, as did the "Cartier school" (named after Macdonald's lieutenant), which urged more tolerance of religious diversity and a more limited role for the church.[21] However, the church commanded more power in Quebec than it did in other Catholic societies. Until the Quiet Revolution, whatever there was of French Quebec's liberalism paled when placed next to the liberalism of English Canada. In the paternalistic traditions of the parish and seigneurial systems, the press was servile to the church until *Le Devoir*'s appearance in 1910. The church organized both the *caisses populaires* and the labour unions so as to isolate them from their more radical Anglo-American counterparts and, in the 1930s, it pointed to fascist Spain and Portugal as corporatist models, an idea embraced by the "reformers" in the Action libérale nationale.[22] As a measure of Quebec's slow socio-economic development in this ideological milieu, only 30 per cent of fifteen- to nineteen-year-olds were in school as late as the 1950s.[23]

On the partisan front, the provincial and federal Conservative parties, the *bleus*, dominated politics for the first three decades after Confederation, consistent with the adage delivered at pulpits that "Heaven is blue and hell is red."[24] Federal Conservative party support, but not conservatism, began to unravel in the 1880s with Louis Riel's execution and, soon after, the Manitoba schools question. The party's naval and conscription policies during the First World War sealed the decline. The provincial Liberals, no less conservative than the Conservatives, governed from the 1890s until an even more conservative Union Nationale held the reins of government from 1936 until 1960, save for a wartime interregnum.

The liberal Quiet Revolution reformulated classical conservatism's social solidarity, but the older conservatism still found voice in the federal Créditistes, whose program was designed to resurrect the past and preserve those elements from being eclipsed by modernization.[25] After the provincial Liberals designated the state as the economy's "*moteur principal*," the Parti Québécois went further and styled Quebec a "corporatist state" modelled on a form of social democratic "corporatism."[26] The PQ brought together leaders of the province's peak economic associations of capital and labour, along with the premier and senior Cabinet minsters, to formulate collectively a societal agenda, something alien to the competitive pattern of labour–management relations in English North America. Liberal and PQ governments together built Canada's largest stable of Crown corporations, symbols of state–societal entanglement and the enmeshment of their interests.

A largely peripheral tendency and with only modest popular support, neoconservatism emerged in Quebec in the 1980s with the completion of the Quiet Revolution's modernization. Students, forsaking the classics, theology, and philosophy for business studies, led the way. Where in the 1970s, 90 per cent of graduates from the École des hautes études commerciales went into government positions, by 1985 only 5 per cent did. That said, many of them were now heading the quasi-public institutions that had become such an important part of Quebec's economy.[27] Governments sought to move away gradually from the welfare state (l'état providence) and state capitalism (l'état entrepreneur) to encourage venture capitalism, but étatisme remained a constant. There was little support for the provincial state taking a free-market approach to the provision of social services or for the state's detachment from economic development.

Religious attendance in Quebec (along with British Columbia) is now lower than elsewhere in Canada, with the French language and the provincial state having attained something like the spiritual equivalence of older church doctrine. The powerful religious past lingers visually in Quebec's grand cathedrals and a landscape dotted with aging church spires, as well as in the National Assembly where a crucifix continues to hang above the Speaker's chair. Even if secularism now dominates public discourse, Quebec nationalism retains some reverence for the distant conservative past; it offers a conception of community solidarity quite different from the nationalism and individualism that characterize other parts of the country.

Some neoconservative articulations cut across partisan lines in the 1980s and 1990s to work their way into Quebec's political conversation. While the PQ government had designated a minister for social solidarity and another for state planning, the Liberals had created a ministry responsible for privatization and, as the federal Progressive Conservative leader in 1997, Jean Charest campaigned on an economic platform similar to that of the Reform Party.[28] To gain and maintain power as Quebec's premier, however, Charest had to backtrack and defend the public institutions (Crown corporations), social programs (heavily subsidized day care and university tuition fees), and policies (on the environment, justice, and a progressive income tax regime) of his PQ predecessors. He, like them, appointed a minister of social solidarity.

The Action Démocratique du Québec (ADQ) appeared in the National Assembly and clearly espoused neoconservative ideas but, after becoming Quebec's official opposition in 2007, its steep decline in the following year's election suggested that initial support for it reflected a disappointment with the established major parties rather than endorsement of its neoconservative policy agenda. Some *péquistes* proved receptive to neoconservatism's message; a group of Quebec public intellectuals, most notably former PQ premier Lucien Bouchard and former *péquiste* Cabinet minister Joseph Facal, denounced Quebec's deep-seated "unhealthy suspicion of business," and Facal bemoaned the public's inconsistency in electing politicians who promise generous public services and defeating politicians who propose raising user fees to fund them.[29]

A neoconservative group, Réseau Liberté-Québec, debuted at the end of 2010 to preach the virtues of smaller government, balanced budgets, and free enterprise. The group's founder, a journalist for the conservative Quebecor media chain and former advisor to the Canadian Alliance, compared the Réseau to the United States Tea Party movement "in that we are very grassroots."[30] However, the popular base for the Réseau's core ideas appears limited and, unlike the Tea Party, there was no Christian fundamentalist element to the group. The Réseau skyrocketed in the polls when pollsters hypothetically cast it as a political party but, as in the case of the ADQ, these rumblings on the right signalled a rejection of the established parties rather the popular embrace of its ideology. In 2012 a new right-of-centre party, Coalition pour l'avenir du Québec led by former *péquiste* Cabinet minister François Legault, absorbed the ADQ and attracted some defecting PQ members of the National Assembly. Federally, Quebec MP Maxime Bernier has served as a strident neoconservative voice in the Conservative caucus, but public opinion in the province has been unsympathetic to his party's positions on crime and punishment, arts and culture funding, the environment, foreign, and defence policies.

Québécois have become more like English Canadians by measures of home ownership, suburbanization, and the decline of the traditional extended family. However, their high rates of abortion, low rates of marriage and fertility, and relative tolerance for the sins of old, such as homosexuality and teen sex, suggest a social liberalism distant from the social conservatism associated with neoconservatism and the emphasis on the family in the Catholic social teaching that had underpinned Quebec's classical conservatism.[31] By a wide margin, Quebecers are the most supportive among Canadians of the idea that the equality of social classes is more important than personal freedom.[32]

Ontario

Unlike their Quebec conservative counterparts and as in the Maritimes, Ontario's conservatives were not cut off from Europe. A Loyalist residue continues to cling to provincial emblems: the Union Jack on the flag, the crown on automobile licence plates, and the provincial motto: *Ut incepit sic permanet fidelis* (As it began, so it remains faithful). Ontario's Conservatives served as the pioneers and standard-bearers of Canadian economic nationalism after the 1860s.

Fewer Loyalists settled in Upper Canada than in the Maritimes, but their influence was greater in Ontario because they were, as in New Brunswick, the charter settler group. The French Revolution and the War of 1812 reinforced their conservatism and anti-Americanism amidst fears of "mobocracy." The Family Compact, a powerful high tory right grouping of colonial administrators, clergy, judges, and financial barons at the heart of Upper Canada's Conservative Party, considered itself the specially appointed guardian of the British connection and the colonial equivalent of the British Tory party.

Geographically, the party's historical base is in eastern Ontario, where the Loyalists settled. Some towns and townships there have voted Conservative cross-generationally since the nineteenth century. The Irish constituted the largest group of immigrants coming to Upper Canada in the first half of the nineteenth century, but it was tory and fiercely anti-Catholic Ulstermen who drove politics. The power of their Orange Order was such that it induced John A. Macdonald to become an Orangeman, and Victorian Ontario had more urban parades organized by the Order than did any other national-religious community.[33] The Conservatives often showed no hesitation to align themselves with extreme Protestant elements.

Conservative Premier James Whitney, often referred to as the "father of progressive conservatism," won four lopsided majorities in the early twentieth century and introduced a number of policies identified with red toryism: the creation of publicly owned Ontario Hydro, workers' compensation, cheaper schoolbooks, and prison and hospital reforms. When the party inaugurated another long period in government in 1943 (lasting forty-two years), its platform was unabashedly red and radically tory. It promised mothers' allowances, pensions, "the fairest and most advanced labour laws," and "economic and social security from the cradle to the grave."[34] Aided by Bay Street, the Conservatives came to embody continuity, staidness, sobriety, and moderation.

The party regenerated itself by changing leaders every decade, projecting experience and business acumen. Leslie Frost sought to run government as he had run his family business; MBA graduate John Robarts called himself a "management man" and operated like a corporate CEO; and Bill Davis assembled a "kitchen cabinet" of business titans, senior party officials, some bureaucrats, and a few labour leaders. Under Davis, who observed of his success that "bland works," Ontario's brand of conservatism and his Conservatives appeared predictable, stolid, and consensus seeking, an image reinforced by his entente with Liberal prime minister Pierre Trudeau on economic and constitutional issues. During their dynasty, the Conservatives successfully bridged Old Ontario – agrarian, rural, small town, white, Protestant, and conservative – with the New Ontario – an increasingly urban, cosmopolitan, poly-ethnic, and multiracial liberal society. In the 1980s, John Wilson observed that "the fact that power has changed hands so infrequently at Queen's Park lends support to the idea that those values which have been assigned to the whole of English Canada – 'ascriptive, 'elitist,' 'hierarchical,' 'stable,' 'cautious,' and 'restrained' – belong only to Ontario." He characterized the provincial political culture as "progressive conservative" and the Conservatives as masters of such a fusion.[35]

The progressive and inoffensive image of Ontario's conservatism soon shattered. The Conservatives' defeat in 1985 and their subsequent third-party status – a first in the party's history – under a red tory leader, Larry Grossman, led to a radical ideological makeover. His successor's neoconservative election manifesto and *cri de coeur*, the Common Sense Revolution, challenged any prior understanding of the party and of Ontarian conservatism. Mike Harris cultivated ideological polarization to partisan advantage, appealed to the entrepreneurial instincts of the province's new visible minorities, and successfully depicted his NDP predecessors' affirmative action programs as discriminatory quotas. The philosophically remodelled Conservatives, promising to reward the skills, ambitions, and efforts of individuals and to cut taxes and downsize government, cast aside all vestiges of the hierarchical, elitist, and communitarian traditions associated with Ontario toryism.

Ontarians turned their backs on the neoconservatism of the provincial Conservatives after the millennium, but this did not fundamentally shift the thinking of the province's leading Conservatives. Prominent Harris acolytes – Jim Flaherty, Tony Clement, and John Baird – appeared in Stephen Harper's federal Conservative Cabinet and they continued to sing the praises of fiscal prudence, tax cuts, and small government. John Tory, Davis's principal secretary, served briefly as provincial Conservative leader but was undone by his urban and tory image, which made him unpopular with his own caucus. His party's support for funding religious schools also put it offside with the party's rural voter base. Defeated, Tory withdrew and left the party leadership to another Harris-era minister, Tim Hudak, who proposed to cut taxes and government spending and to impose a wage freeze in the public sector.[36] The public, however, rejected his agenda in the 2011 election.

In common with tories, Ontario's neoconservatives long for a certain past, but theirs is a celebration of the lifestyle of the suburban middle-class nuclear family before the rise of a drug culture, officially sanctioned gambling, previously illicit sex and pornography, and identity politics. They yearn for certain elements of the Calvinistic puritanism of a bygone era, but they do not campaign by pressing issues such as abortion, capital punishment, or homosexuality and focus instead on lower taxes and reduced constraints on the free market. They spotlight the independent responsible taxpayer who works hard and eschews government support.

The West

The West has no one conservative tradition; there is a singularity to each provincial case. What the western provinces share are anti-establishment impulses common in contemporary neoconservative thinking but are alien to toryism. A region of the mind, the West has been marked by utopian fantasies such as British Columbia's self-image as a lotus land, Alberta Social Credit's "funny money" schemes, and a constitutionally hallucinatory Triple-E (equal, elected, effective) Senate designed on the American model. Manitoba, the only western province where the Conservatives have elected members of the Legislative Assembly in every decade since the nineteenth century, has been the most reticent about such sorties, while social democratic traditions have helped to shape Saskatchewan's self-image.

Ontario's founding stamp on Manitoba – every premier save one between the 1880s and 1988 was born in Ontario or of Ontarian parentage – helps to explain why in the west this province has been the least supportive of neoconservatism. John A. Macdonald's son, Hugh, served as Manitoba's premier during the turn of the twentieth century when the province was receptive to tory ideas. Toryism persisted for much of the century – from premier Sir Rodmond Roblin's castigation of direct legislation (the initiative, referendum, and recall) as "a Socialistic and Un-British Plan ... a form of degenerate republicanism," to premier Sterling Lyon's objection to the Charter of Rights and Freedoms as a "a republican system ... an experiment with a concept foreign to our tradition."[37]

Sir Rodmond's grandson Duff Roblin, premier from 1958 to 1967, reflected the provincial political culture's tory touch. A Co-operative Commonwealth Federation MLA lauded his progressive measures as "the very things we have been calling for over the years,"[38] and tory George Grant dedicated *Lament for a Nation* to Roblin's British-born clerk of the Cabinet. In contrast, Lyon, premier from 1977 to 1981, was an unabashed neoconservative on fiscal issues. Dubbed "The Margaret Thatcher of Manitoba," he preached "acute, protracted restraint," but his government ran the largest deficits on record and the electorate repudiated his agenda at the end of a single term.[39] Under Gary Filmon, Lyon's successor and the last Conservative premier, the Conservatives represented a synthesis of the older Roblin tory sensibility and the harder neoconservative line of Lyon.

Saskatchewan's provincial Conservatives hugged the electoral margins for most of the twentieth century. Nine successive elections between the 1930s and 1970s yielded only one MLA, and the party's popular vote sank as low as 2 per cent. In the first half of the century, they gave voice to anti-immigrant and anti-Catholic prejudices in this the most Catholic of English Canada's provinces and the province with the greatest concentration of Europeans. They aligned their biases with the Ku Klux Klan's religious and racial prejudices in 1920s, and 96 per cent of their MLAs, candidates, and constituency officials were Anglo-Saxons in the 1930s and 1940s.[40] In the 1950s, however, when John Diefenbaker opened the federal party to the increasingly integrated, intermarried, and assimilated third- and fourth-generation European ethnic minorities, Conservative federal hegemony (as Progressive

Conservatives, Reform/Alliance, and Conservative) took hold and has persisted.

The provincial Conservatives took a populist neoconservative turn in the 1970s and won office in the 1980s. Eager to nourish a pro-business entrepreneurial culture, they cut social programs and vowed to pursue privatization aggressively, but the popularity of co-operative ventures and provincial Crown corporations proved a formidable challenge to executing that part of their agenda.[41] As an example, Saskatchewan's farmers voted to maintain the Canadian Wheat Board's monopoly on wheat and barley sales, while Alberta's farmers voted for an openly competitive and unregulated marketing system.[42] Grant Devine's Conservatives preached fiscal prudence but came close to bankrupting the province and self-destructed in a scandal that implicated over a dozen Conservative MLAs and resulted in the (eventual) conviction and imprisonment of the deputy premier.

The Saskatchewan Party is now neoconservatism's provincial face, its first leader a former Reform MP, its current premier, Brad Wall, a former Progressive Conservative ministerial assistant and candidate. Although very popular, the party has treaded cautiously on privatization and successfully fought a proposed foreign takeover of the provincially headquartered and world-leading Potash Corporation. In the 2011 election, it captured an unprecedented 64 per cent of the popular vote.

Populism, Christian fundamentalism, and neoconservatism have been stronger in Alberta than elsewhere in Canada. In good measure, this is because of the formative influence of Americans in provincial settlement. As early as 1908, the *Calgary Daily Herald* reported that American and central Canadian "evangelists seem to have a grip on the city."[43] Americans outnumbered Britons in all fifteen of Alberta's rural census divisions, and they constituted nearly a third of Alberta's immigrants between 1900 and 1920. As late as 1921, American-born immigrants made up more than a fifth of the population, almost certainly the largest concentration ever of Americans in any foreign jurisdiction.[44] The radical populist ideas of Americans such as farm leader Henry Wise Wood, dubbed the "uncrowned king of Alberta"[45] by his biographer, and J.W. Leedy, the former populist governor of Kansas, gained wide currency and popular legitimacy. Only in Alberta did a provincial Conservative party endorse free trade with the United States in the landmark federal election of 1911.

Neither Loyalism nor toryism had much purchase in Alberta. To be sure, Alberta's first prime minister, R.B. Bennett, hailed from

Loyalist New Brunswick and was something of a tory. Un-American in his outlook, he was knighted, retired to, died in, and was buried in Britain. Bennett became prime minister, however, despite Alberta. His Conservatives captured a lower percentage of the vote in Alberta than in any other province, including Quebec, in the 1930 election in which anti-Americanism was an issue and which brought him to power. In Alberta, notions popular in the United States took hold. A survey of Alberta's public school teachers in the 1930s, for example, revealed they saw "the American nation not as a foreign but a kindred folk." In contrast, the "almost unanimous view" of Maritime educators was "vigorous insistence that there is no good reason why Canadian pupils in schools should have their attention called to events in the United States any more, for example, than to French or German development."[46]

At the provincial level, Alberta's Americanized strain of conservatism found expression in a Social Credit government between the 1930s and 1970s.[47] At first a radical and socially conservative regime, it expressed a republican view of democracy when it refused to appear before the Royal Commission on Dominion–Provincial Relations and addressed its brief to "the Sovereign People of Canada."[48] One American-born Social Credit MLA complained that Alberta's legislature had spent too much time discussing the coronation festivities of 1937 at the expense of discussing monetary reform, a sentiment inconceivable at Queen's Park or in Atlantic Canada. Under Ernest Manning, Social Credit anointed itself as the province's chief protagonist in the fight against socialism during the Cold War.

Peter Lougheed's Conservatives captured Social Credit's ideological and social bases of support in the 1970s. However, he behaved as a modernizing technocrat, not a "people versus elites" populist promoter. In the 1990s, Ralph Klein's Conservatives embraced more unequivocally the tenets of neoconservatism. They enthusiastically took on privatization and deregulation, adopted the logic of an international market economy, and redefined citizens as "customers."[49] Although few of its members were originally from Alberta, a neoconservative "Calgary school" emerged at the city's university; one of its professors, Tom Flanagan, served as the Reform party's director of policy and managed Harper's leadership and national election campaigns, while another, Ted Morton, served as the provincial finance minister after having been elected as a Conservative senator-in-waiting.

What distinguishes Alberta from the other western provinces is the prominence of religiously infused moral conservatism. All three leaders of the Reform/Alliance and the new federal Conservative party have been evangelical Christians and have come from Alberta, where their parties have been stronger than in any other province. At the provincial level, the Conservatives have long juggled neoconservative suspicion of state authority with moral conservatism. Despite the anti-government political rhetoric of the Conservatives, however, their government spends liberally on health and education. The party is now competing on the right with a new neoconservative standard-bearer, the Wildrose Alliance, which presents itself as the authentic voice of conservatism and whose election campaign manager in 2012 was Flanagan. In contrast, the new Conservative premier, Alison Redford, projects a red tory image.[50]

American influence has been weaker and British influence stronger in British Columbia than in Alberta. BC represented Greater Britain on the Pacific with many Old World tories and socialists settling there in the first decade of the last century, tripling the population at a time of escalated class tensions, the rise of trade unionism, and the founding of the Britain's Labour party. BC replicated those forces. As in the Maritimes, British Columbians closely followed British politics, but it was Britain's new industrial politics, not its old pre-industrial order, that influenced developments in a corporate frontier setting unlike the prairies' agricultural frontier.[51]

A powerful left-right ideological dynamic imitative of early twentieth-century British and Australian politics arose in BC. In order to stem the success of labour-socialist forces, conservatives coalesced around different partisan labels. They represented a business-backed centre-right coalition to fend off a centre-left labour-backed challenger. Wiped out electorally in the 1930s, the Conservative party signed on as a junior partner in a Liberal-led coalition administration in the 1940s whose raison d'être was to foil the British-inspired CCF. Conservative-minded voters then shifted en masse to a Social Credit coalition from the 1950s until the 1990s. W.A.C. Bennett's conservative government (1952–72) demonstrated a red tory willingness to use the state as an instrument of economic development, most dramatically by creating BC Hydro and BC Ferries as Crown corporations. Neoconservatism has been an especially powerful current in BC since Bill Bennett's regime (1975–86), and Canada's most prominent right-wing think tank, the Vancouver-based Fraser Institute, has had its greatest influence in shaping public policy in BC. In the 1990s, some of the province's conservatives voted for a provincial Reform Party while most threw their lot in with the Liberal party. In 2010, a resurrected provincial Conservative party, led by federal Conservative MP John Cummins, emerged as a putative but as yet untested right-wing challenger to the right-wing BC Liberals. Until 2012 it prominently styled itself "BC's only true conservative party," and more recently has deployed the phrase "common sense vision" to describe its policy outlook.[52]

Religious diversity and secularism are particularly striking in BC, where older, established Christian faiths such as Anglicanism and Roman Catholicism, identified with classical conservatism, have steadily lost ground. There is a noticeable minority of evangelical Christians, especially in parts of the interior, who were politically visible in the late 1990s in response to policy changes recognizing lesbian and gay rights. Evangelicals are a less obvious political force now, and BC sports the highest provincial percentage (36) of atheists and agnostics in the land.[53] A strong current of social democracy has reinforced secularism, as has the strength of free enterprise individualism. In a provincial society of ambitious parvenus, where more residents were born outside than in it, neoconservative thinking attracts many of BC's entrepreneurial Chinese and Indian immigrants, who had begun to shift their support to the federal Conservatives and to vote for whatever provincial party most clearly embraces neoconservatism.

Conclusion

Distinctive provincial conservative traditions contribute to potential ideological tensions within the national conservative movement and the federal Conservative party. Stephen Harper's federal Conservative party, however, has been successful in reconciling the ideological fissures that characterize the different regional conservative traditions. At the party's founding in 2004, for example, Harper's neoconservative, Alberta-anchored Canadian Alliance merged with and consumed the smaller Progressive Conservative party, whose leader, Peter MacKay, hailed from the more tory Maritime region. The merger led some in the older tory mould, including former Conservative prime minister Joe Clark and former Cabinet ministers Flora MacDonald (who was born in Nova Scotia) and Lowell Murray (from New Brunswick), to exit the new party with the claim that it had left them.

This synoptic reconnaissance of provincial conservative traditions and Conservative parties reveals that they emerged from no single intellectual cauldron and that they evolved in disparate historical, partisan, and societal contexts. Diverse national and social groups with dissimilar ideological and religious orientations informed the various provincial conservative traditions and drove their Conservative parties in different directions. Not cut from a single piece of ideological cloth, provincial conservatives and Conservative parties adopted agendas that reflected their contrasting bases of support, policy orientations, and leadership.

NOTES

1 Gad Horowitz, *Canadian Labour in Politics* (Toronto: University of Toronto Press, 1968), chap. 1.
2 Analysts in the United States tend to use *neoconservative* to describe the same political and economic orientation that European analysts tend to characterize as *neoliberal*. Canadian analysts use both terms, and the analysis in this chapter considers them interchangeable while acknowledging that, in other contexts and in the hands of other analysts, there can be substantial differences between the two.
3 J. Murray Beck, "Nova Scotia: Tradition and Conservatism," in *Canadian Provincial Politics: The Party Systems of the Ten Provinces*, 2nd ed., ed. Martin Robin (Scarborough: Prentice-Hall, 1978), 200.
4 Frank MacKinnon, *The Government of Prince Edward Island* (Toronto: University of Toronto Press, 1951); Wayne Mackinnon, *The Life of the Party* (Summerside: Williams and Crue, 1973); and J.M. Bumsted, "The Only Island There Is: The Writing of Prince Edward Island History," in *The Garden Transformed: Prince Edward Island, 1945–1980*, ed. Verner Smitheram, David Milne, and Satadal Dasgupta, 11–38 (Charlottetown: Ragweed Press, 1982).
5 Nevertheless, a Conservative Acadian paper (*Le Moniteur acadien*), launched in 1867, continues to circulate.
6 Frank MacKinnon, "Prince Edward Island: Big Engine, Little Body," in Robin, *Canadian Provincial Politics*, 237.
7 Gordon O. Rothney, "The Denominational Basis of Representation in the Newfoundland Assembly, 1919–1962," *Canadian Journal of Economics and Political Science* 28, no. 4 (1962): 557–70; and E.A. Aunger, *In Search of Stability: A Comparative Study of New Brunswick and Northern Ireland* (Montreal and Kingston: McGill-Queen's University Press, 1981), 48, 62, 67, 75.
8 Hugh G. Thorburn, *Politics in New Brunswick* (Toronto: University of Toronto Press, 1961), 181.

9 Harold D. Clarke, Jane Jenson, Lawrence LeDuc, and Jon Pammett, *Political Choice in Canada* (Toronto: McGraw-Hill Ryerson, 1980), 97; and Agar Adamson and Ian Stewart, "Changing Party Politics in Atlantic Canada," in *Party Politics in Canada*, 8th ed., ed. Hugh G. Thorburn and Alan Whitehorn (Toronto: Prentice Hall, 2001), 309.

10 Peter F. Neary, "'A More than Usual ... Interest': Sir P.A. Clutterbuck's Newfoundland Impressions, 1950," *Newfoundland Studies* 3, no. 2 (1987): 258.

11 Rand Dyck, *Provincial Politics in Canada: Towards the Turn of the Century* (Scarborough: Prentice-Hall, 1996), 47–8.

12 Michael Adams, *Sex in the Snow: Canadian Social Values at the End of the Millennium* (Toronto: Viking, 1997), 204–5.

13 Warren Clark, "Pockets of Belief: Religious Attendance in Canada," *Canadian Social Trends*, catalogue no. 11-008 (Ottawa: Statistics Canada, 2003), 3.

14 Peter Clancy, James Bickerton, Rodney Haddow, and Ian Stewart, *The Savage Years: The Perils of Reinventing Government in Nova Scotia* (Halifax: Forman, 2000); and "MacAulay Praised as PEI 'Cash Cow,'" *Globe and Mail*, 14 October 2002.

15 Robert L. Stanfield, "Conservative Principles and Philosophy," in *Politics: Canada*, 8th ed., ed. Paul Fox and Graham White, 307–11 (Toronto: McGraw-Hill Ryerson, 1995); and Rodney S. Haddow, *Poverty Reform in Canada, 1958–1978: State and Class Influence in Policy Making* (Montreal and Kingston: McGill-Queen's University Press, 1993), 167.

16 Centre for Information and Research on Canada, *The Charter: Dividing or Uniting Canadians?* (Montreal: Montreal, 2002), 30, fig. 9.

17 Lowell Murray, "Don't Do It, Peter," *Globe and Mail*, 23 June 2003.

18 Quoted in "In Depth: Danny Williams," CBC News, 17 October 2006, http://www.cbc.ca/news/background/williams_danny/.

19 Frank McKenna, "Atlantic Canada: A Vision for the Future" (address to the Atlantic Vision Conference of Atlantic Canadian Premiers, Moncton, 9 October 1997), http://www.aims.ca/site/media/aims/vision.pdf.

20 Brian Lee Crowley, *Fearful Symmetry: The Fall and Rise of Canada's Founding Values* (Toronto: Key Porter Books, 2009); Roland T. Martin, *Equalization: Milestone or Millstone?* (Halifax: Atlantic Institute for Market Studies, 2001); David Murrell and Bruce Winchester, *Could Do Better 2* (Halifax: Atlantic Institute for Market Studies, 2006).

21 Paul-André Linteau, René Durocher, and Jean-Claude Robert, *Quebec: A History, 1867–1929*, trans. Robert Chodos (Toronto: Lorimer, 1983), 232–3.

22 Damien-Claude Bélanger, "Quebec History: Biographies of Prominent Quebec Historical Figures; Paul Gouin (1898–1976)," Marianopolis College,

2003, http://faculty.marianopolis.edu/c.belanger/quebechistory/bios/gouin.htm.

23 Luc Bernier, "The Beleaguered State: Québec at the End of the 1990s," *The Provincial State*, ed. Keith Brownsey and Michael Howlett (Peterborough: Broadview, 2001), 144.

24 Vincent Lemieux, "Quebec: Heaven Is Blue and Hell Is Red," in Robin, *Canadian Provincial Politics*, 248.

25 Michael B. Stein, *The Dynamics of Right-Wing Protest: A Political Analysis of Social Credit in Quebec* (Toronto: University of Toronto Press, 1973), 231.

26 Clinton Archibald, "Corporatist Tendencies in Quebec," in *Quebec: State and Society*, ed. Alain-G. Gagnon, 353–64 (Toronto: Methuen, 1984).

27 Alain-G. Gagnon and Khayyam Z. Paltiel, "Toward *Maître chez nous:* The Ascendancy of a Balzacian Bourgeoisie in Quebec," *Queen's Quarterly* 93, no. 4 (1986): 740.

28 Luc Bernier, "State-Owned Enterprises in Québec: The Full Cycle, 1960–1990," in *Québec: State and Society*, 2nd ed., ed. Alain-G. Gagnon (Scarborough: Nelson, 1993): chap. 14; and *Designing a Blueprint for Canadians: Guiding Principles and Policy Priorities of the Progressive Conservative Party of Canada* (Ottawa: Progressive Conservative Party, 1996), 5–7.

29 Lucien Bouchard et al., *For a Clear-Eyed Vision of Quebec*, 19 October 2005, 9, http://www.pourunquebeclucide.info/documents/manifesto.pdf; and Joseph Facal, *Quelque chose comme un grand people* (Montreal: Boréal, 2010).

30 Eric Duhaime, quoted in Philip Authier, "Rumblings on the Right in Quebec," *Montreal Gazette*, 8 November 2010.

31 The Gallup Poll, vol. 60, nos 18, 28, and 30 (7, 8 March and 18 April 2000), and vol. 61, nos 17, 22, and 85 (8 March, 18 April, and 12 December 2001).

32 Centre for Research and Information on Canada, *The Charter: Dividing or Uniting Canadians?* (CRIC: Ottawa, 2002), table 6, 30.

33 Peter G. Goheen, "Symbols in the Streets: Parades in Victorian Urban Canada," *Urban History Review* 18, no. 3 (1990): 237–43.

34 "The Constructive Platform of the Progressive Conservative Party in the Province of Ontario, July 3, 1943," *Globe and Mail*, 9 and 17 July 1943; quoted in Dyck, *Provincial Politics in Canada*, 338.

35 John Wilson, "The Red Tory Province: Reflections on the Character of Ontario Political Culture," in *The Government and Politics of Ontario*, 2nd ed., ed. Donald C. MacDonald (Toronto: Van Nostrand Reinhold, 1980), 214.

36 "Tim Hudak's 10 Ideas to Create Jobs in 2010: Bring Public Sector Agreements in Line with Reality," 10 for 2010, http://10for2010.ca/bring-public-sector-agreements-in-line-with-reality/.

37 Rodmond Roblin, *Initiative and Referendum*, 27 January 1913, R.A.C. Manning Papers, Provincial Archives of Manitoba; and *Federal-Provincial Conference of First Ministers on the Constitution, Verbatim Transcript*, Ottawa, 8–13 September 1980 (Ottawa: Canadian Intergovernmental Conference Secretariat, n.d.).

38 Quoted in Nelson Wiseman, *Social Democracy in Manitoba* (Winnipeg: University of Manitoba Press, 1985), 72.

39 Quoted in Frank B. Edwards, "Call It Meaningful, or Call It Mean, He Believed in the Right-Wing Rhetoric," *Globe and Mail*, 26 January 2011.

40 Seymour Martin Lipset, *Agrarian Socialism: The Co-operative Commonwealth Federation in Saskatchewan* (1950; Garden City: Anchor, 1968), table 36, 235.

41 Leslie Biggs and Mark Stobbe, eds., *Divine Rules in Saskatchewan: A Decade of Hope and Hardship* (Saskatoon: Fifth House, 1991); and James Pitsula and Ken Rasmussen, *Privatizing a Province: The New Right in Saskatchewan* (Vancouver: New Star Books, 1990).

42 "Producer Vote Supports Single-Desk Sale of Barley," *Agrivision*, April 1997; and "One Vote Could Decide Barley Marketing," *Agriweek*, 11 November 1997.

43 Eric Crouse, "The 'Great Revival': Evangelical Revivalism, Methodism and Bourgeois Order in Early Calgary," *Alberta History* 47, no. 1 (1999): 18.

44 *Census of Canada, 1921*, vol. 2, table 50, 298–330, table 53, 334–40, and table 71, 480–2; Howard Palmer, *Patterns of Prejudice: A History of Nativism in Alberta* (Toronto: McClelland and Stewart, 1982), 67; and Canada, Bureau of Statistics, *Origin, Birthplace, Nationality and Language of the Canadian People: A Census Study Based on the Census of 1921 and Supplementary Data* (Ottawa: Bureau of Statistics, 1929), table 46, 99.

45 William Kirby Rolph, *Henry Wise Wood of Alberta* (Toronto: University of Toronto Press, 1950), chap. 8.

46 Mark McClung, "The Outlook of Teachers in Alberta," and H.L. Stewart, "The Views of Teachers in the Maritime Provinces," *Canada and Her Great Neighbor: Sociological Surveys of Opinions and Attitudes in Canada concerning the United States*, ed. H.F. Angus (1938; New York: Russell & Russell, 1970), 114 and 117.

47 Nelson Wiseman, "The American Imprint on Alberta Politics," *Great Plains Quarterly* 31 (Winter 2011): 39–53.

48 Government of Alberta, *The Case of Alberta – Addressed to the Sovereign People of Canada and Their Governments* (Edmonton: 1938).

49 Peter Smith, "Alberta: Experiments in Governance: From Social Credit to the Klein Revolution," in Brownsey and Howlett, *The Provincial State in Canada*, 303.

50 Josh Wingrove, "Will Redford's Cabinet Help or Hinder Her Relationship with Ottawa?," *Globe and Mail*, 18 October 2011, http://www.theglobe andmail.com/news/politics/will-redfords-cabinet-help-or-hinder-her-relationship-with-ottawa/article2203991/; and Chantal Hebert, "You Want Change? So Try Voting," *Toronto Star*, 18 October 2011.

51 Gordon S. Galbraith, "British Columbia," in *The Provincial Political Systems: Comparative Essays*, ed. David J. Bellamy, Jon H. Pammett, and D.C. Rowat (Toronto: Methuen, 1976), chap. 5; Martin Robin, "British Columbia: The Company Province," in Robin, *Canadian Provincial Politics*, chap. 10; and Martin Robin, *Radical Politics and Canadian Labour, 1880–1930* (Kingston: Industrial Relations Centre, Queen's University, 1968), 290.

52 BC Conservatives now regularly make use of the "common sense" terminology that was so central to the Ontario Conservatives under Mike Harris (http://bcconservative.ca/). Until at least February 2012, the tag line that was most prominently attached to the party name was the "only true conservative party" (site accessed 10 February 2012).

53 Statistics Canada, "Population by Religion, by Province and Territory (2001 Census)," http://www.statcan.gc.ca/tables-tableaux/sum-som/l01/cst01/demo30c-eng.htm.

12 American Protestantism and the Roots of "Populist Conservatism" in Alberta

CLARK BANACK

Seymour Martin Lipset argued that the distinct religious histories of Canada and the United States have helped to shape the unique political values of each country.[1] America, following its revolutionary break from Britain, embraced a congregational and voluntary style of Protestantism that encouraged a participatory and egalitarian populist spirit prone to protest when encountering traditional hierarchy. Canada resisted revolution and thus maintained strong links with Old World churches and their hierarchical structures that encouraged deference to traditional sources of authority among adherents. Surely this is an oversimplification but, within this chapter, I want to build slightly on the general dichotomy presented by Lipset and suggest that the unique variant of conservatism that has dominated Alberta politics for nearly a century, which I label "populist conservatism," owes much of its essence to religious interpretations that emanated out of the American, rather than British, Protestant tradition. Thus, from its very beginning, Alberta's politics has been infused with a conservatism that is at odds with the British-based "tory" conservatism that played such an important role in the ideological development of much of the rest of English Canada.

Tory conservatism was grounded in a broad desire to preserve those institutions such as the British monarchy or the Anglican Church that promoted the moral order demanded of the Christian God. Such a goal required the acceptance of certain social hierarchies that could curtail the inclinations of the weak-willed commoner and thus ensure social stability. Inside Canada, this tory variant dominated the early federal Conservative party, which, from Macdonald until at least Diefenbaker, embraced a collectivist and protectionist ideology that allowed the state to restrain certain individual liberties in the name of tradition and the common good. Correspondingly, America's whole-hearted embrace of individualism and democracy was viewed with great suspicion.[2] Alberta's populist conservatism shares this Christian foundation and thus also sought to preserve the institutions capable of spreading this moral message in the name of social stability but it did so from an individualistic and egalitarian perspective that rejects the hierarchical tendencies of tory conservatism. Indeed, there has always been a radical populist streak within Alberta conservatism that stresses the capacity of the common individual and the need to ensure his or her freedom from the oppressive nature of certain established authorities.

Of course, it is widely acknowledged that Alberta has been strongly influenced by patterns of American republican political thought that developed largely in opposition to such tory sentiment. Nelson Wiseman, in a critique of C.B. Macpherson's class-based interpretation of Alberta politics, noted the "radical populist liberalism" carried north by the wave of "Great Plains" American farmers that "played an influential role in Alberta that was unparalleled in Canada." This was "a more militant, more radical, less tory form of petit-bourgeois liberalism than was the Canadian norm."[3] However, by labelling the ideology of such settlers as a straightforward "populist liberalism," we have overlooked the significant Protestant Christian foundation of American agrarian populism and the conservative tendencies it encouraged.[4] This chapter seeks to rectify this gap by demonstrating the links between the broad American Protestant tradition and early Alberta political thought within the United Farmers of Alberta (UFA) and the Alberta Social Credit League who together ruled the province for fifty of its most formative years.[5] Despite important differences, this shared "American Protestant" heritage ensured both parties were built upon a similar populist conservative foundation that grew out of this religious tradition. The remainder of this chapter expands on this assertion by first providing a brief overview of the populist conservatism that emerged out of the American Protestant tradition before considering in more detail the manner by which this American religious perspective influenced the thought of Henry Wise Wood of the UFA and William Aberhart and Ernest Manning of Alberta Social Credit. The chapter concludes with some thoughts on the persistence of the populist conservative sentiment within contemporary Alberta.

The Populist Conservatism of American Protestantism

To grasp the nature of the conservatism encouraged by American Protestantism it is necessary first to acknowledge the influence of the

Puritans who, in the mid-seventeenth century, planted the first seeds of a religion that would grow to be a distinctly American version of what George Marsden labels a "dissenter Protestantism."[6] Dissent in this context refers to the seriousness with which early American Christians believed they were "completing the Protestant Reformation" on American soil, something the Europeans, stuck in their hierarchical class structures and traditions, had left unfinished.[7] Central to his act of "completion" was a rededication by the Puritans to two key Protestant tenets: the sole authority of the Bible and the necessity of developing a personal relationship with God built upon a conversion or "rebirth." The revivalism of the First Great Awakening in the first half of the eighteenth century built upon these dual tenets but did so in a manner that further emphasized the Protestant ideal by rejecting the expertise of the highly educated Puritan clergyman and insisting upon the layman's ability to interpret scripture and experience a personal conversion in an emotional revival setting rather than within a formal church. The result was a shift away from an English-based Puritanism towards an indigenous American evangelicalism that laid the necessary groundwork for the rapid expansion of "populist" religious practices following the Revolution.[8]

In the course of documenting religiosity in post-Revolution America, Nathan Hatch has demonstrated how increasingly assertive common people, building on the gains of the First Great Awakening, demanded unpretentious pastors, down-to-earth sermons, and local control of churches.[9] It was out of this growing demand that the Second Great Awakening emerged during the early nineteenth century, a period of intense large-scale revivalism that generated many new and diverse religious sects led by "folksy" pastors that urged much congregational involvement, thereby further facilitating democratic sentiment by creating important new avenues for direct local participation.[10] One of these newly created sects was the Disciples of Christ, a progressive movement dedicated to the reconciliation and unification of the various denominations of the Protestant Church by stressing a return to "primitive Christianity" based solely upon the teachings of Christ.[11] It was within this sect that long-time UFA president Henry Wise Wood, born and raised in Missouri, was immersed in the American evangelical ideals that rejected the formal and hierarchical nature of traditional Christianity and its tendency to elevate the learned clergy.

The empowerment of the common people was supported further by the theology of Charles Finney, a leading revivalist between 1825 and 1835 who began explicitly promoting the notion of conversion as an act of choice by a free individual rather than one completed solely by God. The adoption of this interpretation of spiritual conversion, which represented a revolutionary split from the Calvinist doctrine of the Puritans, had no trouble gaining support, as it coalesced rather neatly with the broader republican ideals that were prominent in post-Revolution America.[12] This emphasis on individual capacity, which was aided in America by the popularity of the Scottish Philosophy of Common Sense – which emphasized the capabilities of the "common man" to interpret reality by way of his "common sense" – was essential, for it provided a philosophical foundation for the American Christian to personally experience God and freely choose to accept his grace through conversion, thus fulfilling a fundamental requirement for salvation.[13] Of course, the flip side of this coin has been, according to Richard Hofstadter, a tendency towards anti-intellectualism, "a resentment and suspicion of the life of the mind and those who are considered to represent it," in American life.[14] It was out of this anti-intellectual sentiment that Christian fundamentalism, based upon an extreme biblical literalism, began to grow into a significant force that opposed the more progressive sects in America following the Civil War.[15] It is this particular religious perspective that would eventually influence the political thought of William Aberhart, founder of the Alberta Social Credit League.

Obviously, the above synopsis fails to do justice to the rich and diverse development of American religious history, but it does, I think, highlight the manner by which American Protestantism encourages a conservative worldview at odds with the British "tory" tradition. The more familiar aspects of this conservatism are not hard to uncover. From the Puritans, through the First and Second Great Awakenings, and into the contemporary period, the absolute authority of the Christian Bible has remained paramount. This continuity has ensured a long-running adherence to a particular moral code derived from the word of God that places divine restrictions on the conduct of individuals. Beyond specific biblical commandments, American Protestantism emphasized the need for an "orderly life" built upon sobriety, discipline, and hard work, upon which a proper family could be raised.[16] Given the fallen nature of humanity described in scripture, the societal stability and order necessary for the further spreading of God's word required the constant protection and maintenance of institutions that could both educate and police individuals with respect to God's laws. It is in this spirit that one finds religious groups from nearly any period of American history praising the church and family as the central pillars of society due to their function as moral/religious educators, while occasionally demanding the state enact legislation that can assist with such guidance.

Of course, "tory" conservatism also begins from a general Christian foundation that acknowledges the sinful nature of humanity and the corresponding need for traditional institutions and certain laws to ensure social order. However, American Protestantism did not bind these concerns to a belief in a natural social hierarchy, a staple of tory conservatism. Rather, American Protestantism, with its individualistic conception of faith and strong emphasis on the intellectual and moral capacity of the "common man," radically challenges such hierarchical relationships. Unsurprisingly, such an outlook produces a strong populist ethic among followers who, in their quest for personal religious experience, seek political structures that allow for the individual freedom required to live their faith. Yet this individualism, and the corresponding anti-establishment sentiment, remains restricted by a sacred code of conduct derived from the Christian Bible.[17] As Phillip Hammond has argued, American Protestantism "saturated America with the idea that people should be free to do pretty much as they like, as long as they look out for themselves ... and, of course, behave."[18] The result is an individual-based populist conservatism that was eventually imported to Alberta, not simply by the migration of American settlers but more concretely in the political thought of two devout men whose Christian outlook would form the foundation of two unique and influential political movements.

Religion and Political Thought in the UFA

Henry Wise Wood, president of the UFA from 1916 until 1931, was easily the movement's most philosophical and influential figure, despite the prominent role played by many others in the organization. Consequently, he has garnered a large amount of interest from scholars eager to make sense of the UFA's participatory nature, its support for economic co-operatives, and its peculiar advancement of "group government." However, aside from mentioning his background in the Missouri branch of the Disciples of Christ, academics have largely glossed over the influence of his particular Christian perspective.[19] The Disciples, a progressive sect that emerged from the revivalism of post-Revolution America, rejected the hierarchical nature of traditional churches in favour of a co-operative, egalitarian, and participatory structure founded upon the social teachings of Christ. Central to this structure was a strict adherence to a "populist hermeneutic" that viewed the common individual as possessing the intellectual capacity required to interpret the teachings of Christ on his or her own.[20] Within this section I will attempt to provide a brief account of the relationship between this religious perspective and the political thought of Wood.[21]

Wood, following English evolutionary philosopher Herbert Spencer, viewed human beings as naturally social beings whose destiny was to construct a proper social system within which they could flourish. The march towards this social system was guided by the ongoing cosmic struggle between two opposing forces, the true and false laws, those of co-operation and competition. Eventually, these forces would collide one final time, producing a definite victory of good over evil, co-operation over competition.[22] It was up to humanity, however, to ensure the spirit of co-operation would prevail. The precise articulation of this spirit, what Wood deemed "the realm of spiritual science," became the central focus of his social thought.[23]

Given his American Protestant background, it should come as no surprise that Wood accounts for the ills of society by stressing the fallen nature of humanity. He argued that the individual was initially guided by "the animal spirit," that of competition, and until he or she responded to "the call of nature for co-operation," society could not change for the better.[24] Building upon the theology of the Disciples, Wood believed this "call" was found in the teachings of Christ, who demanded that individuals live according to the principle of co-operation, which represented "the climax of the true principles governing individual relationships."[25] Doing so would enable the literal Kingdom of Heaven to be established on earth. However, the individual must first complete a personal regeneration and become a co-operative rather than a competitive being before he or she is ready to contribute to the construction of the coming Kingdom of Heaven, the perfect social system.

Because he emphasized the concrete societal benefits to be derived from the gospels, Wood has often been grouped together with other prominent prairie "social gospel" advocates such as Salem Bland, J.S. Woodsworth, and William Irvine. However, these religious progressives blamed capitalism, not "original sin," for the economic oppression of the people and therefore sought change on an institutional rather than personal level.[26] As Macpherson has noted, Wood's theory assumes that humans are naturally "trading animals" and thus he never considered the merits of an economic system built upon anything other than the market [27] However, he believed that the false law of competition dominated the economic system, and the terms of trading had thus been engineered to favour the creation of monopolies that exploited the common individual. The solution, therefore, did not lie in socialism but rather in a straightforward shift in spirit on behalf of, first, individuals and second, the groups they participate in. Indeed, Wood returned to the teachings of Christ to offer a solution to the economic troubles the masses were facing: "Until the problems of trade are solved according to the laws of Christ, His will cannot maintain on earth, and His great prayer cannot be answered. The solutions of the economic problems must be spiritual, rather than intellectual. Henry George cannot solve them, neither can Carl Marx [sic]. Both may, and will give valuable assistance, but the solution is beyond them. Christ can and must solve them."[28]

Wood's concrete proposal for ensuring that Christ's law of co-operation would overtake the economic and political realm was his demand for "group government." In an effort to lessen the political influence of those who profited excessively through competitiveness he called for the replacement of traditional political parties by occupational groups. The particular economic interests shared by the members of each group would encourage them to co-operate with their fellows and thus resist the seductions of the industrial lobby and contribute to an authentic democratic dialogue. The organization of politics around these occupational groups represented for Wood the initial stage of the social regeneration whereby the true social law of co-operation is introduced into the political realm by a collection of "regenerated" commoners who occupied these groups. It was for this reason that Wood continually stressed that the UFA was not a political party but rather an occupational group and that the overall goals of the organization were not simply the immediate improvement of economic conditions for agrarians but also the broader goal of working to establish Christ's kingdom by practising the law of co-operation. Indeed, the notion of co-operation was the moral essence of the organization.

From this brief overview of Wood's thought it should be clear that it grew directly out of his Christian interpretation. Surely this interpretation was economically and democratically progressive, as were many of the subsequent political goals of the UFA, but it also contained important conservative elements. Adhering to the central tenets of American Protestantism, Wood insisted that only through an individual rebirth in Christ could society improve. This required personal study of the

Gospels and an individual dedication to the moral code demanded by Christ. The most obvious lesson to be derived was that of co-operation, but the UFA also focused much energy on educating agrarian youth on the parables of Christ and the broader Protestant ethic, including hard work and self-discipline required to become proper, contributing citizens.[29] By demanding individual responsibility, guided by basic Christian precepts, the UFA could conserve the institutions of democratic governance and commercialism that were "natural" but in need of reform. On the other hand, the appeal to the individual's capacity to interpret both the moral lessons of the Bible and the nature of political and economic problems the agrarians faced offered a radical challenge to the more traditional attitude of deference to established power present within orthodox versions of conservative political thought. In fact, it was only through the common individual's spiritual conversion, which did not require the blessing of the traditional clergy, that a society dominated by competitive elites become more "co-operative" and thereby allowed the common individual to find freedom from political and economic oppression. Thus, Wood's political thought, derived from his religious perspective, maintained both the conservative morality and the "populist" and egalitarian orientation that blossomed in post-Revolution America.

Religion and Political Thought in the Alberta Social Credit League

Like Wood, William Aberhart and his protégé Ernest Manning were devout Christians whose political thought and action grew out of their religious foundation. A teacher and fundamentalist radio broadcaster by trade, Aberhart rode to political power in 1935 on the promise to end the Depression in Alberta by introducing social credit economics, a controversial plan that would issue "credit" to citizens who lacked the necessary purchasing power required to keep the economy churning. Although Aberhart attempted at times to paint the British-born social credit economic system as a divine plan, this section focuses more closely on the manner by which his and Manning's theology influenced their attitude towards social reform in general terms. Emerging from the same American Protestant tradition that had earlier produced the Disciples of Christ, Aberhart's Christian fundamentalism was grounded in the same general American commitment to "completing the Reformation" and thus placed significant emphasis on both the authority of the Bible and the capacity of ordinary people to interpret it properly as they moved towards a personal conversion. However, a more specific commitment to a strict literal interpretation of the Bible, driven by an increasing displeasure with the interpretations of more progressive Christians, led most fundamentalists, including Aberhart and Manning, towards premillennial dispensationalism.

Dispensationalism was a method of scriptural interpretation based on the notion that history has been divided by God into separate "dispensations."[30] In direct contrast to the progressive religious outlook of Wood, premillennial dispensationalists believed that the literal Kingdom of God was approaching, but it would not occur in the current dispensation, often labelled the "age of grace." The shift to the "millennial" dispensation, wherein Christ would establish his kingdom, would occur solely at the bequest of God, not through the works of individuals committed to social reform. Therefore, the responsibility of humankind within the current dispensation was not to perfect society but rather to seek and accept the righteousness that God freely offers. This required a personal "rebirth" in Christ that rectified one's sinful nature and prepared one for the millennial reign of Christ.

Because the coming of the Kingdom of God was understood to be completely outside the realm of human agency, many have assumed that the overarching logic of this outlook was a complete rejection of social action.[31] However, as Marsden has argued, premillennialists have in many cases supported public and private social programs so long as they were understood as complementary to the regenerating work of Christ that aimed to "save souls."[32] This openness to social action is not "antithetical" to the logic of premillennialism but rather is a consequence of the one further earthly task required of "reborn" Christians: evangelization, the dispensing of the word of God to those not yet "saved." The desire to do so was a central component of the larger "love thy neighbour" spirit that would naturally overcome the "reborn" individual. Other worldly acts would follow, especially those related to feeding, clothing, and healing the needy. Importantly, however, these social or charitable acts were never aimed at perfecting society. It is from this perspective that one can begin to see the motivation that lay behind Aberhart's long-time involvement in radio evangelism and sudden interest in social credit economics.[33]

Aberhart's conversion to Major Douglas's social credit economic theories can be understood only within the context of the suffering he witnessed during the Depression. He was introduced to the theory in the summer of a particularly tough year (1932), and by that fall he was enthusiastically supporting social credit within his radio broadcasts.[34] According to Manning, Aberhart's sudden interest in economic reform was due first to his general Christian commitment to be "thy brother's keeper," a natural response for the born-again Christian who was overwhelmed with a love for both God and his people.[35] For Aberhart, the Depression inflicted a wide-ranging poverty that could not be rectified with the "tough love" strategies commonly associated with Christian fundamentalism. Poverty was not the result of individual laziness or ineptitude but rather an economic system that allowed greedy financiers to overcharge for credit. Acting from his Christian sense of duty to his fellows, Aberhart led the charge against this system with the goal of eliminating the poverty that was crushing Albertans. However, this goal was a means to a further, more religious end.

Aberhart understood such poverty as an impingement on the freedom of the individual and his or her development. As Manning would later explain, Social Credit's association with Christianity was based upon its recognition of "the supremacy of the individual as a divinely created creature, possessing, as a result of divine creation, certain inalienable rights that must be respected and preserved."[36] Therefore, the goal of the Social Credit philosophy was "a free society in which the individual would have the maximum opportunity to develop himself." This required addressing the poverty of the Depression, because the "attention to the cultural realm of life was limited by the economic conditions of that time."[37] Douglas had often mentioned the importance of individual development but, from Aberhart's religious perspective, this development was interpreted to be primarily spiritual. Aberhart was already spending much of his time spreading the word through radio, but what good would it do if poverty was preventing the spiritual development of Albertans?

An article from the *Alberta Social Credit Chronicle* captured this concern by noting, "Crushing and demoralizing poverty obscures men's spirituality." Social credit economics would end this poverty and "only then would it be possible to appreciate completely the message of Him."[38] Aberhart seconded this contention during his first electoral campaign when he suggested, "Much of man's selfishness is produced today through the mad scramble to get the necessities of life. We have to trample one another down to do this."[39] Upon encountering the constitutional roadblocks to implementing social credit policies, Aberhart complained, "The money monopolists will not issue the money tickets to enable the great clumsy, outworn financial system to work so the people must suffer privation and want. They must exist in undesirable depressing conditions that cannot improve their spiritual development."[40] And in 1939 he stated bluntly, "I am convinced that dire poverty and want makes people bitter and turn away from God."[41]

Thus, the goal of political action was for Aberhart and Manning significantly different from Wood's. Rather than encouraging the "regenerated" individual to perfect society, Aberhart and Manning simply sought to create the conditions necessary for individual spiritual conversion. No doubt this distinction ensured a radically different political program between the UFA and Social Credit.[42] However, on a broader level, both movements adhered to the basic tenets of the American Protestant tradition and therefore both encouraged a general populist conservatism. The conservative foundation of Social Credit is not difficult to see. The intense devotion to biblical literalism that characterized Christian fundamentalism strongly emphasized the moral laws of God. Aberhart and Manning went beyond Wood in this regard by continually lamenting the declining morality of citizens, displaying distaste for alcohol, cards, dancing, and commercial or sporting events on Sundays, and even attacking journalists for daring to question an organization as divinely inspired as Social Credit. However, the emphasis they placed on the individual's capacity for spiritual rebirth, and especially the conditions such conversion required, committed Aberhart and Manning to an equally intense devotion to individual liberty not typical of tory conservatism. Thus, a certain radical anti-establishmentarianism grew out of their opposition to any institution that impinged on the freedom of the individual required to pursue spiritual rebirth. For Aberhart, this meant attacking the "fifty big shots" whom he understood to be withholding credit and thus causing "poverty in the midst of plenty." For Manning, who would preside over far more prosperous economic conditions in Alberta, this meant supporting the free market in the face of an emerging socialism that threatened to subdue the individual to the collective.[43] Of course, Manning's shift away from social credit economics and towards an uninhibited capitalism has garnered suggestions that he and Aberhart were, ideologically, distinct political animals.[44] However, from the perspective of their shared religious foundation that exalted the common individual and his or her liberty, we see their divergent economic policies were simply circumstantial means towards the same end.

Conclusion: Populist Conservatism in Contemporary Alberta

For both the UFA and Social Credit, Christianity was the foundation from which their political thought and action grew. Of course, Wood drew from a more progressive religious outlook than Aberhart and Manning, and this produced a much more optimistic account of the possibilities contained within political action. Yet, from a broader comparative perspective, they shared a commitment to a general populist conservative sentiment that demanded adherence to a Christian moral code while simultaneously celebrating the moral and intellectual capacities of the common individual and his or her right to be free. This was embodied in the outlook of both the UFA and Alberta Social Credit and sets them apart from those parties in much of the rest of Canada that were built upon the less individualistic and more deferential "tory" conservative tradition.

Up to this point it has been my general argument that such a difference owes much to the unique influence of the American Protestant tradition on early Albertan political thought. I now want to briefly build on this thesis by turning to contemporary Alberta politics, for it is surely this general populist conservatism, rather than the particular religion-based political arguments in favour of "group government" or "social credit economics," that endures today. Of course, despite the existence of pockets of religious-based social conservatism, Alberta is far more secular today than in the time of UFA or Social Credit. A more influential form of contemporary conservatism is therefore characterized by the widespread belief in "individual responsibility," a notion that is understood largely in secular terms, despite its clear Protestant roots.

Noting central aspects of what I have labelled "populist conservatism," Katherine Fierlbeck has described contemporary Alberta's political culture as a "curious combination of market liberalism and the values of evangelical, fundamental Protestantism."[45] Indeed, two dominant Alberta-based political parties, the provincial Progressive Conservatives (PCs) and the former federal Reform Party, seem to embody this "curious combination" of libertarianism and traditionalism. Thus, echoing Hammond's assessment of the legacy of Protestantism in America, I suggest that contemporary Alberta continues to abide by the populist conservative idea that "people should be free to do pretty much as they like, as long as they look out for themselves ... and, of course, behave."

The sudden rise of the Reform Party in the late 1980s and early 1990s certainly owes much to basic regional discontent, but its success in

Alberta was also due to the powerful legacies of its populist conservative foundation. Reform founder Preston Manning, son of Ernest Manning and a devout evangelical Christian himself, certainly tapped into a growing belief among ordinary Albertans of an oppressive and unresponsive federal government, but also a concern for general moral decay within society. Reform's platform demanded increased mechanisms for direct democracy, an end to government interference in the market, and a return to "common sense" approaches to law and order (with a tinge of religion-based social conservatism at its foundation). This was founded upon a belief in the capacity of the ordinary individual and the necessity of ensuring his or her liberty, while at the same time insisting on individual responsibility, protection of the family, and the relevance of a general moral code based on Christianity.

The contemporary provincial PC party of Alberta has similarly demonstrated a commitment to populist conservative themes, especially since confidence in Peter Lougheed's "state-led" economic strategy eroded in the late 1980s and a more blatant pro-market, anti-statist sentiment began to re-emerge. This culminated in the PCs' unleashing a significant reduction in government expenditures under Ralph Klein in the early 1990s, a move that represented a clear desire to re-prioritize the freedom of the common individual within the marketplace. However, as Claude Denis has noted, these dramatic spending cuts were accompanied by a largely unspoken attempt to instil self-discipline in the population, "admonishing individuals and communities to become responsible and independent, [and] castigating as un-Albertan whoever is not inclined or able to join the crusade."[46] The stress on individual freedom, therefore, was paired with the demand, however implicit, that citizens ought to behave in a "responsible" way. This was in addition to the many conservative social policy pronouncements made by the PCs, including a particular reluctance with respect to gay rights, that were structured around the demands of religious conservatives seeking to preserve the "traditional family" in the 1990s and early 2000s.[47]

Perhaps the most interesting recent occurrence in Alberta politics that points towards the continued strength of this populist conservative sentiment is the sudden emergence of the provincial Wildrose Party. Positioning itself to the right of the long-ruling PC's, the Wildrose is an amalgam of fiscal and social conservatives who advocate a further reduction to the size and scope of the state. Although they temporarily polled well ahead of the governing party, including throughout the majority of the 2012 provincial election campaign, the emergence and subsequent electoral victory of new PC leader Alison Redford has seemingly tempered Wildrose support, at least for the moment.[48] Yet as a cloud of fiscal uncertainty forms over the province due to surprisingly low resource revenues, Alberta citizens will eventually be forced to choose between Redford's PCs, who have indicated a willingness to allow a more active state, or the sternly right-wing anti-statism of the Wildrose, whose commitment to individual liberty and demand for personal responsibility now represent the purest form of "populist conservatism" in the provincial arena. Despite the PCs victory in 2012, it remains to be seen if Alberta will return to a lengthy phase of increased state involvement reminiscent of Lougheed's reign in the 1970s and 1980s or will recommit itself to the stern anti-statism now championed most clearly by the Wildrose. Either way, one senses that populist conservative themes related to both individual freedom and personal responsibility will continue to inform the province's politics.

This contemporary debate over the proper size and scope of the state is obviously a long way from Wood's goal of overcoming the hyper-competitiveness of the marketplace or Aberhart's call for the state to issue credit to all citizens. Yet it is important to see these rather distinct economic philosophies, both historically and more recently, as unique answers to the same question: how to ensure the freedom of the common individual while at the same time encouraging him or her to follow a traditional moral code built around individual self-discipline and the maintenance of the traditional family? Of course, examples of this particular sentiment have arisen in other parts of Canada, but nowhere has the embrace of this ideology been as persistent or as complete as it has in Alberta. And, as I have argued, a central reason why this is so can be traced back to the initial influence of American, rather than British, religious interpretations on the formative strands of political thought in Alberta.

NOTES

1 See Seymour Martin Lipset, *Continental Divide: The Values and Institutions of the United States and Canada* (New York: Routledge, 1990), chap. 5.

2 The classic Canadian articulation and defence of this "tory" conservative variant remains: George Grant, *Lament for a Nation* (Toronto: McClelland and Stewart, 1965).

3 Nelson Wiseman, "The Pattern of Prairie Politics," *Queen's Quarterly* 88, no. 2 (1981): 311–12; C.B. Macpherson, *Democracy in Alberta* (Toronto: University of Toronto Press, 1953).

4 For a discussion of the role played by Protestantism in American populist movements, see Rhys H. Williams and Susan M. Alexander, "Religious Rhetoric in American Populism: Civil Religion as Movement Ideology," *Journal for the Scientific Study of Religion* 33, no. 1 (1994): 1–15; and Joe Creech, *Righteous Indignation: Religion and the Populist Revolution* (Chicago: University of Illinois Press, 2006).

5 The UFA held political office from 1921 to 1935. Social Credit ruled from 1935 to 1971.

6 George M. Marsden, *Religion and American Culture* (Orlando: Harcourt Brace Jovanovich, 1990), 45.

7 Frank Lambert, *Religion in American Politics: A Short History* (Princeton: Princeton University Press, 2008), 17.

8 Mark A. Noll, *A History of Christianity in the United States and Canada* (Grand Rapids: Wm B. Eerdmans, 1992), 100–5.

9 Nathan O. Hatch, *The Democratization of American Christianity* (New Haven: Yale University Press, 1989), 6, 9.

10 Donald G. Matthews, "The Second Great Awakening as an Organizing Process, 1780–1830: An Hypothesis," *American Quarterly* 21, no. 1 (1969): 39.

11 Wilfred Ernest Garrison and Alfred T. DeGroot, *The Disciples of Christ: A History* (St Louis: Bethany, 1948).

12 Marsden, *Religion and American Culture*, 52–4.

13 For a more in-depth consideration of the relationship between "common sense" philosophy and evangelicalism, see Mark A. Noll, "Common Sense Traditions and American Evangelical Thought," *American Quarterly* 37, no. 2 (1985): 216–38.

14 Richard Hofstadter, *Anti-Intellectualism in American Life* (New York: Alfred A. Knopf, 1962), 7, and chaps 3–5.

15 George M. Marsden, "Fundamentalism as an American Phenomenon: A Comparison with English Evangelicalism," *Church History* 46 (1977): 215–32. A more detailed history of American fundamentalism is available in George M. Marsden, *Fundamentalism and American Culture*, 2nd ed. (New York: Oxford University Press, 2006).

16 Charles Taylor, *A Secular Age* (Cambridge: Harvard University Press, 2007), 451–2.

17 The conservative and radical tension within American Protestantism is discussed further in William G. McLoughlin, "Revivalism," in *The Rise of Adventism*, ed. Edwin S. Gaustad, 125–30 (New York: Harper and Row, 1974).

18 Phillip E. Hammond, *The Protestant Presence in Twentieth-Century America: Religion and Political Culture* (Albany: State University of New York Press, 1992), 45.

19 See W.L. Morton, "The Social Philosophy of Henry Wise Wood," *Agricultural History* 22, no. 2 (1948): 114–23; William Kirby Rolph, *Henry Wise Wood of Alberta* (Toronto: University of Toronto Press, 1950), 9–11; and Bradford James Rennie, *The Rise of Agrarian Democracy: The United Farmers and Farm Women of Alberta, 1909–1921* (Toronto: University of Toronto Press, 2000), 212–13.

20 Hatch, *Democratization of American Christianity*, 71.

21 A more detailed consideration of religion's impact on Wood's political thought is available in Clark Banack, "Religion and Political Thought in Alberta" (PhD diss., University of British Columbia, 2012).

22 H.W. Wood, "The Significance of Democratic Group Organization: Part One," the *UFA*, March 1922, 5; and Wood, "The Significance of Democratic Group Organization: Part Four," *The UFA*, ed. Terry O'Neill (15 April 1922), 25, 27. An insightful account of Wood's social theory, minus its religious foundations, is available in Macpherson, *Democracy in Alberta*.

23 H.W. Wood, "My Religion," *Winnipeg Free Press*, n.d., file M-255-47, Earl G. Cook Fonds, Glenbow-Alberta Museum Archives, Calgary, Alberta.

24 H.W. Wood, "Social Regeneration" (speech to the Calgary Labour Church, 30 April 1922), file M-1157-102, Walter Norman and Amelia Turner Smith Fonds, Glenbow-Alberta Museum Archives (G-AMA), Calgary, Alberta.

25 Wood, "My Religion."

26 Richard Allen, "The Social Gospel as the Religion of the Agrarian Revolt," in *Riel to Reform: A History of Protest in Western Canada*, ed. George Melnyk, 138-47 (Saskatoon: Fifth House, 1992). For a thorough discussion of the goals of the "pure" social gospel advocates, see Richard Allen, *The Social Passion: Religion and Social Reform in Canada 1914–1928* (Toronto: University of Toronto Press, 1971), 151–2; and Allen, "Salem Bland and the Spirituality of the Social Gospel," in *Prairie Spirit: Perspectives on the Heritage of the United Church of Canada in the West*, ed. D.L. Butcher, C. MacDonald, M.E. McPherson, and R.R. Watts (Winnipeg: University of Manitoba Press, 1985), 227.

27 Macpherson, *Democracy in Alberta*, 34.

28 H.W. Wood, "Observe U.F.A. Sunday, May 27," *Grain Growers Guide*, 18 April 1917.

29 See Irene Parlby, "Mrs Parlby's Address," *Grain Growers Guide*, 29 January 1919.

30 Aberhart's adherence to dispensationalism is explored in David R. Elliott, "The Devil and William Aberhart: The Nature and Function of His Eschatology," *Studies in Religion* 9, no. 3 (1980): 325–37. A detailed history of dispensationalism is available in Ernest R. Sandeen, *The Roots of Fundamentalism: British and American Millenarianism 1800–1930* (Chicago: University of Chicago Press, 1970); and Timothy P. Weber, *Living in the Shadow of the Second Coming: American Premillennialism, 1875–1925* (New York: Oxford University Press, 1979).

31 See David R. Elliott, "Antithetical Elements in William Aberhart's Theology and Political Ideology," *Canadian Historical Review* 59, no. 1 (1978): 38–58.

32 Marsden, *Fundamentalism and American Culture*, 91.

33 A more detailed articulation of this argument is available in Banack, "Religion and Political Thought in Alberta."

34 This chain of events is detailed in John Irving, *The Social Credit Movement in Alberta* (Toronto: University of Toronto Press, 1959), 43–9; and David R. Elliott and Iris Miller, *Bible Bill: A Biography of William Aberhart* (Edmonton: Reidmore Books, 1987), 100–10.

35 Ernest Manning, interview by Lydia Semotuk, Interview 39 (17 May 1982), 27, Ernest Manning Fonds, University of Alberta Archives (UAA), Edmonton, Alberta.

36 Ernest Manning to G.M. Wilson, 18 April, 1962, Premiers Papers, 1977.173 file 394b, Provincial Archives of Alberta, Edmonton, Alberta.

37 Ernest Manning, interview by Lydia Semotuk, Interview 2 (18 December 1978), 14, Ernest Manning Fonds, UAA.

38 "Materialistic and Spiritual Blend in the Social Credit Faith," *Alberta Social Credit Chronicle*, 7 September 1934.

39 William Aberhart, radio address, 18 June 1935, file M-1157-83, Walter Norman and Amelia Turner Smith Fonds, G-AMA.

40 William Aberhart, Sunday radio address, 5 June 1938, file M-1621-6, Fred Kennedy Fonds, G-AMA.

41 William Aberhart, Sunday radio address, 19 March 1939, file M-1621-7, Fred Kennedy Fonds, G-AMA.

42 For an excellent comparison of the political programs of the UFA and Alberta Social Credit, without much focus on their religious founda-

tions, see David Laycock, *Populism and Democratic Thought in the Canadian Prairies, 1910 to 1945* (Toronto: University of Toronto Press, 1990).

43 Manning's defence of the free market is encapsulated within E.C. Manning, *Political Realignment: A Challenge to Thoughtful Canadians* (Toronto: McClelland and Stewart, 1967). For an insightful examination of the religious beliefs operating behind Manning's political thought, see Dennis G. Groh, "The Political Thought of Ernest Manning" (MA thesis, University of Calgary, 1970).

44 This argument is most prominent in Alvin Finkel, *The Social Credit Phenomenon in Alberta* (Toronto: University of Toronto Press, 1989).

45 Katherine Fierlbeck, *Political Thought in Canada: An Intellectual History* (Peterborough: Broadview, 2006), 76.

46 Claude Denis, "'Government Can Do Whatever It Wants': Moral Regulation in Ralph Klein's Alberta," *Canadian Review of Sociology and Anthropology* 32 (August 1995): 374.

47 For a discussion on the provincial Progressive Conservatives' long history of reluctance to legitimize same-sex relationships, see David Rayside, *Queer Inclusions, Continental Divisions: Public Recognition of Sexual Diversity in Canada and the United States* (Toronto: University of Toronto Press, 2008), 56, and chap. 4. Most recently, the Alberta PCs passed Bill 44 in 2009, which made "sexual orientation" protected ground under the province's human rights legislation but simultaneously reinforced the right of parents to prevent their children from learning about sexual orientation, as well as religion and sexuality, in public schools.

48 A 2010 poll found that 42 per cent of Albertans supported the Wildrose Alliance, compared to 27 per cent support for the governing Progressive Conservatives. See "Wildrose Extends Advantage in Alberta," Angus Reid Public Opinion Poll, 13 March 2010, http://www.angus-reid.com/polls/38544/wildrose_alliance_extends_advantage_in_alberta/. More recently, Alison Redford's PCs have regained a healthy lead in public opinion polls. See Dawn Walton, "Redford Gives Alberta Tories Hope for an Even Bigger Majority," *Globe and Mail*, 13 February 2012, http://www.theglobeandmail.com/news/politics/redford-gives-alberta-tories-hope-for-even-bigger-majority/article2337330/?utm_medium=Feeds%3A%20RSS%2FAtom&utm_source=Politics&utm_content=2337330.

13 Albertans' Conservative Beliefs

DAVID K. STEWART AND ANTHONY M. SAYERS

When a Calgary voter told the CBC during a 2009 by-election, "I've been a Conservative all my life like any normal Albertan," she was reflecting one fact about the province's political history and one widespread understanding of its strong political culture.[1] Alberta is unique among Canadian provinces in the comparative absence of a competitive party system and the continuity of a right-wing hold on government.[2] Many observers attribute this to the popular hold of beliefs associated with conservatism. Jared Wesley, for example, points to the central role of successful parties in emphasizing such values as individualism and populism, building on the widespread assumption that Alberta is "the bastion of Canadian conservatism."[3]

In this chapter we explore whether the attitudes of Albertans accord with arguments about the province's political culture, using findings from a survey immediately following the 2008 provincial election.[4] We focus on values generally associated with modern conservatism: opposition to an expansive role for government; support for reduction in state expenditures; an emphasis on individualism; and moral traditionalism. We also add questions that tap populist sentiments and western alienation – two important dimensions associated with conservatism in western Canada.[5] We examine the overall views of Albertans on these dimensions and assess the extent to which those who support provincial parties on the right (Progressive Conservatives and the newer Wildrose Party) are distinctive from one another and from supporters of the provincial Liberals and New Democratic Party.[6] We also explore the influence of such factors as region of residence, place of birth, age, gender, and education on the various dimensions of conservative attitudinal space. What we find challenges views of Alberta political culture held both inside and outside the province, for we find little suggesting that it has a particularly conservative political culture. The re-election of the Progressive Conservative government in the 2012 election on what has been termed its "progressive appeal"[7] provides another indication that Alberta's conservatism may be exaggerated.

Background Analysis

That the most serious challenge in a generation to the Progressive Conservative's dominance of Albertan politics has come from the right-wing Wildrose fits with a long tradition of popular and scholarly analysis portraying Alberta as the heartland of Canadian conservatism. As Wesley points out, "Alberta's most successful party leaders ... have preached individualism, stressing the importance of personal responsibility, free enterprise, private sector development, entrepreneurship, a strong work ethic, the evils of socialism, and the protection of individual rights and liberties."[8] They have also played up elements of populism, deploying the language of "Alberta-first" during campaigns. Nelson Wiseman argues that Albertans' individualism is an essential component of the political culture of the province, rooted partly in the formative role of American settlers in the early political life of the province, and partly in the relative weakness of immigrant waves carrying more collectivist norms.[9] He builds on a longer tradition of argument pointing to the distinctive role of individualistic sentiment in the province, and the comparative weakness of collectivist views on the right and left.[10]

However, the very character of the recent Wildrose challenge to the Progressive Conservatives suggests that the situation is more complicated. During the party's 2009 leadership race, eventual leader Danielle Smith asked potential voters, "Are we going to be a protest party, the NDP of the right? Or are we going to create a big-tent, mainstream right-of-centre, grassroots conservative party that is capable of catching one of those historic waves and sweeping us into government in 2012?"[11] The implicit answer she provided was that a big tent approach was essential to forming a government even in "conservative" Alberta. Her party's emphasis on themes of populism and western alienation were familiar echoes of earlier governing parties, but the party has attempted to present a moderate face, especially on social issues, and it seems to recognize that provincial opinion is by no means uniformly right wing. In the aftermath of the Wildrose defeat in 2012, the party is revisiting some of its policies, a process described by *Edmonton Journal* columnist Graham Thomson as "let's get rid of the extreme policies and intolerant candidates that cost us the election last April."[12]

A strong strand in the academic literature echoes the complicated reality of Alberta's conservatism. Wesley points out that under Premier Lougheed the provincial government invested major state funds in the petrochemical industry through direct business subsidies and the creation of new Crown corporations.[13] And while it is true that most analyses of the party since then would portray it as tracking rightward from Lougheed's days, work by Boessenkool shows that in 2008–9 Alberta had 40 per cent higher per capita government spending than Ontario and 30 per cent higher than British Columbia.[14] When we look at the party's internal leadership elections, we see that in three universal ballots (1992, 2006, and 2011) the most "conservative" candidates have not been able to make it through to the final ballots.[15] David Laycock argues that the media's "faux regionalism ... presents an image of the West as more conservative than other regions."[16] In fact, however, "most of what is unique about the Western perspective simply reflects a desire to 'say no' to a federal government dominated by – and more generous towards – Ontario and Quebec."

More historically, Roger Gibbins argued that "there is little evidence to suggest that Albertans would like to rein in government spending and government expansion; quite the opposite appears to be the case."[17] He also cited public opinion surveys suggesting that the general public is not as unquestioningly supportive of the oil industry as is commonly believed. "We find, for example, that more people disagree than agree with the statement that 'in recent years the oil industry has been overtaxed by Canadian governments' and that by a ratio of almost four to one, respondents agreed that 'foreign oil companies have too much influence with the Alberta government.'"[18] Indeed, after the government announced its retreat from many of the royalty increases in March 2010, polling by Environics revealed majority support for higher royalties.[19]

More recently, Gerard Boychuk's work on attitudes towards health reform reveals that Albertans are hardly right-wing outliers in this area. He points out that they are no more supportive than other Canadians of allowing more room for provinces to escape the strictures of the Canada Health Act, and "less supportive than other provinces of significant changes to the status quo in the funding of health services."[20] When the Ralph Klein government returned dollars from energy surpluses

Table 13.1. Albertans Wishing to See More Spending by Party Support in 2008 (%)

	Health	Environment	Roads	Crime Control	Cities	Welfare
PC	72	67	71	81	58	36
Liberal	89	89	77	73	75	65
NDP	89	86	74	73	76	65
Wildrose	66	46	67	82	58	32

directly to individuals, the experiment was short lived because polls demonstrated that most Albertans preferred that the funds be diverted to infrastructure and social services.[21]

How do the findings of the 2008 survey fit into this array of analytical perspectives? Our evidence suggests that Albertans are not as conservative on most dimensions as would be widely believed and, where they are conservative, it is more reflective of populism and regional alienation than of libertarian views of the state or moral traditionalism. The data also show that there are important areas in which supporters of what was then called the Wildrose Alliance Party[22] stand out from Conservative party supporters, and of course even more from supporters of the Liberals and NDP, but that no party's supporters are either consistently or radically rightwing.

Government Intervention

The survey had several items related to the scope of government activity and the extent of spending. Respondents were asked if they preferred more or less spending in various policy areas and then were faced with an additional four questions that probed their attitudes towards more interventionist and activist government (on issues like rent control, auto insurance, housing, and the maintenance of overall living standards).

Table 13.1 displays the levels of support for increased spending. It covers "welfare," a clearly redistributive policy area as well as health, cities, and the environment (areas where the extent of government activity is contested by many conservatives). It also includes roads and crime: areas of state activity which we imagine have wide support among Conservatives.

The data indicate overwhelming support (over 80%) for increased spending on crime control. Support is noticeably stronger among

Conservatives and Wildrose party supporters, though even among Liberals and New Democrats close to three-quarters say yes. Spending on roads gets almost as much support, and here the rightist parties' supporters are somewhat less enthusiastic than the centre and left – again the differences are modest.

Where we see less overall commitment to spending, and greater partisan divisions, is with respect to welfare. Two-thirds of Liberals and New Democrats support increased spending, in a position taken by only one-third of Conservatives and Wildrose sympathizers. Still, about half of the respondents were in favour of increased spending. Increased spending on "cities" elicited more overall support than welfare, health even more so, with somewhat less polarization between parties than the welfare area. Spending on the environment is supported by a stronger majority, though with especially strong party differences between Wildrose supporters and the centre-left parties.

The general picture displayed here is that in four of these six major policy areas, more than 70 per cent of Albertans favour increased government spending.[23] For cities, average support is over 65 per cent, and it is just over 50 per cent for welfare spending. It is not inconsequential that welfare so starkly divides the population: it may be emblematic of what conservatives most dislike about government spending. Nevertheless, there remains no consensus even there, even among those supporting the Conservatives and Wildrose parties.

On questions of government intervention (as distinct from spending), we find, with one exception (auto insurance), a strikingly consistent three-quarters of respondents favour government action to ensure decent living standards (76%), to ensure adequate housing (78%), and to limit rent increases (76%). Only auto insurance fails to garner majority support for significant government involvement, though even it is evenly split for and against at 46 per cent.

Table 13.2 displays results using indices of clusters of questions on a variety of dimensions associated with conservatism. The first is a four-question cluster using the questions associated with government activity, with an index value of 1 equivalent to disagreement with all of the statements identified above. The average index score was .32, reflecting a moderately strong commitment to state activity. Not surprisingly, there are partisan differences, with the Conservatives and Wildrose supporters noticeably higher in the average scores (averaging .40) than the other parties (averaging around .20). The small number of Wildrose supporters (at the time) makes it hazardous to over-interpret

Table 13.2. Conservatism Indices: Standardized Means (0–1), by Party Support

	Opposition to government activity	Opposition to environmental/ energy regulation	Support for social "conservatism"	Support for individualism	Support for populism	Western alienation	N range
PC	.39	.47	.38	.55	.78	.70	423–545
Liberal	.22	.20	.20	.37	.63	.36	179–217
NDP	.13	.14	.17	.27	.63	.50	74–97
Green	.23	.11	.15	.41	.69	.50	48–57
Wildrose	.44	.48	.66	.69	.86	.78	41–52
None of these	.30	.34	.29	.47	.73	.60	142–193
Total	.32	.35	.31	.48	.74	.61	946–1193

Note: Where necessary, the direction of indices has been reversed to ensure "agree" signals a progressive response.

differences from the Conservatives, but we do see more anti-state senti-ment among the former than the latter. However, even Wildrose sup-porters are below the mid-point on this conservatism index, at .44.[24]

Further analysis of these data indicate no significant variations in pat-terns of support for intervention by region, community size, or place of birth, though we do find that those who have lived in the province for ten years or more are less supportive of government activity than new-comers. Older Albertans are also somewhat more conservative on this dimension than younger cohorts.

Energy and Environment Issues

The 2008 survey posed two questions tapping popular attitudes towards environmental regulation, on whether tougher environmental standards should take precedence over employment, and whether the province needed to take firm action to combat global warming. The latter was an "easier" question in the sense that it did not force a choice between objectives, but is still controversial in a province so dependent on energy production and marketing. It is therefore significant that 82 per cent of Albertans said yes on combating global warming. On environmental standards taking precedence over jobs, an impressive 58 per cent agreed.

Three other questions explored attitudes towards the government's relationship to energy companies, and here too we find what to some would be surprisingly widespread support for government control. An especially striking 69 per cent agreed that oil and gas companies have too much say in provincial politics, with 60 per cent agreeing that oil sands development should be slowed. There is less agreement on the very contentious issue of whether royalties on gas and oil should be increased, but still 56 per cent agree. The Conservative Stelmach gov-ernment drew the ire of the energy industry by raising royalty rates prior to the 2008 election, and the Wildrose has capitalized on dissatis-faction with the government's approach to this issue.[25] Wildrose policy indicates that a government led by their party would "consult exten-sively with industry prior to introducing policies that affect the energy sector" and "communicate with Albertans about the importance of the oil and gas industry to our province's economy and future."[26] On the other hand, after the Conservative government announced a retreat from many of the royalty increases (in March 2010), polling by Environics revealed majority support for the higher pre-announcement rates or increases beyond that level.[27]

Combining our five questions into an environment/energy regulation scale, where 1 represents the most anti-regulative attitude set, the mean result for Albertans was .35 (see table 13.2). There are very strong party differences here, centre and left parties clustered between .11 and .20, and the two rightist parties very close together at just about the mid-point. This is an even more sharply polarized issue area than overall government intervention, but there is still no sign of a strong pull towards completely vacating government's role in regulating the environment and the energy industry.

There are also regional differences, with Calgary residents recording the highest and Edmontonians presenting substantially lower scores. Even in Calgary, primary home to the energy industry, the average score on the anti-regulatory index is below the midpoint. In a pattern similar to that for government intervention, long-time residents are less pro-environment than newcomers. Most Albertans, regardless of age, birthplace, length of residence, or even region are generally pro-environment and not particularly supportive of the energy industry. This contributed to the negative public response to Wildrose leader Danielle Smith's assertion that the "jury was still out" on climate change (during the 2012 election campaign), a response that *Edmonton Journal* columnist Graham Thomson noted was unhelpful.[28]

Individualism

Just as we see less support for the energy industry among Albertans than we might have expected, and more support for state action on the environment and other issues, we also see only modest indications of the kind of intense individualism associated with the province's political culture. Here we have responses to four questions to attitudes on the relationship between the individual and the state. The questions tap three different policy domains and have quite different conceptual wording, so it is not surprising that they elicit quite different responses:

"Most unemployed could find jobs": 71 per cent agree
"Government regulation stifles drive": 48 per cent agree
"Those willing to pay should get medical treatment sooner": 43 per cent agree
"A lot of welfare and social programs unnecessary": 30 per cent agree

The response to the "jobs" question is quite different than to the others, not surprising in the light of how many new jobs being created in the energy sector. What is more telling is the verdict on the other questions, suggesting a population divided on or largely opposed to frameworks that would leave more room for individual choice or self-reliance than currently exists.

Table 13.2 again reports the partisan variations in the index that relies on responses to all four questions. As in the other indices, the party polarization is pretty clear, and differences between parties within each party cluster are even clearer. The NDP stands out in the non-individualist responses to these questions, and the Wildrose is significantly more individualist than the Conservatives. Responses do not vary significantly across regions, community size, length of residency in the province, and age. Women, those with university degrees, and those born in eastern or central Canada score lower than their counterparts.

Social/Moral Issues

Conservatism, perhaps more in Alberta than in any other Canadian province, is widely seen as embodying morally conservative positions alongside the individualistic suspicion of the state embodied in "neoliberalism." We have seen that Albertans in general are not as conservative on the neoliberal dimensions we have explored as is commonly believed, though there are sharp party differences. What about attitudes towards abortion and same-sex marriage? Here, the results present as much of a surprise as they do in any policy area. When asked if abortion was a matter between a woman and her doctor, fully 76 per cent of Albertans agreed. And when asked whether gays and lesbians should be allowed to marry, 62 per cent agreed.

Because these findings fly so strongly in the face of widespread images of Albertans, they are worth a closer comparative examination. In fact, these data dovetail with recent polling data conducted elsewhere in Canada. A 2010 Ekos survey showed that the 33 per cent of Albertans who opposed same-sex marriage was only slightly different from the Canadian average of 28 per cent, and the Ontario average of 29 per cent.[29] Another 2010 poll showed that 30 per cent of Albertans took "pro-life" positions on abortion, only fractionally off the Canadian average of 27 per cent.[30]

Table 13.2 shows the result of combining responses into a single index measuring social conservatism (high scores indicating disagreement with the statements above). The typical response across the province was heavily tilted against restrictions on abortion and gay marriage. There were significant party differences here, with all of the centre-left parties clustering tightly at the choice/equity end of the scale. (Support for moral conservatism is somewhat stronger among northern and southern Albertans and weaker in the two largest cities, among women, and among the highly educated. Those born in Alberta or outside Canada, and older people, recorded higher scores.)

On this dimension more than any other we see a large gap between Conservatives and Wildrose supporters, the latter being very substantially more traditionalist than the former. Conservative identifiers were much closer to the Liberal score than to that of their right-wing rival. This was a major issue during the 2009 Wildrose leadership campaign, with the main rival of the eventual winner, Danielle Smith, portrayed as a staunch social conservative. Smith's victory may well have allowed the party to broaden its appeal beyond the core of social conservatives who supported it in 2008, particularly because she has made a point of moving away from the issues that would drive them.

However, controversy on issues related to social conservatism appeared to damage Wildrose during the 2012 campaign. Comments by candidates that were perceived as racist and anti-gay slowed and helped reverse the party's momentum, adding to the concern about party priorities created by earlier comments by the party leader on climate change. Danielle Smith refused to condemn her candidates and tried to blame the controversy on the intolerance of others.[31] This prolonged the controversy at the crucial late stages of the campaign.

Populism

There are two attitudinal dimensions in which popular stereotypes about Albertans find stronger support in our data – populism and western alienation. "Populism" is difficult to define and precisely measure.[32] In the Alberta context it is often associated with a simple connection with the "common folk" and can be relatively free of content. Drawing on the work of Blake, Carty, and Erickson, we use three questions, each of which elicits majority support for the populist position.[33]

"Trust ordinary people more than experts": 58 per cent agree
"Probably solve most problems if government is brought back to
   grassroots": 75 per cent agree
"Need government with less red tape": 86 per cent agree

Only 6 per cent gave no populist responses to these questions, and 79 per cent responded positively to two or more. Almost half (49%) scored a 3 on this scale and the overall index score of .74 signalled a more distinctly one-side attitude set across the province compared with any of the other dimensions discussed to this point (see table 13.2). There are party differences, but nothing like those that appear on moral issues and some of the other dimensions. Though not as much as on morality, the Wildrose identifiers stand at one pole of the partisan spectrum. However, about two-thirds of the supporters of the three centre and left parties also provide populist responses.

Respondents from Calgary and Edmonton were less likely to provide populist responses while those in central Alberta recorded the highest scores. Community size mattered, but the distinction with the greatest weight was that between the two largest cities and all other parts of the province. Populist responses correlated with length of time in the province, though "immigrants" from other parts of western Canada were not much different from long-time Albertans. Populism was lower among younger respondents and those with higher levels of education.

Western Alienation

At the time of our survey, the Conservative party formed the federal government, every Alberta MP sat on the government side of the House of Commons, Albertans held several key Cabinet positions, and the prime minister of Canada represented an Alberta constituency. Moreover, Prime Minister Harper scored higher (on a thermometer scale assessing popularity) than any of the Alberta provincial party leaders contesting the 2008 election. Still, the indications of widespread alienation – framed as "western alienation" – are solid. Our survey asked four questions that tapped such sentiments, all but one of them securing strong majorities.

"Alberta is treated unfairly by the federal government": 46 per cent agree

"Alberta does not have its fair share of political power in Canada": 62 per cent agree

"The economic policies of the federal government seem to help Quebec and Ontario at the expense of Alberta": 65 per cent agree

"Because parties depend on Quebec and Ontario, Alberta usually gets ignored in national politics": 70 per cent agree

Only the first, on "unfair treatment," was below the majority point and seemed the only indication that the federal party in power at the time was denting this deep current of Alberta sentiment. Most Albertans gave two or more "alienated" answers. The mean score on this index was .61, and more than half of the respondents gave at least three "alienated" responses, while only 19 per cent gave a "not alienated" response. It is clear that Albertans continue to drink deeply from the well of western alienation.

There are important differences between parties on this dimension (see table 13.2). Again, Wildrose supporters defined one pole, with Conservatives not far behind (much as was true with populism). New Democrats and Greens were significantly lower on this scale, but only Liberals fell below midpoint on this dimension – a finding that conforms to an argument made by Roger Gibbins in the 1970s. Western alienation has become strongly identified with conservatism in Alberta, and in his work on the Reform party Laycock argues, "In the West ... , its 'invasion from the right' was facilitated by its regionalist identity."[34]

Western alienation was least evident in Calgary and Edmonton – another finding congruent with Gibbins's earlier argument.[35] Rural respondents and those who had lived in the province for fifteen years or more scored highest on this dimension. Those from other parts of the west were at least as prone to alienated responses as long-time residents. Those born in eastern and central Canada had scores far below those with a western Canadian origin. We found few significant age differences, in contrast to Canada West Foundation's regular survey of regional discontent, which has found that younger Albertans were less alienated than their elders.[36] Higher education was associated with lower levels of alienation.

The Difference That Party Makes

The attitudes of Albertans vary widely on most of the dimensions associated with western conservatism, and on some dimensions they respond in ways that do not generally accord with conservative positions. Only questions related to populism and alienation display patterns consistent with the view that Albertans are generally conservative. Questions about moral issues in particular demonstrate that convergence towards more "liberal" positions has almost eliminated whatever differences there may have been between Albertans and Canadians elsewhere.

There are, on the other hand, clear partisan differences on several dimensions. Using the gap in the index scores of typical partisans as a measure of polarization, we find especially large numbers on moral

Table 13.3. Conservative Tilt from Provincial Average for PCs and Wildrose

	Opposition to government activity	Opposition to environmental/ energy regulation	Support for social "conservatism"	Support for individualism	Support for populism	Western alienation
PC	.07	.12	.07	.07	.04	.09
Wildrose	.12	.13	.35	.21	.12	.16
Provincial average	.32	.35	.31	.48	.74	.61

issues, individualism, and environmentalism. There are smaller differences, indicating more cross-party agreement, on western alienation and notably populism. We find moderate levels of disagreement on government activity, but on that dimension the tilt is away from the usual stereotypes of Albertans.

Not surprisingly, Conservatives and Wildrose supporters most clearly adhere to several dimensions associated with conservatism. There are, however, differences between them, which we display in table 13.3. Here we tabulate the number of index points to the right of the average Albertan for the typical supporter of the Conservative Party and the Wildrose Alliance. A score of .10 for the Conservatives indicates that an average supporter is scored .10 closer to the conservative end of that particular dimension than the average respondent across the province.

What we find here is that Conservative supporters lie between .04 and .12 to the right of the average Albertan on these scales. The average Wildrose supporter, on the other hand, lies between .12 and .35, the most dramatic contrast being on social issues (.35) and individualism (.21). As the Wildrose broadens its membership, these numbers will probably decline, but it suggests that the new party's core holds to some opinions substantially at odds with the provincial majority. The controversies that arose in the midst of the 2012 election, and the resulting slip in its popularity, illustrate this point and suggest the need for rethinking policy positions that seemed to have occurred in the immediate aftermath of that election.

The Relationship between Attitudinal Dimensions

To what extent do attitudes on these various dimensions cohere? In other words, do respondents with conservative positions on morality also hold individualist positions calling for less government and less regulation? The work of Chris Cochrane and Neil Nevitte suggests that positions on economic and moral issues do not particularly coincide in Europe or in Canada.[37] Our data provide mixed evidence on coherence.

Some very strong correlations do not surprise. Populism is closely associated with western alienation (.44); support for government intervention is closely linked to support for environmental and energy controls (.44). However, there are also statistically significant, if weaker, correlations between most dimensions. Social conservatism, in other words, often travels alongside individualism and an antipathy to government activity. In some ways this is a libertarian paradox, though it does reflect the issue combination that some of Alberta's conservative politicians have adopted in the past. Laycock argues that "most fiscal conservatives appear to agree with Ralph Klein ... [when he] suggested that, to be consistent, those who promote individual choice in the market, should at least permit individual choice in the setting of 'moral compasses.'"[38] At some level this is true, given that most Albertans (like most Canadians) do not want greater restrictions on abortion or a rollback on gay/lesbian marriage. But the two attitude sets do tend to be associated with one another. This may be a distinctive feature of conservatism in the province, and perhaps more broadly in western Canada.

Conclusion

The responses of Albertans to the 2008 survey we have been analysing here suggests that despite the electoral evidence and the codes used by political elites, public opinion in the province may be less "conservative" than widely assumed. This survey was limited to one province, but apart from populist sentiments and western alienation, there seems to be merit in Barrie's contention "that the people of Alberta share fundamental values with citizens of other parts of the country."[39] As in other parts of the country, we find some important differences between large cities and small-town and rural environments – in some cases the sharpest contrast being between the two largest cities and the rest of the province. Sparsely populated areas are more individualistic, less supportive of abortion rights and same-sex marriage, and more characterized by attitudes associated with western alienation. The visibility of such constituencies in Alberta politics reinforces perceptions of the whole province as conservative. But as with other parts of the country, Alberta is becoming more urbanized. This was a crucial factor in defeating the Wildrose Party in 2012, which powerfully illustrated the geographic unevenness of partisan support across the province.

We have seen evidence of strong currents of both populist sentiment and alienated responses to questions about Alberta's status within Canada as a whole and its treatment by the federal government. If we go beyond these data, however, we find evidence that Albertans display some of the highest levels of social capital and interpersonal trust in Canada.[40] Although "normal" Albertans may vote "Conservative," it is by no means clear that conservative views are normal in the province if conservatism is equated with an amalgam of moral traditionalism and libertarian economics. If, though, by "Conservative" we mean populism combined with regional alienation, then we go a long way towards understanding both the enduring success of right-wing parties in Alberta and the future character of the Canadian conservative movement.

NOTES

1 As quoted in "Wildrose Alliance Wins Calgary Glenmore," CBC News Online, 14 September 2009.
2 David K. Stewart and R.K. Carty, "'Many Political Worlds: Provincial Parties and Party Systems,'" in *Provinces*, 2nd ed., ed. Christopher Dunn, 97–113 (Peterborough: Broadview, 2006).
3 Jared J. Wesley, *Code Politics: Campaigns and Cultures on the Canadian Prairies* (Vancouver, UBC Press, 2011), 3, suggests that autonomy is generally understood in terms of western alienation, which has been historically identified as a key component in Alberta's opinion mix. See, for example, Frederick C. Engelmann, "Foreword," in *Society and Politics in Alberta*, ed. Carlo Caldarola, ix–x (Toronto: Methuen and Roger Gibbins, 1979); Roger Gibbins, "Western Alienation and the Alberta Political Culture," in Caldarola, *Society and Politics in Alberta*, 143–67.
4 The phone interview survey of Albertans, stratified by region and gender, was conducted by NRG Research Group in March 2008. Funding for the survey was provided by the University of Calgary's Institute for Advanced Policy Research.
5 Edward Bell, Harold Jansen, and Lisa Young, "Sustaining a Dynasty in Alberta: The 2004 Provincial Election," *Canadian Political Science Review* 1, no. 2 (2007): 27–49, review the explanations of Alberta's unique politics and note the important role attributed to "western alienation," 29. Doreen Barrie suggests that the "casting of Ottawa as the Other was not a very difficult task, as the prairie province had long felt victimized by federal politics that discriminated against the region." See *The Other Alberta: Decoding a Political Enigma* (Regina: Canada Plains Research Centre, 2006), 117. Roger Gibbins argues that "western alienation" is the major factor "providing a distinctive cast to the Alberta political culture" and explains that it "embodies a sense of political, economic and, to a lesser extent, cultural estrangement from the heartland of Canada." See Gibbins, "Western Alienation and the Alberta Political Culture," 143, 146.
6 The figures for party identification are PC 46 per cent, Liberal 18 per cent, NDP 7 per cent, Green 5 per cent, Wildrose Alliance 4 per cent, and no identification 18 per cent. Respondents could choose "Other" as well. So

few chose this criterion that we excluded the category, although those respondents are included in the total.

7 Graham Thomson, "Progessive Appeal of Conservatives wins 2012 election," Edmonton Journal Online, 23 April 2012.

8 Wesley, *Code Politics*, 56.

9 Nelson Wiseman, *In Search of Canadian Political Culture* (Vancouver: UBC Press, 2007).

10 C.B. Macpherson, *Democracy in Alberta* (Toronto: University of Toronto Press, 1962).

11 Danielle Smith leadership campaign literature (2009).

12 Graham Thomson, "Wildrose 2.0 Is a Work in Progress," Edmonton Journal online, 25 November 2012.

13 Wesley, *Code Politics*, 89.

14 Ken Boessenkel, "Does Alberta Have a Spending Problem?," *University of Calgary, The School of Public Policy, SPP Communique*, 2, no. 1 (2010): 1.

15 David Stewart and Keith Archer, *Quasi-Democracy: Parties and Leadership Selection in Alberta* (Vancouver: UBC Press, 2000); David K. Stewart and Anthony Sayers, "Leadership Change in a Dominant Party: The Alberta Progressive Conservatives, 2006," *Canadian Political Science Review* 4, no. 4 (2009): 85–107. Evidence for the 2011 ballot stems from elimination of Ted Morton following the first ballot. See "In Alberta, Are 'Conservatives' Dead as a Dodo," *Globe and Mail*, 29 September 2011.

16 David Laycock, *The New Right and Democracy in Canada: Understanding Reform and the Canadian Alliance* (Don Mills: Oxford University Press, 2002), 155.

17 Gibbins, "Western Alienation and the Alberta Political Culture," 158, 159.

18 Ibid., 163.

19 Jason Fekete, "Royalty Debate Divides Alberta," *Calgary Herald*, 13 March 2010.

20 Gerard W. Boychuk, "The Regulation of Private Health Funding and Insurance in Alberta under the Canada Health Act: A Comparative Cross-Provincial Perspective," *University of Calgary, The School of Policy Studies, Research Papers* 1, no. 1 (2008): 35.

21 Wesley, *Code Politics*, 105–6.

22 The party changed its name to the Wildrose party at its convention in June 2011. See "*Wildrose* Stays True to Change Slogan by Dropping '*Alliance*' from Name," *National Post*, 28 June 2011.

23 Two-thirds of respondents wanted to see more spent on cities and municipalities, 74 per cent wanted more on roads, 75 per cent wanted more on the police, 77 per cent wanted more on protecting the environment, and 81 per cent wished to see more funding for health care.

24 It is important to keep in mind that the Wildrose Alliance has changed since the 2008 election. Not only has its support broadened, according to polls, but with its new leader, Danielle Smith, it has adopted what she talks about as a moderate right-of-centre approach.

25 The support for the dominant commodity by Albertans has also been identified as a key component of the provincial political culture. See, for example, C.B. Macpherson's *Democracy in Alberta*; and Gurston Dacks, "From Consensus to Competition: Social Democracy and Political Culture in Alberta," in *Socialism and Democracy in Alberta: Essays in Honour of Grant Notley*, ed. Larry Pratt, 186–204 (Edmonton: NeWest, 1986). See especially Barrie, *The Other Alberta*, 80.

26 Smith, leadership campaign literature.

27 Fekete, "Royalty Debate Divides Alberta."

28 Graham Thomson, "Progessive Appeal of Conservatives Wins 2012 Election," Edmonton Journal Online, 23 April 2012.

29 Ekos Polling, "Support for Same-Sex Marriage Strong and Rising," 25 March 2010, http://www.ekos.com/admin/articles/cbc-2010-03-26.pdf.

30 Ekos Polling, "Canadians Decisively Pro-Choice on Abortion; No Change over the Decade," 1 April 2010, http://www.ekospolitics.com/index.php/2010/04/canadians-decisively-pro-choice-on-abortion-april-1-2010/.

31 Graham Thomson, *Edmonton Journal*, 23 April 2012.

32 Peter R. Sinclair, "Class Structure and Populist Protest," in Caldarola, *Society and Politics in Alberta*, 73–86.

33 Donald Blake, R.K. Carty, and Lynda Erickson, *Grassroots Politicians* (Vancouver: UBC Press, 1991).

34 Laycock, *New Right and Democracy in Canada*, 169.

35 Gibbins, "Western Alienation and the Alberta Political Culture."

36 Mark Lisac, *Alberta Politics Uncovered: Taking Back Our Province* (Edmonton: NeWest, 2004), 98.

37 Christopher Cochrane and Neil Nevitte, "Value Change and the Dynamics of the Canadian Partisan Landscape," in *Canadian Parties in Transition*, ed. Alain-G. Gagnon and A. Brian Tanguay, 3rd ed., 255–78 (Peterborough: Broadview, 2007); and Cochrane, chapter 2 in this volume.

38 Laycock, *New Right and Democracy in Canada*, 170.

39 Barrie, *The Other Alberta*, 81.

40 John Helliwell, "Do Borders Matter for Social Capital? Economic Growth and Civic Culture in U.S. States and Canadian Provinces," National Bureau of Economic Research Working Paper 5863 (1996); Richard Johnston and Stuart Soroka, "Social Capital in a Multicultural Society:

The Case of Canada," in *Social Capital and Participation in Everyday Life*, ed. Paul Dekker and Eric M. Uslaner, 30–44 (London: Routledge, 2001); Mark Pickup, Anthony Sayers, Rainer Knopff, and Keith Archer, "Social Capital and Civic Community in Alberta," *Canadian Journal of Political Science* 37, no. 3 (2004): 339–54.

14 Moral Conservatism and Ontario Party Politics[1]

DAVID RAYSIDE

Introduction

On the morning of 20 April 2010, veteran anti-gay evangelical crusader Charles McVety issued a press release denouncing a new Ontario "healthy sexuality" curriculum and calling for protest against it. One day later, the Conservative Party's leadership used the issue to attack the Liberal government. A year and a half later, during the 2011 provincial election, Conservatives distributed literature attacking the Liberal government for supporting what were characterized as alarmingly confusing sex education messages to young children. This was not supposed to happen. Moral conservatism had seemed to be a declining force in provincial Ontario politics, and even during periods when traditionalist faith communities were most intent on influencing provincial policymaking, they were seen as having only modest or short-lived impact.

The Ontario party system is unique in Canadian jurisdictions for having a stable three-party system. Though Ontario had Progressive Conservative (PC) governments continuously from the 1940s until the mid-1980s, since then the Liberals, the New Democratic Party, and the PCs have each had at least one term in government. From the mid-1990s on, moral traditionalism seemed mostly to take a back seat in Ontario policymaking, even when Conservatives were in power. True, during the 1980s and early 1990s, a series of political controversies over sexual diversity made clear that moral traditionalists could muster considerable pressure on all parties and could count on the sympathy of a majority of the Conservatives caucus. But by the time that the provincial PCs won office in 1995, the preoccupations of the party leadership were almost entirely neoliberal and largely silent on moral issues.

Public opinion seemed to be shifting steadily towards an embrace of lesbian/gay/bisexual/transgender rights, and the PCs' "common sense" revolutionaries seemed to be largely disconnected from religiously conservative advocacy groups. At the same time, anti-gay elements had all but disappeared in NDP caucuses and had been reduced to a small rump among the Liberals.

How, then, do we explain the Conservatives' embrace of the sex education issue, and the Liberal government decision in April 2010 to withdraw part of the new curriculum for a "rethink"? Does it suggest, as Marci McDonald has argued, that the political influence of activist campaigning on moral issues, particularly by religious conservatives, has been underestimated?[2] Does it further suggest that the strength of such groups, and the grassroots supporters behind them, require the attention of provincial party leaders, and particularly Conservatives? Or were there other factors at play in leading the Conservatives to take up the sex education issue and inducing a sudden retreat for the Liberals?

After outlining the controversy over sexuality in April 2010 and chronicling the emergence of the religious right as an organized force in Ontario politics, this chapter explores the role of moral traditionalism in the party system, first in the PCs. It will argue that the party's shift away from pragmatism under Mike Harris, even if focused on reducing taxation and the role of government, retained a sizeable constituency of religious conservatives and may well have attracted new support by its swing away from pragmatic centrism. The leadership has therefore remained susceptible to seizing on "controversies" in which the mobilization of religious conservatives is seen (rightly or wrongly) as having broader than usual appeal.

The Liberals have important roots in rural and small-town Ontario, and their pragmatism has allowed them to retain the support of some social conservatives. This has manifested itself much less in the party's leadership since the 1980s than before, and the caucus has few members clearly identifiable as moral traditionalists. But in an electoral system with three strong parties and considerable volatility, the Liberals remain anxious about any issue that risks losing them essential rural seats and weakening support among some morally traditional ethnocultural minorities. The New Democrats have certainly gone through difficult internal debates over sexuality, but since the 1980s they have evolved towards the most solidly progressive position of the three parties.

The Sex Ed Story in Brief

Education is unlikely to provoke the kind of culture wars that have characterized the United States, but contention around schools is a recurrent feature of Ontario politics, often centred on funding for faith-based schools. Questions related to youth and sexuality, too, are unlikely to be debated calmly, since they evoke large questions lying at the heart of what schools are meant to accomplish.

Early in the week of 26 September, in the midst of the 2011 provincial election, the Institute for Canadian Values placed a full-page ad in the *National Post* and then in the *Toronto Sun* raising alarm bells about sex education in Ontario. The leading text read:

> Please! Don't Confuse Me.
> I'm a girl. Don't teach me to question if I'm a boy, transsexual, transgendered, intersexed or two spirited.
> Why are teachers forced to teach this curriculum?
> My mommy says she is not allowed to withdraw me from class.
> Mr McGuinty, Mr Hudak and Ms Horwath, please tell me you will stop teachers from confusing me.

Shortly afterwards, just three days before the election, there were media reports of Conservative candidates distributing flyers with the title "Cross-dressing for 6-year-olds" and urging parents to vote against the "McGuinty agenda."[3] The Liberals responded immediately by pointing out that the flyers utterly distorted the provincial healthy sexuality curriculum, which remained the same as what had been put into place under an earlier Conservative government. This helped to marginalize the issue. In fact, most of the media coverage of the incident painted the Conservatives as pandering to homophobia, suggesting that this kind of campaigning would no longer work in Ontario. However, the conclusion that these appeals no longer have currency was premature.

Changes to the way sexual education is taught in Ontario's schools was bound to come up, sooner or later. Despite important gains in the legal recognition of lesbian/gay relationship rights, attention to sexual diversity in Canadian schools had expanded only slightly.[4] Pressure for change had been building, particularly since the late 1990s, but with only slow response, and dramatically uneven application of new policies across schools within even the most forward-thinking boards. Lethargy and resistance to change have been particularly evident in the paucity of policies addressing sexual diversity at the provincial level. This was true not only of Ontario, but across Canada. Curricular inclusiveness has been particularly difficult to effect in formal policy, and there remains widespread timidity in any teaching associated with sexuality.

Public schooling was on then-Liberal premier Dalton McGuinty's agenda from his first taking office in 2003. He styled himself the "education premier" partly in response to policies enacted under the Harris premiership that curtailed school spending and introduced tax credits to compensate parents for private school tuition. There is no evidence that McGuinty included sexuality in his schools agenda, but in September 2006, he named Kathleen Wynne to the education portfolio, someone with a major interest in issues related to equity and diversity – an interest that very much included sexual orientation and gender identity.

In the election held one year after Wynne's appointment, the Conservative leader John Tory pushed schooling issues to the forefront of the campaign by promising an extension of government funding to private religious schools. This, combined with Tory's candidacy in Wynne's riding, intensified the Liberals' self-presentation as defenders of public education. The Liberals won provincially and in Wynne's constituency, and the school funding issue was given major credit for that outcome.

Work had already begun within the education ministry on school safety (since 2004), but Wynne's promotion to minister sped up moves that explicitly addressed sexual diversity. The 2008 report, *Shaping a Culture of Respect*, recommended that a comprehensive school climate strategy be developed that included sexual orientation and gender identity, and urged curricular reform as a part of that strategy.[5] Within a year, legislation and regulations had been approved to address equity in general, and bullying and harassment in particular – with sexual diversity forcefully included.

In the midst of these developments, revisions to the health and physical education curriculum were in the works.[6] Preparations and elaborate consultations had begun in 2007, almost a decade after the last revision, as part of a routine curricular revision cycle. This revealed considerable support for changing the HPE curriculum, and for pushing the healthy sexuality parts towards a more realistic engagement with the kinds of information that young people were receiving about sex, and about sexual diversity.

From the beginning these discussions included Catholic educators, who seemed no different from public system educators in the numbers of them calling for change in the sex education component to HPE. It was widely understood that the Catholic system had the right to interpret curricular guidelines in a distinctive way, a right applied especially to sex education and religious education. Still, many educators in that system knew full well how much the curriculum had to be updated and more inclusive.

By late 2009, the final version of the HPE curriculum was ready. The vast majority of the long and complex document dealt with physical activity and general health. When it did address sex education, it was not dramatically out of line with the evolution of curricula in other Canadian provinces, and in its overall direction it did not represent a radical break from the previous curriculum. But what was new were the prompts provided for teachers to encourage classroom discussion or answer student questions. Here there was encouragement and assistance given to discussing sexual diversity and sexual activity honestly, though in careful language designed to flag what kind of responses were suitable for particular grade levels.[7]

On 18 January 2010, the new curriculum was posted on the ministry's website, and a memorandum was sent to all school boards announcing it – just what would happen with any other new curriculum document. A Cabinet shuffle that same day moved Kathleen Wynne from Education to Transport, replacing her with Leona Dombrowsky, who had been chair of the Roman Catholic School Board in a rural and small-city region of eastern Ontario.

The first sign of protest over sex education was a story on LifeSiteNews, entitled "Mandatory Curriculum for Ontario Schools Promotes Homosexuality, Masturbation."[8] This story on a widely known pro-life website seemed not to spread, and it was an additional six weeks before a mainstream media outlet discussed the new curriculum. On 5 April the *Hamilton Spectator* published a story spawned by a meeting of the Hamilton-Wentworth District School Board, scheduled that day to discuss gender equity policy.[9] Research for this story led the reporter to the new HPE curriculum, which then led to a companion story entitled "Birds and Bees to Be Taught from Grade 3."

Charles McVety, evangelical pastor, president of Canada Christian College and of the Canada Family Action Coalition (CFAC), tireless campaigner on abortion and sexual orientation issues, learned about the revised sex ed curriculum from that story.[10] The Institute for

Canadian Values, responsible for the September 2011 ad on sex education, is housed at McVety's college. Neither it nor the CFAC is a large group, and McVety's relationship with other major evangelical groups has not always been amicable. However, he does have a substantial email list, which includes many journalists and many co-religionists who respond to his calls to action.

At 9:00 on Tuesday morning, 20 April, McVety issued a press release headed by the denunciating line: "Mr McGuinty, Withdraw Explicit Sex Ed for 8 Year Olds." It announced a website (stopcorruptingchildren. ca), claimed support from the leaders of family-focused groups with over a hundred thousand active members, and announced a rally on the Monday after Mother's Day (10 May). McVety quoted himself, saying, "It is unconscionable to teach 8-year-old children same-sex marriage, sexual orientation and gender identity ... It is even more absurd to subject 6th graders to instruction on the pleasures of masturbation, vaginal lubrication, and 12-year-olds to lessons on oral sex and anal intercourse."

That very morning – Tuesday – a reporter asked the premier if the claims made in McVety's press release were accurate. McGuinty, appearing a little unnerved, expressed confidence in the educators who had prepared the curriculum and played down the concerns expressed in the press release.[11] By the next morning, Toronto's two major dailies – the *Globe and Mail* and the *Toronto Star* – both had major stories on the issue and very much framed it as controversial.

That same Wednesday morning, the Conservative leader Mike Hudak challenged the government in question period, vowing to "stand with moms and dads across the province of Ontario" and accusing the government of listening only to "so-called experts and elite insiders."[12] On Wednesday afternoon, the premier once again defended the curriculum, this time with more apparent conviction than in his too-little-scripted response on Tuesday morning.

Then Catholic schooling got tied into the controversy. During ongoing questioning on this issue, the premier indicated that the new program would apply to students in all publicly funded schools, including Catholic – a point reiterated by Minister Leona Dombrowsky. There were soon clarifying statements that the ministry had consulted the Institute for Catholic Education throughout the development of the curriculum and that everyone involved in the process acknowledged that it would have adaptations for Catholic schools. This apparent misstep provided a vehicle for conservative Archbishop Terrence Prendergast of Ottawa to weigh in by emphasizing that parents are children's "first teachers of faith and moral issues" and encouraging them to voice their concerns about the new curriculum.[13]

On Thursday morning, the story was still in the newspaper headlines, and government ministers were still defending the curriculum. Kathleen Wynne described Conservative attacks on it as "despicable," not least because Conservative attacks were linking the curricular changes to the former education minister's own sexual orientation.[14] Even during the course of these assertive counterattacks, however, unease was building inside the premier's office. That afternoon, fifty-four hours after the McVety press release, Dalton McGuinty announced that the sex education segments of the new curriculum were being withdrawn for a "rethink." The next Monday, 26 April, Dombrowsky indicated that her officials were going to be preparing options to "better engage parents on this issue," though indicating no timeline for the preparation of new guidelines on sex education.[15] No one was expecting this review to be completed before the 2011 election, and in the meantime, most Liberals did not want to talk about it. This was an undoubted setback for LGBT advocates and educational reformers. How did it happen?

Faith-Based Activist Mobilization in Ontario

Was the strength of evangelical political networks a decisive factor for any of the important players in the provincial legislature and government? Yes and no. It is fair to say that the deployment of antiquely homophobic rhetoric by Charles McVety has little credibility in the Canadian politics of the 2000s and normally limited reach even among evangelicals. On the other hand, his apparent influence over the medium-term fate of a modest change in the provincial curriculum suggests we take a fresh look at the role of the religious right in provincial politics.

Let us go back to earlier episodes of religious right political organizing directed at provincial policymaking for clues on influence. In the mid-1970s and early 1980s, at the time that American religious conservatives were politically mobilizing around abortion and gay/lesbian rights, there was little equivalent organizing in Canada. After criminal code amendments related to both reproduction and homosexuality were passed by Parliament in 1969, most politicians in Canada were content for a time to treat those issues as resolved or appropriately left to the courts.[16]

This changed in the mid-1980s, when evangelical Protestant and conservative Roman Catholic mobilization around morality politics grew significantly. At the federal level, abortion became a significant political issue as a result of court challenges to remaining restrictions on reproductive choice. The Supreme Court of Canada's 1988 ruling in *R. v. Morgentaler* alarmed pro-life advocates and induced such groups as the Evangelical Fellowship of Canada (EFC) to enhance their federal policymaking presence. They intensified their pressure on Brian Mulroney's Conservative government to restrict abortion access, but the government's attempt to do so failed in 1991, and a further court ruling in 1993 (*R. v. Morgentaler*) substantially limited the capacity for provincial governments to apply restrictions. This essentially eliminated the potential for most hot button reproductive issues to become the focus of provincial politics.

Lesbian and gay rights were different. The prospect of significant gains by LGBT activists in this same period stimulated religiously conservative mobilizing provincially as well as federally. The most important equality provision of the Charter of Rights and Freedoms (section 15) came into effect in 1985, and while it did not explicitly include "sexual orientation," there was growing belief in legal and judicial circles that the courts would see it as a ground analogous to those enumerated in the section. Quebec had already amended its rights charter to explicitly include sexual orientation, and now in Ontario, the constitutional argument was adding to the weight of lesbian/gay activist pressure on the Liberal government of David Peterson elected in 1985.[17]

When that government was persuaded in 1986 to amend the provincial human rights code, evangelical Protestants took the lead in mobilizing grass-roots pressure on provincial politicians, supported by Ontario's Roman Catholic hierarchy. Even though the campaign's core activists had limited resources and political experience, they managed to generate a volume of phone calls, letters, and petitions directed at the provincial legislature that had virtually no precedent.[18] The amendment was approved, but in the face of concerted opposition from all but a few Conservative legislators, and persistent divisions inside the Liberal caucus.

This struggle was replayed in 1994, when the provincial NDP government was persuaded by LGBT activists to introduce a wide-ranging measure to extend relationship rights to same-sex couples. Once again, evangelical Protestants and the Catholic hierarchy took a lead in mobilizing grass-roots opposition.[19] They got full support from the Conservative caucus and were able to play on Liberal and NDP internal divisions. The legislation was defeated, and Christian mobilizing against it was unquestionably an important factor.

Whatever momentum was gained by religious conservatives on this issue, however, was diminished by continuing court victories for sexual minority claimants. In 1999, in a family-law case originating in Ontario, the Supreme Court of Canada ruled that denying rights to same-sex couples that were already accorded to heterosexual de facto couples was unconstitutional (*M. v. H.*). By now the Conservatives were in power and Mike Harris was premier, and his government was obliged to do precisely what they had resisted five years earlier, namely to extend statutory recognition to lesbian and gay couples. This did not mean that full equity had been secured in the province, but a number of very controversial issues were now legally settled.

At the federal level, only marriage was left as a major hot button issue, and it mobilized religious conservatives on an unprecedented scale.[20] As Jonathan Malloy argues, it also forged a more solid coalition among moral conservatives than previous battles.[21] But that opposition was a rearguard action, facing unequivocal court rulings that marriage had to be opened up to same-sex couples. And since it was a federal issue, Ontario's provincial politicians, including provincial Conservatives, were able to stay out of the debate.

The wave of Ontario-specific organizing by Christian conservatives, then, appeared for a time to have come and gone in about a decade. It also seemed increasingly clear that there was less partisan interest in appealing to that electorate by taking strong and visible positions on morality issues. And even at the peak of their political organizing, religious conservatives had far fewer resources than their American counterparts – in Canada generally and Ontario specifically. Evangelical Christians, who represent the core of religious right mobilization on most issues, comprise between one-third and one-half of the population segment that they represent in the United States, and their political fundraising capacity is modest compared to that of their American counterparts.[22] The Roman Catholic hierarchy across Canada is as conservative on these issues as it has been in half a century, and it has been especially crucial in pro-life organizing. On the other hand, there is no indication of significant influence on Catholic popular opinion, which tends to track at about the Canadian and Ontario averages in attitudes towards reproductive and sexuality issues.

In general, Canadian public opinion on both reproductive and sexual diversity issues has swung strongly away from the positions adopted by religious traditionalists. Using Environics data, Amy Langstaff points to significant shifts in attitudes towards sexual diversity (see table 14.1).[23]

Table 14.1. Canadian Public Opinion on Moral Issues (%)

	Same-sex marriage			
	Strongly support	Somewhat support	Somewhat oppose	Strongly oppose
2001	29	26	11	30
2010	43	25	9	20

Abortion: "Every woman who wants to have an abortion should be able to have one."

	Agree	Disagree
1985	53	41
2000	66	26
2010	74	22

Source: Environics Institute, *Focus Canada 2010* (Toronto, 2010), 39

On the other hand, there is a sizeable minority of Ontarians (and Canadians) still either opposed to abortion and the public recognition of sexual diversity or uneasy about such changes. One 2010 poll showed that 39 per cent of Ontarians favour abortion being legal only "under certain circumstances," and 38 per cent support state funding for abortion procedures only in the face of "medical emergencies."[24] The "adamant" anti-gay minority described by Langstaff constitutes about 30 per cent of the population, but until the mid-2000s, about half of Canadians opposed same-sex marriage, as well as adoption by lesbian/gay couples.[25] The urban–rural differences here and elsewhere are significant, so there are parts of Ontario where the hold of traditional positions remains sizeable, even if not a majority. In the right circumstances, and on the right issues, these beliefs or anxieties can translate into substantial political mobilization.

In the case of the 2010 controversy over sex education, there was no high-visibility political mobilization in any way comparable to earlier episodes. The largest of the evangelical groups (Evangelical Fellowship of Canada, Focus on the Family Canada) seem not to have entered the fray in any obvious way, in part because of insufficient time to react. Most MPPs indicated no abnormal level of pushback on this issue – a far cry from the waves of protest that their predecessors received in 1986 and 1994 when sexual minority issues were front and centre at Queen's Park.

However, there was the prospect of unpredictable mobilization. Intense mainstream media attention to the new curriculum in effect did the work of such advocacy groups by repeating the most controversial references in the curriculum, with talk of penises, families headed by two mommies or two daddies, and oral and anal sex. Far beyond the constituencies most readily mobilized by the religious right, these messages tapped potential pools of disquiet about teaching sex to kids.[26] This would include parents who knew perfectly well that their children were being inundated by highly sexualized messages from the world around them, but saw themselves as besieged by that and not at all ready to acquiesce in it. As a result, they saw schools moving into this kind of terrain as adding to the challenge rather than helping. And of course most Ontarians do not have school-aged children, and many do not have day-to-day contact with the kinds of questions that children are asking about sexuality. It was not hard for Conservative strategists to foresee an easy weapon to use against the government in the next election.

The Role of Moral Traditionalism in the Progressive Conservative Party

The fact that the Conservative Party decided to focus on this issue as soon as it became public was critical to the sense of crisis that began to envelop the premier's office, but was far from preordained. Most caucus members remained comparatively traditional on family issues, though for almost all of the period since the mid-1990s, the party leadership was also determined to retain a highly disciplined focus on the neoliberal agenda, intent on preventing outbursts that would flag the religiosity or moral traditionalism of members.

Until the 1990s, the Conservatives generally positioned themselves at the pragmatic centre of Canadian political life. Leaders such as Leslie Frost, John Robarts, and William Davis avoided straying far from centrism or embracing anything that could be easily discerned as a clear ideological position.[27] They embodied what Sid Noel describes as the "operative norms" of Ontario's political culture, including a focus on economic growth while balancing competing interests, and highlighting effective government management.[28] Randall White echoes similar themes, characterizing the post-war Tory dynasty as presided over by centrists who avoided major controversy.[29]

From the late 1960s until the mid-1980s, Ontario's Conservative leaders were able to stay away from reproductive issues by leaving them to federal decision-makers, and from sexual diversity issues because other parties were long reluctant to embrace reformist positions. That said, there could never have been any doubt that most of the party's legislators held traditional views on moral issues related to gender and sexuality. In 1981, when LGBT activists secured enough support in the Ontario legislature to have an amendment to include sexual orientation in the Human Rights Code introduced, only one PC member supported it (out of a caucus of seventy). Mike Harris was among the "no" votes and had been chair of the legislative committee that had examined the amendment in detail.[30] In 1986, when LGBT activists succeeding in getting a sexual orientation amendment included in a package of measures introduced by the minority Liberal government, over three-quarters of the Conservative caucus (forty-one) voted against it (with five abstentions).[31]

At about this time, change was occurring inside the party that would push the Conservatives dramatically to the right, but with a focus on the neoliberal agenda of cutting taxes and reducing the scope of state activity. In the early 1980s, young university-based neoconservatives like Tom Long and Tony Clement took control of the PC Youth Association.[32] They wanted nothing of the pragmatism that had dominated the party's provincial history and rejected the centrism embodied in the federal leadership of Joe Clark. They were, as White points out, free market ideologues.[33] The loss of two provincial elections in the middle of the decade, one under the leadership of the comparative right-wing Frank Miller, the other under the centrist Grossman, created an opening for the "rebels," widened by the decline of the federal PCs. The result was a 1990 victory for Mike Harris, who had sided with the young rebels from a relatively early stage.[34] After losing the election of that year, they consolidated their hold on the provincial party, strengthened by the 1993 decimation of the federal PCs and the success that Ralph Klein was experiencing in Alberta with a platform embodying assertive neoliberalism.[35] The result of their labours was the "Common Sense Revolution," a sweeping program for change made public well ahead of the 1995 provincial election.

The Conservatives won the 1995 election, and Harris lost little time in rolling back NDP policies on welfare, labour, and employment equity. As much as any of his predecessors, he also ensured the primacy of the premier's office in all policymaking.[36] Moral issues were gaining visibility at the federal level, propelled in part by the growth of a Reform Party much shaped by religious conservatives. As Bradley Walchuk points out, however, "The provincial party had no interest in commenting on divisive social issues, and indeed, sought to avoid taking a stance at all costs."[37] Many leaders and strategists would have echoed the words of Ralph Klein when he warned against embracing moral regulation in a new united right (being intensely discussed in the late 1990s). As he put it, "These questions are best left to the internal moral compass found within every Canadian."[38]

However, this is too simplified a picture. After all, Margaret Thatcher and Ronald Reagan, models for most of the conservative revolutionaries in Ontario, were not hesitant to play on morally conservative themes, particularly on LGBT rights. Ralph Klein may well have thought that a national united right had to avoid moral issues, but his own government was prepared to pander to anti-gay sentiments in Alberta by expressing rhetorical anger in the face of LGBT rights gains.[39]

Ontario PC insiders, too, were concerned about the potential for discontents to break away from the party, perhaps by forming a provincial branch of Reform. Woolstencroft points out that there were party strategists who attributed the loss of up to sixteen seats in 1990 to fringe parties on the right.[40] Harris's own roots lay in rural, small-town, and suburban population segments that had little instinctive sympathy with equity claims, especially those from women's groups and LGBT advocates. As John Ibbitson says, Harris appealed to "the traditional values of Ontario's settler culture – self-reliance, low taxes, minimal interference from big-city politics."[41] Many of the party's caucus members were from regions where traditional gender and sexual attitudes remained comparatively unchallenged. Even if they recognized the risks of being tarred as extremist, if faced with an issue like lesbian/gay rights there was no hesitation in standing firm in opposition. For example, in the 1994 debate over NDP legislation to recognize same-sex couples, the Harris Conservatives eagerly presented petitions mobilized by the religious right, and in debate they invoked the familiar American right-wing language of "special interest groups" to marginalize LGBT claims.[42] Among Conservative members who voted that day, not a single one supported the legislation.

By the time the PCs were in government, there were no obvious issues on which they could legislate in the direction of moral traditionalism, and the government was generally intent on avoiding what journalist R. Sheppard characterized as "the messy moral issues" that tended to be seen by Conservatives as "political losers." [43] In 1999, when the Supreme Court of Canada ruled (in *M. v. H*) that Ontario's family law was unconstitutional in its exclusion of gays and lesbians, the Harris government knew it had little choice but to respond legislatively. It then worked behind the scenes to ensure that the bill was debated and passed with as little delay as possible. It was given the grudging title of *An Act to Amend Certain Statutes Because of the Supreme Court of Canada Decision in M. v. H.*, but the deed was done quickly enough to not distract from the government's real priorities.

There were still signals to moral traditionalists that the government understood their views. One example was the government's declaration, soon after assuming power, that it was reassessing an injunction secured by the previous government restricting protests at abortion clinics.[44] That went nowhere, but the PCs did introduce tax credits for parents with children in private schools, and this would unquestionably have pleased those who supported faith-based education.

When Mike Harris stepped down from the party leadership in 2002, Ernie Eves soon became the front-running candidate to succeed him. At times he tried to put some distance between his policy priorities and those of Mike Harris, but he had been a close ally of Harris and an important minister responsible for implementing the Common Sense Revolution. He also did not completely sidestep morality policy, declaring his opposition to same-sex marriage while campaigning in the 2003 provincial election.

The party did seem to revert to more genuinely centrist leadership with the 2004 selection of John Tory to replace Eves (after the electoral defeat of 2003). He was an urban centrist in the mould of earlier party heads, more moderate on fiscal issues than the Harrisites, with no obvious links to morally conservative positions. However, his failure to win office in the 2007 election, and the continuing discontent with his leadership from Harris supporters, led him to resign his position in 2009.

Tim Hudak was then chosen as leader, representing a return to unequivocal neoliberalism. He had been a supporter of Jim Flaherty, the most "Harrisite" of the candidates in the 2002 leadership race. His campaign for the leadership indicated no particular interest in moral conservatism, but in response to a 1995 Campaign Life Coalition survey, he wrote, "I believe that it is the government's role to promote the choice of life in child-bearing decisions" and "to encourage women to carry the babies to term."[45] During the leadership race, Frank Klees was the favoured candidate of many religious conservatives, but one Christian group received a message from a Hudak spokesperson that "made it clear that he is pro-life" and that he strongly agreed that health-care workers should have to right to avoid assisting with medical procedures that violate their conscience.[46] Hudak would also have taken note that Klees got about one-third of the votes cast by PC members in the first ballot of the leadership race, trailing Hudak by only 400 votes. No one in the new leader's circle would have ignored the numerical importance of moral traditionalists in the party's electorate and activist base. And all would have been mindful of the shifting allegiance of religious voters toward the federal Conservatives, and the potential for a similar realignment among provincial voters.[47]

As for the sex education controversy of 2010, the Conservatives saw an opportunity to deploy an issue that flagged traditional family values not only to an important current in the party's traditional base, but also one that might lure many "new Canadians" away from the Liberals. The federal Conservative Party was doing this with some signs of success. The provincial party's leaders did not have the kinds of wedge issues that their federal counterparts have had available to them over recent years (such as same-sex marriage), so the sudden availability of a controversial issue revolving around schools – as important an issue area for ethno-religious minorities as any – increased its appeal.

The fact that even mainstream media outlets that had supported gay-positive initiatives in the past were prepared to treat the new curriculum as controversial, and provide sensationalizing examples for public viewing, made the issue that much more irresistible. In other words, Conservatives could see the issue as one that had enough appeal beyond the recognizable boundaries of the religious right to be deployed as a weapon for beating up the government, not only in 2010, but during the 2011 election. In that election, Tim Hudak defended the use of a sensationalist flyer attacking the Liberals on the sex education issue and repeated the distortions of the Charles McVety attacks of 2010.[48] In 2012, the PC caucus unanimously voted against a government bill aimed at school bullying in favour of their own anodyne measure that avoided specific mention of sexual diversity.[49]

Strategic Anxieties in the Liberal Party of Ontario

Premier McGuinty was widely thought to be personally progressive on most of the hot button issues associated with Christian right organizing. There were far fewer social conservatives in the caucus than there had been one and two decades earlier. Still, there were concerns about strategic vulnerability within important segments of the electorate once

Conservative showed themselves willing to deploy the issue for political gain. Religious and moral traditionalist mobilizing on an issue like sex education, or the threat of it, might affect constituencies that had voted Liberal in the past and that were considered essential for the 2011 election.

In 1981, only 15 per cent of Liberal MPPs had supported adding sexual orientation to the provincial human rights code. When they were in government in 1986, social reformers like Ian Scott had important allies in the Liberal Cabinet, but they faced a significant challenge in securing enough support from their own backbenchers to effect changes in human rights law. When relationship issues were up for debate a decade later, this time under an NDP government, the Liberal leader Lyn McLeod was broadly sympathetic, but opposition among her colleagues forced her to switch sides, and in the end thirty-two of thirty-five Liberals voted against the measure.

The Liberals stayed very close to the centre by choosing the comparatively safe Dalton McGuinty over the more progressive Gerard Kennedy in the 1996 leadership convention. On the one hand, he had staked out a pro-choice position on abortion and seemed receptive to full equality on sexual diversity grounds. On the other, the Liberal leadership knew full well that the party retained voter bases in rural and small-city southwestern Ontario, in traditional corners of eastern Ontario, and in suburban areas where ethno-cultural minorities were amply represented. As Robert Williams has written, the Liberals had endured as a pragmatic party with "something for everyone."[50] They still needed votes in regions where the shift towards fully inclusive sentiments had been slow or partial. Catholic voters mattered, and the premier's chief of staff as well as his education minister (during the sex education controversy) were, like him, practising Catholics. They would have been well enough connected to provincial Catholic networks to sense trouble. More significant was talk of pushback from among "new Canadians" – communities with large numbers of immigrants who had traditionally voted Liberal. The Liberal caucus had several South Asian MPPs, and though most were socially progressive, they would undoubtedly have received some indication of negative reaction to the curriculum. So would MPPs representing areas in the Greater Toronto Area with substantial populations of new immigrants or visible minority communities with strong currents of religious or social conservatism.

A major factor that amplified anxiety within Liberal ranks was the lack of preparedness for controversy inside the offices of the premier and the education minister. Within the ministry, curricular reform had become sufficiently routinized, and the consultations entailed in revision so expert driven, that few if any participants saw any part of this as unmanageably controversial. They may well have been lulled into a false sense of security by the relative lack of controversy that met other steps taken by the ministry over the previous two years to enhance school response to sexual diversity. And while the premier and his office worked more closely on schools issues than others, they had a strong and competent minister in Kathleen Wynne at the time the curriculum was approved, and seemed to have devoted little serious attention to the political risks associated with this issue. This treatment of the curricular update as routine turned riskier with the appointment of a new minister in January. Leona Dombrowsky was a loyal foot soldier but had no personal or principled commitment to the issues at stake here.

The absence of political preparedness to respond to controversy meant that the issue was framed almost entirely by conservative opponents during the first few days after the McVety press release. This left Liberal MPPs and party supporters adrift with too few life preservers. Public opinion polling showed the government to be vulnerable in the lead-up to the 2011 election, and the premier had come under sustained criticism on other policy fronts – most notably the move to harmonize federal and provincial sales taxes. Once it was clear that the Conservatives were willing to seize an issue that posed an especially ominous danger outside the province's big cities, the strategic preference to put the issue to one side for the time being was compelling.

Other Factors

The specifics of the issue at stake also made a difference and may also make generalizing about the political influence of moral conservatives in Ontario hazardous. Educational reformers were also caught off guard by the sudden surge of controversy and had limited resources for a highly public struggle. The media also played an unwitting role in supporting Christian conservative advocates.

The Distinctiveness of Schooling Issues

Part of what made the sex ed controversy a difficult one was the longstanding avoidance of sexual diversity in the vast majority of Canadian elementary classrooms, a fact that most Canadians (and Ontarians) seem either unaware of or unconcerned with. Many Canadians who would count themselves as favourable to educational reform imagine that schools are as inclusive towards sexual minorities as family law is towards same-sex couples. When they hear sensationalized details about what was being implemented in sex ed, they are not well armoured by understanding the schooling experience of LGBT students. Teaching about sexuality has always been difficult, and educators usually approach it with caution. Even parents with children are hesitant to ask what goes on in sex ed classes, and those without children have even less basis for knowing what happens in schools, and less reason to give the matter thought.

All talk of sexual diversity in schools, and of sexuality more broadly, can easily trigger large and unresolved questions about the social and cultural role of schools. Among these are whether schools should convey values that have traditionally prevailed in society or encourage questioning of dominant ideas; whether educators should emphasize what is common to students and the rest of the population or emphasize diversity; whether schools should protect students from aspects of the world around them or fully expose them to even the harsh elements of that world; and whether teachers should defer to and privilege parental authority and leave discussions of such issues as sex and morality to the family.

Reform Activist Limitations

Another factor strengthening the hand of traditionalists was the weakness of educational reformers and LGBT activists. Those who knew about the curricular changes seemed to have anticipated no controversy, and even if they did, they may not have had the resources to respond quickly when the story hit the front pages of the papers. Politicized networks aiming for more LGBT-inclusive schools existed for many years in Toronto, pressing for change with the Toronto School Board in the late 1980s and early 1990s, and then again with the amalgamated Toronto District School Board at the end of the 1990s. These advocates were effective, but their networks were not institutionalized in a form that could be easily mobilized for future controversies. Many LGBT teachers also remained cautious in speaking out on these issues, still insecure about being fully out. Some of Ontario's reform advocates worked inside supportive unions, as in other provinces, but it took until the early 2000s for more than the Elementary Teachers Federation of Ontario to become assertively engaged with these issues.

The process of effecting change in education is also a long and difficult one, requiring sustained pressure within complex administrative systems at the board and ministry levels. Schools-focused advocates have allies in LGBT groups such as Egale Canada and Queer Ontario, and broad reformist groups like People for Education and subject-specific groups like Ophea (Ontario Physical and Health Education Association), but this is a policy area dominated by professionals, and these groups are thinly spread already. Egale has only a few paid staff, and Queer Ontario is a relatively new group operated only by volunteers and with only slight visibility.

In the crucial days of April in which sex ed became controversial, there was no set of networks or groups able to mount an effective response to the sensationalism generated by opponents. There were isolated voices of protest, but they were slow to emerge and insufficient to mobilize the grass roots to create a balance in messages. The one-sidedness of the noise was enough to scare the government, and by the time supporters were organizing a more concerted response, it was too late.

Media Vulnerabilities

As we have already seen, the media strengthened the hands of moral conservatives without necessarily intending to, and put educational reformers on the defensive. The willingness to play up what could easily be seen as sensational guidelines for elementary school teachers helped opponents of the curriculum set the agenda. The absence of any governmental "framing" of the new curriculum meant that in this first flurry of headline stories, even those reporters who were comfortable with LGBT inclusiveness and wary of McVety's obvious homophobia ended up dancing to the tune set out in the original press release, implying throughout that the changes were controversial.

Mainstream media outlets that devote any resources at all to covering provincial politics have only a fraction of the staff they once did. There are also few mainstream media specialists on educational matters anywhere in Canada. So there was arguably not a single noticeable media voice in the crucial first two days of news coverage with any significant background in education policy in Ontario. This is not unique to this policy field, but the complexities of what was being implemented here meant that news editors were vulnerable to treating this story as simply a controversy, with the potential to enliven the front page. Electronic media outlets then simply picked up their cues from those lead stories.

Conclusion

Up to 2010, faith-based political activism in Ontario had secured no significant policy gains since the 1994 defeat of legislation extending recognition to lesbian and gay couples, and even then the victory was given a short life by court victories. Does the outcome of the controversy over sex education in Ontario schools suggest that there is more potential for political influence than this earlier history would suggest? And is there need for a more nuanced analysis of the response to moral conservatism inside Ontario's Conservative and Liberal parties?

Activism born of religious and moral conservatism will continue to be visible in policy debates in Ontario – of that there is no question. True, there are few hot button issues within provincial jurisdiction that have significant mobilizational potential, and the major parties will be generally reluctant to embrace a wide-ranging agenda shaped by moral traditionalism – accurately sensing shifts in Ontario public opinion. Conservatives also remember that they lost the 2007 election in substantial measure because of a promise to extend funding to faith-based schools, and they may well arrive at the conclusion that they lost crucial votes in 2011 by allowing candidates to deploy attacks on the government around sex education. When the Liberal government's school bullying legislation passed over strenuous PC objections in June 2012, Tim Hudak seemed at pains to emphasize that his party did so in favour of its own alternative. He then refused further comment, downplaying the significance of what names to use for school groups, and switching to the state of the economy.[51]

Having said that, the federal Conservative Party has demonstrated that it can retain the loyalty of its evangelical Protestant supporters and make at least moderate gains among practising Catholics and morally conservative ethnic voters by occasionally signalling its support for traditional values, while still retaining its neoliberal preoccupations. The most prominent tool deployed on this front has been its law-and-order agenda, which has an appeal beyond faith communities. But it has also promoted or enacted measures that are more specifically targeted to moral conservatives.[52] This path would appeal to many of Ontario's provincial Conservatives, and the fact that the Liberals "blinked" over sex education in 2010 would reinforce the temptations among strategists to keep an eye out for issues with morally conservative resonance.

What about Liberals? They were clearly set back by the events of April 2010, even while an overwhelming majority of the caucus was sympathetic to the changes being made in the curriculum. The impact of the short-lived McVety campaign, then, was derived in part from scaring Liberals worried about swing ridings important for their hold on government. All it needed was for the major opposition party to show a willingness to take up the issue. When sex education was revived in 2011, the Liberals probably "won" that exchange, but mostly by arguing that they had shelved the changes being complained about. They seemed to stiffen their spine in the face of the debate over Gay-Straight Alliances in 2012, though they were helped by the growing popular and media support for action on homophobic bullying, and by the extent to which the controversy focused (even more than in the sex education debate of 2010) on the resistance of Catholic boards.[53] This weakened the alliance of religious conservatives, not least because it brought to light divisions among Catholic educators themselves. Early in the debate over Bill 13, Charles McVety attacked it as a vehicle for boosting a radical sex education agenda, but grassroots religious right organizing on this never seemed to take off. The government did not "blink" this time, though it has remained notably silent on curricular change since the sex ed flare-up in April 2010.[54]

The influence of conservative faith communities in Ontario, then, is both limited and circumstantial. They are not particularly institutionalized for political action provincially, but they have access to grass roots constituencies that gather weekly in religious services, so individuals and groups have a potentially effective mechanism for political mobilization. Calls to action will not always spark widespread take-up, and even if they do, they will not always have a policy impact. Indeed, as we have seen during federal and provincial debates over sexuality, religious right advocacy can be accurately portrayed as out of touch with public opinion and "mainstream" Canadian values, no matter how many emails they write and telephone calls they make.

But particularly in debates about policy issues as fundamentally unresolved as those related to schooling, there is no reason to think that moral traditionalism and conservative faith-based political intervention will remain permanently on the margins, or that they have no capacities to tap into the concerns of politically relevant sectors of the voting public. The controversy over sex education shows us that even in a province where secularization has been powerfully evident in several decades of public policy change, and in everyday religious practise, faith-based conservatism can still play an influential political role.

NOTES

1 This chapter is part of an ongoing project on the relationship between religiously based activism and Canadian political parties, supported by a grant from the Social Sciences and Humanities Research Council. I could not have imagined telling this story without several people agreeing to confidential interviews. I am also extremely grateful for the assistance of Paul Thomas and Jerald Sabin, both of the PhD program in political science at the University of Toronto. David Docherty provided helpful insights at an early stage in this project, and Mark Bonham at a later state. Over the last couple of years, Chris Cochrane, now a colleague, has been extraordinarily willing to provide me fresh data on several of the analytical questions I delve into.

2 Marci McDonald, *The Armageddon Factor: The Rise of Christian Nationalism in Canada* (Toronto: Random House, 2010).

3 Richard Brennan, "Cross-Dressing for 6-Year-Olds? Hudak Sticks Up for Anti-Liberal Flyer," *Toronto Star*, 3 October 2011. See also Adam Radwanski and Steve Ladurantaye, "Conservatives Slipping, But Looking to Their Ground Game," *Globe and Mail*, 4 October 2011.

4 See my *Queer Inclusions, Continental Divisions: Public Recognition of Sexual Diversity in Canada and the United States* (Toronto: University of Toronto Press, 2008), chap. 8; and Egale Canada, *Youth Speak Up about Homophobia and Transphobia: The First National Climate Survey on Homophobia in Canadian Schools, Phase One Report* (Toronto: Egale Canada, 2009).

5 Ontario Ministry of Education, *Shaping a Culture of Respect in Our Schools: Promoting a Safe and Healthy Relationship* (Toronto: Queen's Printer for Ontario, 2008), 13.

6 At least one newspaper report flagged the potential controversy in the report's recommendation for more detailed sexual health education, and in earlier grades: "New Approach to Sex Ed.," *Toronto Star*, 29 December 2008.

7 For example, in grade three, students are encouraged to respect a variety of parenting patterns, in grade four to recognize bullying, and in grade five to know the right names for body parts and to acknowledge the changes that begin with puberty. In grade six, there is more discussion of puberty and of the inappropriateness of stereotypes associated with sexuality.

8 Patrick B. Craine, 2 March 2010, LifeSiteNews, http://www.lifesitenews.com/news/archive//ldn/2010/mar/10030216.

9 Carmelina Prete, "Sexual Diversity Policy on Agenda," *Hamilton Spectator*,15 April 2010.

10 McVety himself is said to have acknowledged that he heard about the new curriculum from the *Spectator* story.
11 Kate Hammer and Karen Howlett, "The End of Innuendo: Ont. Schools Making Sex Education More Explicit," *Globe and Mail*, 21 April 2010. See also Kristin Roshowy and Robert Benzie, "Opponents to Protest New Sex-Ed Curriculum," *Toronto Star*, 21 April 2010.
12 Robert Benzie, "Ontario and Sex-Ed: We're Starting Over," *Toronto Star*, 27 April 2010.
13 "Archbishop of Ottawa: Sex Ed Standards Can't Trump Catholic Educational Freedom," *Catholic News Agency*, 23 April 2010, http://www.catholicnewsagency.com/news/archbishop_of_ottawa_sex_ed_standards_cant_trump_catholic_educational_freedom/.
14 Marcus McCann, "Roll Out," *Xtra!*, 6 May 2010.
15 Benzie, "Ontario and Sex-Ed."
16 Access to abortion was opened up but subject to approval by a hospital-based therapeutic abortion committee, in some regions difficult or impossible to access. Homosexual activity between men was decriminalized only if in "private" and by consenting adults twenty-one years of age or older. In practice, "private" was narrowly and discriminatorily policed. See Gary Kinsman, *The Regulation of Desire: Homo and Hetero Sexualities*, 2nd ed. (Montreal: Black Rose Books, 1996).
17 On this, see Didi Herman, *Rights of Passage: Struggles for Lesbian and Gay Legal Equality* (Toronto: University of Toronto Press, 1994); Tom Warner, *Never Going Back: A History of Queer Activism in Canada* (Toronto: University of Toronto Press, 2002); and my own "Gay Rights and Family Values," *Studies in Political Economy* 26 (Summer 1988): 109–47.
18 This view is based on confidential interviews with legislative insiders, conducted for my article, "Gay Rights and Family Values."
19 See my own account of this, *On the Fringe: Gays and Lesbians in Politics* (Ithaca: Cornell University Press, 1998), chap. 5. See also Tom Warner, *Never Going Back*; and Warner, *Losing Control: Canada's Social Conservatives in the Age of Rights* (Toronto: Between the Lines, 2010).
20 See Rayside, *Queer Inclusions, Continental Divisions*, chap. 4; Jonathan Malloy, "Canadian Evangelicals and Same-Sex Marriage," in *Faith, Politics, and Sexual Diversity in Canada and the United States*, ed., David Rayside and Clyde Wilcox, 144–65 (Vancouver: UBC Press, 2011).
21 Malloy, "Canadian Evangelicals and Same-Sex Marriage."
22 Tom Warner's analysis of social conservatism in Canada highlights several instances of evangelical Christian campaigning against purported threats posed by gay activists in schools, in *Losing Control*.

23 Amy Langstaff, "A Twenty-Year Survey of Canadian Attitudes towards Homosexuality and Gay Rights," in Rayside and Wilcox, *Faith, Politics, and Sexual Diversity*, 49–66. See also Scott Matthews, "The Political Foundations of Support for Same-Sex Marriage in Canada," *Canadian Journal of Political Science* 38 (2004): 841–66; and my own *Queer Inclusions, Continental Divisions*, chap. 2. Most polls show Ontarians as close to the Canadian average on these issues, less supportive of LGBT rights than Quebecers, British Columbians, and Atlantic Canadians; more supportive than residents of the three Prairie provinces.

24 Angus Reid (August 2010). Reported in Chris Selley, "Hudak Could Find Support on Abortion," *National Post*, 20 July 2011.

25 Langstaff refers to this as an "adamant" minority, "Twenty-Year Survey." On adoption, see Rayside, *Queer Inclusions, Continental Divisions*, chaps 2 and 6; and Rachel Epstein, ed., *Who's Your Daddy? And Other Writings on Queer Parenting* (Toronto: Sumach, 2009).

26 See Langstaff, "Twenty-Year Survey."

27 See Robert Williams, "Ontario Party Politics in the 1990s: Comfort Meets Conviction," in *Government and Politics of Ontario*, 5th ed., ed. Graham White, 216–35 (Toronto: University of Toronto Press, 1997).

28 Sid Noel, "The Ontario Political Culture: An Interpretation," in White, *Government and Politics of Ontario*, 49–70.

29 Randall White, *Ontario since 1985* (Toronto: Eastendbooks, 1998).

30 Chris Bearchall, "Ontario Finally Says No," *Body Politic* 80 (January / February 1982): 8–9. See also Warner, *Never Going Back*.

31 The party leader at the time, Larry Grossman, was one of only four who supported the amendment, though he waited until the last minute to declare himself.

32 John Ibbitson, *Promised Land: Inside the Mike Harris Revolution* (Toronto: Prentice Hall, 1997); Peter Woolstencroft, "More Than a Guard Change: Politics in the New Ontario," in *Revolution at Queen's Park: Essays on Governing Ontario*, ed. Sid Noel, 38–54 (Toronto: Lorimer, 1997).

33 White, *Ontario since 1985*, chap. 5.

34 See Williams, "Ontario Party Politics in the 1990s"; and especially Peter Woolstencroft, "Reclaiming the 'Pink Palace': The Progressive Conservative Party Comes in from the Cold," in White, *Government and Politics of Ontario*, 365–400.

35 White, *Ontario since 1985*, chap. 5.

36 Ibid., chap. 9.

37 Bradley Walchuk, "Intra-Party Federalism and the Progressive Conservative Parties of Alberta and Ontario, 1943–2008" (MA thesis, Brock University, 2008).

38 "Klein Warns Conservatives of Reform-Style Excesses," *Globe and Mail*, 20 February 1999.

39 After the Supreme Court of Canada "read in" sexual orientation to the province's human rights code in its 1998 decision in *Vriend*, Klein mused about invoking the Charter's "notwithstanding" clause. Even if he had no intention of doing that, he created room for a torrent of homophobic abuse, kept alive for some time by promises to contain the impact of the ruling.

40 Woolstencroft, "Reclaiming the 'Pink Palace.'"

41 Ibbitson, *Promised Land*, 20–1.

42 See my *On the Fringe*, chap. 5.

43 Quoted by Claire Farid, "Access to Abortion in Ontario: From *Morgentaler 1988* to the *Savings and Restructuring Act*," *Health Law Journal* 5 (1997): 131.

44 Ibid.

45 Shelley, "Hudak Could Find Support on Abortion."

46 The Association for Reformed Political Action (ARPA) Canada, cited in Tanya Talaga, "Hudak Admits to Once Supporting Anti-Abortion Petition," *Toronto Star*, 16 July 2011.

47 See my "The Conservative Party of Canada and Its Religious Constituencies," in Rayside and Wilcox, *Faith, Politics, and Sexual Diversity*, 279–99.

48 Brennan, "Cross-Dressing for 6-Year Olds"; and Radwanski and Ladurantaya, "Conservatives Slipping."

49 Bill 13 (Accepting Schools Act, 2012) toughened penalties for bullying in schools and required boards to support student initiatives to confront bullying, including that based on sexual diversity. Most controversial of all was the requirement that publicly funded boards, including Roman Catholic, accept group names with explicit LGBT references, including Gay-Straight Alliances. See Andrea Houston, "Mission Accomplished," *Xtra!*, 14 June 2012. The Conservative alternative was Bill 14 (Anti-Bullying Act).

50 Robert Williams, "Ontario Party Politics in the 1990s," in White, *Government and Politics of Ontario*, 231.

51 Houston, "Mission Accomplished."

52 See my "The Conservative Party of Canada and Its Religious Constituencies"; and Warner, *Losing Control*, chap. 7.

53 Kate Hammer and Karen Howlett, "Catholic Schools Fear Fallout from Bill 13," *Globe and Mail*, 5 June 2012.

54 Tanya Talaga, "Anti-Bullying Bill a Front for 'Sex Ed,' Religious Groups Say," *Toronto Star*, 6 December 2011.

15 The Blue Electorate in Quebec and Support for the ADQ and the CPC

ANDREA LAWLOR AND ÉRIC BÉLANGER

The province of Quebec has seen a number of successful right-leaning political parties in its past.[1] The Conservative Party dominated Quebec's provincial electoral scene for most of the first thirty years of the Canadian Confederation. The provincial Conservatives returned to power in 1936 under the banner of the Union Nationale and the leadership of Maurice Duplessis, who remained premier until his death in 1959, with only a short Liberal interruption between 1939 and 1944. At the federal level, Quebec's provincial wing of the Social Credit Party won a sizeable number of seats during the 1960s and 1970s under the leadership of *créditiste* Réal Caouette, while in the 1980s Brian Mulroney became prime minister of Canada in good part as the result of vast support his Progressive-Conservative Party received in Quebec.

In this context, the right-wing provincial party Action démocratique du Québec's (ADQ) impressive success in vote intention polls in 2002 and its rise to Official Opposition status following the outcome of the 2007 election raised the question of whether the province was witnessing a re-emergence of the right. The subsequent decline of ADQ in the December 2008 election, and its absorption three years later into the more moderate new party Coalition Avenir Québec, indicate that the party's short-lived success may have been an anomaly in what was otherwise a relatively stable provincial party system.[2] Yet, during that period, the ADQ were not alone in their electoral upsurge. At the federal level, the Conservative Party of Canada (CPC) also made significant inroads in the Quebec electorate in both 2006 and 2008, sparking debate on whether the two parties shared the same constituency.

This chapter poses three questions. First, is there a "blue" electorate in Quebec in attitudinal terms, and if so, how large is it? Second, to what extent did this electorate provide support for both the ADQ and the CPC in recent provincial and federal elections? Finally, was there a party-level link between the provincial ADQ and the federal Conservatives, and if so, what features characterized it? Thus, we anticipate the linkages between the ADQ and the CPC to manifest themselves through two channels: the attitudes and vote patterns of Quebec voters, and through the connections between the parties themselves.

In this chapter, we focus on the Quebec electorate's conservative attitudes and its electoral support for both provincial and federal conservative parties. As such, we are interested primarily in the attitudinal manifestations of conservatism: whether some Quebecers are wary of state intrusion, or have a preference for more efficient government, for a more restrictive approach to minority accommodation, and for maintaining traditional family values and family structure, and whether these attitudes fuel electoral support for conservative political parties. These are some of the dimensions of conservatism that are salient in the current discussion of conservatism in Canada, and each is tapped by the survey data we use throughout this chapter.

Mapping Quebec's Blue Electorate

The roots of Quebec's conservatism have often been traced back to France's Old Regime, which was in place during the French settlement of the seventeenth and eighteenth centuries, and then to the dominant Catholicism of the nineteenth and early twentieth centuries.[3] Traditional Catholic conservatism, which was the prevailing ideology in Quebec in the 1950s and earlier, can be characterized by a wariness of the state and its authority, as well as clerical and parochial dominance.[4] It was marked by a substantial dose of traditionalism with an emphasis on the family and on the preservation of French Canada's language and values.[5] With the secularization that accompanied the Quiet Revolution of the 1960s, Catholicism and its brand of conservatism quickly lost its hold on Quebec. The pro-market views of the rising francophone bourgeoisie slowly acquired more prominence in the province.[6] Since the 1990s, Quebec economic and social conservatism has become more evident, often linked to a fervent need for economic growth that reaffirms its cultural heritage. Indeed, the accompanying desire for greater autonomy and sovereign authority over its own affairs has encouraged Quebec to embrace international trade (notably with France and the United States, but also more broadly), in addition to, and at times in lieu of, intra-provincial trade. This economic dimension has become even more salient following the end of the consensus on the "Quebec model" of the welfare state inherited from the Quiet Revolution.[7] In addition, modern conservatism in Quebec has been characterized by anti-pluralist views in the wake of the debate surrounding the "reasonable accommodation" of cultural minorities.[8]

In empirical terms, we may ask how widespread such conservative views are among the Quebec population at the beginning of the twenty-first century. What factors account for those conservative attitudes? To explore these questions, we use post-electoral survey data comprising two independent samples of respondents that have been interviewed in 2007 and 2008 ($N = 2175$ and 1151, respectively).[9] These representative surveys targeted residents of Quebec who were of voting age at the time of each of the 2007 and 2008 provincial elections and provide questions about the respondents' voting history at the federal and provincial level, socio-demographic characteristics, and attitudes towards issues relevant to each election.[10]

Figure 15.1 reports the distribution of answers to six items that refer broadly to the role of the state: private sector involvement in health care, privatization of Hydro Québec, government intervention (on poverty and the environment), opinions on labour unions and government waste of tax funds. Figure 15.2 presents the distribution of answers to a series of questions tapping moral conservative views: emphasis on traditional family values, religious service attendance, same-sex marriage, and opinions on reasonable accommodations (the last asked in 2007 only).

Figure 15.1. Views on the Role of the State

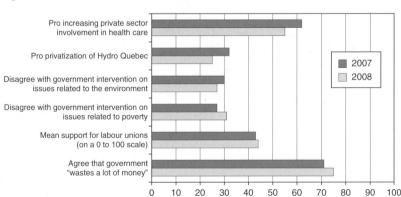

Figure 15.2. Views on Moral Traditionalism and Minority Groups

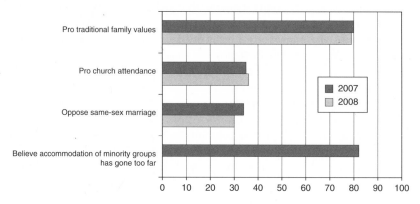

The data from figure 15.1 indicate that, on average, Quebecers have mixed views on the role of the state. On one hand, fewer than a third of the respondents agree with the idea of privatizing Hydro Québec and with the notion that state intervention on issues related to the environment and poverty is not beneficial. On the other hand, around 60 per cent agree with an increase of the private sector's involvement in health care; barely 40 per cent or so support labour unions. Quebecers are also very critical in general of governments' financial management, with around 70 per cent agreeing that governments waste a significant portion of tax money. Although an index made up of the first four agree/disagree statements indicates that, on average, the Quebec electorate situates itself close to the centre-left on a state intervention spectrum (a mean score of 0.40 on a 0–1 scale running from left to right), the answers given to some of the six items suggest that many Quebecers are nonetheless open to some ideas from the political and economic right, such as curbing the influence of labour unions, adopting a more stringent approach to government spending, and allowing some private involvement in the delivery of health-care services.

As Figure 15.2 reveals, the picture appears similarly mixed when it comes to describing the extent to which the Quebec electorate embraces views associated with moral conservatism. Unsurprisingly, given the quick secularization of the province following the Second World War and the onset of the Quiet Revolution, not many Quebecers support church attendance. A related finding is that only a third or so of respondents oppose same-sex marriage. That being said, close to 80 per cent of the survey respondents want more emphasis on traditional family values and about as many believe that accommodation of minority groups has "gone too far."[11] An index constructed from the answers to the first three questions found in figure 15.2 indicates that, on average, Quebecers situate themselves close to the centre on this moral conservatism scale (a mean score of 0.45 on a 0–1 scale running from low to high). However, as indicated by the data, this middle value conceals some important variation in the Quebec population's views on issues related to moral conservatism.[12]

We can briefly explore the correlates of these conservative values with the multivariate regression models presented in table 15.1. The dependent variables in these models each comprise the two indices introduced above: the anti-interventionism scale and the moral conservatism scale.[13] The findings from table 15.1 indicate that negative views on state intervention are more likely to be observed amongst younger individuals, women, francophones, and people residing outside of Montreal. Moral conservatism is more likely to be found amongst older people, men, less wealthy individuals, as well as more religious people. Lower levels of education are associated with both indicators of right-leaning views. Finally, nationalism appears negatively associated with conservatism: autonomists and, to a even greater extent, federalists display more conservative views than sovereigntists. While there are many "blue nationalists" in Quebec, the truth remains that nationalists, and even more so sovereigntists, tend to share a strong collectivist vision of Quebec's state and society that contrasts with the more individualistic views generally associated with the economic and social right.[14]

Each variable is measured as follows: Anti-Interventionism = 0–1 scale going from pro- to anti-state intervention (see text); Moral Conservatism = 0–1 scale going from low to high (see text); Age = three-category variable (18–34 = 0; 35–54 = 1; 55+ = 2); Income = three-category variable (< \$39,999 = 1; \$40,000–\$69,999 = 2; > \$70,000 = 3); Female, Post-Secondary, Francophone, Quebec City = dummy variables; Other Regions = dummy variable (0 = Montreal or Quebec City, 1 = otherwise); Religiosity = response to question "Not counting weddings and funerals, how often do you attend services at your place of worship?" (every week or more often = 1; twice a month = 0.75; once every month = 0.5; once or twice a year = 0.25; hardly ever or never = 0); Autonomist, Federalist = dummy variables based on a nationalism scale (see text).

What about those Quebecers who are conservative on both the state intervention and moral conservatism dimensions? To isolate this core

Table 15.1. Correlates of Conservative Values in Quebec

	Anti–interventionism (standard error)	Moral traditionalism (standard error)
Age	−0.03*** (0.00)	0.06***(0.01)
Female	0.03*** (0.01)	−0.06*** (0.01)
Post-secondary	−0.05*** (0.01)	−0.08*** (0.01)
Income	−0.00 (0.00)	−0.02*** (0.01)
Francophone	0.03*** (0.01)	−0.02 (0.02)
Quebec City	0.03*** (0.01)	0.01 (0.01)
Other regions	0.02*** (0.01)	0.02 (0.01)
Religiosity	0.01 (0.01)	0.38*** (0.02)
Autonomist	0.04*** (0.01)	0.02** (0.01)
Federalist	0.06*** (0.01)	0.08*** (0.01)
Year 2008	−0.02*** (0.01)	−0.03*** (0.01)
Constant	0.38*** (0.02)	0.41*** (0.02)
R^2	0.06	0.35
N	2702.38*** (0.02)	2079.03*** (0.01)

* $p < 0.1$; ** $p < 0.05$; *** $p < 0.01$.

constituency we first created a new multiplicative scale combining our two indices of anti-interventionism and moral conservatism. We then identified as "core conservatives" only those individuals who scored higher than one standard deviation unit from the new scale's mean.[15] About 15 per cent of the sample could thus be labelled as holding strongly conservative attitudes across a wide range of issues. While it is not possible to pinpoint the exact core conservative voter, typically the group encompasses full-time, salaried, working-age (above thirty) voters. This group does not comprise francophones exclusively, but most reside either in the Quebec City area or outside of the greater Montreal region. The voting preferences of this core conservative constituency will be explored further in the next section.

The Blue Electorate's Support for the ADQ and the CPC

Have the conservative attitudes found within the Quebec population in 2007–8 translated into strong support for both the ADQ and the

CPC at the ballot box? Our survey data allow us to shed light on this issue. We test two specific questions. First, what are the relevant socio-demographic characteristics and issue attitudes of ADQ and CPC voters? Are determinants of the vote consistent between the two groups? Second, during this period, did supporters of ADQ actually vote for the CPC, and vice versa?

Our comparison of the two electorates relies on separate models that explain vote choice in both the provincial and federal elections,[16] and that include socio-demographic characteristics and cleavages that are relevant in the literature on Quebec voting: age, gender, education, income, occupation, language, and region.[17] We also test the impact of religiosity, partisanship, and factors more specific to Quebec politics such as evaluations of ADQ leader Mario Dumont and positions on the national debate (federalist, autonomist, sovereigntist). We finally include a set of attitudes normally associated with right-wing party support (anti-interventionism, anti-unionism, government efficiency, moral traditionalism). Logit coefficients from these vote regressions appear in table 15.2, as does an estimate of the change in predicted probabilities of supporting the ADQ (or the CPC) based on a change from the minimum to the maximum value of the variables.[18]

Looking first at the group of socio-demographic variables, we note that the two party clienteles share a number of characteristics. First, both clienteles have a similar occupational profile. Generally speaking, conservative voters are salaried workers (as opposed to unemployed individuals), including self-employed voters. This class dimension to vote choice is consistent with right-wing support more generally and with each party's ideological profile, with the "tax-paying middle class" being at the forefront of their concerns.[19] Second, both parties obtained greater support among francophones. Third, region turns out to have a strong explanatory power over most other socio-demographic variables, given that both parties found their support concentrated in the same geographic areas such as the mostly rural "Québec tranquille" and the "Québec réfractaire" (urban but not Montreal), which demonstrated particularly strong support for the ADQ in the past.[20] Pinard and Rafail show that a similar regional dynamic was at work for the CPC in 2006.[21] In both models the Quebec City effect is the strongest, given that this was the main area where both parties were able to hold onto seats in the 2008 elections. Voters outside of Quebec City and Montreal also demonstrate significant support for conservative parties, just not as much as those living in the Quebec City area.

Table 15.2. ADQ and CPC Vote Choice Models

	ADQ	Min–Max	CPC	Min–Max
Age	−0.14 (0.11)	−0.04	0.16 (0.10)	0.05
Female	−0.22 (0.15)	−0.03	−0.45*** (0.14)	−0.07
Post–secondary	−0.02 (0.17)	−0.00	0.00 (0.16)	0.00
Middle income	0.01 (0.16)	0.00	−0.05 (0.14)	−0.01
Salaried	0.37** (0.17)	0.05	0.28* (0.16)	0.04
Self-employed	0.49* (0.27)	0.07	0.26 (0.24)	0.05
Francophone	0.56* (0.30)	0.06	0.38* (0.23)	0.05
Quebec City	1.11*** (0.21)	0.16	1.44***(0.19)	0.26
Other regions	0.42** (0.21)	0.05	0.32*(0.19)	0.05
Religiosity	−0.70** (0.29)	−0.08	−0.30 (0.25)	−0.04
Autonomist	0.77*** (0.17)	0.11	0.80*** (0.17)	0.14
Federalist	−0.03 (0.19)	−0.00	1.46*** (0.17)	0.26
Dumont evaluation	5.70*** (0.40)	0.70	1.93*** (0.27)	0.29
Strong party identification	−0.90*** (0.30)	−0.13	−0.32 (0.27)	−0.29
Anti–interventionism	1.77*** (0.41)	0.26	1.55*** (0.37)	0.27
Union support	−0.85*** (0.27)	−0.11	−1.29*** (0.24)	−0.19
Government efficacy	1.58*** (0.33)	0.14	0.61** (0.27)	0.09
Moral traditionalism	0.87** (0.34)	0.11	1.29*** (0.30)	0.21
Year 2008	−0.42** (0.18)	−0.05	0.14 (0.15)	0.02
Constant	−7.08*** (0.64)		−5.02*** (0.52)	
R^2	0.39		0.26	
N	1635		1655	

* $p < 0.1$; ** $p < 0.05$; *** $p < 0.01$.

Variables are measured as follows: Middle Income = dummy variable ($40,000–$69,999 = 1; otherwise = 0); Salaried, Self-Employed = dummy variables; Dumont Evaluation = 0–100 feeling thermometer scale (rescaled 0–1); Strong PID = dummy variable (respondent feels very close or fairly close to one of the registered political parties = 1; otherwise = 0); Union Support = response to question "On a scale from zero to a hundred, how do you feel about labour unions in general?" (rescaled 0–1); Government Efficacy = response to question "Do you think that people in the government waste a lot of the money we pay in taxes, waste some of it, or don't waste very much of it?" (a lot = 1, some = 0.5, not very much = 0); all other variables are coded as in table 15.1.

That said, the two voter clienteles do differ in some respects. For instance, there is a clear gender gap associated with voting for the CPC, but no such significant gap in the case of the ADQ. Women were simply less likely to support the CPC, whereas there was no perceptible gender difference for the ADQ. Religious individuals were less likely to support the ADQ, whereas this relationship is not statistically significant in the case of the Conservatives. These various patterns are consistent with previous work on these parties' respective vote bases.[22]

Turning to the second group of variables, which includes political attitudes, we observe that the similarities between the two voter clienteles here appear to be even more pronounced. Looking first at the variables that tap parties' respective neoliberal agendas and their position on state governance, we see that both parties significantly attract support from Quebecers who are less in favour of state intervention, are less in favour of unions, and think that the government is wasting money. The last measure taps overall dissatisfaction with "how government operates," which of course has been a staple of the *adéquiste* discourse[23] but also of the CPC. As both parties were poised as an alternative to years of Liberal (both federal and provincial) and Parti Québécois (provincially) hegemony, this measure may more closely get at the idea of "doing government differently." We finally observe that individuals scoring high on the moral traditionalism scale are significantly more likely to support the ADQ and the CPC over the other competing parties, as one might expect.

When we isolate the segment of the population that is notably conservative on both the anti-interventionism and moral conservatism dimensions, we find some differences between ADQ and CPC support. The voting preferences of this 15 per cent core conservative portion of the sample are displayed in figures 15.3 through 15.5, which show that support for the federal CPC is about twice as large among this core conservative constituency as among the rest of the population. At the provincial level support is also nearly twice as large for the ADQ among this group. At the federal level, close to a quarter of core conservatives support each of the Bloc and the Liberals, about half the proportion who support the CPC. In provincial elections fewer core conservatives go to the PQ (15%), and correspondingly more (35%) support the Liberals. Figure 15.5 finally indicates that cross-level support for the CPC and the ADQ is twice as large among the core conservative constituency as among other voters, and that more than two-thirds of the "non-conservatives" supported neither party.

Figure 15.3. Core Conservative Constituency by Federal Vote Choice

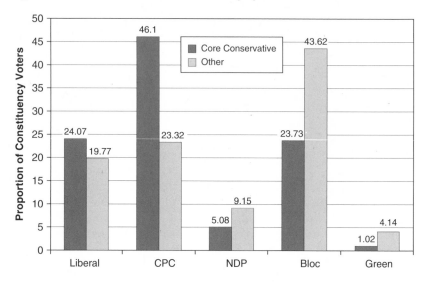

Figure 15.4. Core Conservative Constituency by Provincial Vote Choice

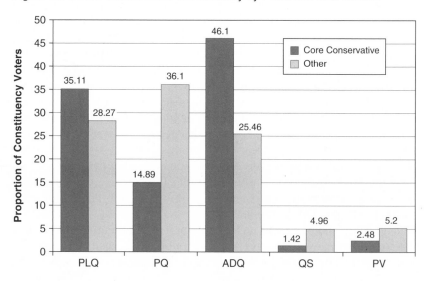

Figure 15.5. Core Conservative Constituency and Cross-Level Vote Choice

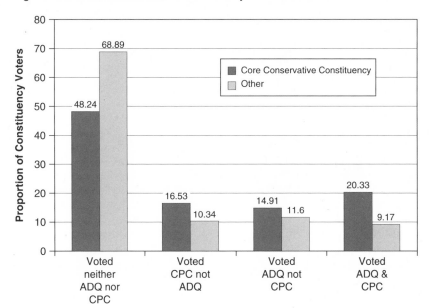

One attitudinal variable not included in table 15.2's vote choice models – as it is available only in the 2007 survey – is the question that refers to "reasonable accommodation" of ethno-religious minorities. As table 15.3 indicates, the ADQ is the party whose voters were least in favour of accommodating cultural minorities in Quebec. However, both PQ and PLQ voter clienteles were also very much against accommodation. Supporters of Québec Solidaire and the Green party were less opposed to such accommodation, though a majority of each still responded favourably to the statement that "we have gone too far in accommodating cultural minorities." These findings conform with the extent to which Dumont and the ADQ played on this sensitive issue during the few months leading up to the 2007 election campaign in Quebec.

Going back to the vote models of table 15.2, we see that two other important factors are significant in motivating vote choice for each party. First, the "Dumont effect": the popularity of the ADQ leader is widely cited as having had an instrumental impact on the ADQ vote.[24] An individual's evaluation of Mario Dumont thus unsurprisingly has a strong effect on a vote for ADQ (a 70 percentage point increase in the

Table 15.3. The Issue of Minority Accommodation in the 2007 Quebec Provincial Election

"Have gone too far in accommodating minorities"	Provincial vote (%)					
	All respondents	ADQ	PVQ	QS	PQ	PLQ
Strongly agree	47	58	29	29	46	45
Somewhat agree	34	35	36	40	37	27
Somewhat disagree	12	5	20	24	13	16
Strongly disagree	5	1	5	9	4	11

Note: Opinions refer to the following statement: "In recent years, we have gone too far in accommodating cultural minorities in Quebec." Cell entries are column percentages.

likelihood of supporting the party). It also has a positive effect on support for the CPC (a 29 point increase), even though Dumont was not the actual leader of the Conservatives. This finding underlines the fact that, at least during that period, Dumont was very well regarded by both constituencies.[25]

As is the case for all Canadian elections, strength of party identification matters for voting patterns. For the ADQ and the CPC in Quebec, there is an expectation that voters who have a weaker sense of party identification would be more likely to support these parties for two reasons. First, both parties were relatively new at the time, giving the voter less time to form a strong adherence. The ADQ truly entered the National Assembly only in 2003 (despite Dumont's earlier personal success); the CPC, now the only federally conservative option, was still in its infancy and is a breed very different from its Progressive-Conservative ancestor. Although the CPC may be closer to the Reform and Canadian Alliance parties, these groups had no electoral success in Quebec in their day.[26] In addition, we expect those with weak party identification to be more likely to vote ADQ and CPC, given that some of the votes for these two parties over previous elections are likely to be in direct response to not wanting to vote for the mainstream parties – in other words, a protest vote.[27] These expectations are borne out partially by the findings of table 15.2. Each party attracts support from individuals not holding a strong party identification, although the relationship is statistically significant only in the case of the ADQ.

In terms of the impact of political attitudes on vote choice, we can discern one notable difference between the clienteles, which has to do with an individual's nationalist position. In these vote models, as in table 15.1, this opinion is tapped through dummy variables measuring "federalist" and "autonomist" positions (with "sovereigntist" being the reference category). As can be seen in table 15.2, both parties receive support from autonomist voters; the latter are about 11 to 14 percentage points more likely to support the ADQ (or the CPC at the federal level) than sovereigntist voters. But contrary to the ADQ, the CPC also attracts the vote of federalist voters (a 26 percentage point increase). In sum, the data in table 15.2 suggest that there was a core of CPC-ADQ voters in Quebec and that the ADQ and CPC electorates were not perfectly aligned with each other. In other words, the ADQ and CPC clienteles shared some important features, but they also differed in some respects.[28]

This phenomenon of partial overlap is reflected in the cross-level vote patterns of Quebecers, as table 15.4 shows. According to the pooled data, about 14 per cent (338 out of a total of 2375) of the survey respondents supported both the CPC and the ADQ in these elections. These voters represent about half of the CPC electorate (52%, see column percentages) and about half of the ADQ electorate (53%, see row percentages). Almost all other Conservative voters supported the provincial Liberals. As for ADQ voters, those who did not support the CPC mostly turned towards the Bloc Québécois (26%), but some also voted for the federal Liberals (9%) or the NDP (10%). Most of these numbers are of course higher in the 2007 survey than in the 2008 one, as a result of the collapse of ADQ in the latter election (e.g., only 35% of Conservative voters supported ADQ in 2008, as opposed to 60% the year before, and cross-level ADQ-CPC vote choice reached 17% in 2007, but dropped to 9% a year later).

We may further ask whether previously supporting the Conservative Party (in 2006 or 2008) significantly leads to voting for the ADQ in the following (2007 or 2008) provincial election, everything else being equal. To answer that question we re-estimated the ADQ vote choice model of table 15.2, adding a dummy variable for whether the individual voted CPC or not in the previous federal election. The results indicate that a CPC vote is significantly and strongly linked to an ADQ vote, above and beyond all other voting motivations – again confirming the close connection between the two parties at the voter level and thus the existence of a clearly identifiable "blue electorate" in Quebec.[29]

Table 15.4. Cross-Level Vote Choice

Provincial vote	Federal vote					
	Liberal	CPC	NDP	Bloc	Green Party	Total
PLQ	49.26% 78.11% (364)	34.37% 39.20% (254)	7.58% 28.14% (56)	7.04% 5.32% (52)	1.76% 15.48% (13)	100% 31.12% (739)
PQ	3.65% 6.22% (29)	5.67% 6.94% (45)	4.66% 18.59% (37)	84.51% 68.61% (671)	1.51% 14.29% (12)	100% 33.43% (794)
ADQ	8.76% 12.02% (56)	52.90% 52.16% (338)	9.86% 31.66% (63)	26.45% 17.28% (169)	2.03% 15.48% (13)	100% 26.91% (639)
QS	4.12% 0.86% (4)	3.09% 0.46% (3)	28.27% 14.07% (28)	55.67% 5.52% (54)	8.25% 9.52% (8)	100% 4.08% (97)
PV	12.26% 2.79% (13)	7.55% 1.23% (8)	14.15% 7.54% (15)	30.19% 3.27% (32)	35.85% 45.24% (38)	100% 4.46% (106)
Total	19.62% 100% (466)	27.28% 100% (648)	8.38% 100% (199)	41.148% 100% (978)	3.54% 100% (84)	100% 100% (2375)

Note: Cell entries are row percentages followed by column percentages, with the number of cases in parentheses. For example, the uppermost left cell indicates that, according to the survey data, 49.26% of provincial Liberal voters supported the federal Liberal Party, whereas 78.11% of federal Liberal voters supported the provincial Liberal Party.

ADQ–CPC Party Linkages

While the preceding section demonstrates that the two parties' constituencies overlapped substantially, this voter-level relationship was necessarily fostered in part by these parties' concerted strategic efforts, despite not sharing the exact same ideology or party structure. Indeed, the Canadian party system in general is notable for having inconsistent party structures at the provincial and federal level.[30] In the mid-1980s, Blake concluded that the federal nature of Canadian politics has led to "two political worlds" that exist concurrently but ultimately separate from one another.[31] While acknowledging that these worlds may live apart, other scholars have intimated that they nonetheless do share some fundamental connections.[32] Quebec can boast a history of parties that have no federal counterpart, but who are quite successful at the provincial level – the Union Nationale and the Parti Québécois being prominent examples. The ADQ is one of the most recent Quebec political phenomenon to exist without a federal counterpart; however, the relationship between the ADQ and the CPC proves that the Canadian model is, yet again, one that can allow the development of informal cross-level ties between the parties. Even where parties do not share a history or ideological roots, there remains room for collusion.

In both the 2007 and 2008 provincial elections the ADQ identified with the federal Conservatives as a political ally. According to the media, "The party [ADQ] long ago tied its wagon to the Conservative party and Stephen Harper relied heavily on the ADQ electoral machinery during the last [2008] federal election."[33] The link between the Conservatives and the *adéquistes* was based on two ties: common viewpoints on salient issues and the organizational linkages between the two parties.

For the ADQ, to form even an informal alliance with the Conservatives was to link with a party that was perceived at the time to understand the value of a partnership with Quebec and whose policies could easily fit in with the ADQ's brand of provincial autonomy. Such a link could benefit the party's image among voters who were warming to the fresh image of the CPC. Moreover, building a partnership with the federal governing party could potentially place the ADQ in a unique position to negotiate aspects of Quebec's future with a government that was sympathetic to their desired style of governing. However, did the policy prescriptions of the ADQ parse with those of the CPC?

Comparing the campaign platforms of the CPC in 2005–6 and the ADQ in 2007 yields considerable similarity. Both parties advocated a relationship of open federalism and provincial autonomy. That this was the ADQ's point of differentiation from the other provincial mainstream parties made the possibility for an informal alliance with the CPC particularly evident. Particular examples of Stephen Harper's desire to assign additional powers to the province of Quebec were obvious. Harper intended to increase direct funding to regional development agencies such as the Canada Economic Development for the Quebec Region, to promote intergovernmental mechanisms to facilitate provincial involvement in areas of federal jurisdiction where provincial jurisdiction is affected, and most frequently cited in the press, to invite Quebec to play a role at UNESCO and other bilateral forums for negotiation where provincial jurisdiction is affected.[34] The ADQ advocated bilateral relations with Ottawa, indicating their willingness to eventually reopen the issue of signing the Constitution if certain conditions were met in recognizing the autonomy of Quebec.[35] Also comparable was the parties' desire to deal with the fiscal imbalance, a perpetually salient topic in Quebec at the time. The CPC allowance of provincial opting out of any new shared-cost federal programs with compensation, as long as the province offers a similar program with similar accountability structures, fit in nicely with the ADQ's desire to balance their provincial budget, rectify the fiscal imbalance, and prevent federal fiscal incursion into provincial affairs.

From a social policy perspective, the CPC was aware that they had to reach out to Quebec without alienating their base. Their approach was twofold: first, through direct measures, such as promoting the Official Languages Act, ensuring equal rights and privileges in using French and English in all public institutions[36]; second, through fiscally conservative policies such as giving parents a monthly stipend of $100 for day care, a policy that the ADQ looked upon favourably and offered in its own platform a year later.[37] Opting into two-tier or a mixed health care was another controversial but uniquely right-wing policy advocated by both the ADQ and CPC, seen in Quebec as catering to citizens who were tired of the long wait lists encountered in universal public health care. Showing their morally traditional stripes, Dumont and the ADQ were at the forefront of the "reasonable accommodations" and immigration debates. No less controversial, the Harper team's 2006 platform included multiple references to tightening security around

immigration and border control, citing a need for an "immigration policy that responds to Canada's economic needs."[38]

The policy platform story in 2008 is not significantly different, even
though the context certainly was. Following their relative success in
2006, the Conservatives knew that they had to either break through in
Quebec and capture additional seats in the Quebec City and Montreal
South-Shore regions, or abandon their frontal attack on winning Quebec
votes altogether. Lacking visibility and experience, the ADQ caucus had
been performing marginally as the Official Opposition, and the party
had taken a twenty-point dive in the polls between September 2007 and
May 2008.[39] From a platform perspective, open federalism and the fiscal
imbalance were still on the menu, as was regional development. Both
parties continued to advocate strong provincial representation on fiscal
issues, as well as policies that targeted families through tax decreases and
individual child-care support.[40] However, the Conservatives' bold declaration in their 2008 platform that support for federalism in Quebec was
at a modern-day high may have been a bit premature, as the announce-
ments of federal cuts to the arts inspired public outcry in Quebec for
having failed to recognize the distinct cultural heritage of Quebec.[41]

What is said in party platforms and what voters see during a campaign
from the media can be two very different visions. Yet vibrant rumours
circulated behind the scenes in political and media backrooms, specu-
lating on an alliance between the CPC and ADQ. The parties' respective stars appeared to be on the rise at the same time. Harper's success
in Quebec in 2006 opened up a new avenue for partnership: "During
the 2005–06 federal election campaign, Harper brought his version of
autonomy directly to Quebecers ... That promise helped Harper to
win seats in Quebec. Now that same formula has helped to catapult
Dumont into the position of Quebec opposition leader."[42] By March
2007, an ideological link as well as a publicly recognized political
friendship had been noted by many. Jean-Claude Rivest, former advisor to Quebec Premier Robert Bourassa, boldly proclaimed the strength
of the alliance, stating that "a vote for Action démocratique du Québec
can be directly translated into a vote for the federal Conservatives in a
future federal election."[43] This notwithstanding, is there clear evidence
that the two party organizations developed relatively close ties over
that time period?

Signs of organizational partnership had garnered speculation much
earlier than the 2006 election. As early as 2004, it was rumoured that the
Conservative Party sought organizational ties with the ideologically

aligned ADQ in the run-up to the next election. Alain Sans Cartier, chief political aide to Mario Dumont, noted, "There are, in fact, what we could refer to as similarities among our supporters ... Many of our supporters are also members of the Conservative Party."[44] The Conservatives, without a formal Quebec lieutenant as the Liberals have, may have suspected that such an alliance would be akin to a presence in Quebec ridings where ADQ support was strong both during the campaign and pre-campaign period. Building a strong organizational team that was unique to the CPC may not have been possible, given the party's standing in Quebec at the time and the signal that it would send to core supporters that resources would be employed to garner support in Quebec – a perpetually sensitive topic for the party's more conservative base. Using shared organizational resources with the ADQ alleviated the financial burden while capitalizing on the ADQ's phone lists and organizational staff (even though the ADQ's organization was never as substantial in size or experience as that of the PQ and the PLQ). From the Conservative side, campaign co-chair John Reynolds offered that the party had "spoken with everyone, but obviously, there are a great number of ADQ members who like our party and our people ... So we will work with them," leading many to believe that an alliance was pending and looked upon favourably by both sides.[45]

Dumont and Harper were thus able to capitalize on each other's organizational strengths to break into regions of Quebec where ideological right-wing ideas were starting to become more welcome. The ADQ, who were criticized for having weak organizational ties that cost them in the 2003 election, had strengthened their support base geographically and were able to assist the CPC, who shared the same weak organizational ties in key areas where they could make gains.[46] Quebec candidates of the CPC such as Josée Verner, Steven Blaney, Jacques Gourde, and Daniel Petit were cited as potential "bridgers" between the two parties, lobbying for a positive relationship between the two formations that could include sharing organizational strengths and acting as policy advocates.[47] The personal relationships formed between the leaders and key party members were publicly perceived as a guarantee to the pursuit of similar policies. In 2007 the two party leaders met a number of times, and in the lead-up to the 2008 federal election the CPC drew from a "tight circle of aggressive Quebec strategists, drawn from provincial Action démocratique du Québec party ... notably Quebec war room chief Michel Lalonde and Mr Harper's press secretary and Quebec adviser, Dimitri Soudas."[48]

The strongest tie may, however, have also been the greatest liability. One prominent ADQ–CPC connection was Conservative Senator Leo Housakos, a long-time friend of Dimitri Soudas, a self-described ADQ chief fundraiser from 2001 to 2008. A senior Conservative organizer, Housakos was president of the ADQ's fundraising commission until he left the position in December 2008, in a move that was attributed largely to the ADQ's poor performance in that month's election. Shortly after, Harper named Housakos to the Canadian Senate.[49] By 2009, problems arose around irregularities with ADQ finances, one of the factors attributed to the quick resignation of new ADQ leader Gilles Taillon. Despite his replies to the contrary, Housakos was speculated to have been involved in a $1.4-million stimulus contract awarded to a Montreal engineering firm where he once worked. Weeks later, the ADQ announced it would cut off ties with members of the Conservative party, including Housakos. If the parties' respective poor performances were not enough to end the alliance, perceptions of financial scandal and possible legal liability finally ended the troubled relationship.

Conclusion

Through analysis of the attitudes and vote patterns of Quebecers, as well as the party linkages developed in recent years between the ADQ and the CPC, this chapter has shown that a significant portion of the Quebec electorate adopts a conservative outlook on state intervention and morality. However, two important caveats apply. First, Quebecers' values were found to be mixed. On some issues, such as private delivery of health-care services, government efficiency, promotion of traditional family values, and cultural minority accommodation, Quebecers very much espouse conservative views. On other issues, however, they appear to be much less conservative. Second, these mixed conservative attitudes did not translate into electoral support for conservative parties as much as might be expected. The ADQ and CPC constituencies did not entirely overlap in their attitudinal profiles. In particular, it was found that Conservative voters in Quebec were much more federalist than ADQ voters and tended to support the Liberal Party as much as the ADQ in provincial elections.

While this chapter does show that there is an "électorat bleu" in Quebec who supported both right-wing parties in 2006–8, despite their being very distinct party entities, it is also clear that this "blue voter" base is too small to allow both parties to grow and become more prominent than they have recently been in Quebec politics. Both parties have experienced a decline in Quebec since 2008, the ADQ more than the CPC. Political pundits have speculated that, among other institutional and psychological factors, the actual relationship between the ADQ and the federal CPC is a prime contributor to this decline.[50] Our analysis suggests a two-pronged explanation for the rise and decline of these two parties: at the party level, the ADQ's alignment with Stephen Harper and the federal Conservatives first helped both parties gain ground, but eventually their individual weaknesses compounded in their effect on both parties.

An additional consideration is that, in the context of Québécois nationalism, there may be electoral costs to a provincial party for getting "too close" to a federal party, whether it is open to Quebec's interests or not – unless that federal party is a distinctly nationalist one like the Bloc Québécois.[51] In our analysis of vote choice in the 2006–8 period, the mere fact that federalist voters were more likely to support the CPC federally level but were no more likely than sovereigntists to vote for the ADQ provincially is a reminder of the particular dynamics of cross-level partisanship in Quebec.

As noted at the outset, Quebec has seen its share of conservative parties. Looking forward, one will have to take into consideration the changing provincial party system in Quebec and the CPC as a viable federal option in that province. With the departure of Mario Dumont as party leader, it had become clear that the ADQ would no longer constitute the robust third option that it did in the 2003 and 2007 elections. In fact, the ADQ had no independent presence in the 2012 provincial election. As of early 2012, the party has ceased to exist, having merged with François Legault's party, the Coalition Avenir Québec (CAQ). The merger allowed for the continuation of some of the ADQ's core ideas – namely fiscal conservativism – that were shared by Legault and his followers. Yet the CAQ is presenting itself as a more moderate option than the ADQ, closer to the ideological centre; Legault himself has sometimes referred to his program as representing the "efficient left." What becomes of the "électorat bleu" in this context will necessarily depend on whether one of the mainstream parties can recapture its vote. The same is true of the CPC constituency in Quebec. CPC support shrank significantly in the 2011 federal election (down to 16.5%), and most Quebecers seem to have lost confidence in Harper and turned their back on him, just as he is perceived to have done to the province of Quebec. While the 2012 election of Pauline Marois and the Parti

Québécois to a minority government may indeed suggest that protest politics are still in play, the strong performance of the CAQ does shed light on how much of this electorate is still drawn to the strong leadership style as seen in Mario Dumont, the open-federalism promises of Stephen Harper, and the desire to carve out a position for the conservative core in Quebec.

NOTES

1 We thank the editors and the anonymous reviewers for their helpful comments on a preliminary version of this chapter, which was nominated for the 2010 Robert H. Durr Award from the Midwest Political Science Association.

2 Éric Bélanger and Richard Nadeau, *Le comportement électoral des Québécois* (Montreal: Presses de l'Université de Montréal, 2009).

3 Xavier Gélinas, "La droite québécoise en contexte," *Droite et démocratie au Québec: enjeux et paradoxes*, ed. Nelson Michaud, 55–93 (Quebec: Presses de l'Université Laval, 2007).

4 Luc Turgeon, "Interpreting Québec's Historical Trajectories," in *Quebec: State and Society*, 3rd ed., ed. Alain-G. Gagnon, 51–67 (Peterborough: Broadview, 2004).

5 For more on this, see Michaud, *Droite et démocratie au Québec*; Linda Cardinal and Jean-Michel Lacroix, eds., *Le conservatisme: le Québec et le Canada en contexte* (Paris: Presses Sorbonne Nouvelle, 2009); Frédéric Boily, *Le conservatisme au Québec: retour sur une tradition oubliée* (Quebec: Presses de l'Université Laval, 2010).

6 Kenneth McRoberts, *Quebec: Social Change and Political Crisis*, 3rd ed. (Toronto: McClelland and Stewart, 1993).

7 E.g., Luc Godbout, ed., *Agir maintenant pour le Québec de demain: des réflexions pour passer des manifestes aux actes* (Quebec: Presses de l'Université Laval, 2006).

8 E.g., Mathieu Bock-Côté, *La dénationalisation tranquille* (Montreal: Boréal, 2007).

9 The 2007 survey includes a web sample and a telephone sample, while the 2008 data were collected entirely online. Data collection was conducted by Montreal-based polling firm Léger Marketing under the direction of Professors Éric Bélanger (McGill University) and Richard Nadeau (Université de Montréal). The two surveys were funded by the Social Sciences and Humanities Research Council of Canada and by the Institute for Research on Public Policy.

10 For more details, see Bélanger and Nadeau, *Le comportement électoral des Québécois*.

11 Aligning the belief that accommodation has gone too far as an *exclusively* conservative value is a somewhat tenuous suggestion in Quebec, as it may also reflect a dissatisfaction with the handling of the reasonable accommodation debate by party leaders that is not uncommon with Liberal and PQ supporters or voters for other parties (see also the results from table 15.3 in the next section).

12 Factor analysis confirms that the items in both the state intervention and moral traditionalism indices each load on a single factor with an Eigen value greater than 1. Additionally, the Pearson's *r* correlation between the two indices remains relatively low at 0.12, suggesting that the two dimensions operate fairly independently of one another (a finding that is consistent with that reported in Christopher Cochrane's chapter 2 in this volume).

13 These models are estimated with ordinary least squares. Since not much difference was found in the distribution of answers between the 2007 and the 2008 data (as can be seen in figures 15.1 and 15.2), the two surveys are pooled for the remainder of the chapter in order to simplify the results, with a control for the year of the surveys being introduced in all the regression models.

14 Michel Sarra-Bournet, "L'infortune politique de la droite québécoise après 1960," in Cardinal and Lacroix, *Le conservatisme*, 177–87.

15 The combined scale's mean is 0.18 with a standard deviation of 0.16. Hence, any individual scoring 0.34 or higher on the combined scale was considered as being part of Quebec's core conservative constituency.

16 The 2006 and 2008 Canadian Election Study surveys provide information on only provincial vote intentions, as opposed to actual vote choice. For this reason, we prefer using Bélanger and Nadeau's provincial studies, which provide reported vote at both levels.

17 See Bélanger and Nadeau, *Le comportement électoral des Québécois*.

18 Each model is estimated with binomial logit on the pooled dataset. Analyses conducted separately for each survey (2007 and 2008) show that the two sets of results are very similar.

19 We acknowledge that salaried workers represent a large and heterogeneous category of social class; unfortunately the survey data at hand do not provide a more fine-grained measure of occupation or class.

20 Pierre Drouilly, "La structure des appuis aux partis politiques québécois, 1998–2008," in *Les partis politiques québécois dans la tourmente: mieux comprendre et évaluer leur rôle*, ed. Réjean Pelletier, 131–68 (Québec: Presses de l'Université Laval, 2012).

21 Maurice Pinard and Pat Rafail, "L'énigme des succès de la droite à Québec," in Michaud, *Droite et démocratie au Québec*, 121–38.

22 Elisabeth Gidengil, André Blais, Joanna Everitt, Patrick Fournier, and Neil Nevitte, "Back to the Future? Making Sense of the 2004 Canadian Election outside Québec," in *Canadian Journal of Political Science* 39, no. 1 (2006): 1–25; Bélanger and Nadeau, *Le comportement électoral des Québécois*.

23 See Maurice Pinard, *Un grand réalignement des partis politiques au Québec*, Les Cahiers du CRIC (Montreal: Centre de recherche et d'information sur le Canada, 2003); Frédéric Boily, *Mario Dumont et l'Action démocratique du Québec: entre populisme et démocratie* (Quebec: Presses de l'Université Laval, 2008).

24 Pinard, *Un grand réalignement des partis politiques au Québec*; Bélanger and Nadeau, *Le comportement électoral des Québécois*.

25 Note that the survey data do not provide a measure of feelings towards Stephen Harper, which is why we include Dumont's evaluation as a predictor of CPC vote.

26 See Éric Bélanger and Jean-François Godbout. "Why Do Parties Merge? The Case of the Conservative Party of Canada," *Parliamentary Affairs* 63, no. 1 (2010): 41–65.

27 A. Brian Tanguay, "The Stalled Realignment: Quebec's Party System after the 2003 Provincial Election," in *Quebec and Canada in the New Century*, ed. Michael Murphy, 83–106 (Montreal and Kingston: McGill-Queen's University Press, 2007); Bélanger and Nadeau, *Le comportement électoral des Québécois*.

28 We can observe that the models' explanatory value (R^2) is higher for the ADQ than for the CPC. This seems mostly due to at least two factors: the evaluations of Dumont obviously having a greater pull for ADQ than for CPC, and the fact that the survey data we use were designed primarily to study provincial vote choice.

29 The results are not shown for space reasons but are available from the authors upon request.

30 David Stewart and R.K. Carty, "Many Political Worlds? Provincial Parties and Party Systems," in *Provinces: Canadian Provincial Politics*, 2nd ed., ed. Christopher Dunn, 97–113 (Peterborough: Broadview, 2006).

31 Donald E. Blake, *Two Political Worlds: Parties and Voting in British Columbia* (Vancouver: University of British Columbia Press, 1985).

32 E.g., Emily Clough, "Two Political Worlds? The Influence of Provincial Party Loyalty on Federal Voting in Canada," *Electoral Studies* 26, no. 4 (2007): 787–96; Laura B. Stephenson and Éric Bélanger, "Loyalty across Levels: Provincial and Federal Partisanship in Canada" (paper presented

at the annual meeting of the Canadian Political Science Association, Ottawa, 2009).

33 "What's Next for the ADQ?," *Macleans.ca*, 11 March 2009, http://www2.macleans.ca/2009/03/11/ we-just-want-to-know-that-you-love-us/#more-42593.

34 Conservative Party of Canada, *Stand Up for Canada*, 42.

35 Action démocratique du Québec, *Une vision, un plan, une parole*, February 2007, 5.

36 Conservative Party of Canada, *Stand Up for Canada*, 43.

37 Tasha Kheiriddin, "The Right Place at the Right Time: The Rise of Mario Dumont and the ADQ," *Policy Options* 28, no. 4 (2007): 53–8.

38 Conservative Party of Canada, *Stand Up for Canada*, 36.

39 Bélanger and Nadeau, *Le comportement électoral des Québécois*, 93.

40 Action démocratique du Québec, *Donnez-vous le pouvoir*, November 2008, 57–9.

41 Conservative Party of Canada, *The True North, Strong and Free*, September 2008.

42 Thomas Walkom, "Harper, Dumont Share Vision of Future," *Toronto Star Online*, 28 March 2007, http://www.thestar.com/article/196767.

43 "Dumont True Winner, Regardless of Election Outcome," Canwest News Service, 25 March 2007, http://www.canada.com/nationalpost/news/ story.html?id=3ed783b9-7be0-4f51-bdc8-2009cbec5a6f.

44 "Conservative Party Seeks ADQ's Help in Quebec," CTV News, 3 May 2004.

45 Ibid.

46 Walkom, "Harper, Dumont Share Vision of Future."

47 "Dumont True Winner, Regardless of Election Outcome," Canwest News Service.

48 "Le premier ministre du Canada chez Mario Dumont," *La Presse*, 8 December 2007; "Once Dreaming of Gains, Tories Praying for a Soft Landing in Quebec," *Globe and Mail Online*, 11 October 2008, http://www.theglobeandmail.com/news/politics/once-dreaming-of-gains-tories-praying-for-a-soft-landing-in-quebec/ article1063797/.

49 "Scandals Rock Quebec's ADQ, Liberals," CBC News, 11 November 2009, http://www.cbc.ca/news/canada/montreal/story/2009/11/11/quebec-adq-leadership-trouble.html.

50 E.g., Chantal Hébert, "L'amicale de l'ADQ," *Le Devoir*, 25 May 2009, http://www.ledevoir.com/politique/quebec/252019/l-amicale-de-l-adq.

51 Vincent Lemieux, *Le Parti libéral du Québec: alliances, rivalités et neutralités*, 2nd ed. (Quebec: Presses de l'Université Laval, 2008).

16 Epitaph for a Conservative Insurgency in Quebec: The Rise and Fall – and Rise and Fall – of the Action démocratique du Québec, 1994–2008[1]

A. BRIAN TANGUAY

Since 1970, provincial elections in Quebec have largely been contests between two major party coalitions: the nationalist and left-leaning Parti Québécois (PQ), on the one hand, and the federalist, business-oriented Parti libéral du Québec (PLQ) on the other. During this time, conservative voters in the province were generally compelled to cast their ballots at election time for one or the other of these major parties, depending on their own predispositions towards sovereignty and the constitutional status quo. Voters who rejected the Manichean constitutional debate between sovereignty and the status quo, or who called for the restoration of traditional morality in this most secular of provinces, or who were interested in more radical attempts to scale back the welfare state than were on offer from the PLQ, were generally out of luck. Even on economic questions, the nominally free-enterprise Liberals were untrustworthy allies for conservatives: no matter what party leaders said during election campaigns, when in government (1970–6, 1985–94, 2003–12) the PLQ appeared to value social peace more highly than making a concerted effort to restructure the welfare state apparatus.

With the appearance on the political scene of the Action démocratique du Québec (ADQ) in the mid-1990s, conservative voters had a seemingly credible third option for the first time since the demise of the Union Nationale (UN) in the early 1980s. Promising both a moratorium on future referenda on sovereignty – what some wags have called the "never-endum" – and the elimination of the most interventionist and *étatiste* elements in the province's economic model, the ADQ also articulated a conservative worldview that placed the family and individual responsibility at the centre of political discourse. On two separate occasions the ADQ appeared poised to make a breakthrough to major (and even governing) party status, in the fall of 2002 and just after the 2007 election, when it managed to win the second-most seats in the National Assembly. Each time, however, support for the ADQ receded almost as quickly as it had surged.

How are we to explain this rise and fall, and rise and fall again of the ADQ? What does the fate of the ADQ mean for conservative voters in Quebec and the possible fate of future conservative parties in the province? This chapter seeks to shed some light on these questions and to situate the ADQ's trajectory in the broader context of the evolution of conservative ideology in Quebec. I hope to show that there is indeed a conservative constituency in the province, albeit one that is mobilized primarily around certain neoliberal economic prescriptions rather than conservative positions on social issues such as the family and morality. To the extent that there is any support at all for moral traditionalism in Quebec, it is limited mainly to questions of immigration and the accommodation of ethnic minorities, issues that were key factors in propelling the ADQ to its stunning breakthrough in the 2007 election.

This chapter will also argue that the theoretical concepts elaborated by Maurice Pinard and others to explain the rise of minor parties – in particular, the notion of the issue unresponsiveness of the major parties – are useful for understanding the successes of the ADQ.[2] In order to make sense of its failures, however, we need to examine the strategic responses of the two major parties to the electoral threat posed by the ADQ, and here we draw on the recent work of Bonnie Meguid.[3] We also explore the role played by organizational factors within the ADQ itself – the question of leadership and of the leader's relations with caucus – in blunting its effectiveness.

The chapter has five sections. In the following, I describe the two partisan realignments of 1935–6 and 1968–76, focusing on what happened to conservative ideology and political parties during each of these periods. Sections 2 and 3 examine the two distinct ADQ "moments" (1994–2002 and 2003–7) and offer explanations for the rise and fall (first moment) and fall and rise (second moment) of the party during each. The fourth section explains the stunning collapse of the ADQ in the 2008 election, only twenty months after its dramatic breakthrough. A brief concluding section, in addition to summarizing the argument, will explore the possibility that a substantial portion of the Quebec electorate is still alienated from the Liberals' version of neoliberalism and the PQ's sovereignty project, and thus open to appeals from a new, right-wing successor to the ADQ, the recently formed Coalition Avenir Québec (CAQ).

Party System Change and the Evolution
of Conservative Ideology in Quebec

Since Confederation in 1867, the provincial party system in Quebec has experienced two major realignments during which the "partisan deck" was shuffled, so to speak, and new parties emerged to replace long-established ones in relatively short order. The first of these critical realignments occurred in 1935–6, when the Union Nationale was created out of an electoral alliance and eventually a merger between a breakaway faction of dissident Liberals, the Action libérale nationale (ALN), led by Paul Gouin, and the provincial Conservative Party, under the leadership of Maurice Duplessis. Duplessis managed to outmanoeuvre his rival Gouin and quickly take control of the new party, which became the dominant force in provincial politics for the next twenty-five years. The UN's ideological blend of conservative nationalism, laissez-faire economics, and vigilant anti-communism, combined with a well-oiled patronage machine and a gerrymandered electoral map that favoured rural ridings and small towns at the expense of Montreal and Quebec City, propelled it to majority governments in the 1936, 1944, 1948, 1952, and 1956 elections.[4]

During the lengthy period of UN rule, which critics of the Duplessis administration characterized as the "great darkness," the dominant ideology articulated by the governing party, clerical leaders, and many lay intellectuals was strictly conservative on social questions.[5] These intellectual elites fought a rearguard action against the rapid industrialization and urbanization that had occurred in Quebec since the 1920s. Even in the 1950s, much of Quebec's intelligentsia was preaching that French Canadians still had a spiritual mission in life. Ideally, they should remain on the farms, shun the big cities and factories where the English predominated, and devote themselves to a Catholic way of life. Duplessis's regime combined this rural nostalgia with a vigorous defence of the free market. The premier himself enjoyed very close ties to the Anglo-American corporate elite, and he sought to portray the province as an ideal target for foreign investment, given its rich store of natural resources and its docile workforce. When labour strife did erupt, as it did in the bitterly violent strikes at Asbestos (1949), Louiseville (1952), and Murdochville (1957), the Duplessis government made certain to send in the provincial police to protect private property and the rights of management.[6]

Another important source of the UN's electoral appeal was its approach to the division of powers within the federal system. In

Duplessis's view, Quebec was one of two "founding nations" and thus merited special constitutional status. His government strongly resisted any attempt by Ottawa to intrude into areas of provincial jurisdiction and clamoured for increased powers of taxation in order to fund Quebec's own programs in these areas.

By the 1950s this conservative ideological edifice, which had been built on top of a relentlessly modernizing socioeconomic foundation, was ready to topple. Opposition to the Duplessis administration gathered force in certain sections of the trade union movement, in the world of journalism (*Le Devoir*), and among a new generation of political activists such as Pierre Trudeau, René Lévesque, and Pierre Vallières. This period of social and political ferment culminated in the "Quiet Revolution" of the 1960s. One of the casualties of this Quiet Revolution was the Union Nationale itself, which went into rapid decline after the death of Duplessis in 1959. Although the UN did manage to win the election of 1966, thanks in large part to the unreformed electoral map and the backlash against certain features of the state-driven modernization undertaken by the Liberal governments of Jean Lesage, by the early 1980s it had disappeared from the party system, replaced by another new party, René Lévesque's Parti Québécois.

The second major realignment in Quebec's twentieth-century history was, like the first, partly the product of a schism within the Liberal Party. In 1967, Lévesque, the popular minister of natural resources in Lesage's Cabinet, bolted the PLQ when his attempt to persuade the party to adopt a resolution in favour of sovereignty-association for Quebec was rebuffed. Along with a small number of left-leaning Liberals, Lévesque formed a new organization, the Mouvement souveraineté-association (MSA). Within a year, this new entity had joined forces with other pro-sovereignty organizations in the province, both on the left (Pierre Bourgault's Rassemblement pour l'indépendance nationale, or the RIN) and the right (Gilles Grégoire's Ralliement nationale, or RN) to create the Parti Québécois. The new party was proudly social democratic, trumpeting its "favourable prejudice towards labour" and advocating much higher levels of state intervention in the provincial economy, along with an expanded social security network.

This second realignment of the party system took place gradually over the course of four elections from 1970 to 1981. In the first election contested by the PQ, in 1970, the new separatist party garnered 23 per cent of the vote, which translated into a paltry seven seats. The 1973 election netted 30 per cent of the vote, but one less seat. In the

1976 election, however, the PQ swept to a stunning victory, obtaining 41 per cent of the popular vote and seventy-one seats. Their accession to power was facilitated by another brief resurgence of the UN under the leadership of Rodrigue Biron, a small-business owner who would later defect to the PQ and sit as a Cabinet minister in Lévesque's government after 1981.

Despite the fact that the PQ candidates who were first elected to the National Assembly in 1970 and 1973 came from working-class ridings in Montreal, the new party was by no means a labour party in the traditional sense of the term.[7] As a number of observers pointed out, the PQ was a vehicle for an ascendant francophone new middle class – civil servants, journalists, social scientists, and the employees of the state-run health, education, and welfare bureaucracies.[8]

In an effort to consolidate a cross-class coalition in favour of Quebec sovereignty, the PQ enacted a remarkable array of sweeping social, political, and economic reforms during its first mandate (1976–81): revision of the Labour Code, imposition of the Rand Formula to strengthen the financial base of trade unions, anti-scab legislation (the first of its kind on the continent), nationalization of part of the province's automobile insurance industry, state takeover of Asbestos Corporation, reform of election finance law to prohibit corporate donations to political parties, and the enactment of the Charter of the French Language (better known as Bill 101). Although attacked from the left for its supposed timidity, the social democratic measures adopted by the Lévesque administration in the face of unrelenting hostility from the business community were indeed impressive.

During the Quiet Revolution and since, Quebec society secularized rapidly. Levels of church attendance are the lowest in North America. Attitudes towards soft-drug use, same-sex marriage, and abortion are more liberal than in the rest of Canada. Quebec now has a much higher rate of common-law unions than do the other provinces and territories, except for the Northwest Territories.[9] As Taras Grescoe points out in his engaging portrait of contemporary Quebec, over 80 per cent of Quebecers strongly agree that people have the right to lead different lifestyles, compared to under 60 per cent in the rest of Canada.[10] Since the early 1970s, neither of the major parties has sought to question this secularization or take measures harkening back to an earlier social order. As a result, the policy prescriptions generally associated with moral traditionalism have been largely absent from political debate, at least until recently.

On economic issues, however, conservative voters in Quebec have had a seemingly credible option at election time: to cast their ballots for the Liberal Party. When Robert Bourassa returned from a brief exile in Europe to assume the leadership of the PLQ for a second time in 1983, he sought to focus the party program on the economy, in particular the need to ensure economic growth by scaling back a bloated provincial state. Prior to the 1985 election campaign, the PLQ published a program in which it inveighed against excessive bureaucratic regulation of citizens' lives, which "tramples on individual liberties, restricts the rights of property and discourages individual initiative."[11] The Liberals advocated extensive deregulation, increased market discipline, and sweeping privatization in order to guarantee economic growth. Having won the provincial election of 1985, however, the Liberals shied away from wholesale rollbacks of the social democratic reforms adopted by their predecessors. On the anti-scab law, for instance, which constituted one of the business community's biggest irritants in the 1980s, Bourassa eventually admitted that his government would do nothing to weaken the legislation, for fear of endangering social peace – an admission that he did not wish to risk antagonizing the province's powerful labour movement.[12]

Thus by the early 1990s there was certainly sufficient room in partisan space in Quebec for a consistently neoliberal party that could articulate a coherent critique of the *étatiste* and collectivist features of the "Quebec model." This is precisely what the Action démocratique du Québec would seek to do, although there were other factors contributing to its emergence, aside from neoliberal economic prescriptions, as we shall see in the next section.

The First ADQ "Moment": From New Party to Near Breakthrough, 1994 to 2002

The Action démocratique du Québec emerged in the early 1990s, a time of profound constitutional crisis in the country. In the wake of the collapse of the Meech Lake Accord, which, among other things, would have recognized Quebec as a distinct society and entrenched this recognition in the Constitution, public and elite opinion in that province radicalized on the question of sovereignty. On the day after the accord lapsed, which happened to be Quebec's *fête nationale* (24 June), Premier Robert Bourassa stood up in the National Assembly and proclaimed, "No matter what anyone says or does, Quebec has always been, is now and will always be a distinct society, free and capable of taking responsibility for its destiny and development."[13] Pressure to hold a referendum on sovereignty escalated, but Bourassa out-manoeuvred opponents within his party by securing Liberal endorsement of the Charlottetown Accord, and agreement to conduct a province-wide referendum that would be held concurrently with the national referendum on the agreement in October 1992. Bourassa's "duplicity" provoked a split within the Quebec Liberal Party, and among the departures was Mario Dumont, the twenty-two-year old president of the party's youth wing. This group would form the nucleus of the ADQ, which was formally established in 1994.

On economic questions, as Pinard and others have pointed out, the ADQ was clearly on the right, in fact well to the right of the median voter.[14] The party's overriding objective was to liberate individual autonomy from what it calls an invasive and "paternalistic" state apparatus, and to inculcate in these autonomous individuals an understanding of their responsibility both for their own actions and for their fellow citizens.[15] The party was highly critical of the "Quebec model" of comparatively high taxation combined with extensive state intervention in the economy, and called for a scaling down of the provincial state apparatus. To these ends, the ADQ has advocated at various times:

- the abolition of school boards – their powers would be assumed by municipal governments – and the institution of school vouchers (the latter was dropped from the program in 2007);
- a flat tax (also dropped after the 2003 election, in favour of lightening the taxation burden on individuals); and
- "two-tier" health care – a greater role for the private sector in furnishing medical services.

The party did not embrace social conservatism. In fact, its electoral program was silent on such deeply divisive questions as the right to abortion, same-sex marriage, the definition of the family, the right to die, and so on, which have mobilized the religious right elsewhere in this country and even more in the United States.

The ADQ made little electoral headway in its first seven years. It was, essentially, in the eyes of the electorate and most pundits, a one-man show – a status reinforced by the party's official name, which appeared on the ballot after 1994: l'Action démocratique du Québec/Équipe Mario Dumont. Opinion polls in the fall of 2002, however, showed support for the ADQ spiking to between 35 and 40 per cent (see figure 16.1), with a majority of francophones favouring it. These surveys also demonstrated that Mario Dumont was far and away the most popular party leader, well ahead of Jean Charest of the Liberals and Premier Bernard Landry of the PQ. These favourable survey results came on the heels of surprising by-election victories for the ADQ in four ridings formerly held by the PQ. Three of the four successful ADQ candidates were relatively young, like party leader Mario Dumont, giving the impression that a generational shift in Quebec politics might be in the making.

What explains this sudden surge in support in the fall of 2002 for the ADQ, an entirely untried party? One factor cited by Pinard is the party's neoliberal ideology, which appealed to a larger constituency than most observers at the time might have been ready to acknowledge. A sizeable portion of the electorate in the early 2000s was receptive to the ADQ's anti-state, anti-tax message, especially in light of Quebec's status as one of the most heavily taxed jurisdictions in all of North America. A 2002 CROP poll showed that 59 per cent of respondents favoured reducing the size of the civil service and allowing a greater role for the private sector in the delivery of health care, and 55 per cent

Figure 16.1. Provincial Voting Intentions in Quebec, 2002–2006

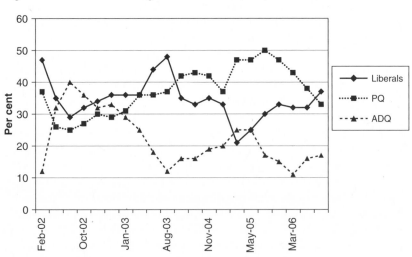

Source: Léger Marketing, http://www.legermarketing.com/admin/voting_int/Provincial_Voting_Intentions_in_Quebec2012.pdf

Table 16.1. Party Support by Neoliberal Attitudes, 2002

Party preference	Reduce size of civil service	Increase private-sector role in health	School vouchers	Flat tax
ADQ (%)	48	48	48	50
Liberal (%)	26	27	27	23
PQ (%)	26	25	25	27
N	267	266	260	183

Source: CROP (2002)
Note: Each column contains only those voters who either agree or agree strongly with each of the items in question; their party preferences, in percentages, are included in each cell of the table.

favoured school vouchers.[16] Only the flat tax failed to secure majority support, with only 36 per cent agreeing and 56 per cent disagreeing. Table 16.1 shows the popularity of the ADQ among those responding favourably to these policy proposals.

A neoliberalism scale can be created by using the average responses to these four questions (in table 16.1), with scores ranging from 1 to a neo-liberal high of 4. The mean for the total sample was 2.6. ADQ supporters averaged 3.0, noticeably more neoliberal than Liberals (2.5) and PQ supporters (2.3). This suggests the persistence of a sizeable minority reflecting what Pinard referred to as "the traditional economic conservatism" among francophone voters.[17]

In addition to its neoliberal ideology, the ADQ benefited from its strategic ambiguity on the constitutional question, which constituted the ADQ's "niche" issue during the first phase of its development.[18] Harkening back to an older form of conservative nationalism, very much in the spirit of Maurice Duplessis's Union Nationale, the ADQ described its preferred constitutional option as a "third way" between the polarized positions of status quo federalism and sovereignty proposed by the two main parties. The ADQ advocated "an autonomist vision," calling for a radical constitutional decentralization.[19] The ambiguity of this positioning provided a significant opening to the majority of francophone voters who by 2002 refused to identify themselves as either federalists or sovereigntists.[20] In addition, most sovereigntists and federalists believed that the ADQ favoured their side in the constitutional debate. Another key source of appeal, arguably the greatest single source of electoral support, was its promise of a ten-year

Table 16.2. Party Support in Quebec by Age Cohort, 2002

Party preference	18–24	25–34	35–44	45–54	55–64	65+
ADQ (%)	28	38	33	48	52	35
Liberal (%)	33	35	27	19	23	41
PQ (%)	39	28	40	32	25	24
N	46	69	106	103	52	63

Cramer's $V = .154$ ($p < .05$)

Source: CROP (2002)

Note: Column percentages add to 100.

moratorium on any future referendum. This pledge had strong appeal in a constitutionally fatigued electorate.

Following Pinard, we can also cite Mario Dumont's considerable personal popularity, widespread dissatisfaction with the incumbent PQ government, and deepening political disaffection among Quebec's voters as three additional contributors to the ADQ's increased popularity. According to Pinard, "Voters who expressed their disaffection with politics constituted a majority [in Quebec] and it is within this majority that the ADQ got its largest support."[21]

A final factor that may have contributed to the surge in support for the ADQ in 2002 was the age of its most visible representatives. Those elected in by-elections that year were young, creating the potential for drawing in younger voters disenchanted with the established parties. In fact, the party did not consistently elicit support from young voters. As table 16.2 indicates, the ADQ appealed disproportionately to older voters. This does not necessarily undercut the argument that the *image* of youthfulness benefited the party. Older voters may well have felt the need for renewal as strongly as any, and their comparatively high turnout rates stood to benefit the party at the polls.

With so many factors in its favour, the ADQ *ought* to have done well in the 2003 provincial election, but as we shall see in the next section, its victory party was not imminent.

The Second ADQ "Moment": From Disappointment to Near Victory, 2003–2007

In the election of 14 April 2003, the ADQ managed to win only four seats, on the basis of 18 per cent of the popular vote. For the next four years, until the run-up to the March 2007 provincial election, support for the ADQ would oscillate between 10 and 20 per cent in public opinion polls, with just a few exceptions (see figures 16.1 and 16.2).

In the election of 26 March 2007, however, Dumont and his party exceeded expectations – and surprised most pollsters – by winning forty-one seats with just over 30 per cent of the vote, becoming the Official Opposition in the process. Jean Charest's Liberals barely clung to power (forty-eight seats on 33% of the vote) with a minority government, the first in the province since 1878. As for the PQ, it declined to the lowest share of the popular vote (28%) since its electoral debut in 1970, taking only thirty-six seats.

What factors can we cite to explain this fall (2003) and rise (2007) of the ADQ? The ADQ's declining fortunes after November 2002 were partly attributable to self-inflicted wounds. Some of the ADQ's neoliberal proposals, such as two-tier health care and a flat tax, came under increased scrutiny and heavy criticism during the election campaign. There were also indications of internal dissension or incoherence.

Figure 16.2. Quebec Voting Intentions, 2006–2010

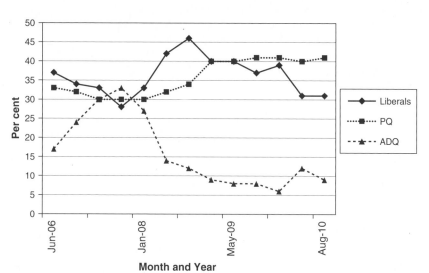

Source: Léger Marketing, http://www.legermarketing.com/admin/voting_int/Provincial_
Voting_Intentions_in_Quebec2012.pdf

Marcel Dutil, a high-profile entrepreneur and supporter of Mario Dumont, criticized the party's flat tax policy as regressive in a presentation to the ADQ's 2002 convention.[22]

Just as the ADQ's support was wavering, the leaders of the other parties were improving their performances. In the televised leaders' debates, the Liberals' Jean Charest raised the sovereignty issue, apparently to his advantage, and was also drawing in some supporters simply wanting a change in governing party. In a more polarized setting, Dumont and his party seemed to struggle to find a distinctive niche and ran a less organized campaign than the others.

However, by the time the 2007 election was called, a number of factors combined to provide the ADQ with another chance at a major electoral breakthrough. Chief among these was the deep unpopularity of the Charest government. In 2005, barely two years into its mandate, only 20 per cent of voters indicated that they would cast their ballots for the PLQ if an election were held (see figure 16.1). Seventy per cent of Quebecers said that they were dissatisfied with the Liberal government's performance, and 84 per cent of francophones were unhappy with the Charest administration. While it is true that Charest's popularity recovered somewhat by the time the 2007 election was held, he nonetheless remained the least respected among the three party leaders – and Mario Dumont was by far the most popular.[23]

What had happened since 2003 to turn most voters against Charest and his government? In addition to backing away from many of their bolder promises from the 2003 campaign, the Liberals had made some very controversial decisions in the early part of their mandate. One high-profile example was the "de-merger" of municipalities. After promising to democratize the process, the Liberals ended up setting up metropolitan-wide councils dominated by the large central cities "from whose grips the de-merged cities had only recently escaped."[24] The final result satisfied almost no one.

Another example was the government's attempt to roll back elements of the "Quebec model." Many centrists and progressives were angered that the government tried to shift policy on labour law, university tuition, and the very popular five-dollar-per-day child-care program. Fiscal conservatives were displeased with the government's unwillingness to press through with major reforms when confronted with opposition and protests from students, workers, and other activist groups.[25] Tasha Kheiriddin, then executive vice-president of the

Montreal Economic Institute, a right-wing think tank, criticized the Charest government for its string of broken promises: failing to reduce taxes by \$1 billion a year, not reining in program spending, failing to "re-engineer" the provincial state apparatus or to downsize the civil service.[26] As in 2002, then, the ADQ was able to play the neoliberal card, promising to ease the tax burden on Quebec's middle class. For the first time, the ADQ's economic message was reaching voters in the suburbs around Montreal – the "450 belt" – who were struggling to make ends meet and unhappy with what they saw as the poor quality of public services purchased with their taxes.[27]

The sovereignty issue also played into Mario Dumont's hands. André Boisclair, who had replaced Bernard Landry as leader of the PQ in 2005, was saddled with a hard-line program calling for another "public consultation" on sovereignty (the document studiously avoided the use of the word *referendum*), which a solid majority of all voters, whatever their linguistic background, simply did not want. Boisclair also suffered from appearing too "cosmopolitan," having admitted to snorting cocaine while a Cabinet minister. He was also dismissed by some critics as too "Montréalais," which one journalist speculated was code for "gay."[28] In the 2007 election, a split between Montreal and the regions over so-called lifestyle issues was a key determinant of voting behaviour, one that yielded enormous electoral benefits for Dumont and the ADQ outside of Montreal.

One other issue that played a particularly important role, enough to produce electoral gains that surprised most pundits, was the question of the extent to which cultural and religious minorities ought to be accommodated. In the months prior to voting day, Quebec was convulsed by a debate over what is referred to in the province as "reasonable accommodation" – for example, whether a Sikh police officer could wear a turban while on the job or a female soccer player wear the hijab while on the pitch.[29]

A number of incidents received intense media scrutiny in 2006 and 2007: a *cabane à sucre* outside of Montreal was criticized for removing the pork from its pork-and-beans to meet the dietary needs of a visiting Muslim family, and a Montreal YMCA came under attack for agreeing to frost its windows so that students at a nearby Hasidic Jewish school would not be able to see women in exercise gear.[30] In January 2007, Hérouxville (population 1200), an overwhelmingly francophone village located in the Mauricie about fifty kilometres from Trois-Rivières, adopted a "code of conduct" (*normes de vie*) for immigrants. This document, which some observers tried to soft-peddle as a humorous expression of regional dissatisfaction with Islamic immigrants, noted among other things that it was illegal in "our community" to stone women for committing adultery or to burn them alive for any reason.[31]

The eruption of an intense debate over the reasonable accommodation of ethno-religious minorities, and more broadly over the nature of the Quebec identity, wrong-footed the leaders of the two major parties. Both Charest and Boisclair sought to downplay the Hérouxville Code as an isolated incident. Dumont, by contrast, suggested publicly that the Québécois had gone far enough in accommodating the cultural sensitivities of immigrant communities. He published an open letter in several major French-language newspapers in which he called on Quebecers to "'get rid of the old minority reflex [of] continu[ing] to submit when we should keep our chin up high.'" And to return to their "European roots."[32]

Dumont's evocation of the roots of Quebec identity struck a responsive chord in certain segments of the electorate, especially outside of Montreal. As journalist Alain Dubuc has pointed out, the controversy over reasonable accommodation in Quebec was fuelled in part by simmering resentment in the regions directed at elitist and cosmopolitan Montreal: "Even if Hérouxville's approach skirts the xenophobic, immigrants are probably not the main target of their anger and unhappiness. There is something else at play, and that something else is a rural revolt against the 'Big City,' its ideas, its way of life, and its growing influence."[33] By the time the 2007 election was called, Charest's Liberal Party and, even more obviously, the PQ under André Boisclair were identified by many voters in rural ridings and small towns as being too closely associated with Montreal. Dumont's continuing personal popularity and widespread scepticism directed at the two main parties were both intensified by an identification with the "traditional," European-based values that were thought to be under siege.

The election gave the ADQ 31 per cent of the provincial vote, just behind the Liberals (33%) and ahead of the PQ (28%). This translated into 41 seats in the 125-seat National Assembly. There were 13 new seats from suburban Montreal – 8 in Laval and the North Shore and 5 on the south shore. It added these to its already strong base in the region around Quebec City and its electoral fortress in the administrative region of Chaudières-Appalaches, which includes the Beauce.[34] This stunning success, however, was not to last.

Collapse and Demise of the ADQ, 2008–Present

A number of observers were convinced that the 2007 results presaged a third major party realignment in Quebec, with the ADQ eclipsing the PQ as the partisan vehicle for soft-nationalist francophone voters in the province.[35] On the other hand, Henry Milner, while acknowledging that the Quebec party system could well have been on the verge of another realignment similar to those that occurred in the 1930s and 1970s, also cautioned that "there is no reason to assume that history will repeat itself this time."[36]

As we now know, Milner's scepticism was warranted, for the ADQ failed abysmally to capitalize on its 2007 breakthrough. Another election was called by the Charest government a little more than a year-and-a-half into its mandate, and the results for the ADQ on 8 December 2008 were bitterly disappointing: it was reduced to seven seats and just over 16 per cent of the vote. Dumont resigned both the leadership of the party and his seat immediately after the vote.

Recent research by Bonnie Meguid helps shed some light on the fate of the ADQ in the 2008 election.[37] She points out that the strategic policy responses of the mainstream competitors to the electoral threat posed by the new "niche" parties is critical to explaining their relative success.[38] These can range from "accommodative," in which a mainstream party adopts a position similar to that of the niche party on the principal issue that drives its success (e.g., immigration, separation, the environment) through "dismissive," in which a mainstream party communicates to voters that the issue championed by its niche competitor is trivial or irrelevant, to "adversarial," in which a mainstream party adopts the opposite position.[39]

Having failed to dismiss the controversy over reasonable accommodation in 2007 as a series of isolated incidents of limited significance, both the PLQ and the PQ quickly moved towards the ADQ's position on the Quebec identity in order to block the electoral threat. Even before the 2007 election was held, the Charest government tried to steal some of Dumont's thunder on this issue by creating the Consultation Commission on Accommodation Practices Related to Cultural Differences, better known as the Bouchard-Taylor Commission after its co-chairs, historian Gérard Bouchard and philosopher Charles Taylor. The commission issued its report in May 2008. After affirming that the furore over reasonable accommodation in 2006–7 was stoked in large part by irresponsible media reports on isolated incidents, the commission made a number of modest recommendations, among them the creation of an Office of Intercultural Harmonization and the insertion into the Quebec Charter of Human Rights and Freedoms of "an interpretative clause that establishes gender equality as a core value of our society."[40] The commission also recommended that "the crucifix must be removed from the wall of the National Assembly, which, indeed, is the very place that symbolizes the constitutional state."[41]

Signs that both the Liberals and PQ were prepared to accommodate themselves to the ADQ position emerged before the commission delivered its report, with increased talk of asserting Quebec identity. In October 2007, Pauline Marois introduced a private member's bill, the Quebec Identity Act, which would have required immigrants "to have an 'appropriate' working knowledge of French to be sworn in as Quebec citizens."[42] Soon after the publication of the report, the National Assembly also adopted Bill 63, An Act to Amend the Charter of Human Rights and Freedoms, which received royal assent on 12 June 2008. This piece of legislation expressly stated that Quebec's Charter rights were guaranteed equally to women and men, thus heading off any attempt by minority groups to subordinate gender equality to freedom of religion. Also in the wake of the Bouchard-Taylor Report's release, an all-party resolution was adopted by the National Assembly affirming the attachment of les Québécois "to our religious and historic heritage represented by the crucifix." Premier Charest observed at the time that "the crucifix is about 350 years of history in Quebec that none of us are ever going to erase and of a very strong presence, in particular, of the Catholic church, and that's our reality."[43]

In short, Dumont and the ADQ lost their *ownership* of the issue of reasonable accommodation after the 2007 election. The ADQ was no longer able to use this wedge issue to highlight differences between it and the mainstream parties. Combined with Dumont's singularly ineffective performance as leader of the opposition, and his inability to rein in his caucus, the ADQ's electoral fortunes took a nosedive. Shortly before Charest called an election for 8 December 2008, two members of the ADQ caucus crossed the floor and joined the Liberals. One of them, Andre Riedl, accused Dumont of running a one-man show – long a criticism of the ADQ leader. In the wake of the disastrous 2008 election, ADQ fortunes plummeted even further, as a series of resignations and leadership changes – Gilles Taillon, Dumont's successor as leader of the ADQ, resigned his post in November 2009, after less than a month in the job – robbed the organization of its legislative effectiveness.

In 2010–11, under the leadership of Gérard Deltell, a former journalist, the ADQ slowly regained some of its former appeal, drawing the support of between 13 and 18 per cent of decided voters in opinion polls. This modest resurgence was curtailed, however, by the emergence of a new right-of-centre organization, the Coalition pour l'avenir du Québec, which was formed in February 2011 under the leadership of former PQ Cabinet minister François Legault and businessman Charles Sirois. On 14 November 2011, the CAQ transformed itself into an official political party with a slightly reworked moniker, the Coalition Avenir Québec. Its "Action Plan" declared that the constitutional debate was "at an impasse," that neither independence nor renewed federalism was possible under existing circumstances, and that Quebecers urgently needed to abandon this increasingly sterile debate. Instead, the CAQ called on the province's voters and elected representatives to "have the courage to adopt the bold measures necessary to pull the province out of the quiet decline into which it has fallen."[44] Among these measures were the abolition of school boards and regional health agencies, a strengthening of the powers of the Office de la langue française, a tightening of the rules governing the tendering of contracts in the public sector, and a limit of 45,000 on the number of new immigrants allowed annually into Quebec.[45]

In its initial months of existence, the CAQ appeared to be wildly successful. It immediately became the most popular party in the province, capturing about one-third of the votes in opinion surveys, with both the PQ and PLQ mired in the low to mid-twenties. In December 2011, one fairly high-profile member of the PQ, François Rebello, joined four other independent MNAs – two former *péquistes* and two former members of the ADQ – in switching to the new party. In January 2012 what was left of the ADQ membership formally voted to join the CAQ. In the months leading up to the provincial election of September 2012, opinion polls showed some slippage in support for the new party, perhaps due in part to heightened scrutiny of some of its more controversial proposals, including those that proposed opening up the collective agreements covering the province's medical doctors and teachers in order to restrain public-sector wage increases.[46] Nonetheless, the newly minted party managed to win just more than 27 per cent of the vote, while the PQ and the Liberals took 32 and 31 per cent respectively. The CAQ's sizeable share of the vote translated into only nineteen seats, however – 15 per cent of the total – illustrating yet again the penalties that the first-past-the-post electoral system inflicts on third parties.

Nonetheless, the CAQ's creditable performance helped to deprive the PQ of its much sought-after majority, and in the context of a precarious minority government, the new party's influence and leverage are bound to be heightened.[47] Many of the underlying sentiments that launched the ADQ into the spotlight in two waves of successful campaigning have clearly not disappeared.

Conclusion

The fortunes of conservatism have fluctuated dramatically over the course of the last eighty years in Quebec. Long the dominant ideology in the province, as incarnated in the highly successful Union Nationale administrations of Maurice Duplessis, conservatism went into eclipse during the Quiet Revolution. Quebec secularized rapidly during this period, and between 1970 and 2000 it appeared as though conservative political parties influenced by the forms of moral traditionalism that still shaped important parties of the right in the rest of Canada no longer had potential for revival. There were some signs of the Liberals reaching towards the fiscally conservative right wing, echoing trends at the federal level among the mainstream parties, but in Quebec even that was muted.

However, the ADQ, which was born during the constitutional crisis of the early 1990s, twice appeared to be on the cusp of a dramatic electoral breakthrough to major party status, drawing on a variety of conservative currents and discontents in the population. This chapter has attempted to explain the peculiar up-and-down trajectory of the ADQ and to relate its fortunes to those elements of popular conservatism for which we are able to find evidence. The analysis suggests that while the ADQ's strategic ambiguity on the constitutional question was the key factor in its emergence in the early 1990s, its success in the 2000s arose from a range of influences beyond that, including support for its conservative economic prescriptions, and in 2007 for its mobilization of resentment against "reasonable accommodation." When the PQ and the governing Liberals moved towards the ADQ in partisan space after the 2007 election, eliminating the significant differences among the parties on the issue of the accommodation of ethnic communities and the definition of the Quebec identity, they helped push down support for the ADQ.

The ADQ's absorption into a new and initially quite popular political party, the CAQ, has re-strengthened right-of-centre policy positions in Quebec's political debate. At the same time, the PQ's internecine struggles, along with the Liberal Party's current search for a new leader to replace Jean Charest (who resigned after the 2012 election) and its potential ideological retooling, appear to be enlarging the room for a right-wing party in Quebec's political system, one that would address *both* the place of immigrants in the province and the need to "re-engineer" the Quebec model. Whether Legault's new party will be able to capitalize on these issues will very much depend on his organization's ability to adapt quickly to changing signals from an unhappy and volatile electorate.

NOTES

1 Portions of this chapter draw on my earlier analysis of the ADQ in A. Brian Tanguay, "The Stalled Realignment: Quebec's Party System after the 2003 Provincial Election," in *Canada: The State of the Federation 2005; Quebec and Canada in the New Century*, ed. Michael Murphy, 83–106 (Montreal and Kingston: McGill-Queen's University Press, 2007).

2 Steven J. Rosenstone, Roy L. Behr, and Edward H. Lazarus, *Third Parties in America*, 2nd ed. (Princeton: Princeton University Press, 1996); Maurice Pinard, "A Great Realignment of Political Parties in Quebec," The CRIC Papers, Special Edition (Montreal: Centre for Research and Information on Canada, March, 2003); Maurice Pinard, *The Rise of a Third Party: A Study in Crisis Politics*, enlarged ed. (Montreal and Kingston: McGill-Queen's University Press, 1975).

3 Bonnie Meguid, *Party Competition between Unequals* (Cambridge: Cambridge University Press, 2008).

4 The story of the ALN's emergence and subsequent electoral failure is well told in Patricia Dirks's interesting volume, *The Failure of l'Action libérale nationale* (Montreal and Kingston: McGill-Queen's University Press, 1991); for a detailed account of the UN administration, see also H.F. Quinn, *The Union Nationale: Quebec Nationalism from Duplessis to Lévesque*, 2nd ed. (Toronto: University of Toronto Press, 1979).

5 Alain Gagnon and Michel Sarra-Bournet, *Duplessis: entre la grande noirceur et la société libérale* (Montreal: Éditions Québec Amérique, 1997).

6 Quinn, *Union Nationale*, 95–7, 158–60.

7 Richard Hamilton and Maurice Pinard, "The Bases of Parti Québécois Support in Recent Quebec Elections," *Canadian Journal of Political Science* 9, no. 3 (1976): 26.

8 Richard French, "Governing without Business: The Parti Québécois in Power," in *Theories of Business-Government Relations*, ed. V.V. Murray (Toronto: Trans-Canada Press, 1985), 165–8; A. Brian Tanguay, "Québec's Political System in the 1990s: From Polarization to Convergence," in *Québec: State and Society*, 2nd ed., ed. Alain-G. Gagnon (Scarborough: Nelson, 1993), 177–8.

9 Natural Resources Canada, "The Atlas of Canada: Families with Children Living at Home, 1996 – Common-Law Couples with No Children Living at Home," http://geogratis.gc.ca/api/en/nrcan-rncan/ess-sst/e1dea5ee-8893-11e0-93f0-6cf049291510.html.

10 Taras Grescoe, *Sacré Blues* (Toronto: Macfarlane Walter & Ross, 2001), 9.

11 Parti libérale du Québec (PLQ), *Maîtriser l'avenir, Programme politique* (1985), 94.

12 Tanguay, "Québec's Political System in the 1990s," 187.

13 Quoted in Jean-François Lisée, *The Trickster: Robert Bourassa and Quebecers, 1990–1992*, trans. R. Chodos, S. Horn, and W. Taylor (Toronto: Lorimer, 1994), 7.

14 Pinard, "Great Realignment of Political Parties."

15 Action démocratique du Québec (ADQ), *For a Responsible Government: Action Plan for the ADQ's First Mandate*, Pre-electoral Council, Quebec City, 1 March 2003, 5.

16 Polling was conducted by Centre de recherche sur l'opinion publique (CROP), the data set entitled *Image ADQ [CR0211]*, and accessed at Canadian Opinion Research Archive, Queen's University, November 2002.

17 Pinard, "Great Realignment of Political Parties," 4. Writing some time ago, Pinard characterized this as characteristic of a majority of francophones.

18 Meguid, *Party Competition between Unequals*, 4.

19 ADQ, "Autonomie et identité: Affirmer notre identité sans se séparer," *Pour un Québec autonome*, http://www.adq.qc.ca/dossiers/autonomie-identite/, accessed 14 October 2010.

20 Pinard, "Great Realignment of Political Parties," 2.

21 Ibid., p. 4.

22 Michel David, "La fin d'un cycle: L'année politique au Québec," in *L'annuaire du Québec 2004*, ed. Michel Venne (Montreal: Fides, 2003), 584.

23 James Allan and Richard Vengroff, "The 2007 Election in Quebec and the Future of the Provincial Party System," *Québec Studies* 47 (Spring/Summer 2009): 119–39.

24 Ibid., 126.

25 The Charest government did raise the cost of subsidized daycare from five to seven dollars a day in its first budget.

26 Tasha Kheiriddin, "Charest Has Not Kept Election Promises on Tax Cuts," *Montreal Gazette*, 7 September 2006.

27 Camil Bouchard, "Individuals as Actors in Their Own Civic Life," *Inroads* 22 (Winter/Spring 2008): 97–9.

28 Don Macpherson, "The End of an Error," *Montreal Gazette*, 16 October 2007.

29 Bob Chodos, "From the Melting Pot to Reasonable Accommodation," *Inroads* 22 (Winter/Spring 2008): 44.

30 Ibid., 44–5; CTV News, "Debate over Religious Rights Continues in Quebec," 19 March 2007, http://www.ctv.ca/CTVNews/ Canada/20070319/montreal_ymca_070319/.

31 Christian Rioux, "The Quebec Language Question Is Back," *Inroads* 22 (Winter/Spring 2008): 57; Tim Nieguth and Aurélie Lacassagne, "Contesting the Nation: Reasonable Accommodation in Rural Quebec," *Canadian Political Science Review* 3, no. 1 (2009): 4.

32 Dumont cited in Darryl Lerroux, "Québec Nationalism and the Production of Difference: The Bouchard-Taylor Commission, the Hérouxville Code of Conduct, and Québec's Immigrant Integration Policy," *Québec Studies* 49 (Spring/Summer 2010): 111.

33 Alain Dubuc, "Fear and Ignorance: A Rural Revolt," *Vancouver Sun*, 1 March 2007, http://www.canada.com/vancouversun/news/editorial/ story.html?id=2d10e22f-1e87-4faf-a6dc-15ffebaa8ab7.

34 The ridings in this district are overwhelmingly francophone, rural, with lower than average household income and an undereducated workforce (Tanguay, "Stalled Realignment," 83–106). Interestingly, Nieguth and Lacassagne speculate that some of the ADQ success in the Quebec City region was due to the support it received from "shock jock" Jeff Fillion of CHOI-FM. This radio station drew in alienated, disaffected male voters. Nieguth and Lacassagne, "Contesting the Nation," 6.

35 Pierre Drouilly, "Une élection de réalignement?," in *L'Annuaire du Québec 2008*, ed. Michel Venne and Miriam Fahmy, 24–39 (Montreal: Fides, 2007); Christian Dufour, "Une entrée triomphale, mais longuement préparée," in Venne and Fahmy, *L'Annuaire du Québec 2008*, 75–8; Vincent Lemieux, "Le PLQ peut encore rebondir," in Venne and Fahmy, *L'Annuaire du Québec 2008*, 53–6; Bryan Breguet and François Vaillancourt, "Rupture or Moderation? The ADQ's Social and Economic Policies," *Inroads* 22 (Winter/Spring 2008): 87–95.

36 Henry Milner, "Quebec Politics after the ADQ Breakthrough," *Inroads* 22 (Winter/Spring 2008): 82.

37 Meguid, *Party Competition between Unequals.*

38 Meguid does not use the labels "minor" or "third" party, preferring instead "niche party." Niche parties in Western Europe, in her view, include at least 250 organizations, encompassing "green, radical right and ethnoterritorial parties" (*Party Competition between Unequals*, 3). She contends that these niche parties all share three principal characteristics: they "reject the traditional class-based orientation of politics" and instead "politicize sets of issues that were previously outside the dimensions of party competition." This might be true of the burgeoning anti-immigrant right-wing parties in a number of European countries, but it does not apply completely to the ADQ. Niche parties also raise issues that do not fit neatly into the traditional left-right axis of partisan competition. Finally, niche parties tend to limit their "issue appeals," focusing instead on either a single issue or a limited range of political questions.

39 Meguid, *Party Competition between Unequals*, 26–9.

40 Quebec, Consultation Commission on Accommodation Practices Related to Cultural Differences (Bouchard-Taylor Commission), *Building the Future: A Time for Reconciliation, Report*, 22 May 2008, 267.

41 Ibid., 20.

42 "Marois Defends Quebec Citizenship Proposal," CBC News, 20 October 2007, http://www.cbc.ca/news/canada/montreal/story/2007/10/20/pq-citizenship.html.

43 Kevin Dougherty, "We'll Keep Crucifix Up, Charest Says," *Montreal Gazette*, 23 May 2008, http://www.canada.com/montrealgazette/news/story.html?id=5741f665-1e03-4967-be5b-58b0f04e04d1.

44 Coalition Avenir Québec, *Agir pour l'avenir: Plan d'action présenté par la Coalition pour l'avenir du Québec*, 14 November 2011, 4. My translation of "avoir le courage de prendre des mesures audacieuses pour le sortir du déclin tranquille dans lequel il est engagé."

45 Ibid., p. 16.

46 Kevin Dougherty, "François Legault Wants Mandate for a New Deal with Doctors and Teachers," *Montreal Gazette*, 10 February 2012.

47 For the official results of the provincial election, held on 4 September 2012, see the website of the Directeur-général des elections du Québec, http://www.electionsquebec.qc.ca/english/provincial/election-results/general-elections.php?e=72&s=2#s. For an analysis of the origins and orientation of the CAQ, see Brian Tanguay, "Coalition Avenir Québec: Another New Party Is Poised to Break the Mould of Quebec Politics – Or Is It?" *Inroads* 31 (Summer/Fall 2012): 95–104.

17 Conclusion: The Distinctive Evolution of Canadian Conservatism

DAVID RAYSIDE AND JAMES FARNEY

Is there a distinctively Canadian hue to conservatism, either in the multiple ideas associated with the term or their take-up by political parties? And, in this diverse and decentralized federal system, are we able to see any similarities across regions in the character of conservative politics?

With lessons drawn from chapters in this book, we reiterate our early argument about the multiple currents associated with Canadian conservatism and the ascendancy of neoliberalism among those currents in the contemporary period. There is a striking similarity to this pattern across the country, evident in both federal and provincial politics. That free market core has marginalized other currents, especially the communitarian and hierarchical forms usually referred to as toryism.

This marks the convergence of Canadian patterns to a model that has become widely influential across the industrialized world and finds its archetypal articulation in the modern Republican Party in the United States. Where once conservatism (in both English and French Canada) included prominent voices resisting radical individualism, most of those who now identify themselves as conservative eagerly embrace the free market individualism they associate with the best of the United States. As in other countries, this is tempered by touches of nationalism or the occasional celebration of the traditional family, but these are grafts onto a neoliberal trunk.

To say that there has been convergence to a common model is not to say that all Canadian distinctiveness has vanished. Canadian conservatism includes currents of moral traditionalism, but they are weaker in numbers than in the United States and perhaps less strident.[1] The neoliberalism that is dominant here is less radically individualistic and free-market driven than American counterparts, though more so than in most of Europe. Perhaps most strikingly, Canadian conservatives have more widely retained support for comparatively high levels of immigration than conservatives in the United States, Europe, and Australia.

Foundational Canadian Conservative Ideas in Comparative Context

Individualism is not new to this country's political life. In the nineteenth century, Canada's founding moment, this country's politics were dominated by liberal individualism, even if not quite as much as in the United States. Quebec's francophone population provided a partial exception, in light of social and cultural dominance of a Roman Catholic hierarchy whose conservatism was of a sort that stressed community and hierarchy. There was also a counter-revolutionary tory "touch" in large parts of British-dominated Canada that looked to Britain's more stratified society as a model for Canada.[2] Politicians who called themselves conservative combined elements of such toryism with individualism, and by century's end had developed a form of "brokerage" politics in holding their parties together and securing support in quite different regions. The liberalism they incorporated was tempered by a suspicion of what they saw as individualistic excess in the United States. They valued the British connection and embraced the deployment of state authority to protect Canadian producers in order to secure order (and manufacturing profitability) across a thinly populated expanse. A tory critique of modern individualism and secularism persisted through much of the twentieth century, such as in the influential writings of philosopher George Grant and historian Donald Creighton.[3]

Often this tory tradition was reinforced by religious engagement in politics and by community identities defined in religious terms.[4] Pre-Confederation and post-1867 politics were shaped in part by contrasting views on the relationship between church and state, particularly on educational matters. Wiseman reminds us that in some regions (the Atlantic, for example) denomination mattered a great deal in partisan choice. Banack (like Wiseman) reminds us of the influence of evangelical fervour on Alberta's right wing parties from that province's foundation.

That said, Canadian political party systems were not historically as deeply defined by questions of church–state relations as many European systems, and religious faith less a core definer of political conservatism.[5]

The chasm that separated European Catholic or religion-based parties and their anticlerical liberal and social democratic opponents has no clear-cut parallel in Canada as a whole and was only mutedly present in the contest between "bleu" and "rouge" in Quebec until the Quiet Revolution of the 1960s. Outside of Quebec, and there only until mid-twentieth century, religious divides did not permeate associational life as thoroughly as in Continental Europe. Canadian parties and their leaders were drawn to brokerage in part because of the fear among some party leaders of what sectional divisions would do for this fragile federation, and in part because of the pragmatic requirements of building electoral majorities. For Macdonald's conservatives, this meant constructing a coalition that included both Protestant Orangemen and Roman Catholics.

This brokerage pattern was not unique to Canada. There are traces of the same pattern in the British Conservative Party, as it adapted to major expansions of the franchise. After the Second World War, Christian Democratic parties in Europe became archetypical "catch-all" parties, operating very much like the brokerage parties that dominated in Canada.[6] At one point all of these parties combined elements of what we might call tory conservatism with "business" liberalism, but in a combination that allowed for considerable state intervention and social-welfare policy expansion in Europe. There have certainly been brokerage elements to American parties, too. Until the 1980s, the Republicans' dominant currents were shaped primarily by liberal individualism and suspicion of government but leavened by so-called liberals or moderates who articulated a vision of the welfare state remarkably akin to Canadian or British red tories.

Modern Federal Conservatism

The fading of tory elements marks both the emergence of today's style of conservatism and the reduction of the distinctiveness of the Canadian form, particularly with regards to its prominent American comparator. As George Grant so publicly lamented, the kind of conservatism that he held to had been almost entirely abandoned by the time he reached his last years in the late 1980s. Since then, the contrast between Canadian and American conservatism has diminished further, with free market liberalism and suspicion of government more strikingly shaped by individualism. Where once Canadian partisan conservatives at the federal level and most provinces celebrated Canada's distinctiveness from the United States, now they are more likely to embrace tax reduction and individual responsibility as mantras, using conservative American models as their inspiration.

A few of our contributors point to the strength of neoliberalism at the heart of the federal Conservative Party, most forcibly Steve Patten. This shift is not unusual among parties of the right in the liberal democratic Western polities and is part of a gradual strengthening of economically conservative frameworks (and their advocates) over the last three decades. As Frendreis and Tatalovich point out, Republican governments in the United States and Conservative governments in Canada have not been particularly good at containing deficits – in the American case, Republicans devoted to neoliberalism have presided over most of the worst post-war deficits. What has been more important for such governments on both sides of the border has been tax cutting, intended, over the longer term, to limit the scope of government activity. Karen Bird and Andrea Rowe argue that the free market individualism of the present-day Conservatives in this country also extends to marginalizing equity programs, including those designed to reduce gender inequalities. Strikingly, the federal party's antipathy to equity-seeking initiatives exceeds those of conservative parties in Britain and France.

To what extent have other currents traditionally associated with Canadian conservatism been pushed to one side? Have the neoliberal preoccupations of the federal Conservative Party, for example, meant a complete sidelining of moral traditionalism? There are in fact contradictory signals. Jonathan Malloy argues that there is an important religiously conservative current within the CPC, influential in some policy initiatives (a point also made by Bird and Rowe, and by Rayside elsewhere).[7] He acknowledges, too, that the Conservatives have been prepared on occasion to use polarizing language or to seize on potentially divisive issues in signalling their sympathies to evangelical supporters. Even if the party's leadership keeps a lid on the visible expression of morally conservative sentiments, and especially those explicitly reflecting religious belief, it continues to work on maintaining and building the loyalty of religiously faithful voters.

This strategic goal of securing a more complete realignment of religious believers in federal politics does not at all diminish the free market individualism at the core of the Conservative Party's priorities. We agree with Cochrane in recognizing the ideological distinctiveness of moral traditionalism and economic neoliberalism in the Canadian public. That said, there are strong currents of economic individualism among Canada's evangelical Protestants, who were the most important faith-based constituency at the moment when the new Conservative Party united the Canadian right. There are also many Roman Catholics brought into Conservative circles through pro-life activism who have proven more amenable to the free market than one would expect, given that church's tradition of opposition to it. Canadian religious conservatives are not identical to their American counterparts, but they share much of the American Protestant impulse to combine traditional morality with a suspicion of government and support for the free market.[8] Their determination to prioritize moral or family traditionalism at election time is a pale shadow of what occurs in the U.S. Republican Party but is more evident than in most sister rightist parties in Europe.

Immigration and refugee policy is one area in which the comparative distinctiveness of the federal Conservatives is clearest. As Inder Marwah, Phil Triadofilopoulos, and Steve White argue, there is much continuity in Canadian policy in this area and little sign of the shift to immigration limits and anti-minority language that we find within some Republican circles in the United States and in several centre-right parties in Continental Europe. Tougher measures and certainly stronger language invoked in some instances, such as in response to the arrival of a ship containing Tamil refugee claimants in 2010, are in fact not exemplars of an overall tilt towards a demonization of immigrants. This reflects in part the distinctive immigration patterns in Canada – fewer illegal immigrants, comparatively high education levels, and a broad range of countries of origin – that reduce the popular backlash against migrants and the temptations of party leaders to embrace that backlash.[9] The relative moderation of immigration policy also reflects the Conservatives' goal of increasing their support among visible minorities and immigrants.[10]

Another area in which some might claim that pragmatism or centrism prevails is foreign policy. This is a perspective echoed in the contribution of Bloomfield and Nossal, who cite the Harper Conservatives' record in Afghanistan. This is a plausible view, though we would argue that there is evidence of a clear ideological shift, apparent in a range of policy changes, even if they build on some elements put into place by earlier Liberal governments. There is an increased emphasis on strengthening the Canadian military, on engaging in fighting conflicts, and on celebrating past military exploits in citizenship-related materials destined for newcomers. There has been significant movement towards more unequivocal support for Israel than virtually any of that country's allies, and less engagement in the kind of honest broker diplomacy that characterized at least some of our interventions at the United Nations. Canada has never had a distinguished international record on environmental issues, but the Conservative government has shifted policy even more sharply away from environmental sustainability than its predecessors. In foreign aid, the Conservatives have prioritized national interest more transparently than its predecessors, and have displayed a willingness to pick and choose among aid providers based in part on fit with the government's policy priorities on reproductive issues.

The final current that we have linked to political conservatism is populism, which has played an important role historically in the party politics of both left and right. Populist appeals in recent decades have been more prominently associated with the right, however, and were a key element in the rise of the federal Reform Party during the 1980s and 1990s (even if the party's leadership seemed less committed to substantive change that would reflect those impulses). Tom Flanagan argues that there are, at most, only modest remnants of populism in the Conservative Party, which is characterized by war-like controls imposed by the leader on all aspects of policymaking and party organization. James Farney pursues the theme, finding that federal Conservatives have set a pattern that provincial conservative parties increasingly follow – the adoption of highly disciplined models of party organization, and a few populist appeals with roots in the Reform party experiment, but little engagement with the core problem of democratic disengagement that motivates populists in the first place.

Where once Canadian conservatism stood at some midpoint between a variety of European rightist models on the one hand, and the American on the other, the changes we have explored here move it much closer to the American model. It has developed at its core a clearer ideological commitment to free market individualism than any federal party on the right in Canada's past. It has developed a more muscular nationalist discourse, prioritizing the military and abandoning any pretence of an international brokerage role. It has avoided the explicit invocation of faith and downplayed morality politics, but it has worked to realign party political loyalties by pitching focused appeals to a variety of faith-based or morally traditional constituencies, in line with the Republican model.

Provincial Parallels

What has been said of party politics at the federal level increasingly applies to major parties on the right at the provincial level, though most strikingly west of the Ottawa River. Quebec may be a partial exception, as would parts of Atlantic Canada and the northern territories. But in Ontario and western Canada, the shift towards more free-market-focused individualism has been pronounced, pushing other ideas to the margins.

Ontario has long had a major right party that strongly resembled its federal counterpart. During the long period in which the federal Progressive Conservatives followed the brokerage model, Ontario's PCs did the same. At times in the first four post-war decades, PC premiers like John Robarts and William Davis were prototypical of Canadian centrist (or red) toryism. In the early 1990s, however, Mike Harris's leadership marked a shift towards more assertively individualistic policies. Moral traditionalism remained an important current within the party's electorate and its caucus, but there was no mistaking the priority attached to reconfiguring the role of the provincial government and lowering taxes.

The case of Alberta naturally comes up in any consideration of what has been happening to provincial conservative politics in this country. And because it is such an important case, we have included two chapters devoted entirely to the politics of that province. As we have already indicated, Clark Banack argues, as does Wiseman, that there are in fact distinctive elements in the province's "foundational" political culture, suggesting powerful ongoing currents of individualism, populism, and evangelical faith. Taking a long look back, we can see Alberta's politics dominated by parties of the right (whether Social Credit or Progressive Conservative) displaying all these elements. What we also see in more recent decades, though, is precisely the kind of shift towards prioritizing neoliberalism as we have seen elsewhere, starting with the Ralph Klein premiership in 1992. In the present day, freemarket policies are still a hallmark of the Alberta PCs' program, and even more radically of the Wildrose Party, which has emerged as a challenger for right-wing dominance. The neoliberal shift of Alberta's partisan right is accompanied by a subtle marginalization of moral traditionalism, echoing patterns in the Conservative Party of Canada and Ontario's PCs. There are voters and party supporters who will expect some attention to policies that signal their party's sympathies with traditional family values, but such signals would typically avoid most hot button issues associated with morality politics. The overwhelming focus would be on policies designed to keep taxes low and contain state authority, particularly in the oil and gas industry.

Quebec is a partial exception to this pattern, though the provincial Liberal Party under Jean Charest did attempt to shift public policy towards closer alignment with neoliberal ideas. However, Charest did not go as far as he once promised, faced as he was by massive public protests. As Brian Tanguay points out, there is a neoliberal constituency in the province, a point also made by Lawlor and Bélanger. The Action démocratique du Québec (ADQ) arose as a fleetingly powerful option for the province's voters on two occasions, in part on the basis of neoliberal sentiment. And the new Coalition Avenir Québec draws to some extent on the same currents. During recent years, however, voters have faced and will continue to face parties of the right that look more centrist than counterparts in most other provinces.

Quebec's right is distinctive in the muted expression of morally traditional stances on gender, sexuality, or family. Public opinion polling regularly shows Quebecers to be among the most progressive in Canada on such questions (though usually only slightly more progressive than residents of BC and the Atlantic region). Neither established parties on the right nor upstarts are likely to give even lip service to such traditional beliefs.

The other unusual feature of Quebec's provincial politics is the recurrent prominence given to questions of immigrant "integration." The issue of "reasonable accommodation" was exploited by the ADQ in 2006 and 2007, and it clearly struck a chord that resonated enough in the general public to draw the two major parties towards policy positions that would be hard to find major party support for in other parts of the country. Questions of immigrant integration raise complex issues in a minority linguistic/cultural setting such as Quebec, and as a result support for policies that may fairly be called assimilationist crosses ideological boundaries more than in the rest of Canada. Still, it does give the political right a coloration somewhat different from that in most other parts of the country.

Conservative Beliefs among Canadians

Canadians are much like publics in most other liberal democratic systems in displaying complex and multifaceted belief systems, holding to positions we would identify as conservative on one set of issues but not necessarily on others. Overall, Canadians' beliefs lie between those of most western Europeans and those of Americans. They are less support-ive of expansive state policy than Europeans but more than Americans. By the same token, they are more individualistic than Europeans and more drawn to populism, but not to the extent of Americans. They are more conservative on moral issues than western Europeans but less than Americans (though the gap with the latter is smaller than might be imagined from contrasts in religiosity).[11]

Only on questions of immigration do Canadians occupy other than a mid-Atlantic position. Overall, Canadians are more supportive of comparatively high levels of immigration than Europeans, though Quebecers stand out in expressing doubts about immigration and sen-timents that are wary of or suspicious of Muslims in particular.[12] As we have already suggested, the support for multicultural sentiments across most of Canada has a lot to do with the patterns of migration to this country – the relatively high levels of education and modest numbers of illegal immigrants. Popular beliefs may also be rooted in the comparatively long history of immigration to this country, and the prosperity built in part on those immigrant waves.

What of the variations within Canada? The articles in this collec-tion that talk about the contemporary beliefs of Canadians, Quebecers and Albertans in particular, challenge some of the regionalist stereo-types about this country's politics. Albertans are not as conservative as we may have imagined and Quebecers not as progressive. Canadian regions have very different economic and social origins, so that each can be thought to have had a distinctive form of conservatism as part of its early political culture. How much of that pertains to the present day, however, is unclear. The strength of regionalist sentiment is as power-ful now as it has been in decades, but that does not mean that the belief systems, the political priorities, and the policy outcomes vary nearly as much as Canadians would assume.

What evidence is there that Canadian beliefs have shifted in recent decades towards more conservative positions? To the extent that we can treat Canadians as a whole, Chris Cochrane clearly shows that changes in attitudes have been to some extent out of sync with changes in the most prominent parties on the right. The average Canadian has shifted significantly towards inclusive positions on sexual diversity and towards the pro-choice side of the spectrum on reproduction. The leadership of conservative parties at the federal level and in provinces like Alberta, Saskatchewan, and Ontario no doubt realize this shift but are still prepared to signal their belief in traditional family values.

Most conservative parties in Canada have also shifted towards more radically free-market positions, at least rhetorically, than the average Canadian. Public opinion is complex on this front (as on all others), but there is no evidence to suggest that basic tenets associated with neoliberalism have majority support in any region of the country. There have been uneven shifts towards free market or individualist positions, but not to nearly the ideological positioning staked out by major parties on the right.

How then have conservative parties won office so frequently in recent times, across most of the country? As Cochrane points out, this is in part because non-right parties are not as politically coalesced as contemporary conservatives, who at the federal level learned the stark messages of political division during the 1990s. He also points out that parties on the left have tended to stake out equity-based policy positions on most of the issue dimensions that we associate with the left-right spectrum. In doing so, they are faced with an electorate with more "fragmented" belief systems, sympathetic to one or another of their positions but not with the others. Conservatives have been able to pick up on the discontents embodied in such fragmentation.

Concluding Thoughts

The ideological movement of most of Canada's rightist parties from a record of recurrent centrist pragmatism towards more ideological rigidity has parallels in other countries, including Britain, parts of Continental Europe, Australia, and of course the United States. The shift in Canada is a good deal less radical than that espoused by Tea Party Republicans (and many other Republicans) in the United States, but it adopts much of the anti-tax language and the rhetoric of individual responsibility that has been a hallmark of that party for three decades. This is more radical talk than would be found on the mainstream right in most European countries, where the welfare state is more expansive and popularly supported.

One distinctive element of Canadian partisan conservatism is the place of faith. The absence of an explicitly faith-based or "confessional" party at the federal level and most provinces for most of this country's history marks Canada apart from much of Europe. But the federal Conservatives have built on the realignment of the 1990s by crafting specific, often subtle, appeals to a variety of faith communities. In the process, we may be witnessing a more coherent religious "sorting" of the electorate than we have seen in decades, led by a party that avoids focusing on moral issues – this at a time when politics in most of Europe has been or is becoming more de-confessionalized than ever. There are similarities on this front, and so many others, with the U.S. party system's evolution since the 1970s, away from denominational "sorting" to a partisan differentiation between all people of ardent faith and others.[13] There is still a contrast between the Conservatives in Canada and the Republicans in the United States, evident in the reticence shown by most Canadian conservatives to take up very high-profile hot button issues like abortion. It is also evident in the reluctance of almost all Canadian politicians, including those on the right, to talk personally about faith. But in overall terms the partisan realignments of the 1990s and 2000s in Canada bear strong similarities to those that began in the United States during the 1970s and 1980s.

As we have seen, another distinctive element of major rightist parties in Canada, until now, has been the relative weakness of the anti-immigrant radicalism that is so widespread in Europe and so powerful in parts of the United States. There remains a degree of cross-party agreement on the broad outlines of policy that encourages comparatively high levels of immigration and that avoids targeting ethno-religious minorities as threats to the dominant culture. Quebec is a partial exception to this, but partisan appeals to popular anxieties over immigration are a pale shadow of what has been occurring in France, Italy, Flanders, some states in Germany, and parts of Scandinavia.[14]

Conservatism in Canada, then, has come to be most strongly associated with free market liberalism than with any of other currents we associate with the politics of the right. When in power, conservatives seem ready to proceed incrementally and to avoid taking such radical steps as to jeopardize their chances of re-election. But for most there is a clearer endgame than was evident in conservative parties of the past. There is, then, a form of strategic pragmatism mixed with unequivocal ideological commitment.

If there is any remaining reverence for the past among conservatives, it lies in support for traditional norms on gender and sexuality. This sentiment is not as widespread as in the United States and not as aggressively pursued by politicians. Instead there is a kind of niche marketing strategy to signal a form of moral camaraderie and a deployment of specific issues (like law and order) that will appeal to more than just moral traditionalists. The irony, of course, is that challenges to traditional family forms and ideas that engender such unease among so many Canadian conservatives have been fuelled in part by the spread of precisely the kind of individual autonomy that conservatives celebrate.

The use of targeted messaging is also used to gain support for other elements of conservative coalitions in federal and provincial politics. At the federal level, tough talk on Tamil refugee claimants arriving on the west coast, and publicizing names and photographs of other claimants accused of deceit on their applications for immigrant or refugee status (or of crimes committed before arrival), helps secure loyalty among supporters who are wary of immigration. On the other hand, apologies for past wrongs against Chinese Canadians or South Asians, coupled with messages to selected minority communities on shared conservative moral values, help build support among immigrants and the offspring of immigrants.

This is a form of coalitional politics without the pragmatic brokerage that long dominated the right in most of Canada.[15] There is a clear ideological commitment behind it. For some within the conservative fold, that ideological commitment is to faith-based views about family and schooling in addition to freemarket individualism. For most, though, it is a commitment primarily to a fundamental altering of the role of the state in Canadian society, and to convincing Canadians that the marketplace should be left as unencumbered as possible in shaping the success or failure of individuals and their families.

NOTES

1 See Sam Reimer, *Evangelicals and the Continental Divide: The Conservative Protestant Subculture in Canada and the United States* (Montreal and Kingston: McGill-Queen's University Press, 2003).

2 Gad Horowitz, "Conservatism, Liberalism, and Socialism in Canada: An Interpretation," *Canadian Journal of Economics and Political Science* 32, no. 2 (1966): 141–71.

3 On Grant, see H.D. Forbes, *George Grant: A Guide to His Thought* (Toronto: University of Toronto Press, 2007).

4 On early party formation, see André Siegfried, *The Race Question in Canada* (1907; Toronto: McClelland and Stewart, 1966); John English, *The Decline of Politics: The Conservatives and the Party System, 1901–20* (Toronto: University of Toronto Press, 1977); and Frank Underhill, *In Search of Canadian Liberalism* (Toronto: Macmillan, 1961).

5 Seymour Martin Lipset and Stein Rokkan, eds., *Party Systems and Voter Alignments* (New York: Free Press, 1967).

6 Otto Kirchheimer, "The Transformation of West European Party Systems," in *Political Parties and Political Development*, ed. J. LaPalombara and M. Weiner, 177–200 (Princeton: Princeton University Press, 1967). Even with Christian Democratic parties broadening their appeal as catch-all parties, religion remained a powerful predictor of support for them.

7 David Rayside, "The Conservative Party of Canada and Its Religious Constituencies," in *Faith, Politics and Sexual Diversity in Canada and the United States*, ed. David Rayside and Clyde Wilcox, 279–99 (Vancouver: UBC Press, 2011). See also Jonathan Malloy, "Canadian Evangelicals and Same-Sex Marriage," 144–66, in the same volume, and James Farney, *Social Conservatives and Party Politics in Canada and the United States* (Toronto: University of Toronto Press, 2012).

8 Sam Reimer, *Evangelicals and the Continental Divide: The Conservative Protestant Subculture in Canada and the United States* (Montreal and Kingston: McGill-Queen's University Press, 2003), 144–65.

9 Will Kymlicka, "Marketing Canadian Pluralism in the International Arena," in *The Comparative Turn in Canadian Political Science*, ed. Linda A. White, Richard Simeon, Robert Vipond, and Jennifer Wallner, 99–123 (Vancouver: UBC Press, 2008).

10 This strategy has been effected in part by pitching moral traditionalism to such communities. See Rayside "Conservative Party of Canada and Its Religious Constituencies."

11 See, for example, Rayside, *Queer Inclusions, Continental Divisions: Public Recognition of Sexual Diversity in Canada and the United States* (Toronto: University of Toronto Press, 2008), chap. 2.

12 On Canadian attitudes overall, see Michael Adams, *Fire and Ice: The United States, Canada and the Myth of Converging Values* (Toronto: Penguin, 2003).

13 On this, see Robert Putnam and David Campbell, *American Grace: How Religion Divides and Unites Us* (New York: Simon & Shuster, 2010).

14 Gérard Bouchard and Charles Taylor, *Building the Future: A Time for Reconciliation*, Commission de consultation sure les pratiques d'accommodement reliées aux différences culturelles, Gouvernement du Québec, 2008. On Muslims in the west elsewhere, for example, see Yvonne Yazbeck Haddad, ed., *Muslims in the West* (New York: Oxford University Press, 2002); and Joel S. Fetzer and J. Christopher Soper, *Muslims and the State in Britain, France, and Germany* (New York: Cambridge University Press, 2005).

15 This is an important distinction made by Tom Flanagan, in remarks made during a panel discussion on Canadian party politics, Annual Meeting of the American Political Science Association, Toronto, September 2009.

Bibliography

Ajzenstat, Janet, and Peter Smith. *Canada's Origins: Liberal, Tory, or Republican?* Ottawa: Carleton University Press, 1995.

Archer, Keith, and Faron Ellis. "Opinion Structure of Party Activists: The Reform Party of Canada." *Canadian Journal of Political Science* 27, no. 2 (1994): 277–308. http://dx.doi.org/10.1017/S0008423900017364.

Bellamy, David J., Jon H. Pammett, and Donald Cameron Rowat. *The Provincial Political Systems: Comparative Essays.* Toronto: Methuen, 1976.

Berger, Carl. *The Sense of Power: Studies in the Ideas of Canadian Conservatism, 1867–1914.* Toronto: University of Toronto Press, 1970.

Betz, Hans George. *Radical Right-Wing Populism in Western Europe.* New York: St Martin's, 1994.

Bickerson, James, Alain-G. Gagnon, and Patrick J. Smith. *Ties That Bind: Parties and Voters in Canada.* Toronto: Oxford University Press, 2009.

Black, Conrad. *Render unto Caesar: The Life and Legacy of Maurice Duplessis.* Toronto: Key Porter Books, 1998.

Blake, Donald E., David J. Elkins, and Richard Johnston. *Two Political Worlds: Parties and Voting in British Columbia.* Vancouver: University of British Columbia Press, 1985.

Brodie, Janine, and Jane Jenson. *Crisis, Challenge and Change: Party and Class in Canada.* Toronto: Methuen, 1980.

Campbell, Kim. *Time and Change: The Political Memoirs of Canada's First Woman Prime Minister.* Toronto: Doubleday, 1996.

Campbell, Robert M., and Leslie A. Pal. *The Real World of Canadian Politics.* 2nd ed. Peterborough: Broadview, 1991.

Carty, R. Kenneth. *Politics, Policy, and Government in British Columbia.* Vancouver: University of British Columbia Press, 1996.

Carty, R. Kenneth, William Cross, and Lisa Young. *Rebuilding Canadian Party Politics.* Vancouver: University of British Columbia Press, 2000.

Carty, R. Kenneth, Lynda Erickson, and Donald E. Blake. *Leaders and Parties in Canadian Politics: Experiences of the Provinces.* Toronto: Harcourt Brace Jovanovich Canada, 1991.

Christian, William. *George Grant: A Biography.* Toronto: University of Toronto Press, 1993.

Christian, William, and Colin Campbell. *Party Politics and Ideologies in Canada.* Toronto: McGraw-Hill Ryerson, 1996.

Courtney, John C., and David E. Smith, eds. *The Oxford Handbook of Canadian Politics.* Toronto: Oxford University Press, 2010. http://dx.doi.org/10.1093/oxfordhb/9780195335354.001.0001.

Crosbie, John, with Geoffrey Stevens. No Holds Barred: My Life in Politics. Toronto: McClelland and Stewart, 1997.

Cross, William. *Political Parties.* Vancouver: University of British Columbia Press, 2004.

–, ed. *Political Parties, Representation, and Electoral Democracy in Canada.* Toronto: Oxford University Press, 2002.

Dabbs, Frank. *Preston Manning: The Roots of Reform.* Vancouver: Greystone Books, 1997.

Diefenbaker, John. *One Canada.* Toronto: Macmillan, 1975.

Dobbin, Murray. *Preston Manning and the Reform Party.* Toronto: James Lorimer, 1991.

Donnelly, Murray S. *The Government of Manitoba.* Toronto: University of Toronto Press, 1963.

Elkins, David, and Richard Simeon, eds. *Small World: Provinces and Parties in Canadian Political Life.* Toronto: Methuen, 1980.

Ellis, Faron. *The Limits of Participation: Members and Leaders in Canada's Reform Party.* Calgary: University of Calgary Press, 2005.

English, John. *The Decline of Politics: The Conservatives and the Party System, 1901–20.* Toronto: University of Toronto Press, 1993.

Erwin, Lorna. "Neo-Conservatism and the Canadian Pro-Family Movement." *Canadian Review of Sociology and Anthropology / La Revue canadienne de sociologie et d'anthropologie* 30, no. 3 (1993): 401–21.

Farney, James. *Social Conservatives and Party Politics in Canada and the United States.* Toronto: University of Toronto Press, 2012.

Finkel, Alvin. *The Social Credit Phenomenon in Alberta.* Toronto: University of Toronto Press, 1989.

Flanagan, Tom. *Game Theory and Canadian Politics.* Toronto: University of Toronto Press, 1998.

– *Harper's Team: Behind the Scenes in the Conservative Rise to Power.* 2nd ed. Montreal and Kingston: McGill-Queen's University Press, 2009.

– *Waiting for the Wave: The Reform Party and Preston Manning.* 2nd ed. Montreal and Kingston: McGill-Queen's University Press, 2009, 1995.

Forbes, Hugh Donald. *George Grant: A Guide to His Thought.* Toronto: University of Toronto Press, 2007.

Foster, Bruce. "New Right, Old Canada: An Analysis of the Political Thought and Activities of Selected Contemporary Right Wing Organizations." PhD diss., University of British Columbia, 2000.

Fox, Paul, and Graham White, eds. *Politics: Canada.* 8th ed. Toronto: McGraw-Hill Ryerson, 1995.

Freeden, Michael. *Ideologies and Political Theory: A Conceptual Approach.* Oxford: Clarendon, 1996.

Frizzell, Alan, and Jon H. Pammett. *The Canadian General Election of 1997.* Ottawa: Carleton University Press, 1997.

Frizzell, Alan, Jon H. Pammett, and Anthony Westell. *The Canadian General Election of 1993.* Ottawa: Carleton University Press, 1994.

Gagnon, Alain. *Quebec, State and Society.* Toronto: Methuen, 1984.

Gagnon, Alain-G., and A. Brian Tanguay, ed. *Canadian Parties in Transition.* 3rd ed. Peterborough: Broadview, 2007.

Gagnon, Georgette, and Dan Rath. *Not without Cause: David Peterson's Fall from Grace.* Toronto: Harper Collins, 1992.

Gairdner, William D. *After Liberalism: Essays in Search of Freedom, Virtue, and Order.* Toronto: Stoddart, 1998.

– *The Trouble with Canada: A Citizen Speaks Out.* Toronto: Stoddart, 1990.

– *The War against the Family: A Parent Speaks Out.* Toronto: Stoddart, 1992.

Garr, Allen. *Tough Guy: Bill Bennett and the Taking of British Columbia.* Toronto: Key Porter Books, 1985.

Glassford, Larry A. *Reaction and Reform: The Politics of the Conservative Party under R.B. Bennett, 1927–38.* Toronto: University of Toronto Press, 1992.

Graham, Roger. *Old Man Ontario: Leslie M. Frost.* Toronto: University of Toronto Press, 1990.

Grant, George. *English-Speaking Justice.* Toronto: Anansi, 1985.

– *Lament for a Nation: The Defeat of Canadian Nationalism.* Ottawa: Carleton University Press, 1965.

– *Philosophy in a Mass Age.* Toronto: Copp Clark, 1966.

Grey, Deb. *Never Retreat, Never Explain, Never Apologize: My Life, My Politics.* Toronto: Key Porter Books, 2004.

Gwyn, Richard J. *Smallwood: The Unlikely Revolutionary.* Toronto: McClelland and Stewart, 1972.

Harrison, Trevor. *Of Passionate Intensity: Right-Wing Populism and the Reform Party of Canada*. Toronto: University of Toronto Press, 1995.

– *Requiem for a Lightweight: Stockwell Day and Image Politics*. Montreal: Black Rose, 2002.

Hawkins, John. *Recollections of the Regan Years: A Political Memoir*. Hantsport: Lancelot, 1990.

Hoover, Dennis R. "The Christian Right under Old Glory and Maple Leaf." In *Sojourners in the Wilderness: The Christian Right in Comparative Perspective*, edited by Corwin E. Smidt and James M. Penning, 171–93. Lanham: Rowman and Littlefield, 1997.

Horowitz, Gad. "Conservatism, Liberalism, and Socialism in Canada: An Interpretation." *Canadian Journal of Economics and Political Science* 32, no. 2 (1966): 143–71. http://dx.doi.org/10.2307/139794.

Hoy, Claire. *Bill Davis: A Biography*. Toronto: Methuen, 1985.

Humphries, Charles. *Honest Enough to Be Bold: The Life and Times of Sir James Pliny Whitney*. Toronto: University of Toronto Press, 1985.

Ibbitson, John. *Promised Land: Inside the Mike Harris Revolution*. Toronto: Prentice Hall, 1997.

Jeffrey, Brooke. *Hard Right Turn: The New Face of Neo-conservatism in Canada*. Toronto: Harper Collins, 1999.

Johnson, William. *Stephen Harper and the Future of Canada*. Toronto: McClelland and Stewart, 2005.

Kirk, Russell. *The Conservative Mind: From Burke to Santayana*. New York: Regnery, 1953.

Kitschelt, Herbert, with Anthony McGann. *The Radical Right in Western Europe*. Ann Arbor: University of Michigan Press, 1995.

Knopf, Rainer, and F.L. Morton. *The Charter Revolution and the Court Party*. Peterborough: Broadview, 2000.

Kornberg, Allan, Joel Smith, and Harold D. Clarke. *Citizen Politicians – Canada: Party Officials in a Democratic Society*. Durham: Carolina Academic Press, 1979.

Laycock, David. *The New Right and Democracy in Canada: Understanding Reform and the Canadian Alliance*. Don Mills: Oxford University Press, 2001.

– *Populism and Democratic Thought in the Canadian Prairies, 1910 to 1945*. Toronto: University of Toronto Press, 1990.

Levy, Gary, and Graham White. *Provincial and Territorial Legislatures in Canada*. Toronto: University of Toronto Press, 1989.

Lipset, Seymour Martin. *Agrarian Socialism: The Co-operative Commonwealth Federation in Saskatchewan*. Garden City: Anchor, 1950.

– *Continental Divide: The Values and Institutions of the United States and Canada.* New York: Routledge, 1990.

Lisac, Mark. *The Klein Revolution.* Edmonton: NeWest, 1995.

MacDonald, Donald C., ed. *The Government and Politics of Ontario.* 3rd ed. Scarborough: Nelson, 1985.

MacDonald, L.I. *Mulroney: The Making of the Prime Minister.* Toronto: McClelland and Stewart, 1985.

MacKenzie, Chris. *Pro-Family Politics and Fringe Parties in Canada.* Vancouver: University of British Columbia Press, 2005.

Mackey, Lloyd. *Like Father, Like Son: Ernest Manning and Preston Manning.* Toronto: ECW, 1997.

– *The Pilgrimage of Stephen Harper.* Toronto: ECW, 2005.

Macquarrie, Heath. *The Conservative Party.* Toronto: McClelland and Stewart, 1965.

– *Red Tory Blues.* Toronto: University of Toronto Press, 1992.

Malloy, Jonathan. "Bush/Harper? Canadian and American Evangelical Politics Compared." *Canadian Review of Canadian Studies* 39, no. 4 (2009): 352–63. http://dx.doi.org/10.1080/02722010903319079.

Manning, Preston. *The New Canada.* Toronto: Macmillan, 1992.

– *Think Big: My Adventures in Life and Democracy.* Toronto: McClelland and Stewart, 2002.

Manthorpe, Jonathan. *The Power and the Tories: Ontario Politics: 1943 to the Present.* Toronto: Macmillan, 1974.

Martin, Lawrence. *Harperland: The Politics of Control.* Toronto: Viking, 2010.

Martin, Patrick, Allan Gregg, and George Perlin. *Contenders: The Tory Quest for Power.* Scarborough: Prentice-Hall Canada, 1983.

Massolini, Philip. *Canadian Intellectuals, the Tory Tradition, and the Challenge of Modernity, 1939–1970.* Toronto: University of Toronto Press, 2001.

McDonald, Marci. *The Armageddon Factor: The Rise of Christian Nationalism in Canada.* Toronto: Random House, 2010.

– "Stephen Harper and the Theo-Cons." *Walrus,* October 2006.

Morton, F.L., and Rainer Knopff. *The Charter Revolution and the Court Party.* Peterborough: Broadview, 2000.

Mulroney, Brian. *Memoirs.* Toronto: McClelland & Stewart, 2007.

Noel, S.J.R. *Politics in Newfoundland.* Toronto: University of Toronto Press, 1971.

– *Revolution at Queen's Park: Essays on Governing Ontario.* Toronto: J. Lorimer, 1997.

Noll, Mark A. "What Happened to Christian Canada?" *Church History* 75, no. 2 (2006): 245–73. http://dx.doi.org/10.1017/S000964070011131X.

Oliver, Peter G. *Howard Ferguson: Ontario Tory*. Toronto: University of Toronto Press, 1977.

Pal, Leslie Alexander, and David Taras. *Prime Ministers and Premiers: Political Leadership and Public Policy in Canada*. Scarborough: Prentice-Hall Canada, 1988.

Pammett, John, and Christopher Dornan, eds. *The Canadian General Election of 2000*. Toronto: Dundurn Group, 2001.

–, eds. *The Canadian General Election of 2004*. Toronto: Dundurn Group, 2004.

–, eds. *The Canadian General Election of 2006*. Toronto: Dundurn Group, 2006.

–, eds. *The Canadian General Election of 2008*. Toronto: Dundurn Group, 2009.

Patten, Steve. "The Reform Party's Re-imagining of the Canadian Nation." *Journal of Canadian Studies / Revue d'etudescanadiennes* 34, no. 1 (1999): 27–51.

Perlin, George. *The Tory Syndrome: Leadership Politics in the Progressive Conservative Party*. Montreal and Kingston: McGill-Queen's University Press, 1980.

Persky, Stan. *Fantasy Government: Bill Vander Zalm and the Future of Social Credit*. Vancouver: New Star Books, 1989.

Pickersgill, J.W. *The Mackenzie King Record*. Toronto: University of Toronto Press, 1960.

Pitsula, James, and Ken Rasmussen. *Privatizing a Province: The New Right in Saskatchewan*. Vancouver: New Star Books, 1990.

Plamondon, Bob. *Full Circle: Death and Resurrection in Canadian Conservative Politics*. Toronto: Key Porter Books, 2006.

Quinn, Herbert F. *The Union Nationale: Quebec Nationalism from Duplessis to Lévesque*. Toronto: University of Toronto Press, 1979.

Rae, Bob. *The Three Questions: Prosperity and the Public Good*. Toronto: Viking, 1998.

Rayside, David. *Queer Inclusions, Continental Divisions: Public Recognition of Sexual Diversity in Canada and the United States*. Toronto: University of Toronto Press, 2008.

Rayside, David, and Clyde Wilcox, eds. *Faith, Politics, and Sexual Diversity in Canada and the United States*. Vancouver: University of British Columbia Press, 2011.

Reimer, Sam. *Evangelicals and the Continental Divide: The Conservative Protestant Subculture in Canada and the United States*. Montreal and Kingston: McGill-Queen's University Press, 2003.

Robertson, Ian Ross. "Party Politics and Religious Controversialism in Prince Edward Island, from 1860 to 1863." *Acadiensis* 7, no. 2 (1978): 29–59.

Robin, Martin. *Canadian Provincial Politics: The Party Systems of the Ten Provinces*. Scarborough: Prentice-Hall of Canada, 1978.

Rolph, William Kirby. *Henry Wise Wood of Alberta*. Toronto: University of Toronto Press, 1950.

Schultze, Rainer-Olaf, Roland Sturm, and Dagmar Eberle, eds. *Conservative Parties and Right-Wing Politics in North America: Reaping the Benefits of an Ideological Victory?* Opladen: Leske and Budrich, 2003.

Segal, Hugh. *Beyond Greed: A Traditional Conservative Confronts Neoconservative Excess*. Toronto: Stoddart, 1997.

–*The Long Road Back: The Conservative Journey in Canada, 1993–2006*. Toronto: Harper Collins, 2006.

– *The Right Balance: Canada's Conservative Tradition*. Vancouver: Douglas and MacIntyre, 2011.

Sharpe, Sydney, and Don Braid. *Storming Babylon: Preston Manning and the Rise of the Reform Party*. Toronto: Key Porter Books, 1992.

Slade, Arthur G. *John Diefenbaker: An Appointment with Destiny*. Montreal: XYZ, 2001.

Smallwood, Joseph R. *I Chose Canada*. Toronto: Macmillan, 1973.

Smith, Alexander T., and Raymond Tatalovich. *Cultures at War: Moral Conflicts in Western Democracies*. Peterborough: Broadview, 2003.

Smith, Denis. *Rogue Tory: The Life and Legend of John G. Diefenbaker*. Toronto: MacFarlane Walter & Ross, 1995.

Speirs, Rosemary. *Out of the Blue: The Fall of the Tory Dynasty in Ontario*. Toronto: Macmillan, 1986.

Stein, Michael B. *The Dynamics of Right-Wing Protest: A Political Analysis of Social Credit in Quebec*. Toronto: University of Toronto Press, 1973.

Stevens, Geoffrey. *Stanfield*. Toronto: McClelland and Stewart, 1973.

Tatalovich, Raymond. *The Politics of Abortion in the United States and Canada*. Armank: M.E. Sharpe, 1997.

Taylor, Charles. *Radical Tories: The Conservative Tradition in Canada*. Toronto: Anansi, 1982.

Thomas, Lewis Herbert. *William Aberhart and Social Credit in Alberta*. Toronto: Copp Clark, 1977.

Thorburn, Hugh. *Politics in New Brunswick*. Toronto: University of Toronto Press, 1961.

Thorburn, Hugh, and Alan Whitehorn, eds. *Party Politics in Canada*. 8th ed. Toronto: Pearson, 2001.

Waite, P.B. *John A. Macdonald*. Markham: Fitzhenry & Whiteside, 1999.

Warner, Tom. *Losing Control: Canada's Social Conservatives in an Age of Rights*. Toronto: Between the Lines, 2010.

White, Graham. *The Government and Politics of Ontario*. Toronto: University of Toronto Press, 1997.

Wiseman, Nelson. *In Search of Canadian Political Culture*. Vancouver: University of British Columbia Press, 2007.

Young, Lisa. *Feminists and Party Politics*. Vancouver: University of Toronto Press, 2000.

Young, Lisa, and Keith Archer, eds. *Regionalism and Party Politics in Canada*. Toronto: University of Toronto Press, 2002.

Contributors

Clark Banack is an assistant professor in the Department of Political Science at York University, where he is completing a book that explores the influence of religion on political thought in Alberta, both historically and more recently. His broader research interests include religion and politics in Canada and the United States, provincial politics, Canadian regionalism and federalism, Canadian political thought, and identity politics and group rights.

Éric Bélanger is associate professor in the Department of Political Science at McGill University and is a member of the Centre for the Study of Democratic Citizenship. His research interests include political parties, public opinion, and voting behaviour, as well as Quebec and Canadian politics. He has co-authored *Le comportement électoral des Québécois* (2009), winner of the 2010 Donald Smiley Prize. His articles have appeared in *Comparative Political Studies*, *Political Research Quarterly*, *Electoral Studies*, *Publius: The Journal of Federalism*, the *European Journal of Political Research*, and the *Canadian Journal of Political Science*.

Karen Bird is associate professor of political science at McMaster University, specializing in comparative politics and research methods. Her research focuses on the political behaviour, inclusion, and representation of women and ethnic minorities across industrialized democracies. Recent publications include (with Thomas Saalfeld and Andreas M. Wüst), *The Political Representation of Immigrants and Minorities: Voters, Parties and Parliaments in Liberal Democracies* (Routledge 2010), and "Gendering Minority Participation in Public Life," in *Political Participation of Minorities*, ed. Marc Weller (Oxford 2010).

Alan Bloomfield completed his PhD at Queen's University in 2011. His thesis explored the "strategic culture" of states, using Australia's strategic history as an illustration. He currently holds a Vice-Chancellor's Postdoctoral Research Fellowship at the University of New South Wales in Sydney. He has published on matters ranging from strategic culture to Australian Labor Party foreign policy trends to the meaning of the term *Islamofascism*.

Christopher Cochrane is an assistant professor of political science at the University of Toronto Scarborough. He studies the impact of ideology on political decision-making and party competition in Canada and other democratic countries. His research on this topic has appeared in the *Canadian Journal of Political Science* ("Left/Right Ideology and Canadian Politics") and in *Party Politics* ("The Asymmetrical Structure of Left/Right Disagreement").

James Farney is assistant professor of political science at the University of Regina, having been a visiting professor and postdoctoral fellow at Queen's University. His interests include Canadian and American politics, religion and politics, and the politics of education. His *Social Conservatives and Party Politics in Canada and the United States* was published by the University of Toronto Press in 2012.

Tom Flanagan is professor of political science at the University of Calgary and a fellow of the Royal Society of Canada. He has contributed frequently to Canadian media, especially the *Globe and Mail* and the CBC. His experience as national campaign manager for the Conservative Party of Canada is described in his book *Harper's Team: Behind the Scenes in the Conservative Rise to Power* (2007). *Beyond the Indian Act: Restoring Aboriginal Property Rights* (co-authored with Christopher Alcantara and André Le Dressay, 2010), was nominated for the Donner-Canadian Prize in 2011.

John Frendreis is professor of political science at Loyola University Chicago. His teaching and research interests include economic policy, environmental politics, and American political parties and elections. His publications include articles in the *American Political Science Review, American Journal of Political Science, Journal of Politics, Comparative Political Studies, Political Research Quarterly, Social Science Quarterly*, and *Polity*, and he is co-author of the book *The Presidency and Economic Policy* (2008).

Andrea Lawlor completed her PhD at McGill University as a member of the Centre for the Study of Democratic Citizenship. She was awarded a SSHRC postdoctoral award to attend the University of California at Berkeley. Her research focuses on Canadian and comparative public policy and public opinion. Other interests include immigration and citizenship, party financing, and Quebec politics. Her work has appeared in the *Canadian Journal of Public Administration* and *Electronic Media and Politics*.

Jonathan Malloy is chair of the Department of Political Science at Carleton University. His research and teaching focus on Canadian political institutions and the politics of evangelical Christians, especially in comparative perspective. Recent work on the latter has appeared in the *American Review of Canadian Studies, Politics, Religion and Society,* and *Faith, Politics and Sexual Diversity in Canada and the United States* (ed. David Rayside and Clyde Wilcox, 2011).

Inder Marwah is in the midst of a SSHRC postdoctoral fellowship based in political science at the University of Chicago. His research focuses on political exclusion in liberal political thought and practice, and includes contemporary explorations of social and political inclusion in culturally and religiously diverse states. His work has been published in *History of Political Thought, Kantian Review, Hypatia,* and *Social Theory and Practice*.

Kim Richard Nossal is a professor in the Department of Political Studies at Queen's University. He is the author of a number of works on Australian and Canadian foreign and defence policy. His latest book, co-authored with Stéphane Roussel and Stéphane Paquin, is *International Policy and Politics in Canada* (2011).

Steve Patten is associate professor in the Department of Political Science at the University of Alberta. His research and teaching has explored the political ideas and policies of the partisan New Right, the dynamics of party system change, theoretical perspectives on the changing character of public policy, and the implications of neoliberal culture and governance for citizenship and democracy. He has written a number of articles for edited volumes and academic journals, as well as co-editing (with Lois Harder) *The Chrétien Legacy: Politics and Public Policy in Canada* (McGill-Queen's University Press 2006). His research examines the challenge of democratizing policymaking in parliamentary systems of government.

David Rayside is professor of political science at the University of Toronto and has long been associated with the Mark S. Bonham Centre for Sexual Diversity Studies (serving as founding director until 2008). Among his publications are *Faith, Politics, and Sexual Diversity*, co-edited with Clyde Wilcox (UBC Press 2011), and *Queer Inclusions, Continental Divisions* (University of Toronto Press 2008). He has served on the governing bodies of both Canadian and American political science associations.

Andrea Rowe is a PhD candidate in comparative public policy at McMaster University. Her research interests include innovation policy, internationalization of public policy, and the role of gender in public policy and administration. She has a master's in public administration from the University of Victoria.

Anthony M. Sayers is associate professor of political science at the University of Calgary. He has written on Canadian and Australian politics – on political parties, elections, parliaments, and federalism – and has taught in both countries. He is author of *Parties, Candidates and Constituency Campaigns in Canadian Elections* (UBC Press 1999) and has published articles in *Party Politics*, the *Australian Journal of Political Science*, the *Canadian Journal of Political Science*, the *Canadian Political Science Review*, *Electoral Studies*, and the *International Journal of Canadian Studies*.

David K. Stewart is professor of political science at the University of Calgary. He has taught at seven universities in the four western provinces. His research interests have led to work on political parties, leadership selection, provincial party systems, parliamentary government, and political realignment. He has published in journals such as the *Canadian Journal of Political Science*, *Party Politics*, *Canadian Political Science Review*, and *Publius: The Journal of Federalism*, and is the co-author of *Conventional Choices: Parties and Leadership Selection in the Maritimes* and *Quasi-Democracy?: Parties and Leadership Selection in Alberta* (2007).

A. Brian Tanguay is professor of political science at Wilfrid Laurier University. His main areas of interest are Quebec politics, Ontario politics, political parties, interest groups and social movements, and electoral reform. He is the co-editor (with Alain-G. Gagnon) of *Canadian Parties in Transition* (the third edition of which appeared in 2007).

In 2003–4, he worked for the Law Commission of Canada, drafting its report, *Voting Counts: Electoral Reform for Canada*.

Raymond Tatalovich is professor of political science at Loyola University Chicago. He received his PhD from the University of Chicago, where he studied public policy analysis under Theodore J. Lowi. His specializations are moral conflicts and economic policy. Among his recent publications are *Moral Controversies in American Politics* (M.E. Sharpe 2011) and *The Presidency and Economic Policy* (Rowman & Littlefield 2008).

Triadafilos Triadafilopoulos is associate professor of political science at the University of Toronto, where he teaches courses in public policy and conducts research in immigration and citizenship politics and policymaking. He is the author of *Becoming Multicultural: Immigration and the Politics of Membership in Canada and Germany* (UBC Press 2012), and editor of *Wanted and Welcome? Policies for Highly Skilled Immigrants in Comparative Perspective* (Springer 2013). Recent articles have appeared in *Social Politics*, the *Journal of Ethnic and Migration Studies*, and the *Review of International Studies and Social Research*.

Stephen White is postdoctoral research fellow on diversity and democratic citizenship with the Centre for the Study of Democratic Citizenship and the Department of Political Science at Concordia University. His research focuses on Canadian public opinion and political behaviour, and immigrant political attitudes and behaviour. His most recent work has appeared in the *Canadian Journal of Political Science* and *Political Research Quarterly*.

Nelson Wiseman, associate professor in the Department of Political Science at the University of Toronto, specializes in Canadian government and politics. In 2009, *Choice* designated his book, *In Search of Canadian Political Culture* (UBC Press 2007) as an Outstanding Academic Title. The author of a monthly column for the *Hill Times*, he has appeared as an invited witness before committees of the Canadian House of Commons and Senate, and the Legislative Assembly of Ontario. In 2010, he wrote an invited brief for the United Kingdom House of Lords Select Committee on the Constitution.

Index